Kälin and Kochenov's

QNI
Quality of Nationality Index

An Objective Ranking of the Nationalities of the World

Kälin and Kochenov's

QNI Quality of Nationality Index

An Objective Ranking of the Nationalities of the World

Kälin and Kochenov's Quality of Nationality Index (QNI) is designed to rank the objective value of world nationalities, as legal statuses of attachment to states, approached from the perspective of empowering mobile individuals interested in taking control of their lives. The QNI looks beyond simple visa-free tourist or business travel and takes a number of other crucial factors into account: those that make one nationality a better legal status through which to develop your talents and business than another. This edition provides the state of the quality of nationalities in the world as of the fall of 2018.

Edited by Dimitry Kochenov and Justin Lindeboom

·HART·

HART PUBLISHING

Bloomsbury Publishing Plc

Kemp House, Chawley Park, Cumnor Hill, Oxford, OX2 9PH, UK

HART PUBLISHING, the Hart/Stag logo, BLOOMSBURY and the Diana logo are trademarks of Bloomsbury Publishing Plc

First published in Great Britain 2020

Copyright © Dr. Christian H. Kälin and Prof. Dimitry Kochenov, and contributing authors, 2020

Dr. Christian H. Kälin, Prof. Dimitry Kochenov have asserted their rights under the Copyright, Designs and Patents Act 1988 to be identified as the Authors of this work.

All rights reserved. No part of this publication may be reproduced or transmitted in any form or by any means, electronic or mechanical, including photocopying, recording, or any information storage or retrieval system, without prior permission in writing from the publishers.

While every care has been taken to ensure the accuracy of this work, no responsibility for loss or damage occasioned to any person acting or refraining from action as a result of any statement in it can be accepted by the authors, editors or publishers.

All UK Government legislation and other public sector information used in the work is Crown Copyright ©. All House of Lords and House of Commons information used in the work is Parliamentary Copyright ©. This information is reused under the terms of the Open Government Licence v3.0 (http://www.nationalarchives.gov.uk/doc/open-government-licence/version/3) except where otherwise stated.

All Eur-lex material used in the work is © European Union, http://eur-lex.europa.eu/, 1998–2020.

A catalogue record for this book is available from the British Library

ISBN: HB: 978-1-50993-323-5

Typeset by Kevin Connolly

Printed and bound in Great Britain by Ashford Colour Press Ltd

To find out more about our authors and books visit www.hartpublishing.co.uk. Here you will find extracts, author information, details of forthcoming events and the option to sign up for our newsletters.

The coffee-table book for citizenship aficionados

Contents

Contents

What is the QNI? The Creators' Preface	1
Ranking Nationalities, Not States	1
How Does It Work? The QNI in a Nutshell	2
The Creators, Editors, and Authors of the QNI	6
List of Contributors	7

Part 1 Laying Down the Base 9
By Dimitry Kochenov and Justin Lindeboom

1	The QNI's Task: Demystifying Citizenship through Clear Data	10
2	What Is Citizenship or Nationality?	13
3	Who Decides Who Is a National?	16
4	How to Decide Who Is a National	18
5	Nationalities Are Not Equal	22
6	A Country's Power and Citizenship Quality: The Lack of Correlation	26
7	Each Nationality Is Global: The Rise of Intercitizenships	28

Part 2 Methodology 37

8	Deploying a Clear Methodology to Tell a New Citizenship Story	38
9	Nationalities Included in the QNI	39
	'Non-Citizens' of Latvia	39
	Israeli Laissez-Passer	39
	British Nationalities	40
	Citizenship of the European Union	42
	Territories That Do Not Possess a Separate Nationality	43
	Statuses and Documents Excluded from the QNI for Failing to Meet the Criteria of a Nationality	46
10	Time of Measurement	49

11	Composition of the QNI	50
	Human Development	51
	Economic Strength	53
	Peace and Stability	56
	Diversity of Settlement Freedom	57
	Weight of Settlement Freedom	60
	Diversity of Travel Freedom	61
	Weight of Travel Freedom	63

Part 3 The QNI General Ranking — 67

12	Introduction to the QNI General Ranking	68
	QNI General Ranking	68
	Quality Tiers	68
13	Nationalities of the World in 2018	70
14	QNI General Ranking 2018	72
15	Movement between Tiers in 2014–2018	77
16	Risers in 2014–2018	81
	Croatia	81
	Romania	82
	Bulgaria	82
	United Arab Emirates	83
	Colombia	83
	Grenada	84
	Peru	84
	Timor-Leste	84
	Georgia	85
	Moldova	85
17	Fallers in 2014–2018	86
	Yemen	86
	Libya	87
	Syrian Arab Republic	87
	Qatar	88

Part 4 Regional and Thematic Rankings — 91

18	Europe	92
19	Americas	95
20	Middle East and North Africa	97
21	Sub-Saharan Africa	99
22	Asia and the Pacific	102
23	European Union	105
24	Mercado Común del Sur	108
25	Organisation of Eastern Caribbean States	110
26	Gulf Cooperation Council	112
27	Economic Community of West African States	113
28	North Atlantic Treaty Organization	114
29	Eurasian Economic Union	116
30	Association of Southeast Asian Nations	118
31	Commonwealth of Nations	120
32	Largest Countries by Area	123
33	Microstates	124
34	Best Countries According to Perception	127
35	Most Powerful Countries According to Perception	129
36	Non-Recognized States	131

Part 5 Expert Commentary — 135

37	North versus South or Integrated versus Isolated? Notes on the Global Grouping of Nationalities *By Yossi Harpaz*	136
38	Population Density, Wealth, and Refugee Flows: New Perspectives of the Quality of Nationality Index *By Benjamin Hennig and Dimitris Ballas*	146

39	The Quality of Statelessness *By Katja Swider*	154
40	Citizenship-by-Investment (*Ius Doni*) *By Christian H. Kälin*	161
41	Twenty-Four Shades of Sovereignty and Nationalities in the Pacific Region *By Gerard Prinsen*	171
42	Passports, Free Movement, and the State in South America *By Diego Acosta Arcarazo*	183
43	The Quality of African Nationalities *By Andreas Krensel*	191
44	Two Sticks, Half a Carrot: External and Domestic Divisions in the Post-Soviet Space *By Ryhor Nizhnikaŭ*	199
45	Post-Yugoslav Nationalities *By Elena Basheska*	210
46	Citizenship of the European Union and Brexit *By Dimitry Kochenov*	216
47	Canadian Nationality: The Value of Belonging *By Jacquelyn D. Veraldi*	222
48	Mexican Nationality *By Pablo Mateos*	228
49	French Nationality *By Sébastien Platon*	232
50	Nationality of the Kingdom of the Netherlands *By Jeremy Bierbach*	238
51	Bulgarian Nationality: Dire Straits? *By Kamen Shoilev*	246
52	'Non-Citizens' of Latvia *By Aleksejs Dimitrovs*	253
53	Georgian Nationality *By Laure Delcour*	256
54	Israel: Citizenship, Residence, Taxation: A View from Practice *By Eli Gervits*	262

55	China and India	265
	By Suryapratim Roy	
56	Myanmar: The Unflinching Law of the Ethnic Citizen and the 'Mixed Blood' Other	269
	By José-María Arraiza	

Part 6 End Matter   277

Endnotes	278
Bibliography	287
Methodological Annex	298
Glossary of Terms	301
Alphabetical Index of Nationality Quality Charts Included in the Text	303
Acknowledgments	305

What is the QNI? The Creators' Preface

Ranking Nationalities, Not States

Kälin and Kochenov's Quality of Nationality Index (QNI) is designed to rank the objective value of all the world's nationalities as legal statuses of attachment to states. Looking beyond simple visa-free tourist or business travel rights, the QNI takes several other crucial factors into account to demonstrate that the world's nationalities are not equal, and that some nationalities afford a better legal status than others to develop one's talents while living a rewarding life. The emerging picture reveals that while some nationalities are welcomed bundles of rights, others — the majority, in fact — are clear liabilities for their holders.

The QNI ranks *nationalities* — legal statuses of attachment to states — rather than states per se. It takes into account the increase in world migration flows and the lack of correlation between the nationalities held by a growing number of active individuals and the countries in which their businesses are established and their lives are lived. Such considerations fundamentally distinguish the QNI from the majority of other indexes and rankings, which take states — that is, sovereign territorial entities — somewhat too seriously. In today's globalized world, the legal status of millions of nationals extends their opportunities and aspirations far beyond their countries of origin: the confines of the state simply are not the limit of one's ambitions and expectations.

A country's positive characteristics, such as its economic strength or its level of human development, are not always reflected in the practical value of that country's nationality to its citizens. Economically strong countries can have relatively unattractive nationalities, such as China and the Chinese nationality, for instance, whereas microstates, such as Liechtenstein, for example, can offer nationalities of great value. It is not a secret that our nationalities directly impact our lifestyles, freedom to think independently, do business, and live longer, healthier, and more rewarding lives. While the extremes are well known — a child in Somalia or the Democratic Republic of Congo is 50 times more likely not to survive beyond its first five years than a child in Japan or Finland, and Liberian and nationals of the Democratic People's Republic of Korea are infinitely less likely to experience an excursion to Paris, New York, or Moscow than, say, Singaporeans and Argentineans — a single source has been missing that ranks the worth of nationalities. This QNI provides this single source.

The reality that the QNI describes is regrettable in many respects: in most cases our nationality plays an important role in establishing a highly arbitrary ceiling, one that determines our opportunities and aspirations. This ceiling reflects the core aspect of being a national of some specific place: nationality is based on a random act of birth that bears no correlation to any person's achievements, ideas, feelings, and desires — instead, it is the result of a 'birthright lottery', in

the memorable phrase of Ayelet Shachar. This is something that the designers of the QNI do not endorse but nevertheless observe as part of the day-to-day global reality and that the Index aims to document. The QNI, updated annually, is the source of a dynamic understanding of the quality of world nationalities as measured by a set of clear and transparent criteria.

How Does It Work? The QNI in a Nutshell

Everyone has a nationality (citizenship) of one or more states. States' characteristics differ greatly — the landmass of the Russian Federation is huge, while that of Eswatini (formerly Swaziland) is small; Luxembourg is rich, Mongolia less so. Just as states differ, so too do nationalities themselves. The key premise of the QNI is that it is possible to compare the relative worth of nationalities, not simply of countries. We believe that because a nationality is a legal status that significantly impacts its citizens' lives both inside and outside the territory of the conferring state, knowing the comparative value of a nationality is hugely important.

For a reliable comparison of nationalities, it is important to consider both internal and external factors. Internally, we look at how successful the country is in terms of human development, economic prosperity, and stability and peace. It is preferable to have the nationality of a country with long life expectancy, a good education system, and a high level of prosperity, such as Australia, than that of a country that offers less security and poorer education and health care to

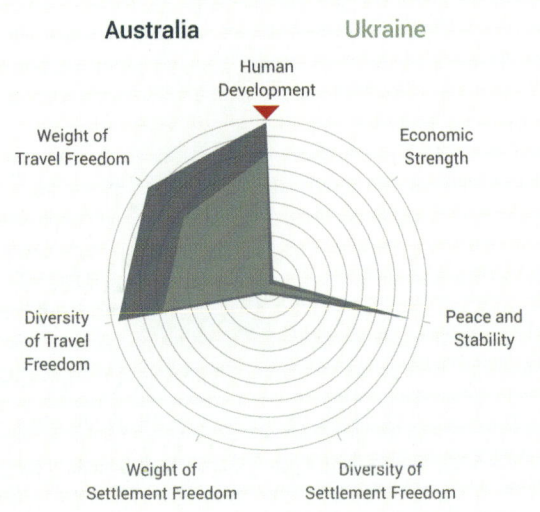

its nationals, such as Ukraine. It is better to have the nationality of a country with a large economy, like the United States — and as a consequence, enjoy the rights to work and reside in it — than in a tiny country, however prosperous, like San Marino. It is better to have the nationality of a peaceful and stable country, like Denmark, than that of a country with security risks, like Venezuela. The QNI takes three internal factors into account:

- Economic Strength
- Human Development
- Peace and Stability

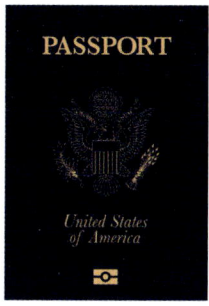

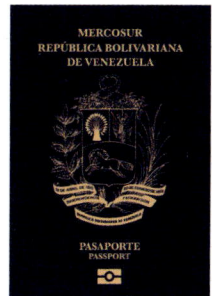

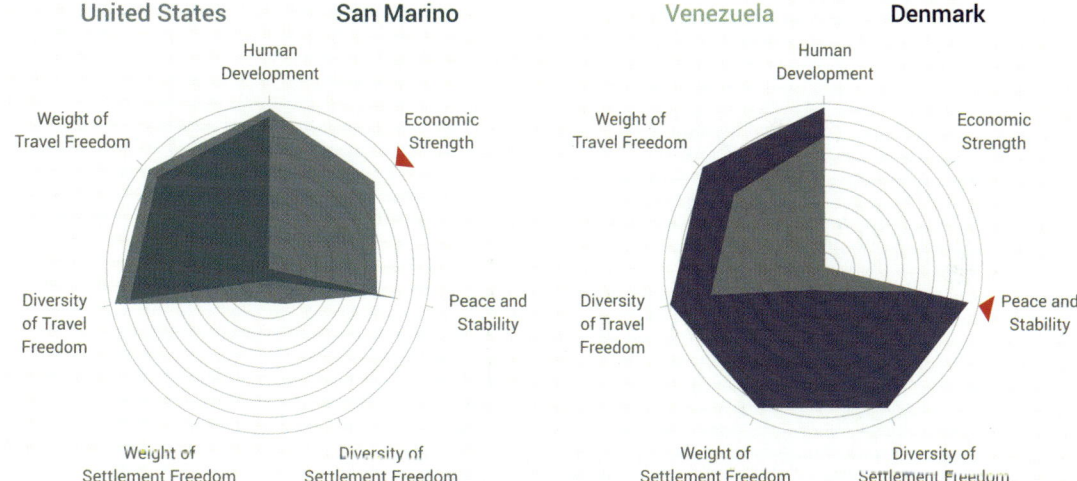

External factors are no less important, however: some nationalities allow their holders to travel all around the world unobstructed, with no questions asked. Consider the Belgian nationality, for instance, which allows visa-free or visa-on-arrival access to 176 countries and territories. Other nationalities require the acquisition of endless visas for tourist and business travel, and at times make such travel de facto impossible. The Turkmen nationality, for example, enables visa-free or visa-on-arrival access to only 51 countries and territories.

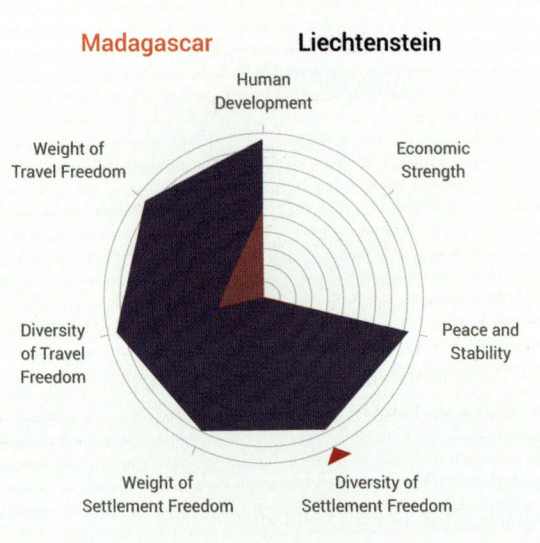 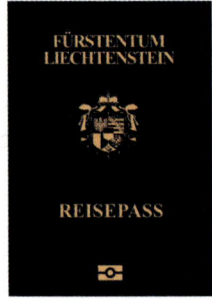 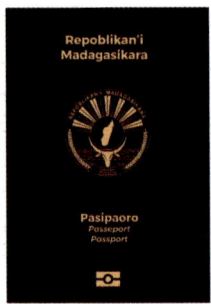

More importantly, however, most of the world's nationalities confer a right on their holders to be welcomed by other countries and societies besides their own — a right to home treatment. In this sense, possessing one nationality can give rise to plentiful rights in a number of states as opposed to in just one, including the right to work and the right to settle. Liechtenstein nationality, although conferred by a tiny country, gives its bearers full access to all the EU Member States and all the countries of the European Economic Area (EEA): Liechtensteiners are at home in 41 countries and territories, enjoying all the rights that the bearers of the local nationalities enjoy. When one compares this with Madagascan nationality, for example, which is associated with no such extraterritorial rights at all, the difference becomes clear.

Two external elements used to evaluate any nationality's worth are therefore extremely important:

- Travel Freedom
- Settlement Freedom

To reflect the added value of both elements in the most effective way, the QNI looks at two criteria for both. The first criterion is the number of other jurisdictions one can travel to or settle in while holding a particular nationality, because the diversity of the places one can live in or visit based on one's nationality has a profound effect on quality of life. In this respect, Liechtensteiner nationality is better than Madagascan nationality, and German is better than Turkmen.

The second criterion takes into account the Human Development level and Economic Strength of every possible country that a person with a particular nationality can travel to or settle in. By this measure, being able to travel to France visa-free is of greater added value than being able to visit war-torn Syria visa-free. The same is true for settlement: having an unconditional right to work and live in Germany, for instance, puts Icelandic nationality above Chinese nationality, since Chinese nationality does not even allow settlement and work in the totality of the territory of the issuing state itself. Indeed, the Special Administrative Regions of Macao and Hong Kong require mainland Chinese nationals to acquire permits to settle in or even visit them.

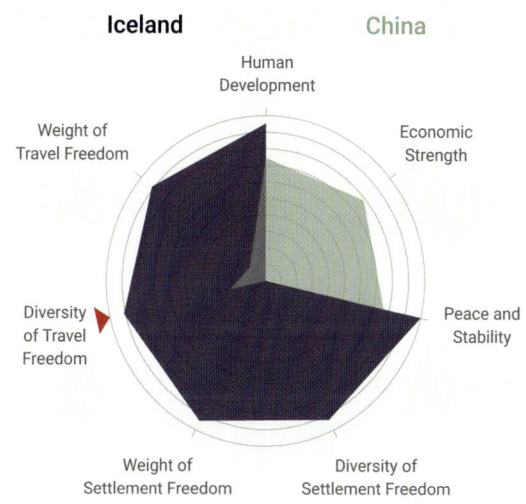

All of these factors were taken into consideration to create the QNI: Kälin and Kochenov's Index allows for an objective and impartial comparative assessment of the worth of all the world's nationalities. By taking both internal and, crucially, external factors into consideration, the QNI offers a clear account of which nationalities are objectively better than others, and disproves a number of unhelpful mythologies — such as that the possession of any nationality is equally fine or that the most prosperous and economically important countries provide their nationals with the best nationality. (As just one example, although China is an economic giant, its nationality has a very modest objective value.) Intuitively, we have suspected all along that some nationalities were great while others were, quite simply, terrible; now we know which are which, and the Index's intuitively understandable round charts allow for easy comparisons. The QNI divides the nationalities of the world into five tiers based on quality: Very High Quality, High Quality, Medium Quality, Low Quality; and Very Low Quality. This division gives a very clear idea of the standing of each of the world's nationalities at a glance, as is done on pages 70 and 71.

This Hart Publishing edition replaces the *Henley & Partners — Kochenov Quality of Nationality Index* and marks a new beginning for the Index. We have updated aspects of the methodology, reassessed years of data, and introduced deep revisions throughout, building on the editions published by Ideos Publications in Zürich annually from 2016 to 2018 and making this edition of the QNI even more reliable. Updating the QNI annually ensures that an up-to-date picture of the quality of the world's nationalities is readily available, illuminating medium- to long-term trends in nationalities' development in terms of quality.

Dr. Christian H. Kälin and Prof. Dimitry Kochenov
Zürich and Groningen

The Creators, Editors, and Authors of the QNI

Kälin and Kochenov's Quality of Nationality Index (QNI) is the result of successful cooperation between Dr. Christian H. Kälin and Prof. Dimitry Kochenov. Kälin is Chairman of Henley & Partners, the world's leading residence and citizenship planning firm, and is the author of *Ius Doni in International and European Law* (Brill-Nijhoff, 2019), the first book-length critical academic account of investment migration. Kochenov is Professor of European Constitutional Law and Citizenship at the University of Groningen, the Netherlands. He is the author, *inter alia*, of *Citizenship* (MIT Press, 2019) and is the editor of *EU Citizenship and Federalism* (Cambridge, 2017).

Moving beyond the general concept, Dr. Justin Lindeboom, who writes and teaches European law and legal theory at the University of Groningen, has been the key editor of the Index together with Prof. Kochenov. Where authorship is not otherwise specified, all parts of the QNI have been co-written by editors Kochenov and Lindeboom in collaboration.

Countless individuals passionate about citizenship and migration made contributions to this project, both large and small, ultimately making this index possible. We would like to thank especially Elena Basheska, Adrian Berry, Suelen Haidar, Nina Hevig Bredvold, Borek Janeček, Ilka Lane, Sinéad Moloney, Alan Murray Hayden, Juliane von Reppert-Bismarck, Kyrill Ryabtsev, Flips Schøyen, Charlie Scott, Peter Spiro, Beata Stachowicz, Daning Xie, and, in particular, Jacquelyn Veraldi.

List of Contributors

Prof. Diego Acosta Arcarazo, University of Bristol
Dr. José-María Arraiza, Åbo Akademi University, Turku
Prof. Dimitris Ballas, University of Groningen
Dr. Elena Basheska, Legal Researcher and EU Affairs Consultant, United Kingdom
Dr. Jeremy Bierbach, Franssen Advocaten, Amsterdam
Dr. Laure Delcour, Fondation Maison des sciences de l'homme, Paris
Mr. Aleksejs Dimitrovs, Lawyer, European Parliament, Brussels and Strasbourg
Mr. Eli Gervits, Eli Gervits Law Offices, Tel Aviv
Dr. Yossi Harpaz, Harvard University and Tel Aviv University
Prof. Benjamin Hennig, University of Iceland
Dr. Christian H. Kälin, Henley & Partners, London
Prof. Dimitry Kochenov, University of Groningen
Mr. Andreas Krensel, IBN Immigration Solutions, Cape Town
Dr. Justin Lindeboom, NYU Law School and University of Groningen
Prof. Pablo Mateos, CIESAS Center for Research and Advanced Studies in Social Anthropology, Guadalajara
Dr. Greg Nizhnikaŭ, Finnish Institute of International Affairs, Helsinki
Prof. Sébastien Platon, University of Bordeaux
Dr. Gerard Prinsen, Massey University, New Zealand
Dr. Suryapratim Roy, Trinity College, Dublin
Mr. Kamen Shoilev, Partner, New Balkans Office, Barrister, Sofia
Dr. Katja Swider, University of Amsterdam
Ms. Jacquelyn Veraldi, Trinity College, University of Cambridge

Part 1

Laying Down the Base

By Dimitry Kochenov and Justin Lindeboom

1 The QNI's Task: Demystifying Citizenship through Clear Data

The demystification and deromanticization of citizenships and nationalities is long overdue (Kochenov and Lindeboom 2017; Kochenov 2019a). Although much ink is spilled in the literature about concrete citizenships' 'values', 'identities', and 'honor' when speaking about citizenship, two fundamental starting points — which underpin the QNI — should always be kept in mind.

Firstly, as a historically sexist and racist 'status of being' randomly assigned by an authority, any citizenship is inevitably arbitrary, messy, and complex. Crucially, it never depends on an individual's wishes: the authority will decide who is a citizen no matter what his or her 'identity' or 'values' may be (Kochenov 2019b). Those who think that a parent's 'blood' or the fact of birth in a particular territory is sufficient justification for the distribution of the crucial rights and entitlements that shape our lives can probably stop reading here: this book is not a neo-feudal nationalist restatement of citizenship's glory — it is anti-feudal. Among the first premises of looking at nationalities critically — replacing nationalist mantras with objective data — is the belief that it is wrong to judge people by the color of their passports rather than by their values, education, or any other factors related to their personality, talents, and achievements. This is the key paradox of contemporary citizenship: in a world where the belief in equal human worth is the key starting point of thinking about justice, citizenship is *ab initio* on the losing side (Carens 2013).

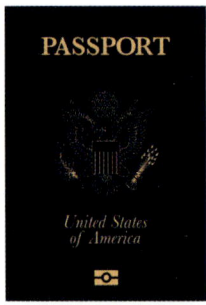   
 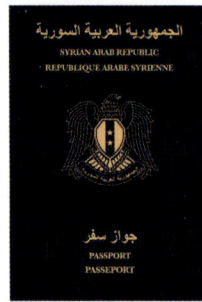  

The second starting point is a consequence of the first. The random distribution of rights and life chances would not be such a problem if discrepancies among the different possible outcomes of the 'birthright lottery' were minimal (Shachar 2009). Because this is not the case, however, the idealized concept of 'separate but equal' citizenship does not work (Spiro 2019a). The Basotho, Kyrgyzstanis, and Nicaraguans know this very well, as do the Austrians, Canadians, and New Zealanders, who are among the lottery's winners. Citizenship's random nature notwithstanding, it is extremely important to hold a 'good' nationality since the determinant of global inequality is now geography, not class, as was primarily the case in the past (Milanovic 2016); on average, the poorest Danes are richer and live longer and more rewarding lives than the most well-off Central Africans.

This volume's visualizations of the world, which are a special contribution by Ben Hennig and Dimitris Ballas, make this point abundantly clear: money travels with the most elite passports, while the majority of the world's population lives with substandard-quality nationalities at best. Because what all citizenships around the world have in common is the right to be admitted to particular places, citizen-

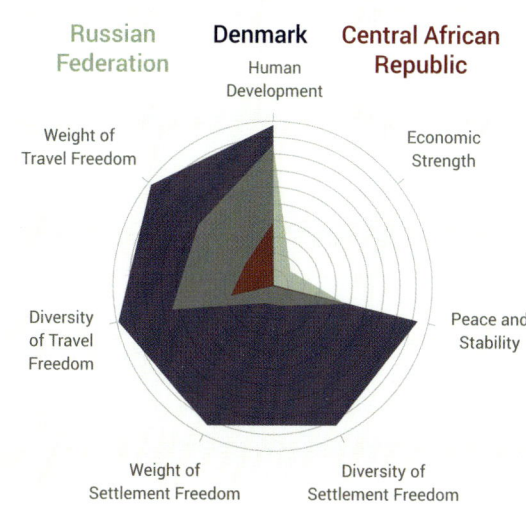

ship — from an instrument of rights-proliferation and protection — has become the fundamental tool of policing and reinforcing global inequality. Central African Republic citizenship is a status that will not grant you many visas. It will more than likely ensure that you will never join the Danes or even the Russians and will die where you are. In comparison, Danish nationals can choose to settle and work without question in 43 of the richest countries and territories in the world, never facing, by virtue of their citizenship status, the problems that frame the lives of citizens of the Central African Republic.

In modern times, being admitted to desirable parts of the world — made possible only by possessing a requisite citizenship — is fundamental to all aspects of one's life: medical care, education, wealth, and basic freedom all depend on citizenship, which is randomly ascribed at birth. The elementary raison d'être of the QNI is thus to debunk three central mythologies that surround our current 'separate but equal' thinking about citizenship and nationality, which are derived from black letter public international law and echo the mantras regarding the sovereign equality of states (Sironi 2013), as well as traditional philosophical and sociological analyses of what citizenship and nationality are and stand for (Marshall 1977).

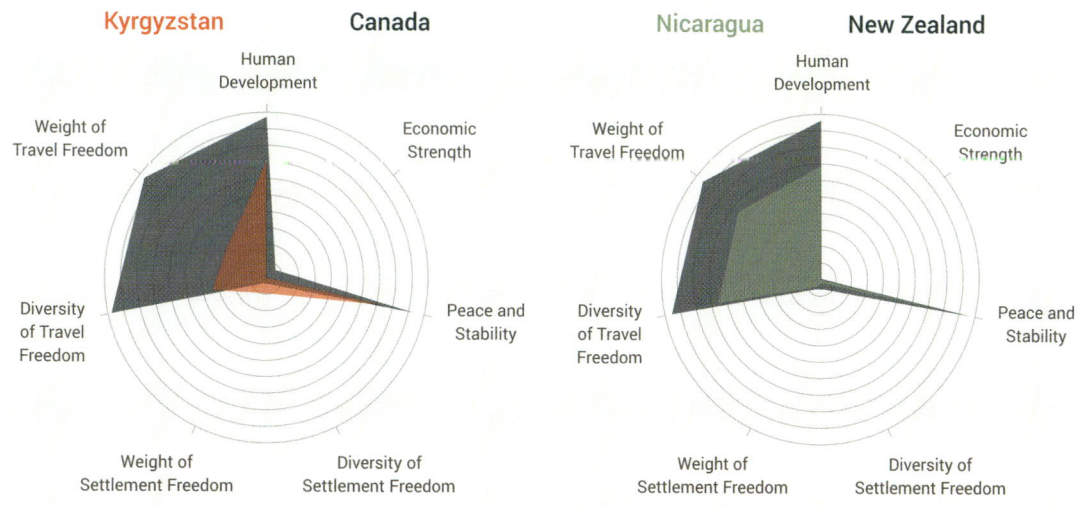

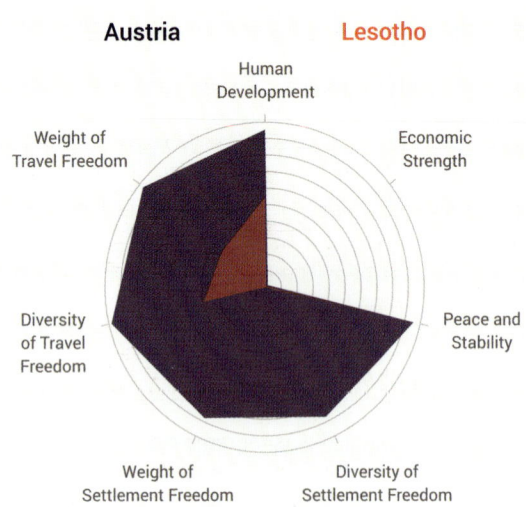

The QNI demonstrates that at least three familiar myths informing our thinking about citizenship and nationality could not be further from the truth. The first myth is that all nationalities are equal, and that it is impossible to compare them because attachment to a country cannot be objectively measured, which reinforces the narrative that 'separate but equal' works. The QNI shows beyond any reasonable doubt that it does not, since comparing the key rights associated with different nationalities reveals huge discrepancies in their quality. The second myth is that there is a direct correlation between the power and the size of a country's economy and the quality of its nationality. This line of thinking is equally misguided: the QNI demonstrates that the nationalities of the world's most militarily and economically powerful countries cannot compare in quality to those of some microstates. The third myth, on which democratic justifications for upholding the 'separate but equal' status quo rest, holds that there is a correlation between the geographical scope of the rights granted by a nationality and the territory of the conferring state. The research informing the QNI demonstrates clearly that this correlation, which was true in the past, does not exist in the 21st century. Some nationalities grant access to key citizenship rights, including the right to work and reside in the territories of dozens more countries than those granting the status in the first place. Some examples are visualized on the map on pages 30 and 31. In helping debunk these three mythologies the QNI opens a Pandora's box of questions, some of which are discussed below and also in Dimitry Kochenov's *Citizenship* (Kochenov 2019b).

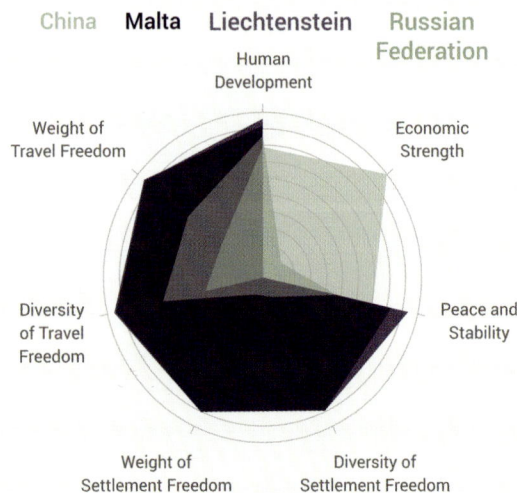

Once citizenship is thoroughly scrutinized, it is evident that the above three mythologies, and many others, are deeply entrenched in how we think about nationality and citizenship and interfere with our capacity to perceive the data showing that each of them has proven to be false. This counterintuitive twist makes the QNI particularly interesting.

2 What Is Citizenship or Nationality?

The idea of measuring and comparing nationalities sounds odd if we believe in the International Court of Justice's (ICJ) description of nationality as

> *a legal bond having as its basis a social fact of attachment, a genuine connection of existence, interests and sentiments, together with the existence of reciprocal rights and duties. It may be said to constitute the juridical expression of the fact that the individual upon whom it is conferred, either directly by the law or as the result of an act of the authorities, is in fact more closely connected with the population of the State conferring nationality than with that of any other State.*[1]

It is a relief to know that the contemporary reality of citizenship and nationality is far removed from this romantic vision (Spiro 2019b). In *Nottebohm*, not finding 'genuine links' allowed the ICJ to endorse robbing a former German of his extensive Guatemalan possessions after the Second World War as a consequence of his naturalization in Liechtenstein, a neutral and prosperous European state, rather than in Guatemala, where he lived most of his adult life. Liechtenstein was not allowed to protect its citizen since the legal link of nationality attachment was not enough for diplomatic protection, according to the Court. Since Mr. Nottebohm did not have any other nationality, Guatemala de facto expropriated all his properties with no due process of law. This case, or its outcome, would not be possible today.

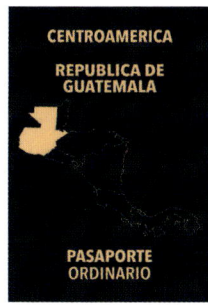

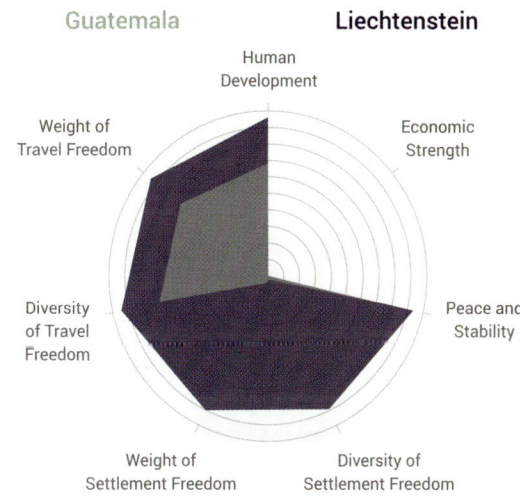

Unlike what *Nottebohm* depicts, citizenship in fact operates (and has always operated) quite differently: making a citizen is an ideology-inspired legal exercise, implying a choice among available bodies that could be useful for the purposes of achieving the goals of the relevant authority at any given time, whatever these may be. Those persons who are less useful are simply excluded and do not exist in the eyes of the law — they are proclaimed non-citizens. Without the *legal* link of nationality, they, like Friedrich Nottebohm himself, cannot possibly have a 'genuine link' with any state that has not claimed them. A legal link of nationality — the essence of this concept — has to be genuine to be meaningful, of course, but this does not imply any connection to the state, its current or past territory, or to the officially proclaimed culture. Instead, when established by the authority the legal link is required and sufficient to establish the connection with the state.

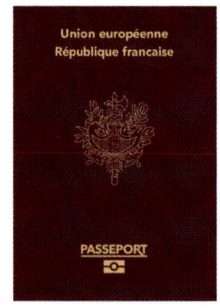
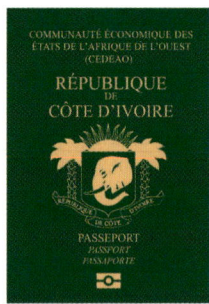

A 'genuine link' in the non-legal *Nottebohm* sense boasts little to no significance in the world where Guatemalan nationality is still infinitely less desirable than the status with which Liechtenstein provides its citizens; this is the reason Mr. Nottebohm chose to acquire Liechtensteiner nationality in the first place, despite the fact that he lived in Guatemala his whole adult life. The meaning of 'genuine links' will not change in the world as long as French expatriates in Côte d'Ivoire will do anything in their power not to be considered as Ivorians in the law of that country (no matter how genuine the links), and as long as Eritrean migrants in Berlin who are not following formal naturalization procedures need to be excluded by the German government from any nationality claims based on general socialization. The worth of these

nationalities is too different to ignore when looking at the lives that people may build in a particular place. This situation is not new, and is the reason why naturalizing in Guatemala did not cross Mr. Nottebohm's mind, no matter how much he desired to be rid of his Third Reich nationality at the start of the Second World War. Internationally, citizenship law is thus not a reflection of deep connections, but of shallow, procedural ones; the QNI is the best illustration of why this is the case. We thus fully agree with Brubaker that national citizenships are today's most important "instrument and object of closure", that is, exclusion (Brubaker 1992, 23). Using this approach, the distinction between nationality and citizenship in many philosophical and sociological works in the field becomes unproductive. Hence, 'citizenship' and 'nationality' will be used synonymously throughout the QNI.

Exclusions can run along any lines: territory of origin, race, religion, education, language, time — name it and a legal-historical example will be found. Citizenship's capacity to exclude is its core function, which means that in the 'golden days' of citizenship — the mythical days of the concept's absolute, just authority — exclusion at the level of *legal* status could only rarely be questioned: equality is *among* citizens, as you may recall. As a consequence, in its relationship vis-à-vis its citizens the authority enjoys an almost universal carte blanche, as the story goes: ethnic electorates are created (Visek 1997), those who are not 'white' enough for its liking are assigned to 'ancestral homelands' and proclaimed to be 'foreigners' (Dugard 1980), and those who are sent away due to their ideological (Chamberlain 2006) or racial deficiencies are declared as non-citizens (Rundle 2009). The long history of flagrant discrimination is rich and diverse, and citizenship has consistently been effective in justifying such discrimination by muting any objections at the outset: "But she was not a citizen!" Under this paradigm the core question, before looking at rights, entitlements, duties, and equality claims, is "*Who* is a citizen in this society?" This is a question to which only the public authority is entitled by its own law to give an answer. Those who are not citizens are per se entitled to nothing, and this is legally and politically right, we are told, even if also frequently morally unjust. Legalization and justification of essentially randomized discrimination is the core function of citizenship, after all.

Contemporary Estonian passport

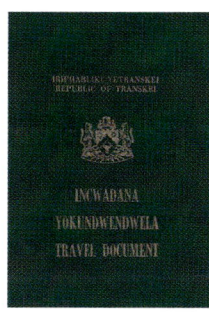
Transkei travel document

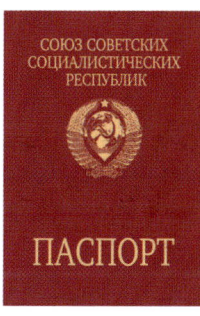
Soviet foreign travel passport

The cover of a German Third Reich passport stamped with the letter "J" (Jude) identifying its holder as a Jew

A nationality for the purposes of the QNI thus emerges as a legal status of belonging to a public authority (usually a state), which may or may not come with a prize of rights and a set of liabilities and duties to fulfill. Links with the territory the authority effectively controls or cultural affinity are of no relevance here: an Italian who has never been to Europe but possesses the right documents is as much a national as an Italian who has never left Macerata.

It is crucial in this context that the official name of the legal status of personal attachment conferred by the authority in question is of no direct relevance. EU citizenship, a legal status of attachment to the European Union bringing with it rights and possibly duties for those designated as its citizens (Kochenov 2009), is therefore as meaningful for the QNI (even though the Union is not quite a state) as the status of 'non-citizen' of Latvia, which is — although the denial is in the name — a classical status of nationality for all intents and purposes. Just as the citizenship of the US, Sri Lanka, or Australia establishes a connection between the status and the state, the status of 'non-citizen' of Latvia connects its holders to the Latvian state, endowing them with both rights and obligations to that state, as Aleksejs Dimitrovs explains in his contribution to this volume.

3 Who Decides Who Is a National?

Due to the intrinsic link between citizenship and state sovereignty, international law is clear that who is a citizen is for states to decide. The 1930 Hague Convention on Certain Questions Relating to the Conflict of Nationality Laws is unequivocal on this issue: "It is for each state to determine under its own law who are its nationals."[2] Thus, nationality can be conferred only by national law — international law as it stands today can only hypothetically influence such state decisions.[3] It certainly cannot separately confer nationality on individuals, even if it theoretically guides states on what is and is not acceptable. Since the famous dicta of the Permanent Court of International Justice (PCIJ) in the cases of *Tunis and Morocco Nationality Decrees* and *Polish Nationality*, where the PCIJ opined that in the future the role played by international law in the sphere of conferral of citizenship rights might increase through new treaty obligations,[4] the reality of national dominance in the citizenship domain has scarcely been altered. Attempts to regulate citizenship issues globally at the international level have been far from successful.

The picture becomes more complicated once the rules on the recognition of nationality under international law are taken into account. Following the ICJ decision in *Nottebohm*, states are not obliged to recognize the nationality lawfully conferred on an individual by another state even if said individual does not have any other. The approach to the framing of citizenship adopted in the international legal documents thus begs for an extremely cautious reading. While states are free to determine who their citizens are, this determination does not always work on the international level and, as a consequence, can have a purely internal effect and deprive people of any access to justice.[5]

Indeed, sometimes uncritically hailed as settled law,[6] the *Nottebohm* judgment should be read with a grain of salt, as the ICJ's dictum on the requirement of nationality being "a genuine connection of experience, interests and sentiments, together with the existence of reciprocal rights and duties" withdraws attention from the actual *ratio decidendi* of the case, which indicates that the judgment's basis is actually rooted in the doctrine of abuse of rights, specifically tailored to the particular facts of the case (Sloane 2009). Moreover, state practice and *opinio iuris* reveal hardly any suggestion that there must be a genuine link between the nationality-conferring state and individual for a nationality to be recognized outside the context of diplomatic protection (Sloane 2009, 29–35; Sironi 2013).[7] With the exception of bizarre examples such as overt discrimination and en-masse extraterritorial naturalizations in passportization schemes,[8] international law simply offers no concrete standards for the acquisition and recognition of citizenship. Rather, while a rudimentary international law of citizenship seems indeed to be developing (Spiro 2011), international regulation of the recognition of nationality is infused with a functional approach, focusing on the objectives of specific international legal regimes[9] and on the protection of individual rights (Sironi 2013, 54), rather than policing a one-state one-person fiction, which inspired *Nottebohm*

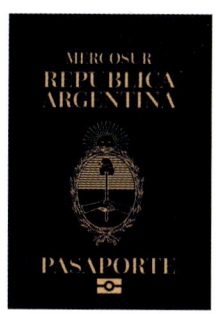  

but could never be observed in practice (Spiro 1997; Spiro 2016). *Nottebohm*, in other words, is not good law any more (Sironi 2013), if it has ever been.[10] This is particularly true of the EU, from which the dubious *Nottebohm* logic has been expressly departed as far back as the 1990s in the *Micheletti* case,[11] and in which the *Nottebohm* perspective on nationality and

citizenship was dismissed as an excursion into the "romantic period of international law", in the words of Advocate General Tesauro.[12] Spain was obliged to recognize the Italian nationality of an Argentinian who had never visited his second country of citizenship before turning to it in order to settle in Spain under the EU's free movement rules.

4 How to Decide Who Is a National

The majority of citizenships are distributed at birth based on the principles of *ius sanguinis* (bloodline) and *ius soli* (place of birth) or, more frequently, both.[13] Directly from the principle of sovereignty flows the limitation that any state can regulate only what happens within its realm, so all it takes is another state's willingness to claim someone as a citizen and the neatness of the Westphalian presentation of reality is gone. Italy made up to a million Latin Americans its nationals since the change of its law at the beginning of the 1990s; many Mexicans hold US nation-

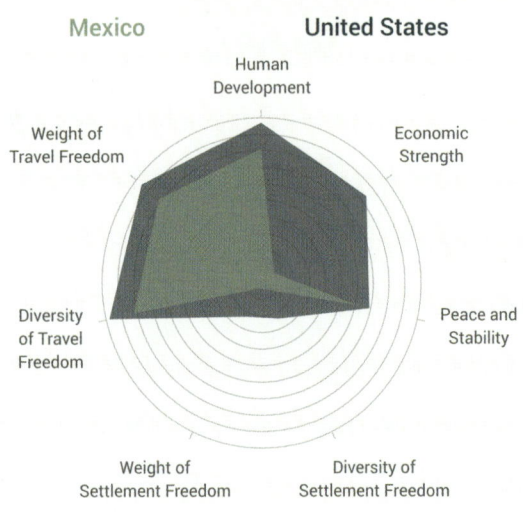

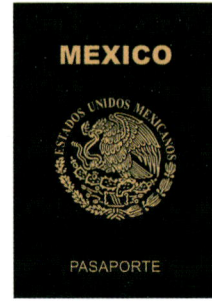 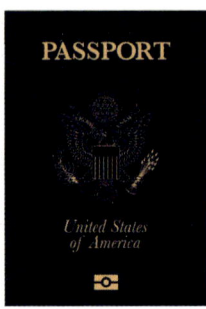

ality since Mexico allowed for dual citizenship towards the end of the 20th century; plenty of Macedonians are also Bulgarians; a huge number of Moldovans are equally Romanians. The toleration of such interpenetrations of citizenship is growing worldwide, as Spiro in particular has masterfully demonstrated (Spiro 2016). Fighting back is a quixotic exercise: Slovakia tried to pressure members of its Hungarian minority *not* to accept Hungarian citizenship by threatening to annul their original Slovak nationality. Although it raised unnecessary international tensions and garnered international ridicule, this policy did not dissuade Slovakia's Hungarians from obtaining passports of the kin-state; rather, it pushed them to do so in secret (Arraiza 2015, 114). Unlike the other examples, however,

 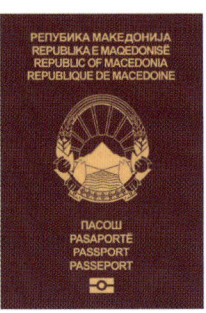

a Slovak gains little by obtaining a Hungarian nationality in terms of objective benefits: the qualities of the two nationalities are very similar, both boasting elite citizenships in the EU, which indicates purely emotional motives for such citizenship acquisition.

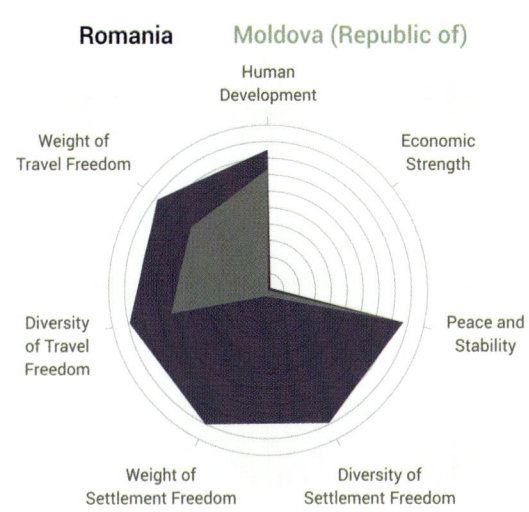

Anyone who asserts that the allocation of citizenships in the world is logical and clearly flowing from the neat separation of the world into well-founded constitutional systems backing the legality of such allocations, would thus not be telling the truth. Local birth is good for Uruguayans but irrelevant to Germans. A tenured professorship in a local university is irrelevant to Germans but until 2008 was a key to immediate Austrian citizenship. Being 'active in the diaspora' is irrelevant to Austrians but can make you a Pole. Having a Lebanese mother is irrelevant to the Lebanese, but the fact of having a Jewish mother — even one without Israeli citizenship — can make you an Israeli. The rules are truly diverse and the examples of this diversity are countless: what is taken for granted as best practice in one country can seem almost outrageous in another.

Such diversity in regulation creates both challenges for many and opportunities for some. Not knowing the rules can result in surprises, and getting the full picture depends on knowing both the nationality rules in a child's country of birth and the rules in the parents' countries of citizenship. A Moscow-born child of a Dane who himself was born outside of Denmark to a naturalized father and a Jordanian mother will be Russian, unable to reside with the parents in Denmark without a residence permit or even to enter the country without a visa. Jordan does not allow for a *ius sanguinis* transfer of citizenship via the mother, and Danish law limits such a transfer to two generations for children born abroad. Consequently, the child — born stateless in this case — will receive citizenship of the Russian Federation by birth, even though the Russian Federation does not recognize *ius soli* in general — that is, unless the child is otherwise stateless. Similar cases are more common than one would expect, illustrating the randomness of citizenship assignment. In other words, the laws of many states, including but not limited to the state of birth of the child, the states of birth of the parents, the states of the citizenship of the parents, the state custodians of the ethnic groups to which the parents belong, the religion of the parents, and other factors will be at play at the moment of citizenship being granted at birth (Kochenov 2019b).

As we have seen, citizenship acquisition at birth is potentially governed by a number of national legal systems, all of which view themselves as endowed with a legitimate claim of authority over the issue. Similarly, naturalizations are equally governed by the combination of laws of a number of states, no matter what each individual state actually says on its books. This is because naturalization rules usually differ depending on the citizenships that the applicant already holds — an Estonian naturalizes two and a half times faster in Italy than a New Zealander does,[14] and a Filipino five times faster in Spain than a Tunisian (Kochenov 2010; Kochenov and Lindeboom 2018). Naturalization rules may also depend on the citizenship rules of the state of original nationality. For instance, Morocco does not allow for the renunciation of its citizenship, which means that any Moroccan naturalizing in a country requiring such renunciation, such as the Russian Federation, will necessarily fall under an exception, since there is no way for the Russian legal system to change Moroccan law.

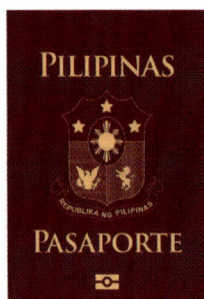

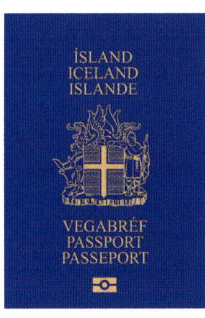 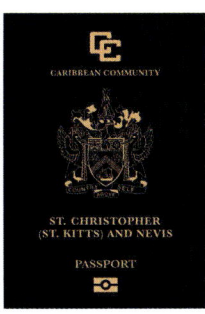

Although 98% of the world's population never undergoes a change of citizenship status once initially assigned, acquisition of citizenship by naturalization tends to be in the spotlight more frequently now. Importantly, naturalization rules are no simpler or more intuitive than those for the acquisition of citizenship status by birth. Some are extremely complex: a special Act of Parliament is still required in Iceland to naturalize anyone. By contrast, some are relatively simple: buy a home of a particular value in the Caribbean or donate to one sugarcane diversification fund or another and you are a citizen of any island of your choice, starting from USD 100,000 per family, with a seasonal hurricane discount (Surak 2016); see also Kälin's contribution to this volume. Some naturalization rules were even easier in the past. As one example, the German States of the Holy Roman Empire used 'presumed naturalization', as reported by Fahrmeir (1997). Residence in a new German state implied, for any foreign German, the acquisition of a new citizenship once the entry fees had been paid and a certain residence period had elapsed.

As already mentioned, the majority of international legal instruments aimed at regulating citizenship issues engaged in 'ghost-hunting': instead of effectively addressing issues of vital importance, such as the imminent need for the reduction of statelessness,[15] they concentrated on combating double nationality,[16] hence focusing on ensuring absolute sovereignty of states over their claimed populations as opposed to protecting human rights and equality. Long gone are the times in which the doctrine of insoluble allegiance reigned, which assumed "a debt of gratitude which cannot be forfeited, cancelled or altered by any change of time, place or circumstance" (Blackstone 1884, 117; Spiro 1997, 1419–30), thereby making either the acquisition of a new nationality or a change of the original nationality virtually impossible. This is because of the rise of human rights and global migration (Bosniak 2000; Joppke 2010; Joppke 2018), coupled with the elimination of gender discrimination in the citizenship laws of the majority of states performing well on the Human Development Index (HDI), which empowered women to pass on their nationality and radically increased the number of multinational children (Bredbenner 1998). Naturalizations and the changing of nationality are both legally recognized realities.[17] Agreeing with Chan, at present "there seems to be a general consensus that everyone is entitled to change his nationality" (Chan 1991, 8). The toleration of multiple nationalities, as wonderfully documented by Spiro, is *the* current norm in international relations (Spiro 2016).

5 Nationalities Are Not Equal

Looking beyond the formalities of black-letter international law, it is clear that nationalities diverge strongly in their practical value. It is not a secret that our nationalities have a direct impact on our lifestyles, freedom to think independently, do business, and live longer, healthier, and more rewarding lives. The extremes are well known: contemporary citizenship is among the key tools

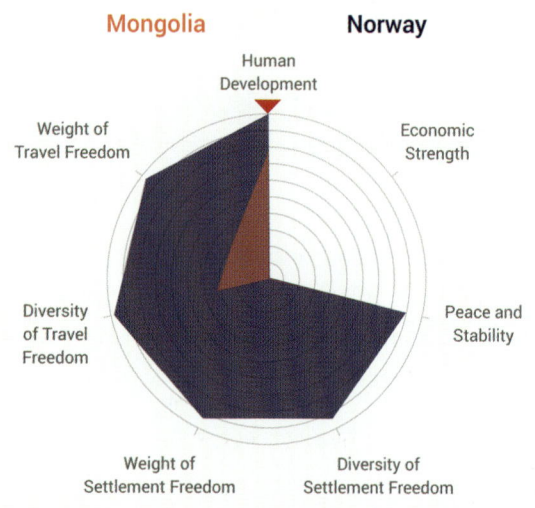

in the preservation of steep global inequality, as Milanovic has masterfully demonstrated (Milanovic 2016). A child in Nigeria is 38 times more likely not to survive the first five years of life than a child in the United Kingdom (UK). Likewise, Afghans and Iraqis are far less likely to experience London, Los Angeles, or Tokyo than, say, Austrians and Australians. Nationalities are not equal on a number of counts. It is better to have the nationality of a country that offers a long life expectancy, good schooling system, and high level of prosperity, such as Norway, than that of a country that offers lower levels of security, schooling and health to its nationals, such as Mongolia. It is better to have a nationality — and, as a consequence, enjoy the rights to work and reside in that country — in a state with a large economy, like China, than in a tiny country, however prosperous, like Andorra. It is better to have

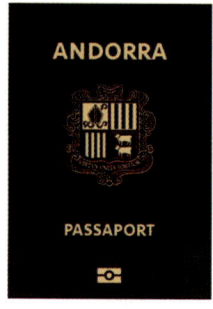 

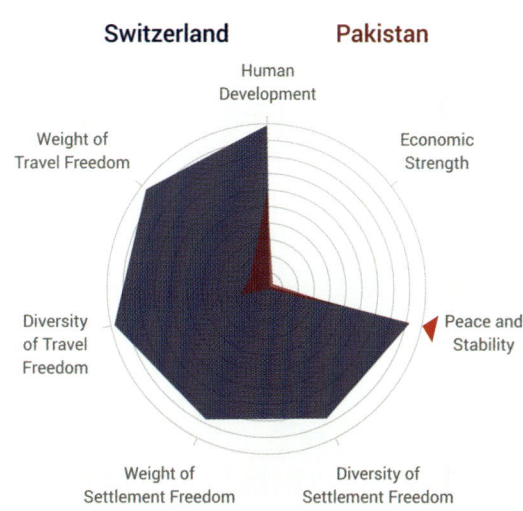

the nationality of a peaceful and stable country, such as Switzerland, than that of a country with security risks, such as Pakistan.

It is difficult to defend the argument that because of the patriotic feelings held by nationals about their country the value of nationalities is unquantifiable. In today's globalized world, identities overlap (Kymlicka 1995; Spiro 2016), members of the population have lived abroad, sometimes for a considerable amount of time, and many are likely to hold more than one passport.[18] Additionally, regardless of the subjective feelings people may or may not have towards their nationality, the living environment in one's home country — welfare, education level, life expectancy, and so on, as well as the global opportunities it affords — are quantifiable, and differences in quality between nationalities are measurable.

The most notable evidence of how distorted — and, in fact, condescending — the claim is that nationalities are fundamentally equal is made manifest by nationalities that are *liabilities* rather than sources of rights and opportunities, which is sadly true for the *majority* of citizenships in the world, certainly those included in the Very Low Quality and Low Quality categories of the QNI. (See the map of the quality of the world's nationalities on pages 70 and 71.) As the QNI demonstrates, a valid comparison of citizenships as legal statuses attached to states, as opposed to a comparison of the states themselves, reveals that most of the world's citizenship statuses are of much lower quality than the ones conferred by a handful of Western European, North American, and other

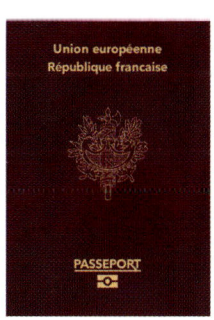
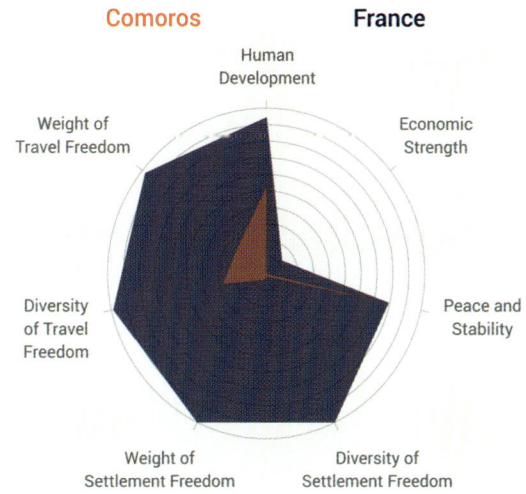

24 • Quality of Nationality Index

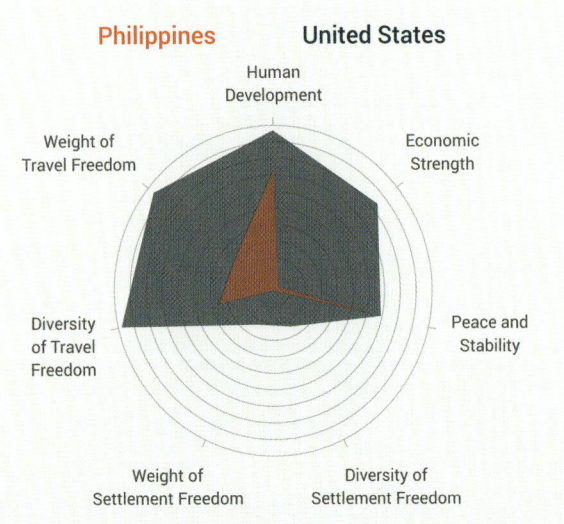
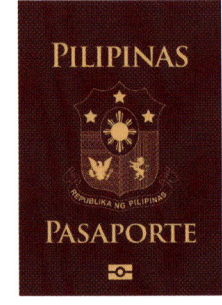
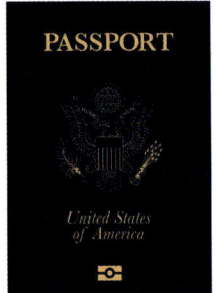

highly developed nations. Any random comparison of the legal statuses of former colonies and former colonizers produces very consistent results. The quality of nationality of the Comoros Islands is overwhelmingly worse than that of France (and Mayotte), the nationality of Suriname is ranked significantly lower than that of the Kingdom of the Netherlands (which includes Aruba), the nationality of Angola is less desirable than that of Portugal, and being a Filipino makes you worse off than being an American.

This basic and predictable finding abundantly illustrated by the QNI has far-reaching implications for the profiling of citizenship as a "right to have rights", *pace* Arendt: many citizenships in the world are so bad that one can possibly talk of liabilities only, not rights. This finding is in tune with economic inequality research: life chances and prosperity are distributed unequally around the world more in special than in class terms. The correlation with citizenships is clear: most people holding the liability statuses ascribed to them by birth are in the world's gutter, and are thus deprived of any rights and opportunities even remotely comparable to those enjoyed by citizens of the Global North (Milanovic 2016). Citizenship is unquestionably the tool used to keep them there. Indeed, it has become one of the crucial tools in ensuring the preservation of spatial inequalities in the world since *all* borders around the world are always locked for the holders of liability-level legal statuses, while remaining open for holders of the elite citizenships of North America and Western Europe.

6 A Country's Power and Citizenship Quality: The Lack of Correlation

Recognizing that all citizenships are not created equal, it would be a grave mistake, however, to identify the quality of nationality with the quality of the conferring state; the quality of a nationality is not always reflected in basic characteristics such as the economic power or development level of the countries with which such nationalities are associated. What your nationality allows you to do *outside* your home country matters at least as much as living standards within it. Thus, economically strong countries can have relatively unattractive nationalities insofar as they do not allow their nationals to freely settle in other countries, such as is true of China and the Chinese nationality and of Canada and the Canadian nationality. Conversely, small economies can offer nationalities of great value (such as Slovenia and the Slovenian nationality, which allows free settlement to 41 countries and territories, and Iceland and the Icelandic nationality, which allows free settlement to 43 countries and territories), precisely because they offer full access to employment and residence in the more than 40 other nations of the EU — Slovenian and Icelandic nationals receive home treatment, in fact, and access to opportunities not offered by the Canadian and Chinese nationalities. Likewise, in 2018, in terms of tourist and business travel, the same tiny Slovenia, with visa-free or visa-on-arrival access to 170 countries, easily surpassed the Chinese nationality, whose mainland Chinese travel document granted visa-free or visa-on-arrival access to only 66 countries. Perhaps the most obvious example can be seen with those possessing Iranian or Yemeni nationalities who were, upon the executive order of President Trump, suddenly confronted with the impossibility of entering the territory of the US visa-free regardless of any personal circumstances or any other nationality they held: it is time to admit that the quality of nationalities varies to the extent that a low-quality nationality can be a *liability*, rather than an empowering bundle of rights.

6 A Country's Power and Citizenship Quality: The Lack of Correlation

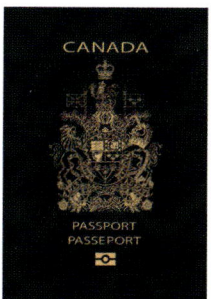
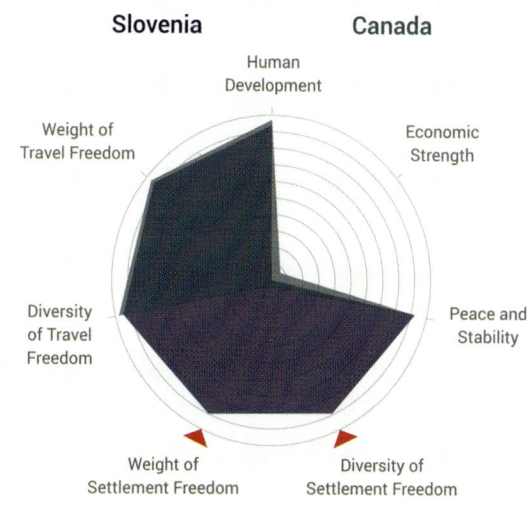

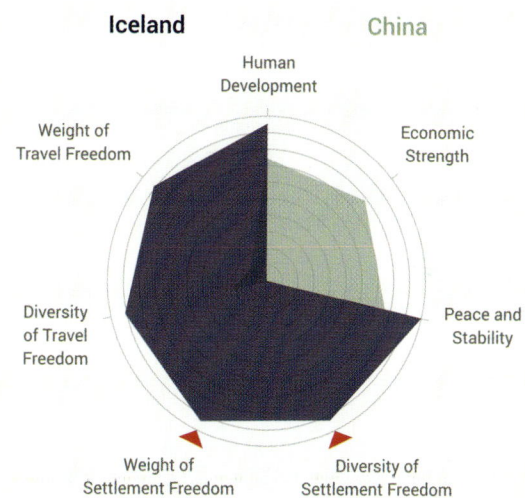

7 Each Nationality Is Global: The Rise of Intercitizenships

It follows from the discussion above that a nationality is not merely a legal relationship between a state and an individual. In fact, nationalities in the contemporary world are global and have a global significance, which is precisely what the QNI attempts to measure: once a nationality is granted to a person, that person is treated and ascribed rights and duties globally according to the nationality they hold. In other words, being an Iraqi or a Swede is not only about you and Iraq or you and Sweden: all the countries in the world will adjust their treatment of a Swede and an Iraqi to the different standards of quality these nationalities stand for. For the Iraqi, the majority

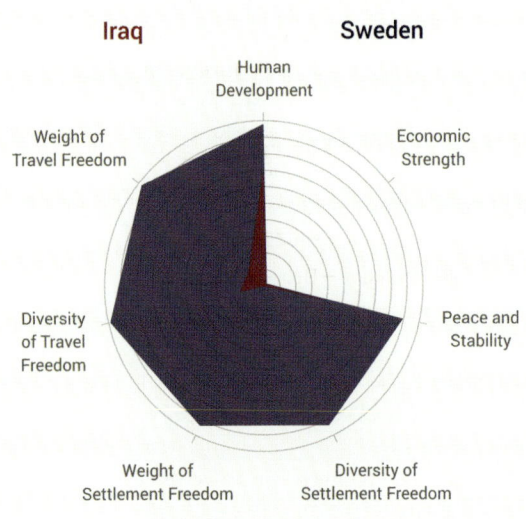

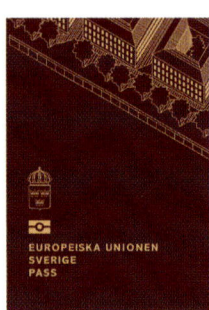

of global doors will be closed. For the Swede, plentiful opportunities will be available. Besides visa-free travel, such opportunities include unlimited access to settle and work in 43 of the world's most developed countries, that have huge GDPs per capita and stellar HDI scores. The Iraqi will have the 'right' to stay in Iraq while visas or residence permits elsewhere will usually be refused. An Iraqi is thus globally humiliated by law through his or her nationality, compared to a Swede, whose horizon of opportunities is boosted: comparing these nationalities is very difficult, since what divides them is an unbridgeable abyss in terms of quality. This abyss is significantly present the world over: a Swede is a Swede everywhere in the world, just as an Iraqi is an Iraqi.

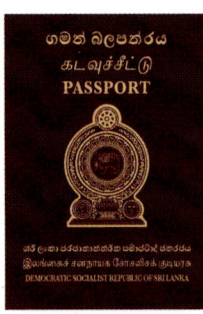

One of the core aspects here — besides the biases in the law of most jurisdictions worldwide against those holding the nationalities of the countries viewed as poor and unstable — is the very idea of a correlation between a citizenship and the territory of rights. The hitherto unquestioned correlation between citizenship rights and sovereign territory is changing in many places. Indeed, any classical citizenship presumes a correlation between the legal status created and enforced by the authority (say, Sri Lankan citizenship) and the territory of rights, in particular political rights and the right to reside and work, corresponding to the

territory of the issuing state (in this case, the Sri Lankan territory).[19] Research shows that in the 21st century this correlation no longer holds true for the majority of jurisdictions around the world (Kochenov and Lindeboom 2017); this core finding is the starting point of this part of the QNI. While a Sri Lankan or Mongolian citizenship still comes with a package of rights that are uniquely invocable in Sri Lanka or Mongolia, respectively (where, on the basis of these statuses, the number of other jurisdictions granting rights to settle and work is zero), the citizenship status issued by more than half of the world's nations is no longer limited to the territory controlled by the issuing authority. The majority of the citizenships of the most highly developed nations are passports to full inclusion in dozens of states, rather than to one state only. This alters a crucial element of the story of citizenship: its scope.

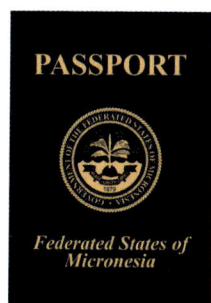

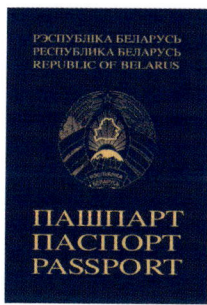

Indeed, the hitherto unquestioned correlation between citizenship rights and sovereign territory is changing in many places: more and more citizenships around the world secure access to key citizenship rights including residence, work and, also not infrequently, political rights (Fabbrini 2017). Such rights are outside the confines of the sovereign territory whose authority is responsible for the grant of the legal status of citizenship in the first place. Importantly, this does not concern only the (quasi-) citizenship of the (formerly) subordinated colonies that, through some version of a "compact of free association" (Keitner and Reisman 2003) with what used to be the 'mother country', would extend the rights of the colonial center to the former colonial subjects: think of the Micronesians in the US (Dang 2011) or — if we are not stretching it — Belarusians in the Russian Federation (Voronina 2013). This global phenomenon is now overwhelmingly widespread.

The logic of opening up the sovereign territory and hence, potentially, access to the citizenship status, as such, for each other's citizens, was first proposed at the end of the 19th century by Albert Venn Dicey, the legendary English constitutionalist, to apply to the British Empire and the US (Dyer 1897); while the proposal found only a cold reception then, today it has come to work well around the world. From the Gulf Cooperation Council (Babar 2011) to Latin America (Acosta and Freier 2015; Acosta and Geddes 2014), West Africa (at least on paper) (Adepoju 2002; Adepoju 2009), the Caribbean (Lancaster and St. George 2015; Berry 2014), the Nordic countries (Kuisma 2007), and more broadly, the EU, what can be observed is an extension of core citizenship rights granted by some nationalities far beyond the territory controlled by the issuing authorities. Dicey referred to his idea as 'intercitizenships'. The dislocation of the citizenship–sovereign-territory correlation has turned into a fundamentally important trend in the contemporary evolution of citizenship, which one might brand, following Dicey, as the rise of intercitizenships penetrating two or more jurisdictions via the same legal status, enhanced through the binding requirement of mutual recognition.

Madagascar, Mongolia, Sri Lanka, and the like are now exceptions, while the norm a hundred years ago used to be the correlation between citizenship, the national territory, and the scope of the rights granted by citizenship that these statuses bestow. Almost half the nations around the world today issue citizenship statuses recognized by other nations in terms of often virtually unconditional access to the national territory for work and settlement. So, a Bahraini is welcome to work and reside in the other five Gulf Cooperation Council states, a Norwegian in 43 European nations, and an Armenian in Belarus, Georgia, Kazakhstan, Kyrgyzstan, and the Russian Federation. From

Map Showing Settlement and Work Rights for Selected Nationalities

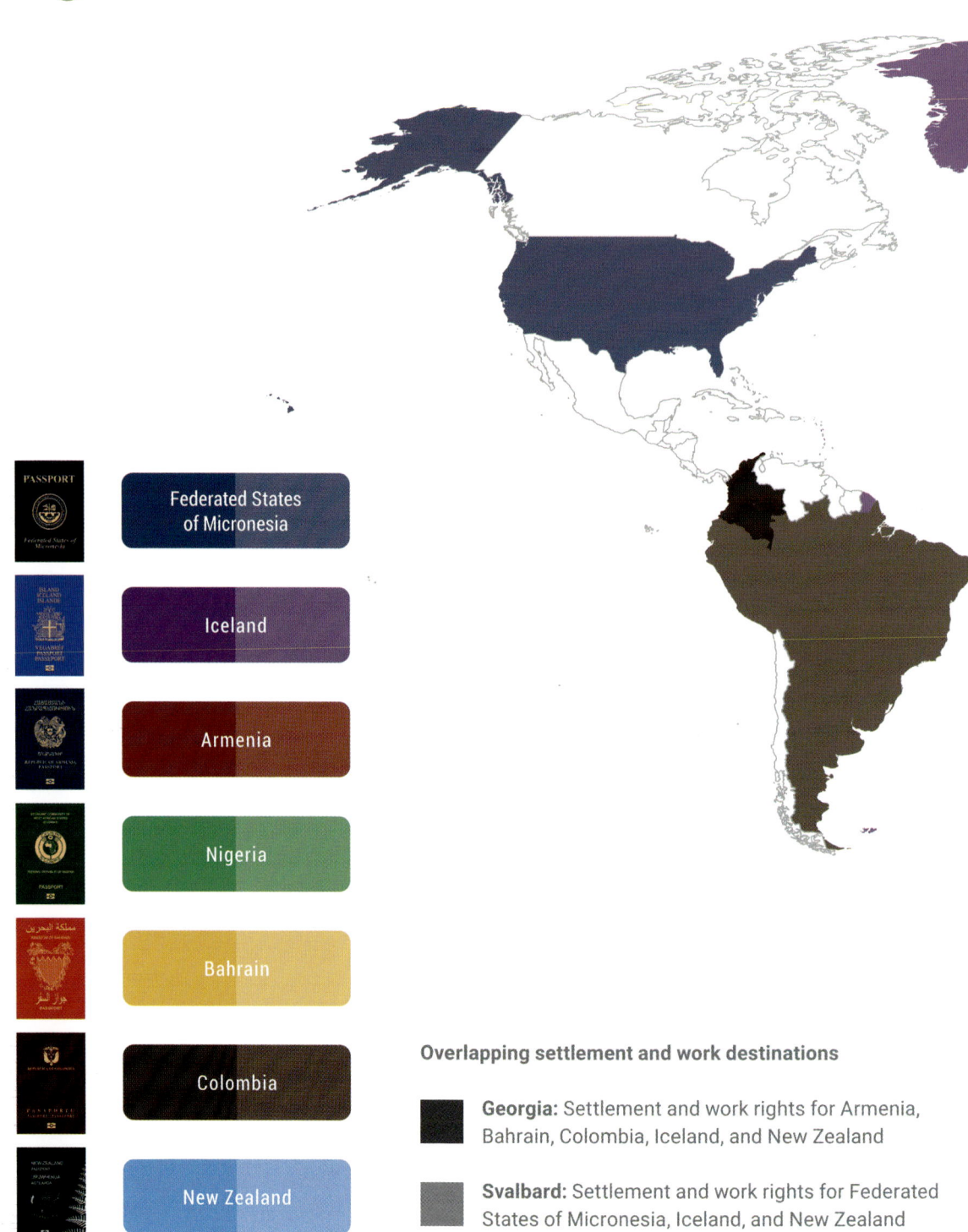

Overlapping settlement and work destinations

Georgia: Settlement and work rights for Armenia, Bahrain, Colombia, Iceland, and New Zealand

Svalbard: Settlement and work rights for Federated States of Micronesia, Iceland, and New Zealand

7 Each Nationality Is Global: The Rise of Intercitizenships · 31

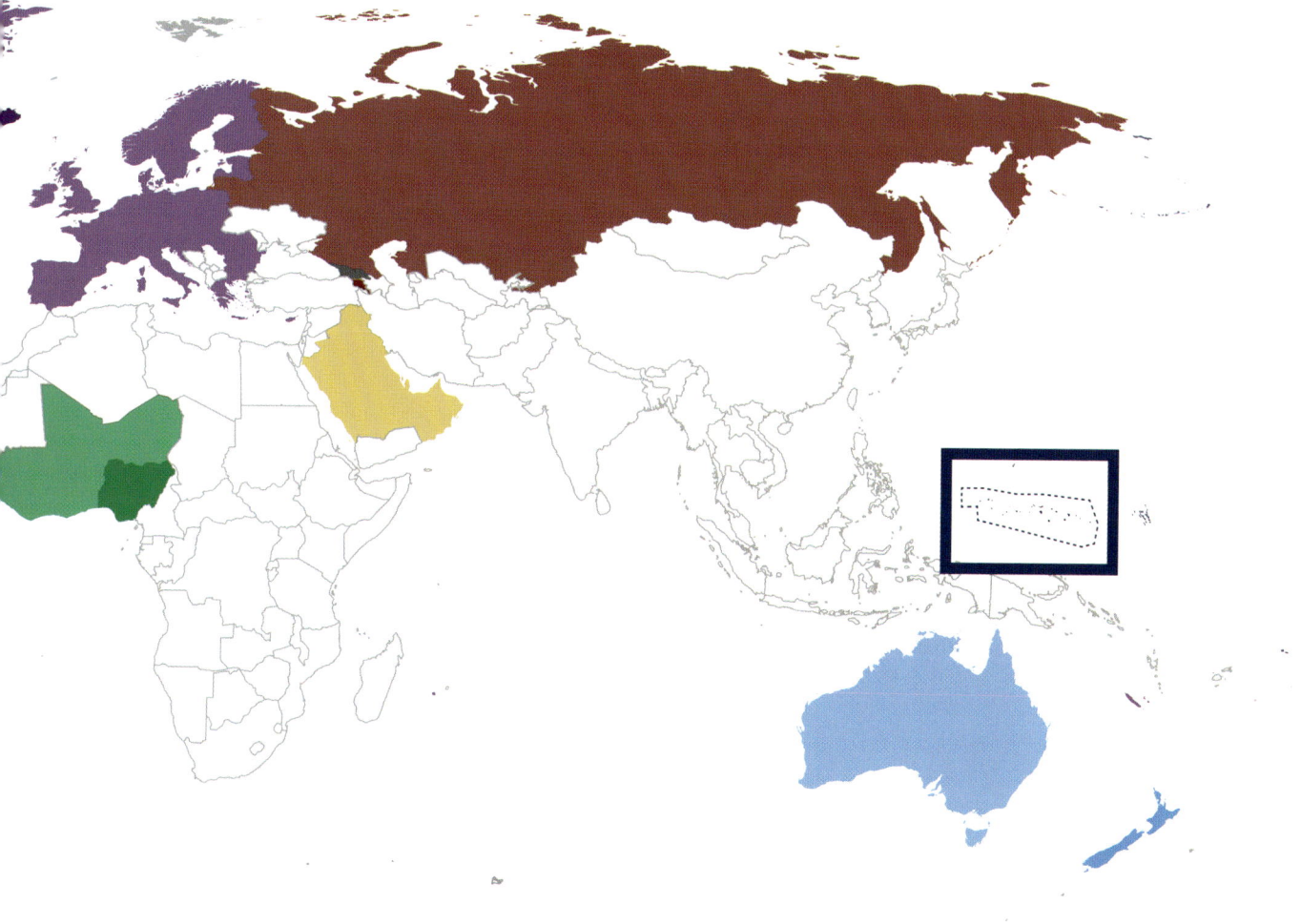

ECOWAS in Western Africa, the OECS in the Caribbean, and MERCOSUR in Latin America to the New Zealand–Australia arrangement, from the core rights granted to Indians in Nepal and Bhutan to the full access to the US territory and labor market granted to citizens of Nauru, Palau, and FS Micronesia, the decoupling of the territory where the core non-political rights of citizenship are enjoyed and the territory of the state granting citizenship is now a universal phenomenon.

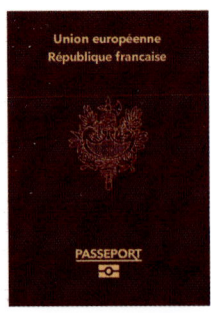

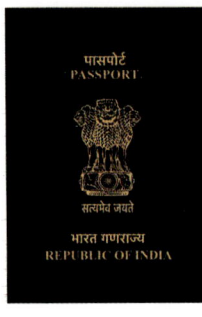

The global phenomenon of citizenship interpenetration at the level of work and residence rights has overwhelming significance for the conceptualization of sovereignty, citizenship, and territory. More and more, states issue legal statuses that increasingly entitle the relevant holders to citizenship rights outside the sovereign realm of the issuing country. The implication of the palette of rights associated with each particular legal status of this kind is that states de facto do nothing less than issue multiple citizenships: that of France gives full access to work and reside in 46 countries and territories; Armenia, five; India, two, and so on. When analyzing the rights of each of the world's nationalities, incorporating the settlement-abroad criterion is indispensable, of course, since a microstate nationality, say that of Liechtenstein or Malta, may grant residence and work rights in dozens of other states, thus boosting the rights value of the citizenship in question. The reverse is also true: the nationality of an important country, such as China, may provide access to zero foreign destinations for visa-free work and long-term residence.

The extremes emerging on the spectrum of rights–territory interconnections replacing the mono-correlation vary, from citizenships granting no residence and work rights per se in any territory at all, such as the British overseas territories citizenship, which is valid only for access to the territory of the issuing entity with a special endorsement unrelated to the holding of the status as such, to citizenships of countries endowing their nationals with no access to the right to settle and work in the territory of foreign states (such as Mongolia, Madagascar, and Sri Lanka, mentioned above), and to, finally, the leaders of the new trend, all of which are European nations. Such leaders, emerging based on the number of foreign states and territories allowing settlement and work, are France, Denmark, and the Netherlands, whose citizens can settle — no questions asked — in the highest numbers of states and territories abroad, which turns these citizenships into legal entitlements of access to more than 40 state territories and labor markets without any pre-authorizations.

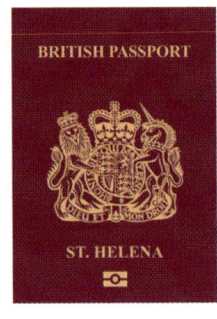

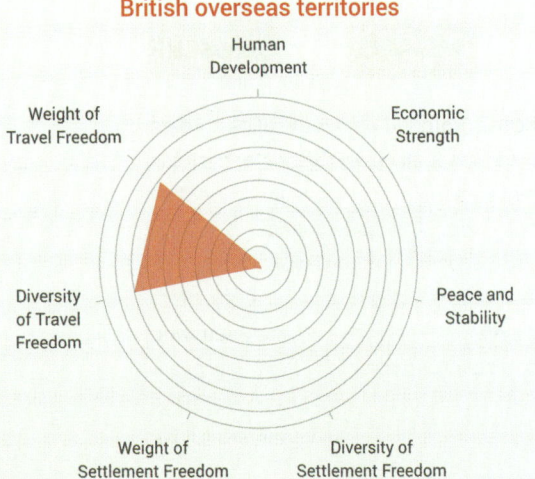

7 Each Nationality Is Global: The Rise of Intercitizenships • 33

Once this new crucial trend in citizenship law and policy is visualized, the map of the world changes to a great degree. This new trend is depicted in the map of the intercitizenships of the world, where the intensity of the country's color depends on the number of foreign states allowing the holders of its citizenship to settle and work in their territories without visas and permits — extending de facto the nation's territory for the holders of those particular citizenships.

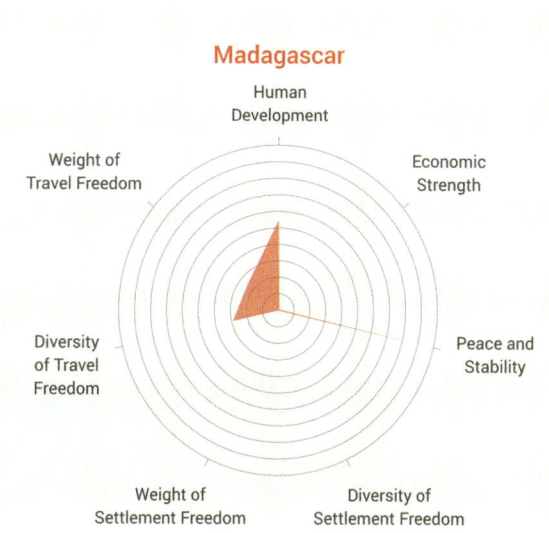

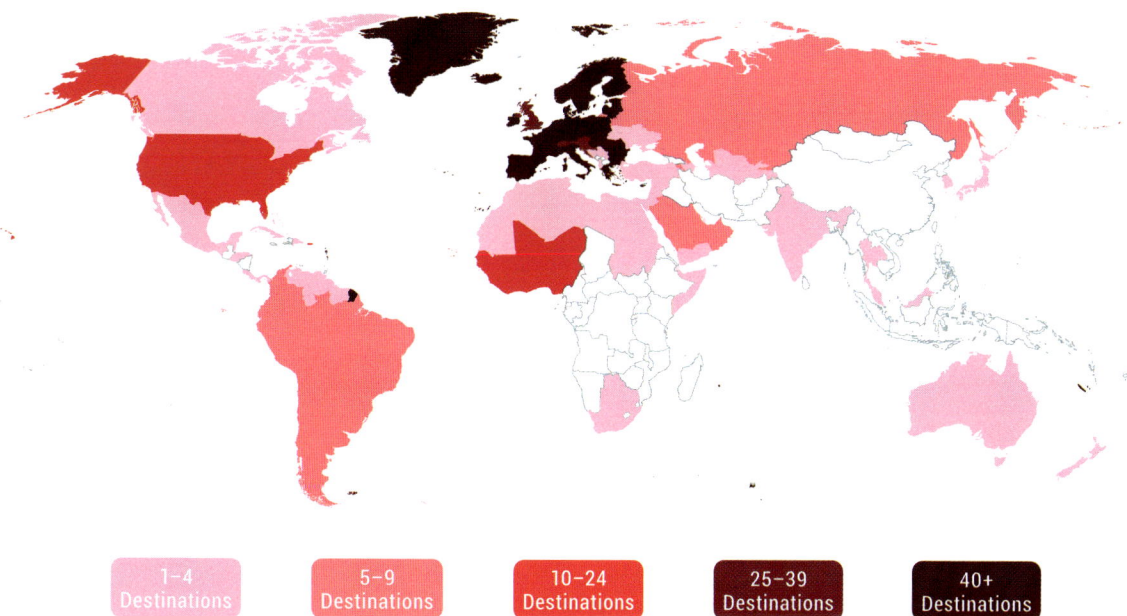

This map allows us to rethink the political maps of the world in a profound way: some of its borders are necessarily illusory from the practical work and residence perspective, which boosts the rights of individual citizens and obviously calls into question the current approaches to understanding the *demoi* in all the countries involved. If the notion of the people — the body politic — endowed with political rights — is to correlate with the territory where the laws are made and enforced, it is on its face problematic to exclude from political life all those who enjoy full access to the territory of the state for life and work by virtue of their foreign citizenship. To inform a Colombian, who has a right, without any pre-authorizations (subject only to a clean criminal record), to be present and to work in Argentina, Brazil, and a number of other Latin American nations (Acosta 2018), that no political rights could ever extend to her since she is a foreigner, is both counterintuitive and problematic: once a single working–living space has been created between countries, and the right to be part of a society other than the one to which you legally belong by virtue of your citizenship is extended based on the same citizenship status, what is at stake, it seems, is the redefinition of the meaning of 'the people' through the profound interconnections between concurrent legal regimes worldwide.

The intercitizenship interpenetration of territorial rights was anticipated by Dicey as long ago as in 1897. Addressing the fellows of All Souls at Oxford, Dicey put forward a proposal for Anglo-Saxon intercitizenship: full mutual recognition of citizenships between the British Empire and the US, to mark the coming of the 20th century.

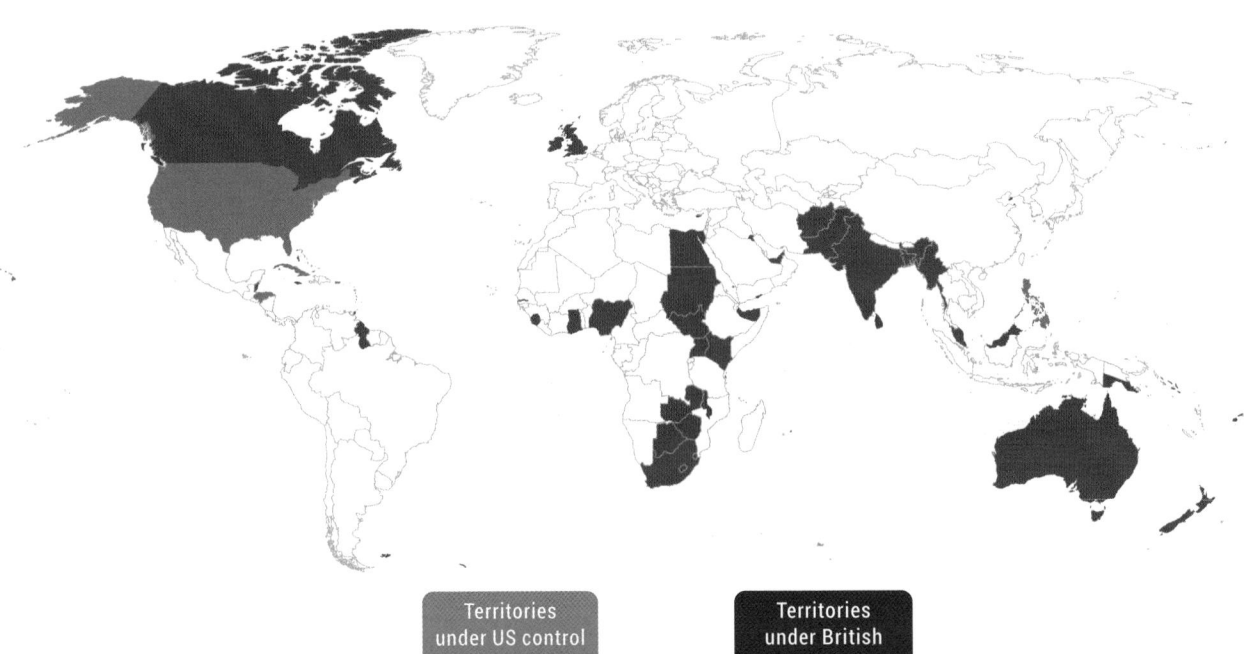

A. V. Dicey's Proposed British–American Intercitizenship, 1900

Although he was not taken seriously at the time, Dicey actually predicted the future: whether we like it or not, the separation of the world into states and of the people of the world into citizens is arbitrary. States with similar cultures and close ties between populations were bound to experience migration and a need to correct or ameliorate the steep exclusions created by the legal proclamation of foreignness affecting their populations. Intercitizenships proposed by Dicey are thus one of the core elements of the citizenship landscape in the world of the 21st century, shaping the rights enjoyed by hundreds of millions of individuals around the globe. To map territories of rights correlating with every citizenship following the new trend is a very useful exercise to show what the geography of work and settlement freedom is actually like for the holders of each particular nationality in a situation where the correlation between citizenship and territory is no more. None of the modern intercitizenships is as expansive in scope as that which Dicey originally proposed, but the trend is much more widespread than even the most courageous minds at the end of the 19th century could have anticipated.

This change can be explained by both the emergence of regional integration blocks (EU, MERCOSUR, ECOWAS) and the gradual deterioration of the former empires — continuing post-colonial ties, as is attested to by the gradually waning intercitizenships of the former Soviet space and between some parts of the former British Empire (India and its satellites, Australia and New Zealand) and the US empire (states in free association, such as FS Micronesia). An intermediate option is also possible, as demonstrated by the Latin American countries that have historical colonial ties and revamped integration in the sphere of migration. Global trends in citizenship development around the world may lead one to conclude that the strict correlation between the state territory issuing citizenship and the geographical scope of the key rights of such citizenship has perished for good; if true, this poses a number of questions that will be crucial for legal theorists and practitioners to address.

Part 2

Methodology

8 Deploying a Clear Methodology to Tell a New Citizenship Story

The QNI turns to numbers to illustrate the notion of citizenship and nationality today in a less textbook-friendly way than usual, refusing to recite the usual commonplaces about citizenship related to its dignity and sacred nature, and the so-called equality among statuses, and looking critically at the connections between the territories, citizenships, and rights. The lessons we learn are very clear: the majority of the world's citizenships do not actually grant rights in any way comparable to the elite 'supercitizenship' of the global North: they are thus about liabilities, not rights. Citizenships have global rather than local significance. In order to tell this new citizenship story — based on objective, quantified data rather than subjective feelings of attachment and romanticized stories about what citizenship represents — we need to turn to the method and results of the QNI. In Part 2 of this volume, we will first explore the composition and sources of the QNI, and subsequently show how our methodology reveals the significant changes in the value of nationalities around the world.

9 Nationalities Included in the QNI

The QNI defines nationalities as heritable legal statuses of attachment to a public authority — usually a state — which entitle the holder to a passport or a passport-like travel document. The overwhelming majority of nationalities worldwide are ranked in this Index. These include practically all United Nations member states plus Kosovo, the Palestinian Territory, Taiwan, Hong Kong, and Macao. Only nationalities for which no reliable data on any of the sub-elements is available are excluded. In addition, the following statuses are also ranked:

- The legal status of the 'non-citizens' of Latvia
- The legal status of the Israeli Laissez-passer
- British nationalities
- Citizenship of the EU

'Non-Citizens' of Latvia

The legal status of the 'non-citizens' of Latvia is granted to former nationals of the Soviet Union belonging to ethnic minorities who were living in Latvia when the Soviet Union collapsed and who do not possess Latvian nationality nor that of any other country. Children of the holders of the Latvian 'non-citizen' status can inherit it, which makes it a real nationality within the meaning of the QNI, notwithstanding the fact that the bearers, not being Latvian citizens, are unquestionably stateless in the eyes of international law.

Israeli Laissez-Passer

The Israeli Laissez-passer travel document is issued in place of a passport for Israeli citizens in exceptional circumstances, including to:

- Israeli citizens who have stayed more than 10 years abroad (once citizens have visited Israel, they are entitled to an Israeli passport)
- Naturalized Israeli citizens who do not demonstrate intent to settle in Israel
- Israeli citizens who have lost or destroyed two or more passports in a period of 10 years

Where such a passport indicates that the holder is a citizen of Israel (and the nationality in the passport is Israeli), visa-free access to 58 destinations is allowed.

British Nationalities

There are eight types of British nationality for the purposes of the QNI:

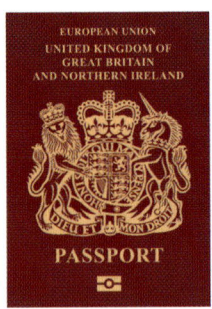

1. British Citizenship

British citizenship was introduced by the British Nationality Act 1981, which replaced Citizenship of the United Kingdom and Colonies (CUKC). This status is usually held through a connection with the UK, the Channel Islands, and the Isle of Man. Until the advent of Brexit, British citizenship automatically carried a right to live and work in the UK free of any immigration controls. British citizens are citizens of the EU until the moment Brexit takes effect. That said, the actual number of EU citizenship rights enjoyed by British citizens depends on their degree of connection to a particular territory with which their citizenship is associated.

2. British Citizenship Acquired in Connection with the Channel Islands and the Isle of Man

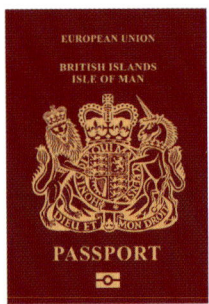 

UK citizenship status acquired through connection with the Isle of Man or the Channel Islands forms a separate category of British nationality for the purposes of the QNI. Although full EU citizens, the holders of such UK citizenship, while enjoying unconditional settlement and work rights in the Isle of Man and the Channel Islands respectively as well as the UK, do not enjoy unconditional rights to work and reside in the other 27 EU Member States unless they spend at least five years in the UK before exercising EU free movement rights. This creates a radically different penumbra of rights for the holders of such statuses, notwithstanding the fact that they are officially British citizens, just like those who acquired the status by virtue of their connection with the UK. This difference in the scope of rights, combined with the fact that different documents are issued to these categories of UK citizens, means that the status they hold acquires a significance of its own for the purposes of the QNI.

3. British Nationals (Overseas) Status

British Nationals (Overseas) status was initially issued in 1987 under the Hong Kong Act to the permanent residents of Hong Kong, who could either register for this nationality or retain their British dependent territories citizenship. The latter, however, could not be renewed after its expiry, and British overseas territories citizens could renew their passports only by registering as British Nationals (Overseas). British Nationals (Overseas) have no automatic right to live or work in the UK and do not enjoy EU citizenship.

4. British Overseas Citizenship

This is a status held by citizens of the UK and its colonies on 31 December 1982, who did not become British citizens or British overseas territories citizens on that date. The holders of the status have no automatic right to live or work in the UK and are not considered UK nationals by the EU, and thus do not enjoy the rights of EU citizenship.

5. British Overseas Territories Citizenship

This is a status held by people connected with British overseas territories, which does not grant by itself the right of residence or work in any of those territories: these rights must be acquired separately. Each UK overseas territory issues a different style of document to the holders of this status residing in its territory. Although the covers of the passports differ, each still confers the same legal status in British law. While the extent of visa-free or visa-on-arrival travel

enjoyed by the holders of this status might vary to some degree depending on the overseas territory issuing the passport, the QNI applies an average score of visa-free travel access enjoyed by the holders of this status, which is justified because the differences are minimal. For instance, unlike the citizens of other British overseas territories, Montserratian passport holders can travel visa-free to Suriname, and the same exception applies to Bermudian passport holders traveling to Montenegro. British overseas territories citizens do not have a right to live or work in the UK. Similarly, British overseas territories citizens are not, generally, EU citizens under EU law. The only exception is the British overseas territories citizenship issued in connection with Gibraltar, which for this reason is considered a special category for the purposes of the QNI.

6. British Overseas Territories Citizenship (Gibraltar)

Unlike other British overseas territories citizens, those who have acquired the status by virtue of a connection with Gibraltar are EU citizens, with some exceptions. This makes the British overseas territories citizenship acquired in connection with Gibraltar radically different from the British overseas territories citizenship acquired in connection with any other British overseas territory, such as the British Virgin Islands or Anguilla. Thus, it is a different category of nationality for the purposes of the QNI.

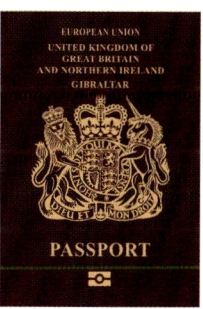

7. British Protected Person Status

This status was originally granted to people who acquired a UK status through connection with the protectorates over which the UK held a mandate. In its current form, the British protected person status is acquired by an individual who, on 1 January 1983, was a citizen or national of Brunei; already a British protected person; or a child born to a British protected person parent who would otherwise be stateless. The British protected person status is lost in most cases through the acquisition of citizenship of any country in the world, including that of a different type of UK nationality. British protected persons have no automatic right to live or work in the UK and are not citizens of the EU.

8. British Subject Status

In its current form, British subject status was acquired by an individual who, on 1 January 1983, was either a British subject without citizenship, that is, who was a British subject on 31 December 1948 and did not become a citizen of the UK and its colonies, a Commonwealth country, Pakistan or the Republic of Ireland; was a citizen of the Republic of Ireland on 31 December 1948 but made a claim to remain a British subject; and some other cases. British subjecthood is one of the most restrictive statuses issued by any country in the world as it comes with no rights whatsoever in the UK: holders of British subject status cannot even enter the UK for short-term tourist or business stays without a visa and enjoy no settlement or work rights either in their country or in the country that issued their status. They are not citizens of the EU.

Citizenship of the European Union

The EU provides the nationals of its 28 Member States with a formal citizenship status that complements their national-level statuses. EU citizenship grants its holders the genuine freedom to pursue their own choices in terms of where they want to live and work within the Member States of the EU. In this respect, it is reminiscent of traditional nationalities. Nevertheless, EU citizenship is in many respects a peculiar concept. It is fully dependent upon the nationalities of the Member States — one cannot become an EU citizen unless one holds an EU Member State nationality. Furthermore, EU citizenship is not embodied in a passport or equivalent travel document: EU citizens must use their national passports to be able to enjoy its value. EU national passports, however, are standardized in many respects. Given the standardization and prohibition of discrimination on the basis of the nationalities of the 28 Member States, EU citizenship behaves, in many respects, like any other nationality considered for the purposes of this Index (see also the special contribution by Dimitry Kochenov in this volume).

Thus, EU citizenship is much like an extra perquisite that particular nationalities grant their holders, which is not embodied in an independent physical document of a single design, although it clearly is a single legal status. The inherently particular nature of EU citizenship, building on the nationalities of the (pre-Brexit) 28 Member States of the EU, implies that the value of being an EU citizen is not absolute — it depends on one's nationality. Therefore, for the purposes of the QNI, EU citizenship is a legal fiction whose value is based on the values of its constituent nationalities, which enables us to measure the average value of being an EU citizen. The value of EU citizenship is calculated as follows:

- In calculating EU citizenship's Economic Strength, the economic strength of its Member States is aggregated.
- For Human Development and Peace and Stability the value of EU citizenship is calculated by the average of its constituting nationalities. That is, the Human Development score of EU citizenship is equal to the average level of human development in the EU as expressed by the average score on the HDI of its current 28 Member States.
- For Diversity and Weight of Settlement Freedom only settlement outside the EU is counted, to ensure that the EU nationality does not receive an undue advantage in the Index. In 2018, almost all EU citizens could freely settle in four countries outside the EU: Georgia, Iceland, Norway, and Switzerland.

- To measure the Diversity of Travel Freedom, the value of EU citizenship is calculated by the average of the Member States' values excluding intra-EU travel. Such exclusion of free intra-EU travel reflects the unitary concept of EU citizenship and its inclusion in the Index alongside the 28 passports of EU Member States.
- For the Weight of Travel Freedom, the value of EU citizenship is calculated by the average of the Member States' values excluding the intra-EU travel weight for each Member State.

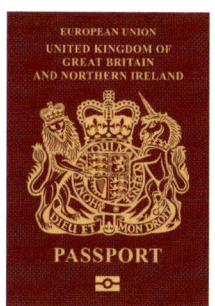  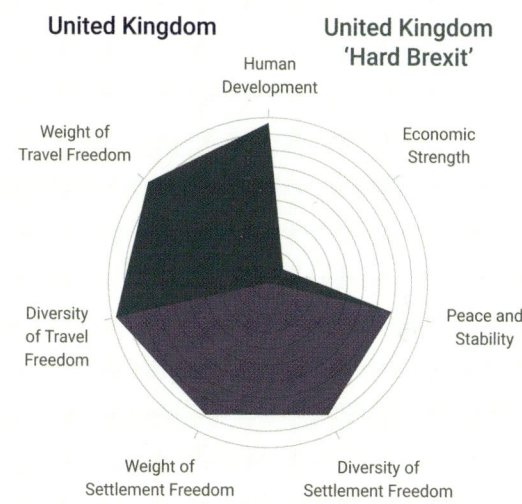

The added value of EU citizenship in terms of additional rights the holders of this status enjoy on top of their EU Member State nationalities is clear when one compares the value of UK citizenship before and after Brexit (based on the optimistic assumption that the British economy will not shrink significantly and that Brexit will affect only Diversity and Weight of Settlement Freedom). The resulting difference is the highest recorded fall in the quality of nationality, superseding even the deterioration of Syrian and Libyan nationality quality as a result of civil war and the rise of ISIS.

Territories That Do Not Possess a Separate Nationality

Some territories, such as the Faroe Islands or Greenland, may count as travel or settlement destinations for nationals of certain states but do not possess a separate nationality themselves, notwithstanding a right to issue passports of their own design, which some of such territories might enjoy. These territories are included in the QNI as destinations insofar as they have independent immigration controls. In that case they are ascribed a minimal destination value so that their presence as travel or settlement destinations does not go unnoticed. This is explained in further detail in 'Composition of the QNI'.

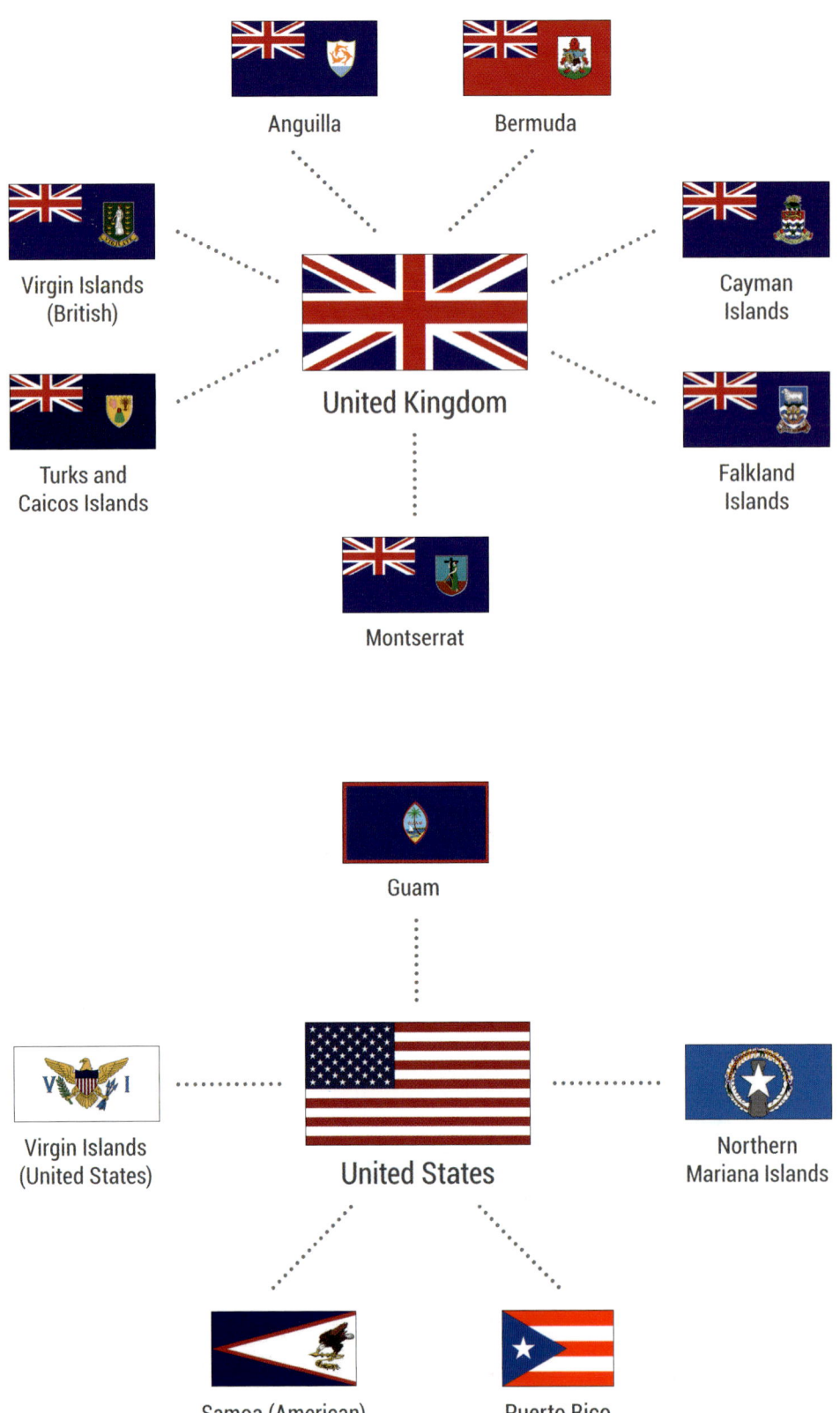

9 Nationalities Included in the QNI · 45

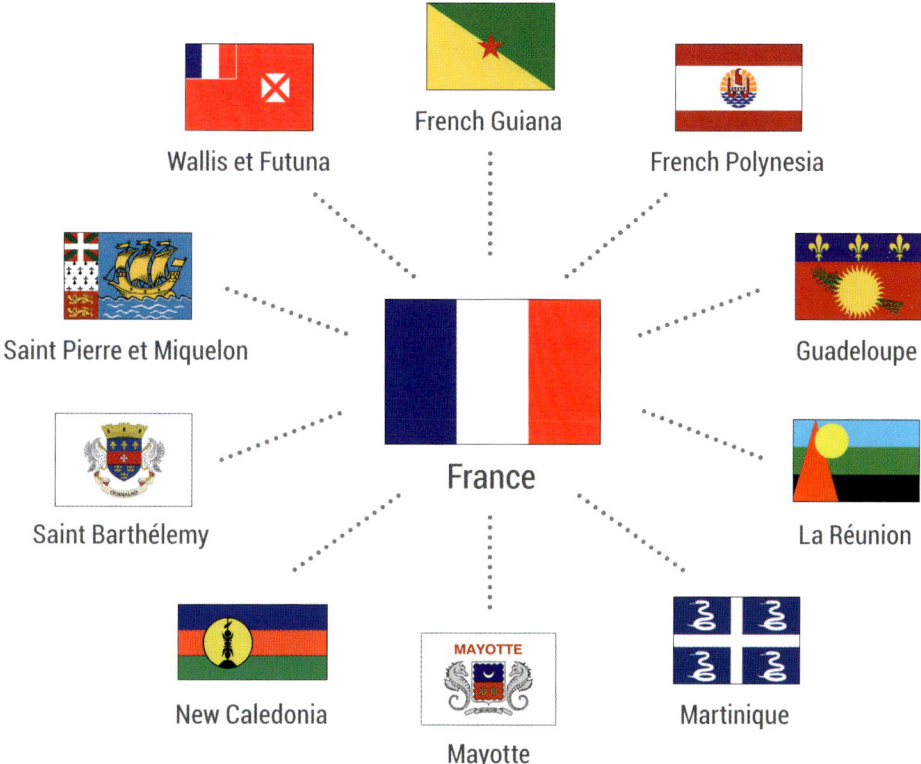

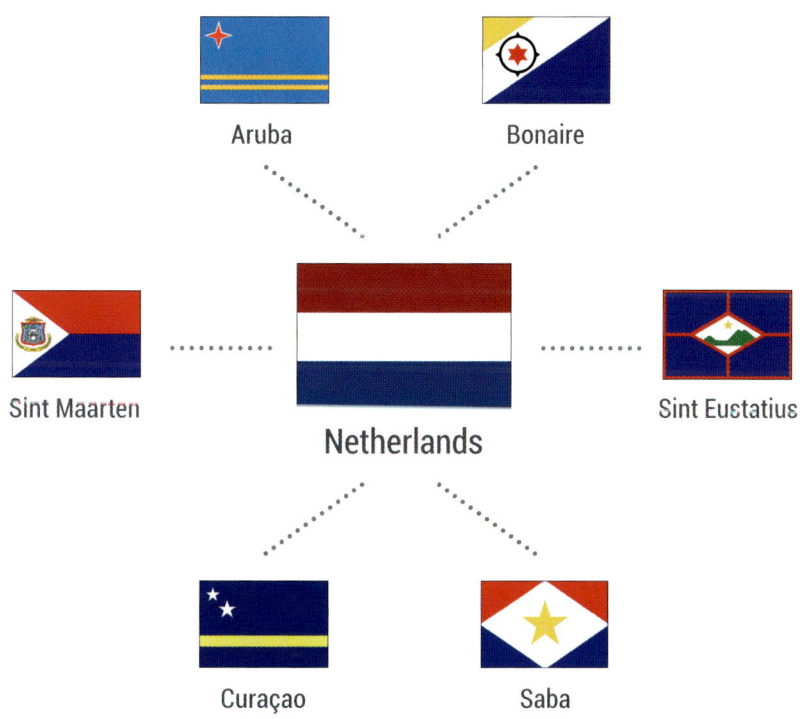

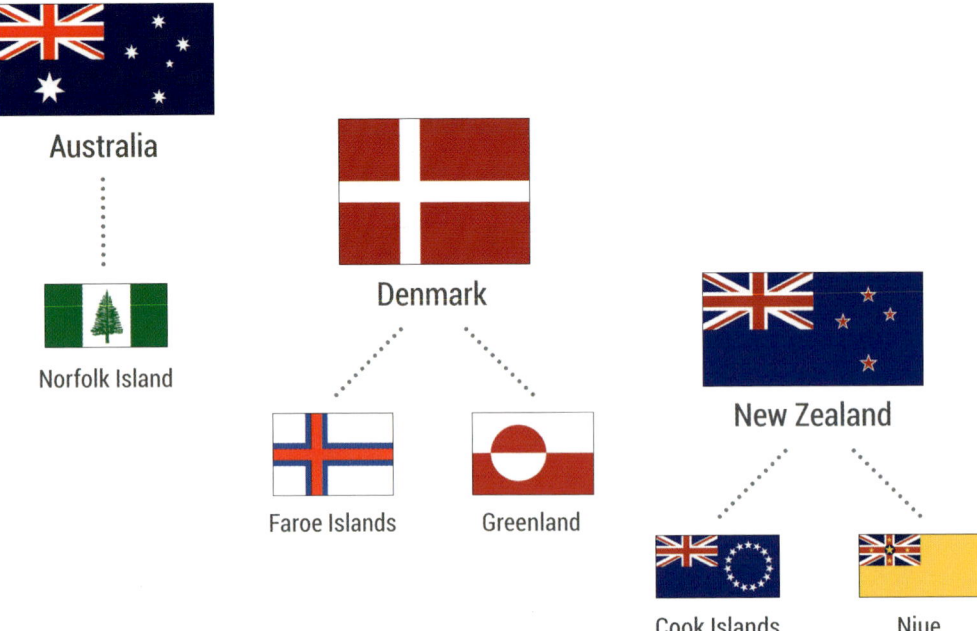

Statuses and Documents Excluded from the QNI for Failing to Meet the Criteria of a Nationality

Excluded from the QNI are all the personal legal statuses granted to specific subcategories of citizens in active military or diplomatic and similar service. These documents attest to the special status of the bearer rather than to only his or her nationality. Similarly excluded is the nationality of the Vatican City State, which cannot be passed on between generations. Given that the ordinary population of citizens is absent from the Vatican, Vatican nationality is not included in the QNI.

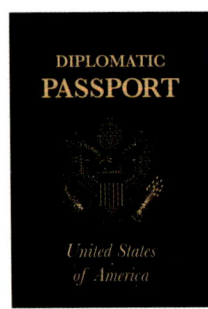 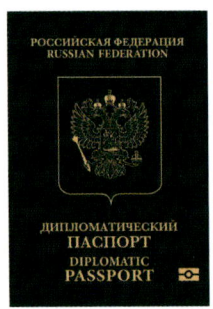 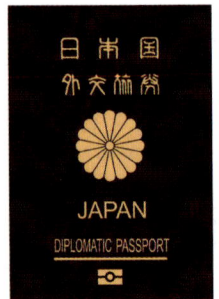 

Also excluded from the QNI are non-heritable or idiosyncratic legal statuses and the travel documents that give them expression, because they do not correlate to possession of a real nationality in the legal sense commonly recognized in international law. Fantasy passports and quasi-nationalities of de facto or de jure non-existent countries are also excluded. Consequently, excluded statuses and documents include, among others:

- All refugee travel documents
- Certificates of identity that can be granted by states to stateless persons or refugees who cannot obtain a valid passport from their state of nationality

- United Nations laissez-passer (UNLP or LP), which is granted to staff of the UN and specific international organizations and can be used as a valid travel document on official missions
- All other laissez-passer documents (except for the Israeli Laissez-passer, which has been rather unsuitably named, as further explained in the special contribution by Eli Gervits on page 262 of this volume)
- 1954 Convention travel documents, which can be granted to stateless persons pursuant to the 1954 Convention Relating to the Status of Stateless Persons

  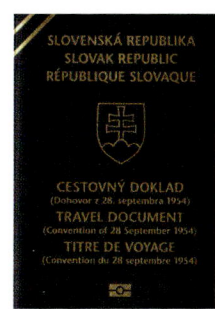 

- Passport of the Sovereign Military Order of Malta, a travel document granted to officials of the Roman Catholic religious order the Sovereign Military Order of Malta and which does not correspond to a nationality in international law, notwithstanding the international legal personality of the order

- Nationalities and corresponding passports of de facto existing countries that have particularly limited recognition, for example the nationalities of Abkhazia, Nagorno-Karabakh, South Ossetia, Transnistria, or the Turkish Republic of Northern Cyprus. However, a separate ranking of various nationalities of non-recognized states can be found below in a separate section on non-recognized nationalities, which is based on various estimations and proxies

- Nationalities and passports issued in the name of occupied territories with no recognized statehood, like Western Sahara
- Passports corresponding to subnational statuses of belonging, such as the passport of the Faroe Islands, which, as long as it corresponds to the Danish nationality, is to be treated as Danish for the purposes of this Index

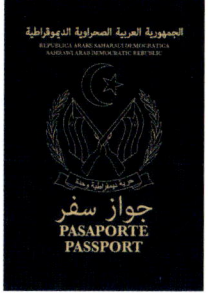

- Camouflage and fantasy passports of de facto and also de jure non-existent countries. These are passports issued in the name of a non-existent country, which, therefore, cannot testify to the possession of any existing nationality. Camouflage passports are mostly used for false identification and/or criminal activities, and are generally issued under the name of a country no longer in existence, for example:

    - British Honduras (now Belize)
    - Ceylon (now Sri Lanka)
    - Ciskei (now part of South Africa)
    - Dahomey (now Benin)
    - Dutch Guiana (now Suriname)
    - Gilbert Islands (now Kiribati)
    - Iraq/Kurdistan Immigration ID Card
    - Rhodesia (now Zimbabwe)
    - Sealand
    - South Viet Nam (now Viet Nam)

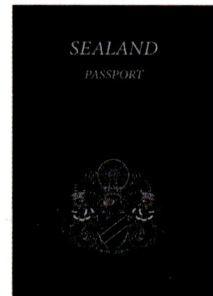

Fantasy passports are used for a variety of purposes, but mostly for making political statements. Some prominent examples:

- *Neue Slowenische Kunst* (NSK) passport
- Aboriginal Nation passport
- Conch Republic passport
- Hare Krishna Consciousness sect passport
- Dynastie et états carolingiens-berniciens diplomatic passport
- World Service Authority passport

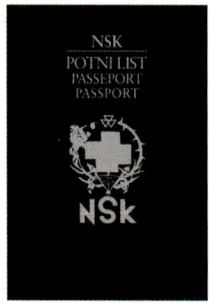

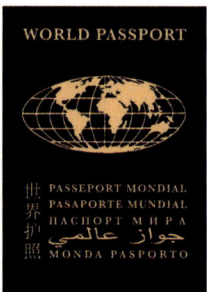

10 Time of Measurement

This edition of the QNI represents the status quo on 1 July 2018. Where up-to-date data as of 1 July is not available, the most recently available data is used. Such deviations in the data are listed in the Annex.

Tourist and business visa regime changes after 1 July 2018 will be integrated into the next edition of the QNI.

11 Composition of the QNI

The QNI comprises seven sub-elements, distinguishing between three sub-elements that measure a nationality's Internal Value and four sub-elements that measure its External Value:

- **Internal Value:** Human Development, Economic Strength, and Peace and Stability
- **External Value:** Diversity of Settlement Freedom, Weight of Settlement Freedom, Diversity of Travel Freedom, and Weight of Travel Freedom

In what follows, we will introduce the individual sub-elements and the manner in which they are measured and calculated, using different examples from the 2018 QNI General Ranking.

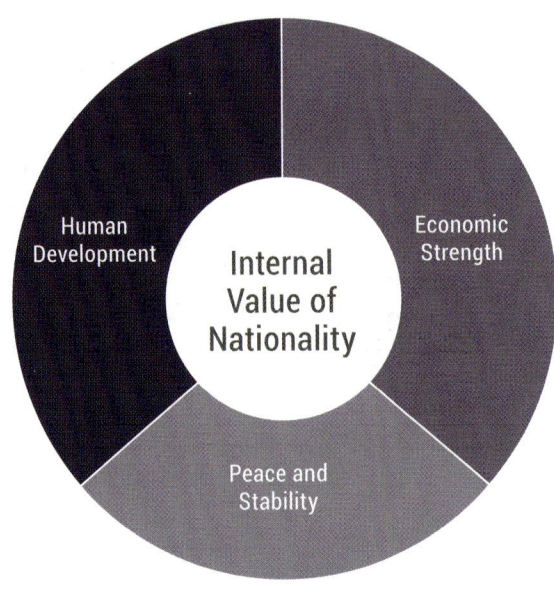

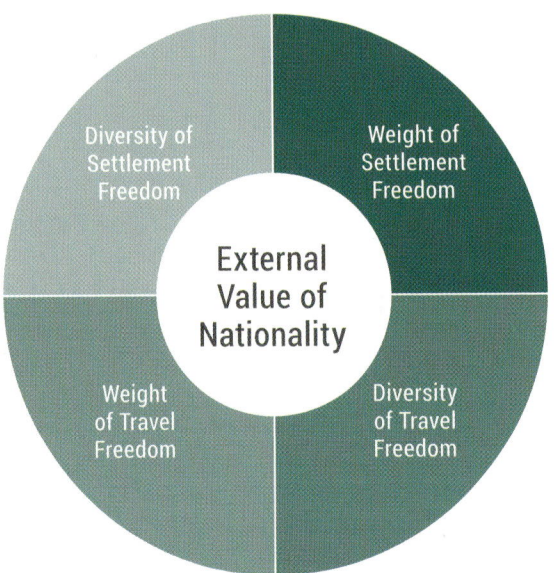

Human Development

The basic level of development associated with a nationality provides a rough prophecy of the average person's life prospects. This is illustrated by substantial disparities between the average life expectancy, level of education, and general welfare of nationals of sub-Saharan countries and those of Western European countries. Therefore, the level of Human Development has a direct impact on the quality of a nationality, especially because a large majority of individuals spend most of their lives in their home country.

The QNI Human Development measurement is derived from the United Nations Development Programme's Human Development Index (HDI), which is today's most authoritative ranking of basic human development. It is derived from three measures, as illustrated in the figure below.

The Three Dimensions of the Human Development Index (HDI)

Health	Education	Standard of Living
Measured by life expectancy at birth, with a minimum value of 20 years and a maximum value of 85 years	Assessed by the mean of the number of years of schooling for adults aged 25 years and the expected years of schooling for school-age children	Measured by gross national income per capita

This annual index is based on the idea that the development of a country is not reflected in its economic strength or growth per se, but in its people and their capabilities. Its methodology was designed by the Pakistani economist Mahbub ul Haq together with a team of economists including Nobel laureate Amartya Sen in order to evaluate non-economic development in the simplest possible manner so as to make it intelligible for a wide audience. The index measures three dimensions of human development: health, education, and standard of living.

- Health is measured by life expectancy at birth, with a minimum value of 20 years and a maximum value of 85 years.
- Education is assessed by the mean number of years of schooling for adults aged 25 years and the expected years of schooling for children of school-entering age.
- Standard of living is measured by gross national income per capita.

HDI scores do not reflect inequalities, poverty, human security, empowerment, or other factors directly, although these factors obviously exert influence on the levels of health, education, and standard of living indirectly. HDI scores are directly mirrored in the Human Development component of the QNI: the higher the country's score on the HDI, the higher the Human Development score of the corresponding nationality.

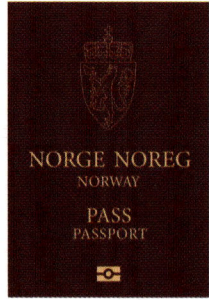  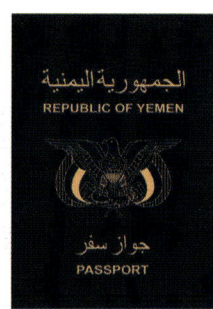

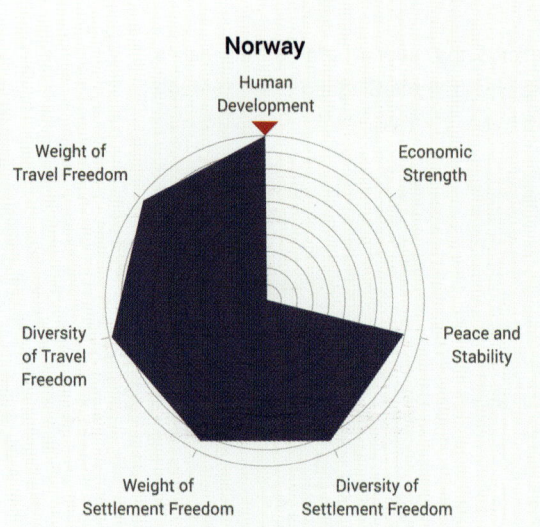

Examples: In the 2018 HDI Ranking, Norway was the highest-scoring country with an HDI score of 0.953 on a 0.00–1.00 scale. For the purpose of the QNI, the Norwegian nationality gets the full 15% score associated with Human Development. Romania has an HDI score of 0.811. As QNI scores are proportionately normalized to a 0%–15% scale, the Romanian nationality has a Human Development score of

$$\frac{0.811}{0.983} \times 15 = 12.76\%$$

Similarly, Yemen's HDI score of 0.452 correlates with a Human Development score of

$$\frac{0.452}{0.953} \times 15 = 7.11\%$$

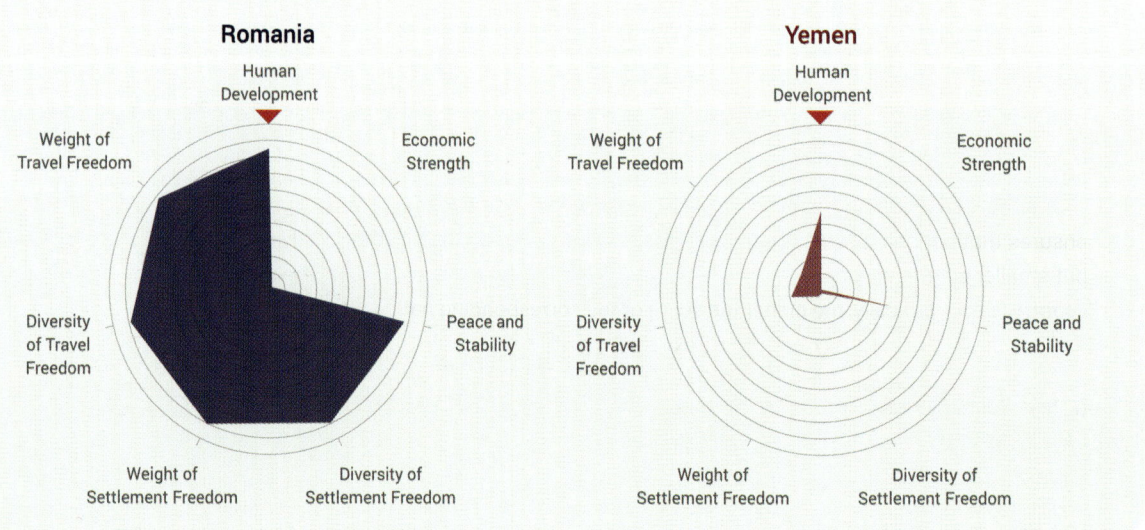

Economic Strength

The contribution of the economic strength of the country to the quality of its nationality is all about scale: stronger economies offer more opportunities in private and professional life, creating more value for their nationals. While the HDI takes welfare and standard of living into account by measuring GDP per capita, the scale of opportunities available to the holders of a nationality is primarily reflected by the size of the associated country. Being a national of the US, for example,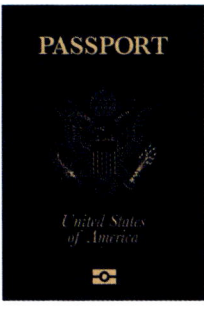
enables someone to pursue endless opportunities without crossing national borders. This makes US nationality more valuable compared to the nationality of, for example, Singapore, even though the countries have a comparable per capita GDP (according to the World Bank, in 2017 the per capita GDP of the US and Singapore were, respectively, USD 58,270 and USD 54,530). Including GDP, which is defined as "the sum of gross value added by all resident producers in the economy

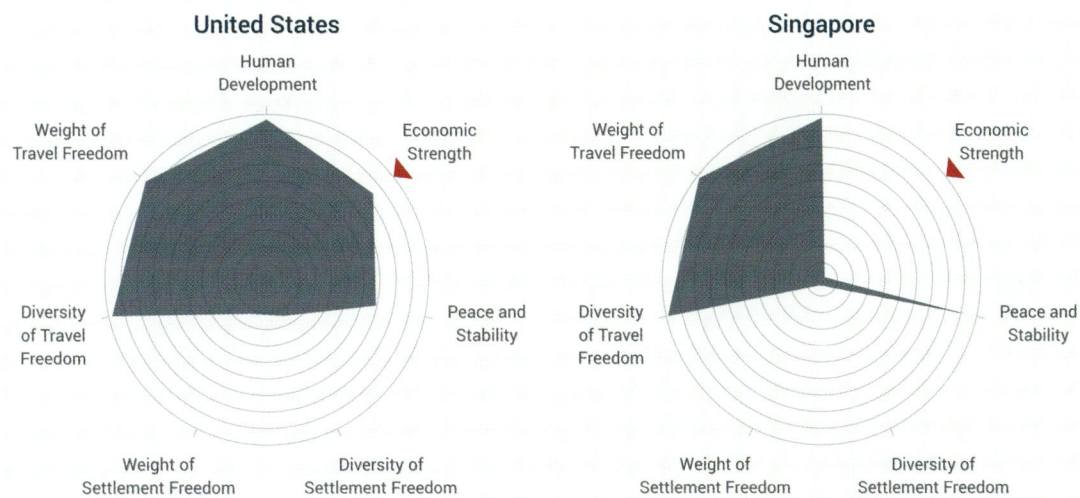

plus any product taxes and minus any subsidies not included in the value of the products,"[20] ensures that nationalities of larger countries are valued higher than economically comparable but smaller countries, reflecting the greater number of life chances they offer. The stronger the country is economically, the higher the score of the corresponding nationality.

Economic Strength is measured by a country's share of world GDP at purchasing power parity (PPP), excluding rents from the exploitation of natural resources — so-called natural resources rents (NRR).

Purchasing Power Parity: Applying PPP converts countries' GDP into international dollars. An international dollar possesses the same purchasing power that a US dollar has in the US. Such conversion makes economies more comparable because the GDP figures reflect the actual size of the economy from a consumer perspective. By using PPP GDP, the QNI gives a more realistic perspective on the economic strength of nationalities for the purpose of valuing their quality. Instead of measuring the formal scale of economies without due regard for genuine purchasing power, the QNI measures the real and comparable opportunities that nationalities offer.

Excluding Natural Resources Rents: NRR is the sum of oil rents, natural gas rents, coal rents (hard and soft), mineral rents, and forest rents. NRR is excluded from the measurement of Economic Strength to avoid substantial distortion of the value of some nationalities. While Economic Strength is principally intended to reflect all economic opportunities granted to holders of a nationality, NRR is not suitable to reflect the genuine scale of a country that works   to the benefit of its nationals. Some African and Middle Eastern countries, for example, have relatively large economies that are substantially dependent on NRR. This distorts the value of their nationalities: their Economic Strength is not reflected in the scale of economic and social opportunities that their nationals enjoy. Including NRR, for example, would inflate the value of the nationality of Algeria, which derives 12% of its GDP from NRR, and Venezuela, with 15% of its GDP from NRR, vis-à-vis the actual assets of their nationalities.

Both PPP GDP data and NRR data have been collected from the World Bank. For some countries, there is either no or only incomplete PPP GDP available in the World Bank database. Where no sufficiently recent or reliable PPP GDP data could be used, the most recent (non-PPP) GDPs from the United Nations Statistics Division, National Accounts Main Aggregate Database, Trading Economics, and the World Bank are applied. Since the countries for which PPP GDP data is unavailable generally have extremely small-scale economies, the use of nominal GDP figures is highly unlikely to have affected their ranking. A list of countries for which non-PPP GDP data was used can be found in the Annex.

Data on PPP GDP (minus NRR) has been normalized to a 0–15 scale in order to collect scores for the Economic Strength parameter of the QNI.

Examples: In 2018 the largest economy was China with an 18% share of the world GDP at PPP excluding NRR. The Chinese nationality accordingly received the full 15% on the Economic Strength parameter. The Mexican economy accounted for ~1.8% of the world GDP excluding NRR. The nationality of Mexico received an Economic Strength score of

$$\frac{1.8}{18} \times 15 = 1.5\%$$

The German economy's ~3.3% share of the world's GDP excluding NRR resulted in an Economic Strength score of

$$\frac{3.3}{18} \times 15 = 2.75\%$$

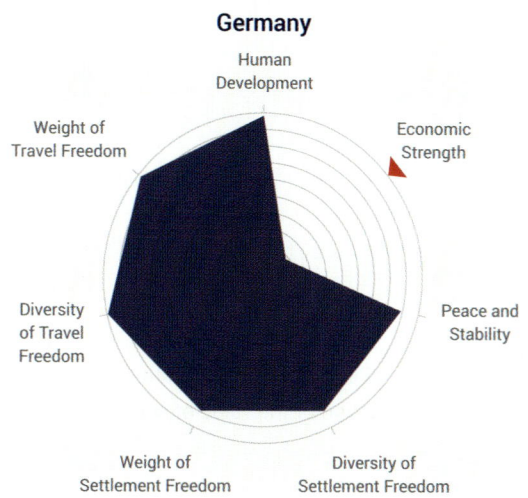

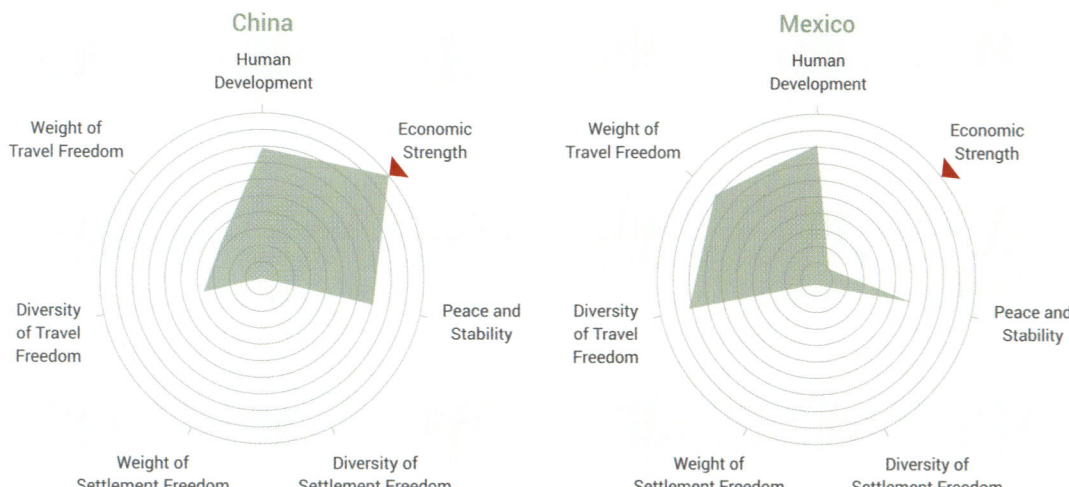

Peace and Stability

A peaceful society is likely to foster human development, welfare, and happiness. Conversely, war and violence can dramatically affect the fate of a person having a particular nationality, especially a nationality that grants its holders few to no global opportunities.

For measuring Peace and Stability, the QNI uses figures from the annual Global Peace Index (GPI) published by the Institute for Economics and Peace. The GPI is an annual ranking that measures the peacefulness, stability, and harmony of countries by looking at 23 indicators of peace that are divided into three domains:

- Ongoing domestic and international conflict, measuring the role, intensity, and duration of a country's internal and external conflicts using six indicators, including the number of deaths from organized conflict and the state's relations with neighboring countries
- The level of harmony within a nation, evaluating 10 indicators of a safe and secure society including low crime rates, minimal terrorist activity, the number of refugees as a percentage of the population, and a stable political scene
- Degree of militarization, incorporating seven indicators such as military expenditure as a percentage of GDP, nuclear and heavy weapons capabilities, and the ease of access to small arms

GPI scores are ranked on a scale from 1.000 (most peaceful) to 5.000 (least peaceful). These scores are converted to the normalized 0–10 scale for the QNI's Peace and Stability parameter: the better a country scores on the GPI, the higher the Peace and Stability score of its corresponding nationality. The nationality of the most peaceful country receives the full 10% score, while a hypothetical score of 5.000 on the GPI would result in a 0% score for Peace and Stability.

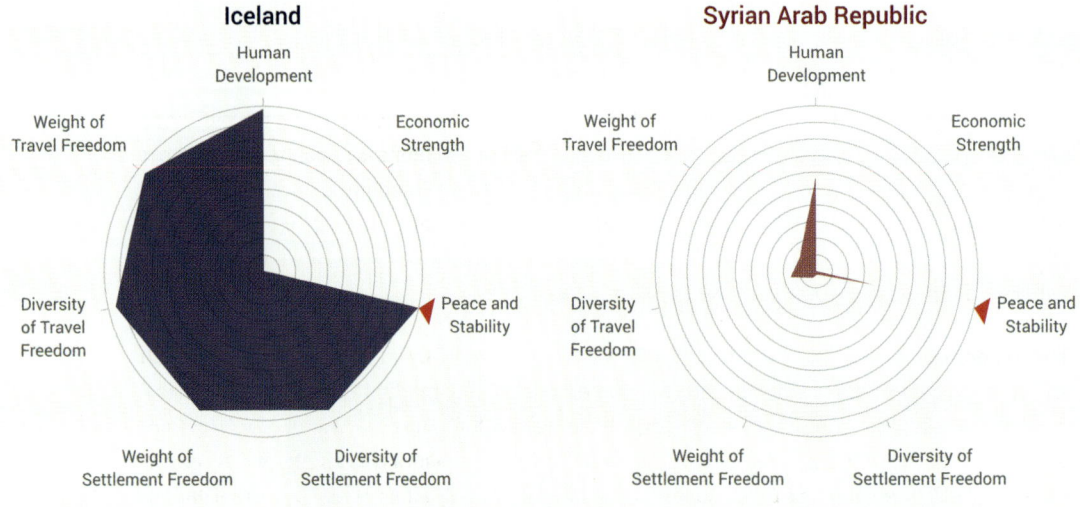

Examples: According to the 2018 GPI, the most peaceful country is Iceland, with a 1.096 score. The least peaceful country, the Syrian Arab Republic, received a score of 3.600. The Icelandic nationality gets the full 10% for Peace and Stability. The scores of other nationalities are calculated by normalizing the GPI bandwidth between 1.096 and 5.000. Hence, the score of the Syrian nationality is arrived at thus:

$$\frac{3.600 - 5.000}{1.096 - 5.000} \times 10 = 3.59\%$$

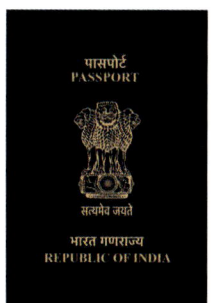

India has a GPI score of 2.504. The Peace and Stability score of the Indian nationality is

$$\frac{2.504 - 5.000}{1.096 - 5.000} \times 10 = 6.39\%$$

Some countries are not included in the GPI; their nationalities have been evaluated in the QNI because reasonable estimations are available based on the average scores of surrounding countries or of the region. A list of these nationalities and the methodology employed for calculating reasonable estimations can be found in the Annex.

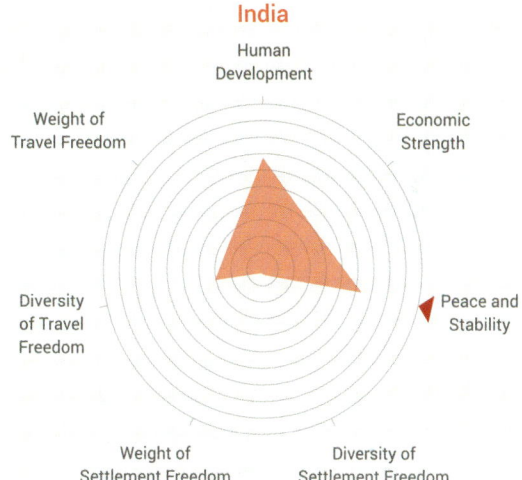

Diversity of Settlement Freedom

An increasing number of nationalities allow their holders to settle freely, not only in the territories of their respective countries. Instead, the scope of their settlement rights is also extended to other countries and territories. The QNI includes Diversity of Settlement Freedom as an inherent part of the quality of nationalities. Consequently, it measures the number of full-access countries — that is, countries where the holder of a particular nationality can freely work and live and is subject to either no or only minimal immigration requirements.

The freedom to settle abroad is constrained throughout the world by numerous limitations, such as access to social benefits, health care insurance, and the labor market. Therefore, 'full access' must be interpreted somewhat loosely because there are virtually no countries in which foreigners are completely assimilated without any conditions. For measuring Diversity of Settlement Freedom, settlement in a particular country is considered possible if an adult holder of a nationality is allowed to work there without having to obtain a visa or with a visa acquired on arrival. Permission to work in that country is either not required or virtually automatic.

In other words, Settlement Freedom does not mean that the holder of a nationality is given carte blanche to settle in a different country. What this sub-element primarily measures is the options to work somewhere else. Furthermore, the following factors are not considered in determining the freedom to settle in another country:

- Entitlement to public pension systems
- Entitlement to health care
- Entitlement to social security benefits
- Potential for family members to join the person in question
- Specific skill qualifications that are required to perform certain professions, particularly of a qualitative nature, such as bar qualifications to practice as a lawyer, medical qualifications to practice as a doctor, or construction-worker qualifications

The QNI also does not take into account any settlement freedom that is based on factors other than nationality itself, such as being in possession of a higher education diploma (as is the case in CARICOM, for instance).

Data on the Diversity of Settlement Freedom is gathered through extensive research of the literature on the legal requirements for settlement throughout the world. Research on the formal legal requirements is complemented with expert consultation in all regions of the world. This ensures that only real and genuine settlement freedom is taken into account; sham legal freedoms are not considered. As no antecedent on this topic exists, the QNI is the only source on global Settlement Freedom worldwide.

The more countries giving full-access settlement to the holder of a nationality, the higher that nationality's score is on Diversity of Settlement Freedom. All data is converted and normalized on the 0–15 scale of the Diversity of Settlement Freedom parameter.

Examples: In 2018, French nationals had the highest degree of Settlement Freedom in terms of diversity, with 46 full-access settlement destinations available. Accordingly, the French nationality received a 15% score on Diversity of Settlement Freedom. Most other EU Member States' nationalities, such as Estonia, Hungary, Poland, and Romania, gave full access to 41 destinations. These nationalities received a Diversity of Settlement Freedom score of

$$\frac{41}{46} \times 15 = 13.37\%$$

The Dutch nationality (45 settlement destinations) received a 14.67% score.

11 Composition of the QNI • 59

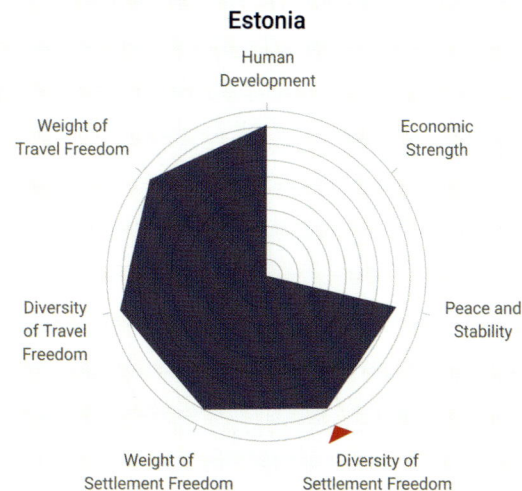

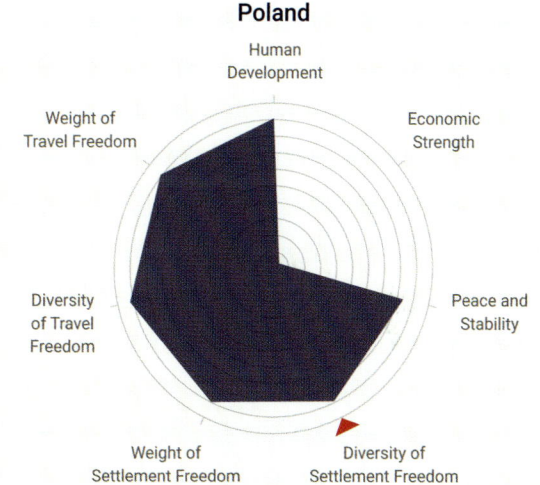
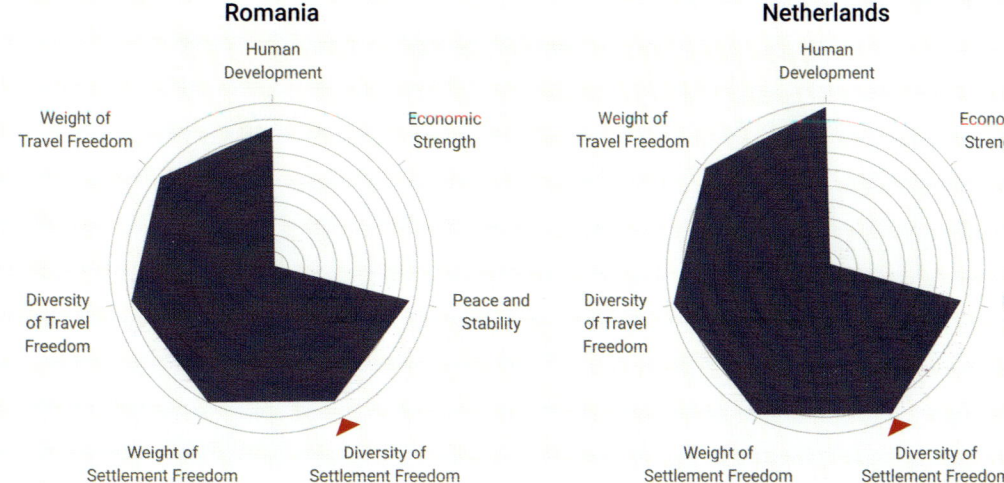

Weight of Settlement Freedom

While Diversity of Settlement Freedom provides intrinsic value to boost freedom and life opportunities, not all destinations are equal. For example, nationals of Nigeria are able to settle freely in 14 other ECOWAS member states, while people from Monaco and New Zealand can settle freely in only three: France, Georgia, and the Norwegian archipelago of Svalbard for Monaco nationals, and Australia, Georgia, and Svalbard for New Zealanders. However, full access to France or Australia for nationals of Monaco or Australia, respectively, will on average provide for more economic opportunities than those available in the individual ECOWAS member states. In addition, both Australia and France provide a higher level of Human Development than any of those countries, making them more attractive as settlement destinations for the majority of people.

Therefore, the QNI also includes a measurement of the combined value of the countries that a nationality allows one to settle in. This Weight of Settlement Freedom value is composed of the sum of all such countries' weighted scores on Human Development and Economic Strength, which both account for 50% of this 'destination value' for each destination. The sum of all these destination values becomes the total Weight of Settlement Freedom for a given nationality. This sum is normalized on a 0–15 scale.

Example: In addition to having the highest number of settlement destinations, the French nationality also scores highest on the aggregate value of its settlement destinations, at 558.66. The French nationality receives the full 15% on the Weight of Settlement Freedom parameter. Cape Verde nationals have settlement access to the 14 other member states of ECOWAS. The aggregate value of these destinations is 88.94. While the number of settlement destinations for Cape Verde nationals is thus roughly 30% of that for French nationals, the aggregate value of settlement destinations for Cape Verde nationals is just under 16% of the aggregate value of settlement destinations linked to the French nationality. The Weight of Settlement Freedom for the nationality of Cape Verde accordingly is 2.32% on the 0–15 scale.

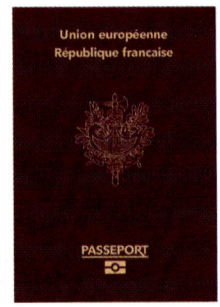
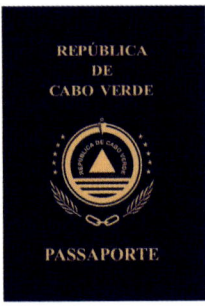

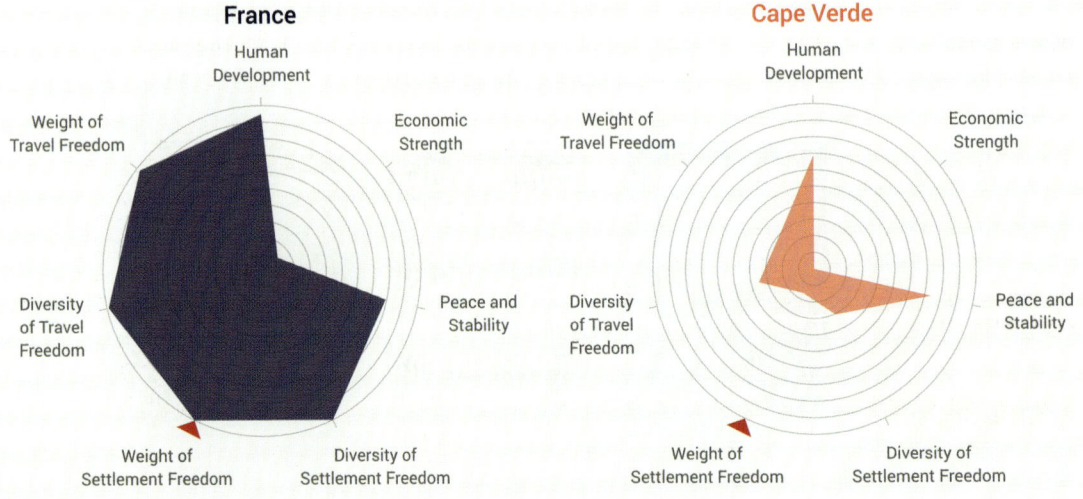

Some of the settlement destinations taken into account for the Weight of Settlement Freedom of particular nationalities do not feature in the QNI themselves because there is no data available on their Human Development and/or Peace and Stability. There are also countries, such as Aruba, New Caledonia, and American Samoa, that are excluded because they lack their own nationality, despite the existence of their own immigration controls. Notwithstanding their own absence in the QNI, for the purpose of this edition of the QNI these countries and territories have been ascribed a minimal weighted score of 10.99, consisting of the sum of the normalized HDI world mean and a normalized, infinitesimal GDP value. Ascribing a minimal weighted score to these countries ensures that the possibility to settle in them does not go unnoticed. All the territories enforcing their own border controls that are assigned such a weight are listed in the Annex.

Diversity of Travel Freedom

Diversity of Travel Freedom measures the number of tourist- and business-access countries the holder of a particular nationality can visit visa-free or with a visa-on-arrival for a short-term stay. Work or recourse to public funds is usually strictly prohibited.

Visa restrictions play an important role in controlling the possibilities for (foreign) nationals to travel freely across borders. Almost all countries now require visas from certain non-nationals who wish to enter (or leave) their territory. A visa allows you to travel to the destination country as far as the port of entry (airport, seaport or land border crossing) and ask the immigration officer to allow you to enter the country. The immigration officer usually also decides how long you can stay for any particular visit. In most countries, a tourist and business access visa allows you to stay in the country between one and three months.

Diversity of Travel Freedom is a valuable aspect of the quality of nationalities. It gauges the extent to which holders of a particular nationality can freely travel without extensive administrative hassles and time-consuming preparation.

 Diversity of Travel Freedom is measured using data provided by the International Air Transport Association (IATA), the trade association of the overwhelming majority of airlines. IATA maintains IATA Timatic, the world's largest, most reliable database of travel information. QNI data is based on the status quo on 1 July 2018. For the QNI, the country scores received by IATA are directly transposed to the corresponding nationality. The more destinations a nationality allows you to visit for tourist or business purposes without requiring a prior visa application, the higher that nationality's value is in terms of Diversity of Travel Freedom, also on a 0–15 scale.

  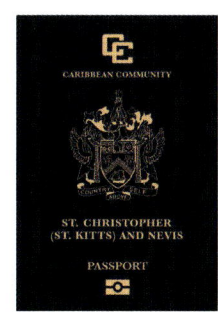 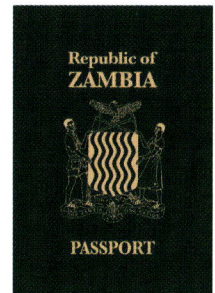

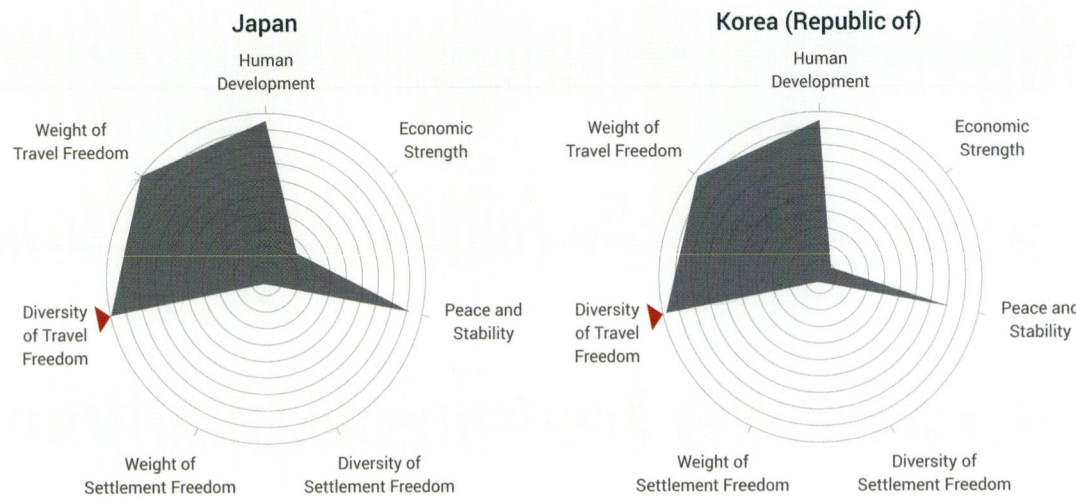

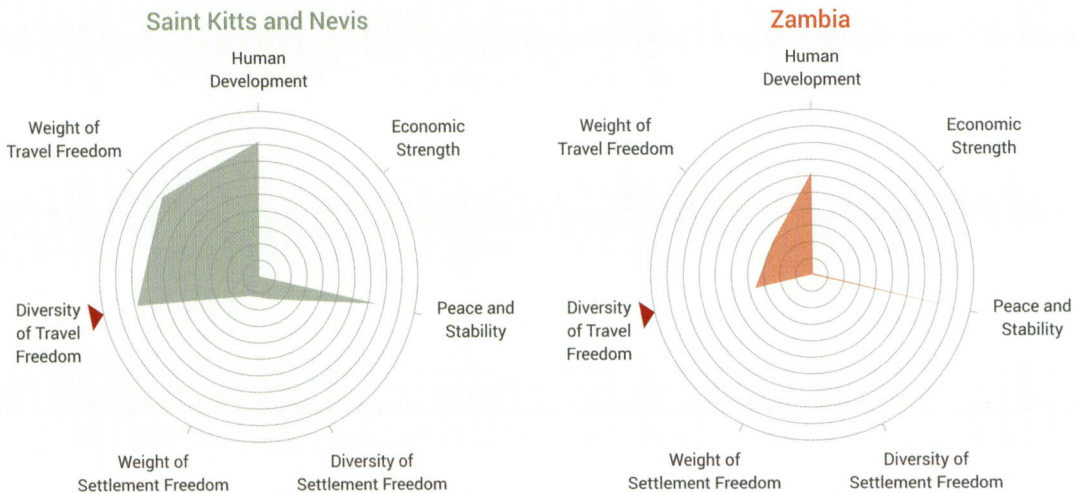

Examples: In 2018, the highest-scoring nationality on Diversity of Travel Freedom was that of Japan, giving visa-free or visa-on-arrival access to 179 destinations. The Japanese nationality received the full 15% on the Diversity of Travel Freedom parameter. A close second was the nationality of the Republic of Korea with 176 destinations, resulting in a normalized score of

$$\frac{176}{179} \times 15 = 14.75\%$$

The nationality of Saint Kitts and Nevis comes with 141 visa-free or visa-on-arrival destinations, which corresponds to a Diversity of Travel Freedom score of

$$\frac{141}{179} \times 15 = 11.82\%$$

Nationals of Zambia have similar travel access to only 65 destinations, corresponding to a 5.45% normalized score.

Some territories count as destinations but are not considered nationalities. These are territories that enforce their own entry requirements but are governed by other countries, and people originating from these territories hold passports issued only by the governing country. The following territories are considered destinations, but not nationalities, for the Travel Freedom part of this Index.

- Territories dependent on the UK: Anguilla, Bermuda, Cayman Islands, Falkland Islands, Gibraltar, Montserrat, Turks and Caicos Islands, and British Virgin Islands
- Territory dependent on Australia: Norfolk Island
- Territories associated with New Zealand: Cook Islands and Niue
- Territories under administration of the US: Guam, Northern Mariana Islands, Puerto Rico, American Samoa, and the US Virgin Islands
- Territories under administration of the Kingdom of the Netherlands: Aruba, Bonaire, Sint Eustatius, Saba, Curaçao, and Sint Maarten
- Territories dependent on France in the Caribbean and in the Atlantic, Indian, and Pacific Oceans

Weight of Travel Freedom

In addition to its diversity, the QNI measures the Weight of Travel Freedom, applying the same principles that are applied for Weight of Settlement Freedom: the combined value of all countries allowing visa-free or visa-on-arrival tourist and business access to the holders of a nationality is composed of the sum of all of these countries' weighted scores on Human Development (accounting for 50%) and Economic Strength (accounting for 50%).

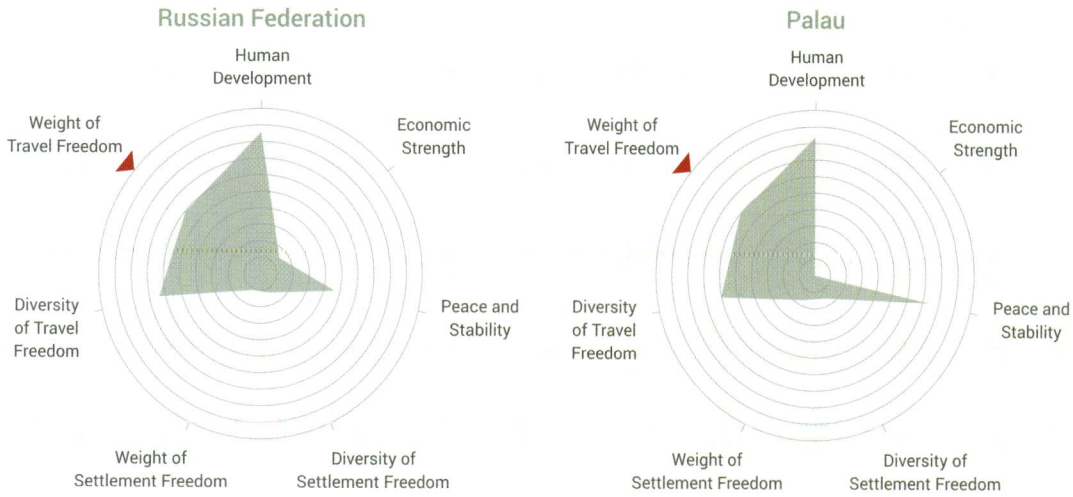

Examples: In 2018 a Russian Federation passport gave visa-free or visa-on-arrival access to 115 destinations. However, a prior visa application is still necessary for Russian nationals to access, among others, the US, EU countries, Australia, Japan, and Canada. The Weight of Travel Freedom for the Russian nationality is therefore comparatively low (8.94% on a 0–15 scale). The nationality of Palau, despite having slightly lower travel diversity with 108 visa-free or visa-on-arrival

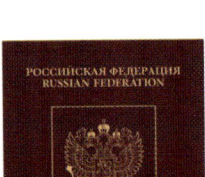 

destinations, ends up with a higher score on Weight of Travel Freedom (8.99%). Nationals of the Marshall Islands, having the same number of visa-free or visa-on-arrival travel destinations as Russian nationals, get more value from the travel destinations available to them, with a normalized score of 9.51%.

As mentioned above, the complete list of specific countries that a particular nationality allows its holders to visit visa-free or by visa-on-arrival is not publicly available. The Weight of Settlement Freedom values are calculated by IATA specifically for the QNI, using the abovementioned formula and based on visa regimes as of 1 July 2018.

Some of the countries that can be visited visa-free or by visa-on-arrival have nationalities that do not feature in the QNI because there is no data available on Human Development and/or Peace and Stability. There are also countries that are not represented in the QNI because they lack their own nationality, despite having their own immigration controls, such as Aruba, New Caledonia, and American Samoa. Notwithstanding their own absence from the QNI, and for the purpose of this edition of the QNI, these countries and territories have been ascribed a minimal weighted score of 10.99, consisting of the sum of the normalized HDI world mean and a normalized infinitesimal GDP value. Ascribing a minimal weighted score to these countries ensures that the possibility to visit them visa-free is not overlooked. All the territories enforcing their own border controls that are assigned such a weight are listed in the Annex.

The World's Countries by Access to Europe's Schengen Area and the United States

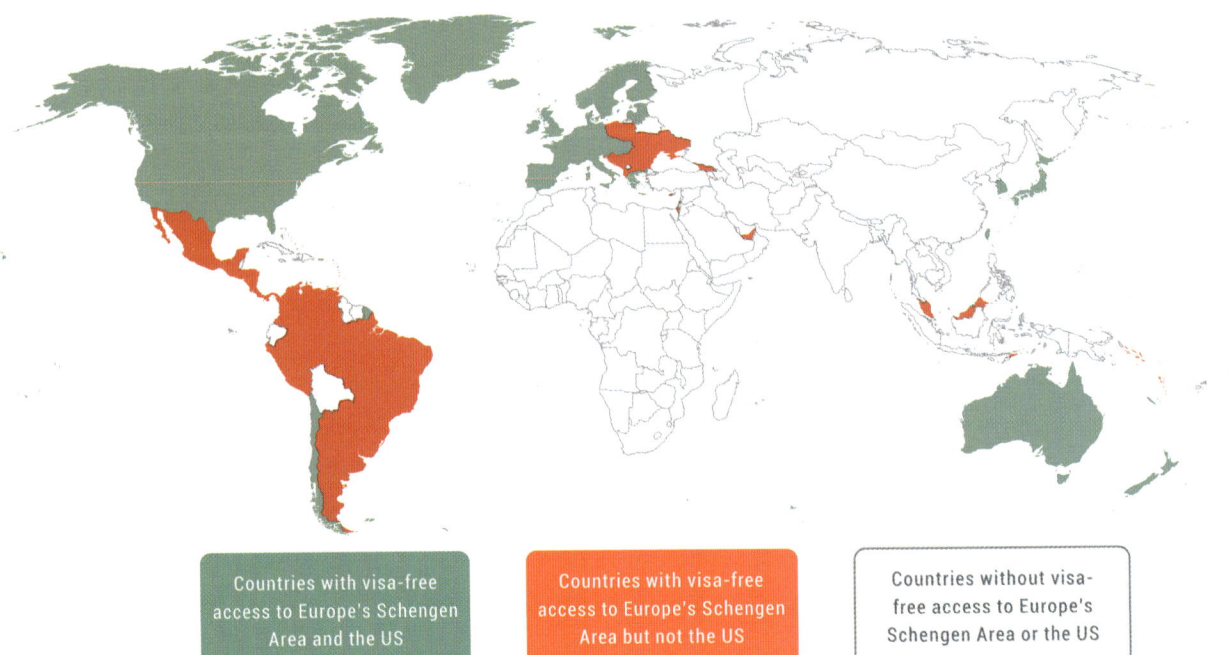

Part 3

The QNI General Ranking

12 Introduction to the QNI General Ranking

QNI General Ranking

The QNI General Ranking ranks nationalities on a scale from 0% to 100%. Scores are rounded to one decimal place. The following weights are attributed to the separate sub-elements:

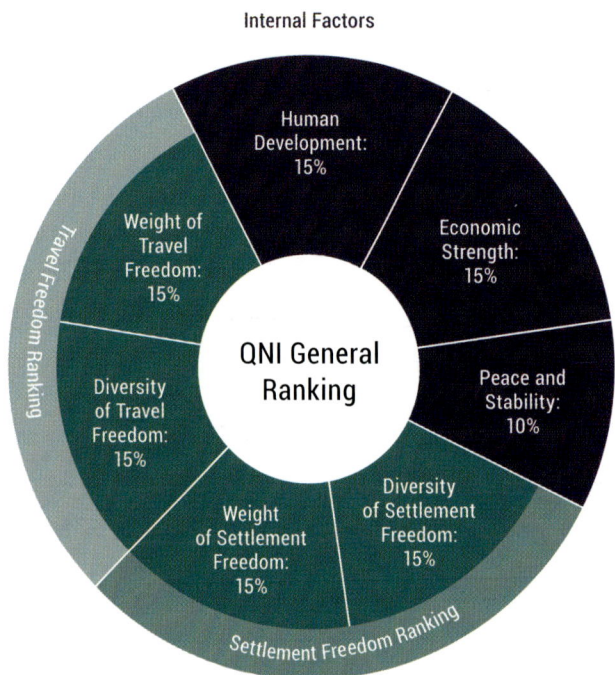

Quality Tiers

Moreover, nationalities are categorized into five tiers:

- **Very High Quality:** nationalities with a value of 75.0% and higher
- **High Quality:** nationalities with a value of between 50.0% and 74.9%
- **Medium Quality:** nationalities with a value of between 35.0% and 49.9%
- **Low Quality:** nationalities with a value of between 20.0% and 34.9%
- **Very Low Quality:** nationalities with a value of 19.9% and lower

While Very High Quality and High Quality nationalities are the ones that the authors of the majority of citizenship textbooks have had in mind, in that they are associated with highly developed and stable countries and provide their holders with a usable bundle of rights, the same cannot be said — to varying degrees — of the nationalities belonging to the three lowest categories. The majority of these cannot compare to the leading nationalities and essentially confer bundles of liabilities, rather than attractive rights, on the populations who hold them.

12 Introduction to the QNI General Ranking • 69

13 Nationalities of the World in 2018

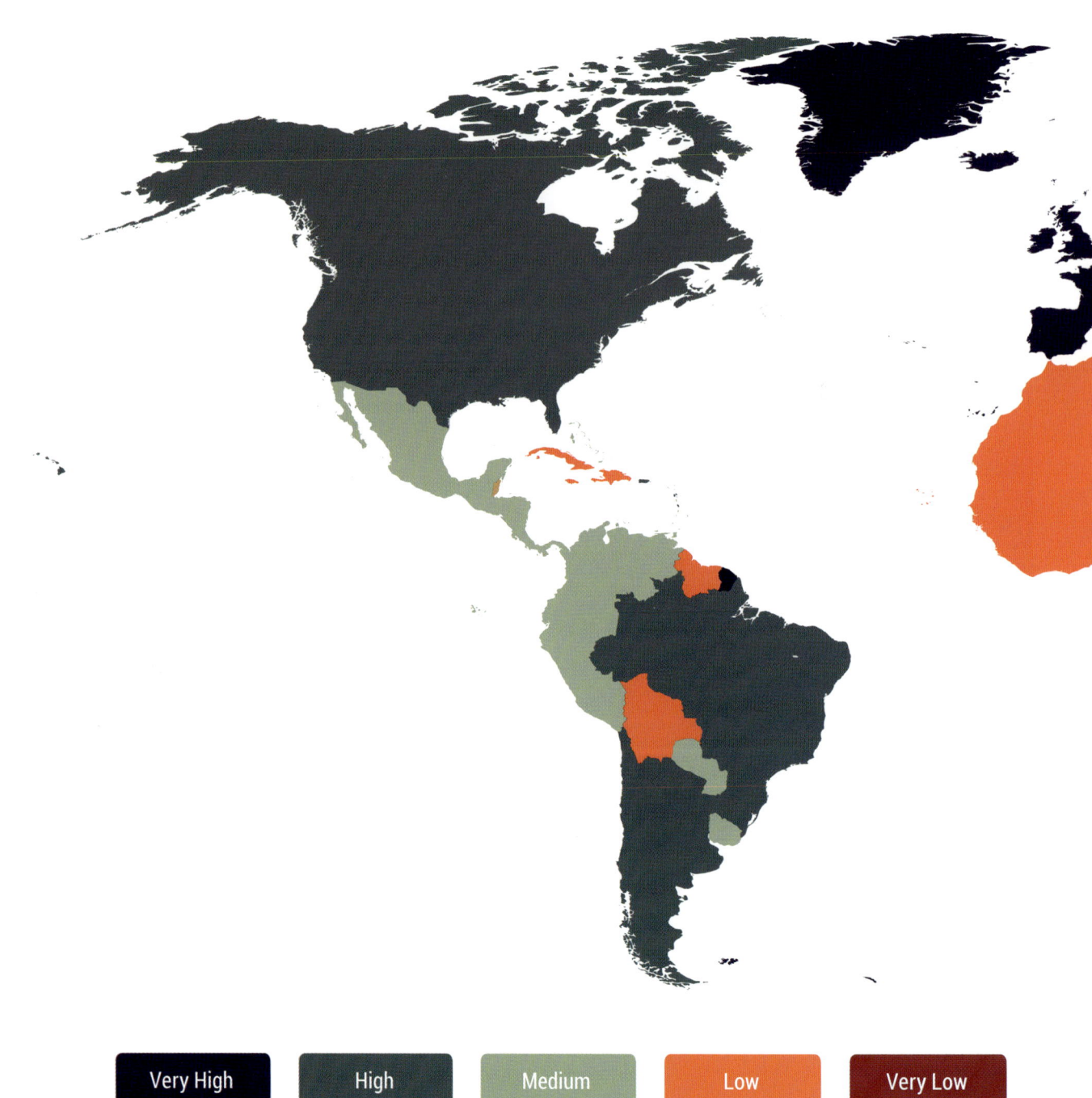

13 Nationalities of the World in 2018 · 71

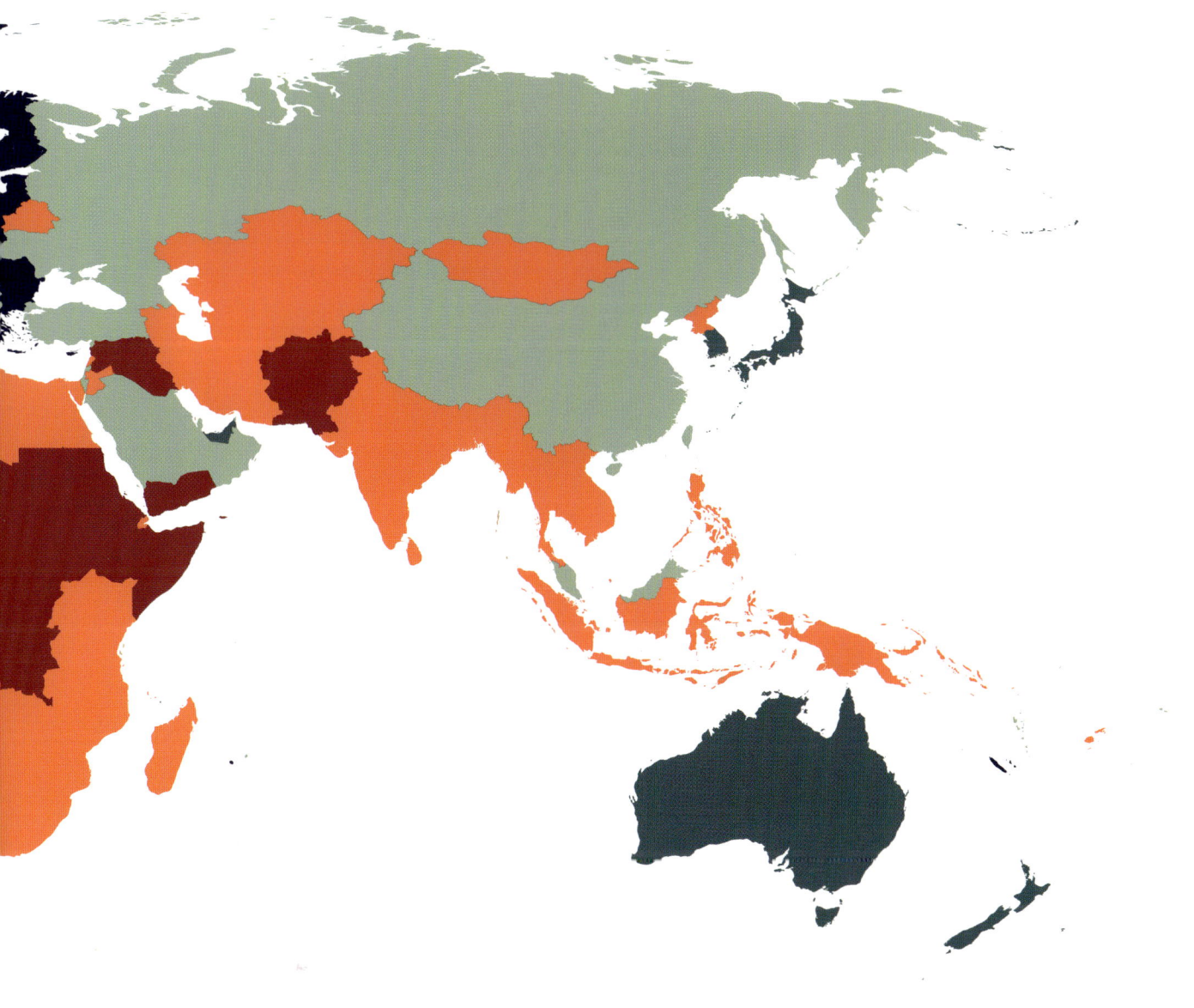

14   QNI General Ranking 2018

Ranking	Nationality	Value 2018	Change in Value 2017–2018	Change in Value 2014–2018
1	France	83.5	−0.3	+0.2
2	Germany	82.8	−0.4	+0.2
2	Netherlands	82.8	+0.3	+0.2
3	Denmark	81.7	−0.3	−0.8
4	Sweden	81.5	−0.1	−0.4
4	Norway	81.5	−0.5	+0.1
5	Iceland	81.4	−0.1	+0.9
6	Finland	81.2	+0.4	−1.0
7	Italy	80.7	−0.5	+0.7
8	United Kingdom	80.3	+0.1	−0.2
9	Ireland	80.2	−0.2	0
10	Spain	80.0	−0.5	+0.4
11	Switzerland	79.8	−0.4	−0.4
11	Belgium	79.8	0	+0.2
12	Austria	79.7	0	+0.1
13	Czech Republic	79.0	−0.2	+1.7
13	Portugal	79.0	−0.3	+0.7
13	Luxembourg	79.0	−0.1	−0.3
14	Liechtenstein	78.9	−0.3	−0.1
15	Slovenia	78.6	+0.7	+1.8
16	Malta	77.6	+0.7	+1.0
17	Hungary	77.5	−0.4	+0.6
17	Slovakia	77.5	0	+0.9
18	Greece	77.3	0	+0.6
19	Estonia	77.1	0	+1.2
20	Poland	77.0	−0.4	+1.4
20	Lithuania	77.0	0	+1.9
20	Latvia	77.0	+0.2	+1.9
21	Cyprus	75.3	−0.1	+2.2
22	Romania	75.2	+0.3	+14.9
23	Bulgaria	75.0	+0.5	+14.3
24	Croatia	73.8	+4.2	+19.6
25	United States	70.0	−0.9	+4.6
	EU citizenship	63.6	−0.3	−5.7
26	Japan	58.4	+0.1	−0.8
27	British overseas territories (Gibraltar)	56.0	+0.3	n/a
28	Canada	55.3	+0.1	+0.3
29	Australia	55.2	−0.5	+0.4
29	Chile	55.2	−0.3	+4.4
30	Singapore	55.1	+0.2	+0.3
31	New Zealand	54.8	−0.4	−0.2

Ranking	Nationality	Value 2018	Change in Value 2017–2018	Change in Value 2014–2018
32	Argentina	54.5	+0.1	+3.2
33	Brazil	54.3	+0.1	+3.8
34	Korea (Republic of)	54.2	−0.2	+1.0
35	Jersey	53.3	−0.6	n/a
36	Guernsey	53.2	−0.6	n/a
37	Isle of Man	53.2	−0.6	n/a
38	Monaco	52.5	−0.4	+1.3
38	Andorra	51.6	−0.6	+2.4
39	San Marino	51.4	−0.9	+0.1
40	Malaysia	51.0	+0.1	+2.0
41	Uruguay	50.5	−0.1	+2.1
42	United Arab Emirates	50.3	+2.4	+12.8
43	Brunei Darussalam	49.2	−0.4	+0.1
44	Hong Kong, China (SAR)	48.9	+0.7	+1.3
45	Antigua and Barbuda	47.7	+0.1	+2.4
46	Saint Kitts and Nevis	47.5	+0.2	+2.4
47	Paraguay	46.8	+0.1	+2.9
48	Israel	46.7	−0.2	+1.6
49	Barbados	46.3	+0.2	+2.7
49	Saint Vincent and the Grenadines	46.3	+0.6	+9.6
50	Seychelles	46.2	−0.4	+4.2
51	Chinese Taipei (Taiwan)	46.1	−0.1	−0.2
52	Mexico	45.7	+0.1	+3.0
52	Grenada	45.7	+0.5	+9.8
53	Peru	45.6	+0.4	+9.5
54	Bahamas	45.5	+0.1	+1.3
54	Costa Rica	45.5	+0.3	+3.5
54	Saint Lucia	45.5	+0.3	+8.5
55	Mauritius	45.2	−0.2	+3.2
56	China	44.3	+0.8	+4.9
56	Venezuela	44.3	+1.9	+3.5
57	Commonwealth of Dominica	43.9	−0.4	+7.9
58	Panama	43.8	0	+2.4
58	Macao	43.8	0	+2.0
59	Colombia	43.3	+0.9	+11.6
59	Trinidad and Tobago	43.3	+0.5	+7.9
60	Palau	42.7	0	n/a
61	Serbia	42.1	+0.3	+3.5
62	Russian Federation	42.0	+0.1	+3.8
63	Marshall Islands	41.8	−0.6	n/a
64	Montenegro	40.9	+0.1	+3.1
65	Micronesia (Federated States of)	40.2	−0.4	n/a
66	El Salvador	39.7	−0.2	+1.6
66	Samoa	39.7	+0.6	n/a
67	North Macedonia	39.3	0	+2.2
68	Honduras	39.2	−0.3	+2.4

Ranking	Nationality	Value 2018	Change in Value 2017–2018	Change in Value 2014–2018
69	Ecuador	39.1	-0.3	+7.6
69	Guatemala	39.1	+0.4	+1.9
70	Kuwait	39	+0.5	+1.6
71	Bosnia and Herzegovina	38.8	-0.1	+2.8
72	Albania	38.7	-0.1	+3.1
72	Tonga	38.7	0	n/a
73	Moldova (Republic of)	38.6	-0.7	+7.7
73	Tuvalu	38.6	+0.3	n/a
74	Nicaragua	38.5	+0.4	+2.3
75	Ukraine	38.2	+0.9	+5.4
76	Turkey	37.7	+0.6	+2.5
77	Georgia	37.5	+0.1	+8.3
78	Qatar	37.1	-0.1	-1.1
78	Vanuatu	37.1	-0.1	n/a
78	Oman	37.1	+0.7	+2.1
79	Kiribati	36.6	+0.2	n/a
80	Solomon Islands	36.5	+0.4	n/a
81	Saudi Arabia	36.2	+0.3	+0.2
82	Bahrain	36.1	+0.5	+0.8
83	Bolivia (Plurinational State of)	35.8	-0.3	+2.0
84	Kazakhstan	35.7	+0.1	+3.8
85	South Africa	35.0	+0.1	+2.5
86	Belarus	34.8	-0.1	+1.5
87	Cape Verde	34.2	-0.4	+2.2
88	Belize	34.1	-0.3	+2.8
89	Ghana	33.9	-0.3	+2.3
90	Guyana	33.6	+0.6	+3.7
91	Fiji	33.2	+0.1	n/a
92	Suriname	33.1	+0.5	+1.6
92	Timor-Leste	33.1	+0.3	+8.4
93	Maldives	33.0	+0.3	+1.7
93	Botswana	33.0	+0.1	+2.7
94	Thailand	32.4	0	+1.5
95	Gambia	32.2	+0.2	+2.0
95	India	32.2	+1.0	+2.7
96	Nauru	32.0	-0.4	n/a
96	Jamaica	32.0	-0.1	+1.6
97	Indonesia	31.8	+0.6	+2.4
97	Benin	31.8	+0.1	+2.4
98	Armenia	31.7	-0.4	+2.3
99	Senegal	31.3	-0.1	+2.0
99	Sierra Leone	31.3	-0.4	+1.9
100	Israeli Laissez-passer	31.0	-0.5	n/a
101	Latvia ('Non-Citizen')	30.8	-0.2	+1.1
102	Kyrgyzstan	30.6	0	+3.1
103	Togo	30.3	-0.8	+1.5

Ranking	Nationality	Value 2018	Change in Value 2017–2018	Change in Value 2014–2018
104	Dominican Republic	30.2	+0.6	+2.5
105	Azerbaijan	30.1	-0.2	+0.4
106	Namibia	30.0	-0.3	+1.8
106	Côte d'Ivoire	30.0	-0.1	+2.6
106	Cuba	30.0	+0.5	+0.5
107	Tunisia	29.9	-0.6	+0.2
107	Guinea	29.9	+0.4	+2.7
108	Burkina Faso	29.8	0	+2.2
109	Mongolia	29.3	+0.2	+1.8
109	Uzbekistan	29.3	0	+0.6
110	Guinea-Bissau	28.8	+0.3	+3.1
111	Papua New Guinea	28.7	0	+2.3
112	Liberia	28.6	-0.1	+1.5
113	Morocco	28.1	-0.2	+1.5
113	Nigeria	28.1	-1.0	+0.8
114	Tajikistan	27.9	+0.2	+1.3
114	Philippines	27.9	+0.1	+1.0
115	Mali	27.8	-1.0	+0.8
115	Eswatini[1]	27.8	+0.2	+2.2
116	Zambia	27.6	-0.5	+1.0
117	Bhutan	27.5	-0.3	+1.2
118	Niger	27.4	-0.3	+1.6
118	Algeria	27.4	0	+0.8
119	Tanzania (United Republic of)	27.0	-0.4	+1.7
120	Kenya	26.9	+0.2	+2.2
121	Gabon	26.8	-0.3	+1.3
121	Jordan	26.8	-0.3	-0.1
121	Viet Nam	26.8	+0.1	+0.5
122	Turkmenistan	26.7	0	+1.1
123	Lesotho	26.6	-0.2	+0.5
124	Malawi	26.4	-0.4	+1.7
125	Sri Lanka	26.2	-0.3	+1.6
125	Iran (Islamic Republic of)	26.2	+0.4	+0.8
126	São Tomé and Príncipe	25.8	-0.3	+1.9
127	Egypt	25.7	-0.4	+0.5
128	Kosovo	25.3	-0.7	+0.9
128	Lao People's Democratic Republic	25.3	0	+0.5
129	British Nationals (Overseas)	25.2	0	n/a
130	Uganda	25.1	-0.2	+1.5
130	Lebanon	25.1	-0.3	0
130	British overseas territories	25.1	-0.2	n/a
131	Zimbabwe	24.9	+0.1	+2.5
132	Equatorial Guinea	24.8	-0.1	+2.1
133	Cambodia	24.6	0	-0.3
134	Madagascar	24.5	-0.3	+1.5

1 Formerly Swaziland

Ranking	Nationality	Value 2018	Change in Value 2017–2018	Change in Value 2014–2018
135	Angola	24.2	+0.6	+2.7
135	Comoros	24.2	−0.5	+2.1
136	Mauritania	24.1	−0.5	+0.9
137	Bangladesh	23.6	0	+1.2
137	Haiti	23.6	−0.3	+1.5
138	Rwanda	23.3	+0.3	+2.9
138	Mozambique	23.3	−0.1	+2.2
138	Congo (Republic of the)	23.3	+0.7	+0.8
139	Palestinian Territory	23.1	0	+0.7
139	Myanmar	23.1	−0.1	+1.6
140	Nepal	23.0	−0.1	0
141	Korea (DPRK)[2]	22.9	−0.2	n/a
142	British Overseas citizens	22.8	+0.2	n/a
143	British protected persons	22.6	+0.3	n/a
143	British subjects	22.6	−0.1	n/a
144	Cameroon	22.4	+0.3	+0.3
145	Djibouti	21.7	−0.6	+0.2
145	Libya	21.7	−0.4	−2.7
146	Chad	20.7	−0.2	+1.7
147	Burundi	20.0	+0.6	+1.2
148	Ethiopia	19.9	−0.1	+0.7
149	Iraq	19.4	+3.8	−0.5
150	Pakistan	19.0	−0.3	+0.5
151	Sudan (Republic of the)	18.9	−0.4	+1.0
152	Eritrea	18.8	−0.3	+0.4
153	Congo (Democratic Republic of the)	18.0	−0.9	+1.3
154	Central African Republic	17.6	−0.1	+1.0
155	Yemen	17.2	−0.7	−3.7
156	Syrian Arab Republic	16.8	−0.1	−1.9
157	South Sudan	15.9	−0.8	n/a
158	Afghanistan	15.4	+0.3	−0.1
159	Somalia	13.8	−0.5	n/a

2   Korea (Democratic People's Republic of)

15 Movement between Tiers in 2014–2018

Between 2014 and 2018, 18 nationalities moved between the QNI's quality tiers, 17 of which moved upwards. Only the Yemeni nationality fell from the Low Quality to the Very Low Quality tier.

Nationality	Movement 2014–2018	2014 Tier	2018 Tier
Bulgaria	▲	High Quality	Very High Quality
Cyprus	▲	High Quality	Very High Quality
Romania	▲	High Quality	Very High Quality
Andorra	▲	Medium Quality	High Quality
Malaysia	▲	Medium Quality	High Quality
United Arab Emirates	▲	Medium Quality	High Quality
Uruguay	▲	Medium Quality	High Quality
Bolivia[1]	▲	Low Quality	Medium Quality
Colombia	▲	Low Quality	Medium Quality
Ecuador	▲	Low Quality	Medium Quality
Georgia	▲	Low Quality	Medium Quality
Kazakhstan	▲	Low Quality	Medium Quality
Moldova (Republic of)	▲	Low Quality	Medium Quality
South Africa	▲	Low Quality	Medium Quality
Ukraine	▲	Low Quality	Medium Quality
Burundi	▲	Very Low Quality	Low Quality
Chad	▲	Very Low Quality	Low Quality
Yemen	▼	Low Quality	Very Low Quality

1 Bolivia (Plurinational State of)

The nationalities of Bulgaria, Cyprus, and Romania moved from the High Quality tier to the Very High Quality tier, showing their superior value across the board. For the Cypriot nationality, Peace and Stability improved over the past few years, as did Travel Freedom. The Cypriot nationality was already in the upper region of the High Quality tier, and this development sufficed for it to gain enough value to pass the 75.0% threshold. The Bulgarian and Romanian nationalities were among the top risers over the past five years of measurement and gained substantial value due to the full integration of these countries in the EU internal market, including full settlement access for Bulgarians and Romanians in other EU Member States.

Nationality	Movement 2014–2018	Value 2014	Rank 2014	Value 2018	Rank 2018
Bulgaria	▲	60.7	24	75.0	23
Cyprus	▲	73.1	22	75.3	21
Romania	▲	60.3	25	75.2	22

See also Risers in 2014–2018 on pages 81–85.

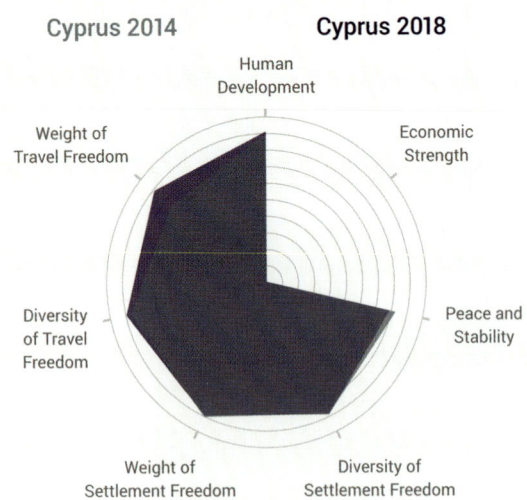

Most nationalities climbing from the Medium Quality to the High Quality tier saw minor improvements in Travel Freedom and Peace and Stability. Of course, the most notable riser in this group is the Emirati nationality, which is one of the top risers over the past five years of measurement, largely the result of numerous visa-waiver agreements.

See also Risers in 2014–2018, pages 81–85.

Nationality	Movement 2014–2018	Value 2014	Rank 2014	Value 2018	Rank 2018
Andorra	▲	49.2	35	51.6	38
Malaysia	▲	49.0	37	51.0	40
United Arab Emirates	▲	37.5	56	50.3	42
Uruguay	▲	48.4	38	50.5	41

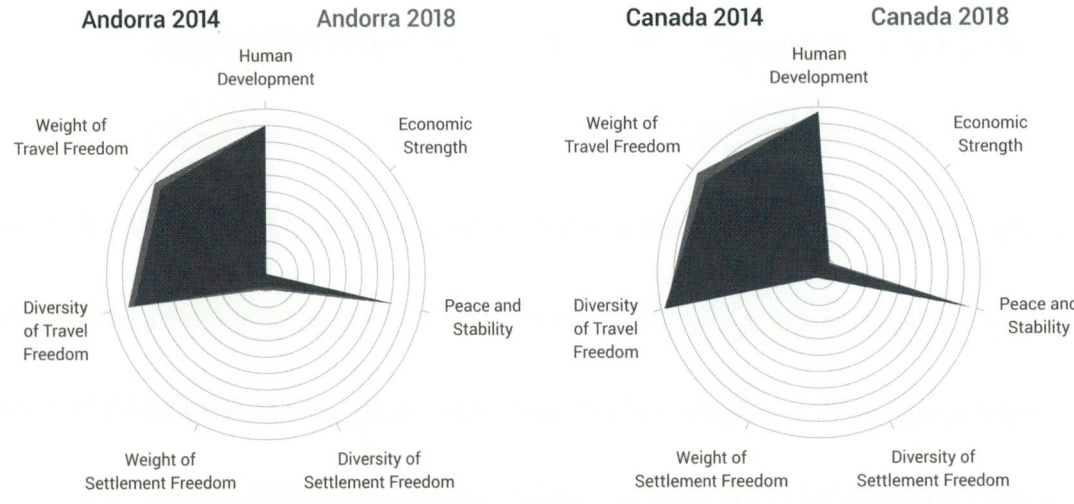

Eight nationalities moved up from the Low Quality tier (20.0%–34.9%) to the Medium Quality tier (35.0%–49.9%). The nationalities of Bolivia, Colombia, and Ecuador gained significant value as a result of the increased economic integration of South American economies. They also saw a large improvement in Travel Freedom: nationals of Ecuador, for example, could travel visa-free or by visa-on-arrival to 89 destinations in 2018, as opposed to 74 destinations in 2014. The nationalities of Georgia, Moldova, and the Ukraine also improved their value significantly because of visa-waiver agreements with Europe's Schengen Area in particular. The Ukraine did notably well on the External Value parameter and was able to climb to the Medium Quality tier in spite of a general deterioration in Peace and Stability over the past four years.

Nationality	Movement 2014–2018	Value 2014	Rank 2014	Value 2018	Rank 2018
Bolivia[1]	▲	33.8	72	35.8	83
Colombia	▲	31.7	78	43.3	59
Ecuador	▲	31.5	80	39.1	69
Georgia	▲	29.2	91	37.5	77
Kazakhstan	▲	31.9	77	35.7	84
Moldova (Republic of)	▲	30.9	82	38.6	73
South Africa	▲	32.5	75	35.0	85
Ukraine	▲	32.8	74	38.2	75

1 Bolivia (Plurinational State of)

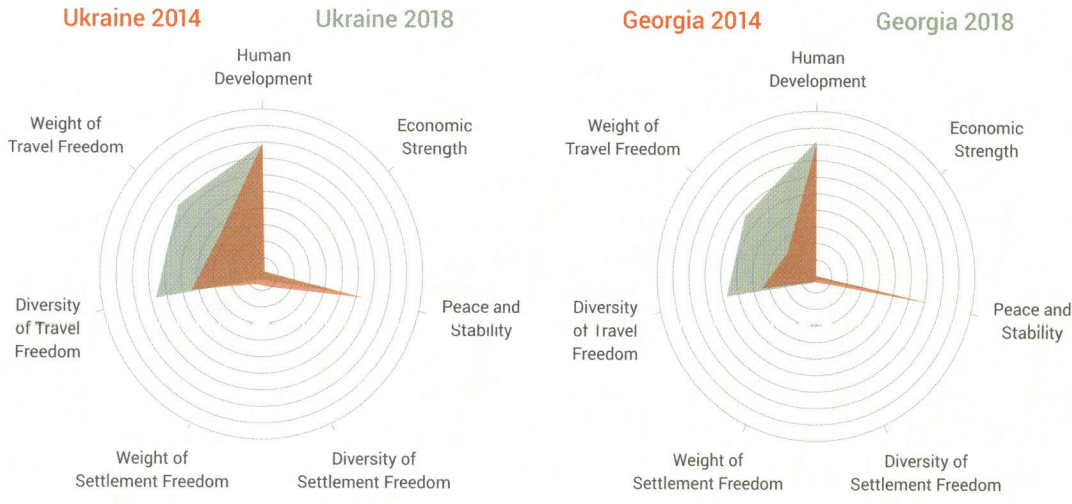

The nationalities of Chad and Burundi gained little value overall and are still of marginal value. However, both of them did pass the 20.0% score because of minor improvements in Travel Freedom. Citizens of Chad could travel visa-free or by visa-on-arrival to 52 destinations in 2018, as opposed to 46 in 2014. For citizens of Burundi, such travel opportunities increased from 41 visa-free and visa-on-arrival travel destinations in 2014 to 46 such destinations in 2018. While these are marginal gains, the two nationalities have added sufficient value to join the Low Quality tier.

Nationality	Movement 2014–2018	Value 2014	Rank 2014	Value 2018	Rank 2018
Burundi	▲	18.8	136	20.0	147
Chad	▲	19.0	135	20.7	146

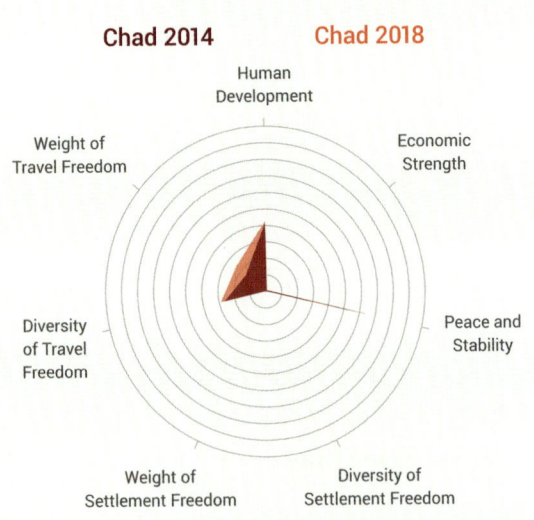

The nationality of Yemen is the only nationality falling to a lower quality tier, in this case from Low to Very Low Quality. This trend requires little explanation: Yemen's civil war has destroyed the country's economy and peace and stability and has further diminished the travel freedom of its citizens. Other nationalities that lost considerable value remained in the same quality tiers. The nationality of Syria, for example, was already of Very Low Quality in 2014, while that of Libya was and still is in the Low Quality tier.

Nationality	Movement 2014–2018	Value 2014	Rank 2014	Value 2018	Rank 2018
Yemen	▼	20.9	131	17.2	155

16 Risers in 2014–2018

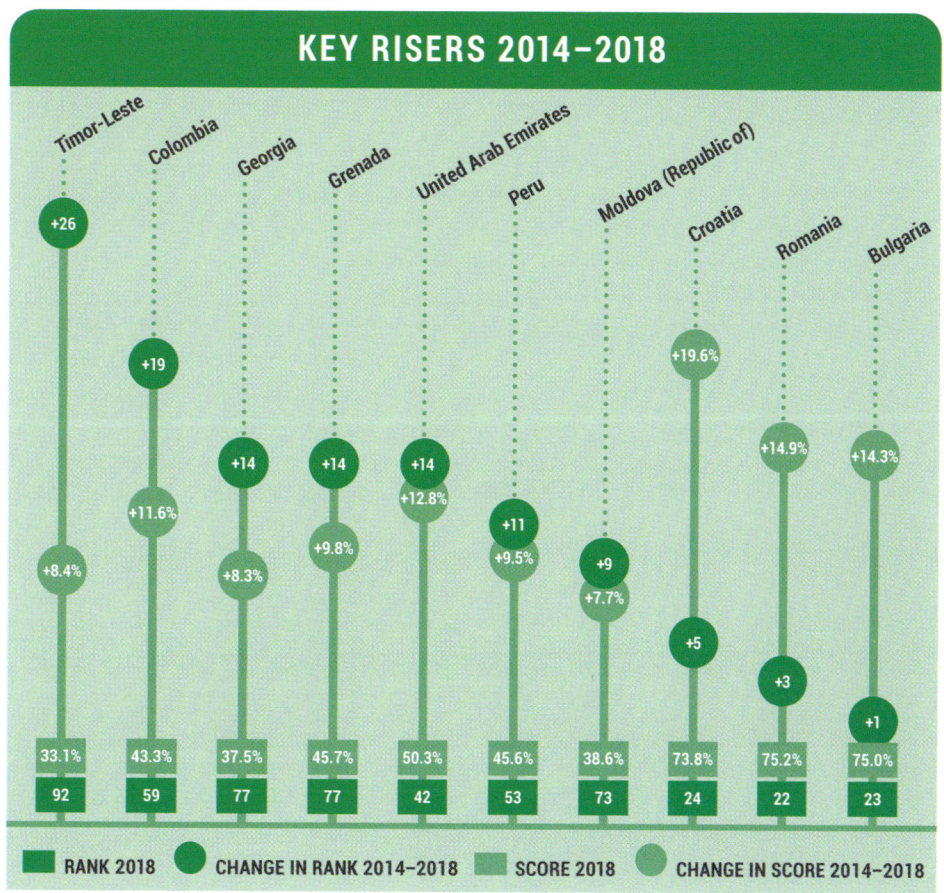

Croatia

Croatia joined the EU on 1 July 2013. Following the Accession Treaty of Croatia, other EU Member States can introduce free movement of workers who are Croatian nationals over a seven-year period. Thus, while in 2014 Croatian nationals had settlement access to 16 other territories, in 2018 this number had increased to 39 destinations, and visa-free or visa-on-arrival travel destinations increased from 129 to 159. As a result, the Croatian nationality's score increased from 54.2% to 73.8% and gained five places on the QNI General Ranking.

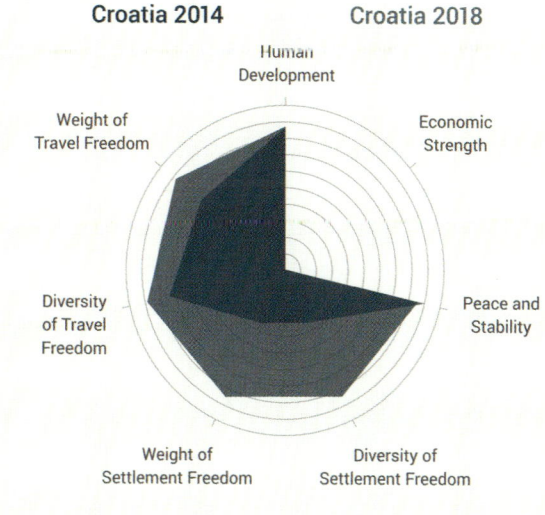

Romania

Romania joined the EU on 1 January 2007. After the seven-year transitional arrangements, Romanian nationals could benefit from full integration in the internal market from 2014 onwards. In the 2014 QNI, the Romanian nationality granted full settlement access to 23 destinations — Georgia and 22 EU destinations — which increased to 41 such destinations after the end of the transitional arrangements. Visa-free or visa-on-arrival travel destinations also increased from 141 to 159. Romania's score on the Global Peace Index improved from 1.68 in 2014 to 1.60 in 2018. All in all, the nationality of Romania improved its QNI score from 60.3% to 75.2% and gained three places on the QNI General Ranking.

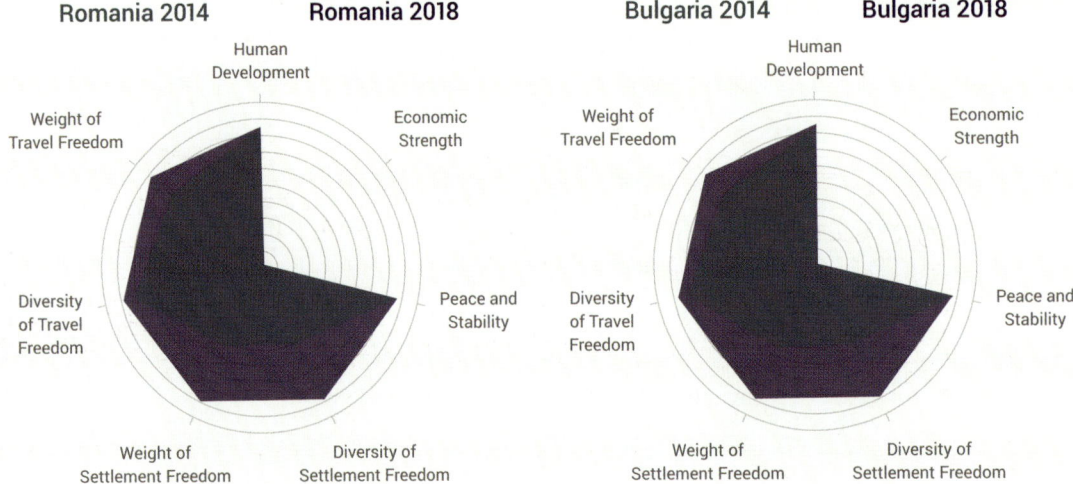

Bulgaria

Like Romania, Bulgaria joined the EU on 1 January 2007. After the seven-year transitional arrangements, Bulgarian nationals could benefit from full integration in the internal market from 2014 onwards. Bulgarian nationals had full settlement access to 24 destinations — Georgia and 23 EU destinations including Spain, the latter to which Romanian nationals had no such access at that time. Bulgarian settlement access increased to 41 such destinations after the end of the transitional arrangements. Visa-free or visa-on-arrival travel destinations also increased from 141 to 159. Bulgaria also saw improvements in Human Development, with its HDI score improving from 0.797 to 0.813. On the QNI General Ranking, the Bulgarian nationality went up from 60.7% in 2014 to 75.0% in 2018, and advanced from the 24th to the 23rd place.

United Arab Emirates

The Emirati nationality gained significant value over the past years, which is mainly attributable to an increase in visa-free and visa-on-arrival travel destinations. Diversity of Travel Freedom increased from 72 destinations in 2014 to 143 destinations in 2018, notably including the visa waiver from the Schengen Area. Meanwhile, the general level of Human Development for this nationality has increased slowly in recent years. The nationality of the United Arab Emirates improved its value from 37.5% in 2014 to 50.3% in 2018, overtaking the Israeli nationality as the most valuable nationality in the Middle Eastern region and firmly establishing itself in the top 50, with the 42nd position in the 2018 QNI General Ranking.

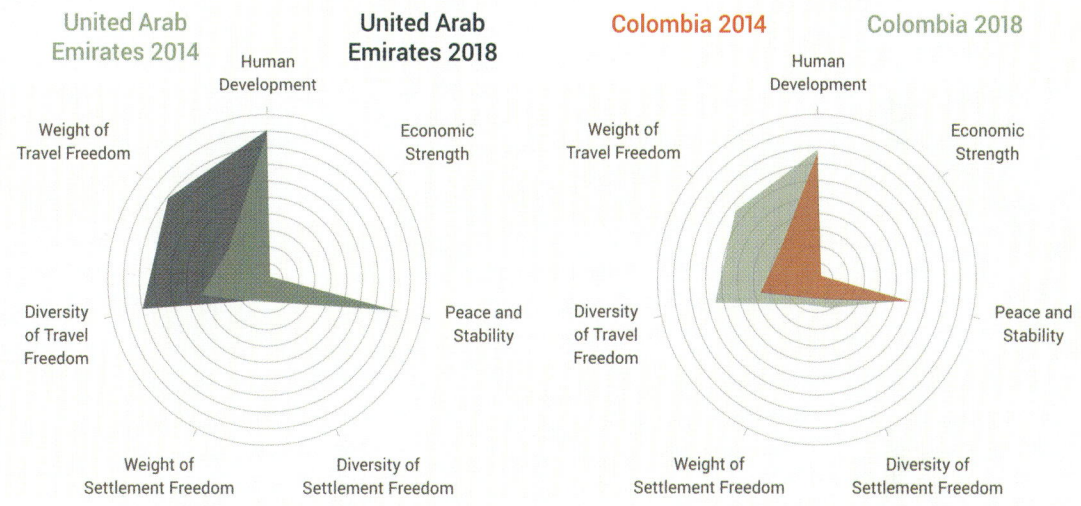

Colombia

The Colombian nationality's value improved by 11.6 percentage points from 31.7% in 2014 to 43.3% in 2018. Human Development levels have increased slightly but steadily over the past years. At the same time, Colombian nationals gained settlement access to Ecuador, Peru, and Svalbard, adding to the existing settlement freedom they had in Argentina, Bolivia, Brazil, Georgia, Paraguay, and Uruguay. Travel Freedom also developed from 63 visa-free and visa-on-arrival destinations in 2014 to 118 destinations in 2018, which has included Europe's Schengen Area since the visa-waiver agreement between Colombia and the Schengen Area countries on 3 December 2015.

Grenada

Grenada and the EU ratified a visa-waiver agreement on 15 December 2015, granting visa-free travel for nationals of Grenada to the Member States of the EU. This agreement fits in the broader trend of Grenadian nationals' travel freedom. Between 2014 and 2018 their visa-free and visa-on-arrival travel destinations increased from 88 to 130. Overall, the value of Grenadian nationality improved from 35.9% in 2014 to 45.7% in 2018, with its ranking increasing from 66th to 52nd.

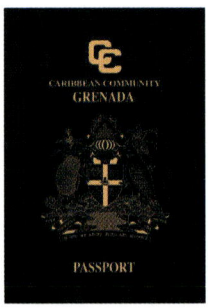

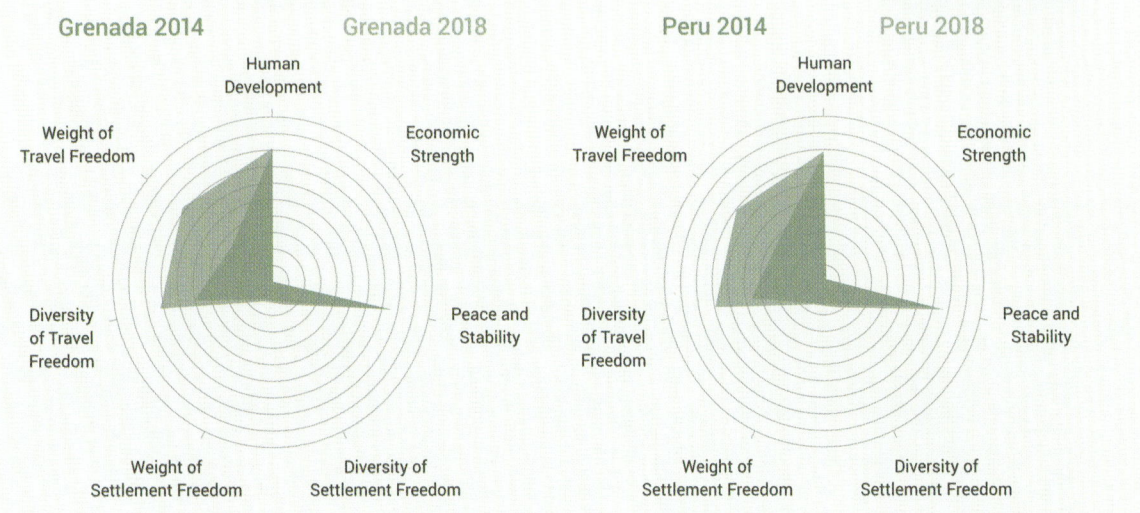

Peru

The nationality of Peru improved its overall value through both internal and external factors. Between 2014 and 2018, Peru's level of Peace and Stability improved significantly, as demonstrated by an improvement from 2.30 to 1.99 on the GPI. Peruvian nationals also gained free settlement access to Ecuador and Svalbard (although losing such access to Georgia). Travel Freedom increased from 88 to 125 visa-free and visa-on-arrival travel destinations. Overall value increased from 36.1% in 2014 to 45.6% in 2018, a sufficient improvement for a jump from 64th to 53rd place on the QNI General Ranking.

Timor-Leste

Nationals of Timor-Leste saw minor improvements in both Human Development (from 0.610 to 0.625 on the HDI) and Peace and Stability (from 1.95 to 1.90 on the GPI). Travel Freedom almost doubled from 48 visa-free or visa-on-arrival travel destinations in 2014 to 88 such destinations in 2018. The overall value of Timorese nationality increased from 24.7% to 33.1%. In 2018, it occupied the 92nd position on the QNI General Ranking, improving by no fewer than 26 places.

Georgia

Human Development in Georgia improved slightly between 2014 and 2018 (from 0.765 to 0.780). The same applies to Peace and Stability, which improved from 2.225 in 2014 to 2.130 in 2018. Its increase in value is largely due to substantial developments in Travel Freedom, from 60 visa-free and visa-on-arrival travel destinations in 2014 to 103 destinations in 2018. In all, the value of the Georgian nationality increased from 29.2% to 37.5%, corresponding to a 14-place improvement on the QNI General Ranking, from the 91st to the 77th position.

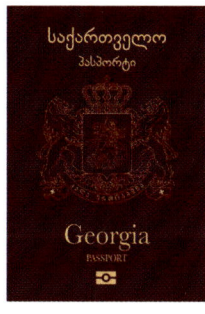

Moldova

The Moldovan nationality benefited from a significant increase in Travel Freedom. While in 2014 its nationals could travel visa-free or by obtaining a visa-on-arrival to only 59 destinations, in 2018 the number increased by 52 to a total of 111 such destinations. Settlement Freedom deteriorated, as Moldovan nationals no longer have full access to Armenia, Kyrgyzstan, and the Russian Federation, leaving only Georgia and Svalbard as settlement destinations. While this last development limited its overall improvement in value, the nationality of Moldova nonetheless gained 7.7 percentage points and 9 places on the QNI General Ranking.

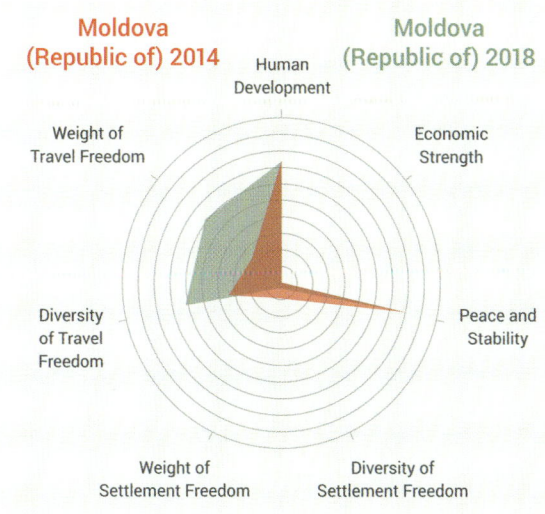

17   Fallers in 2014–2018

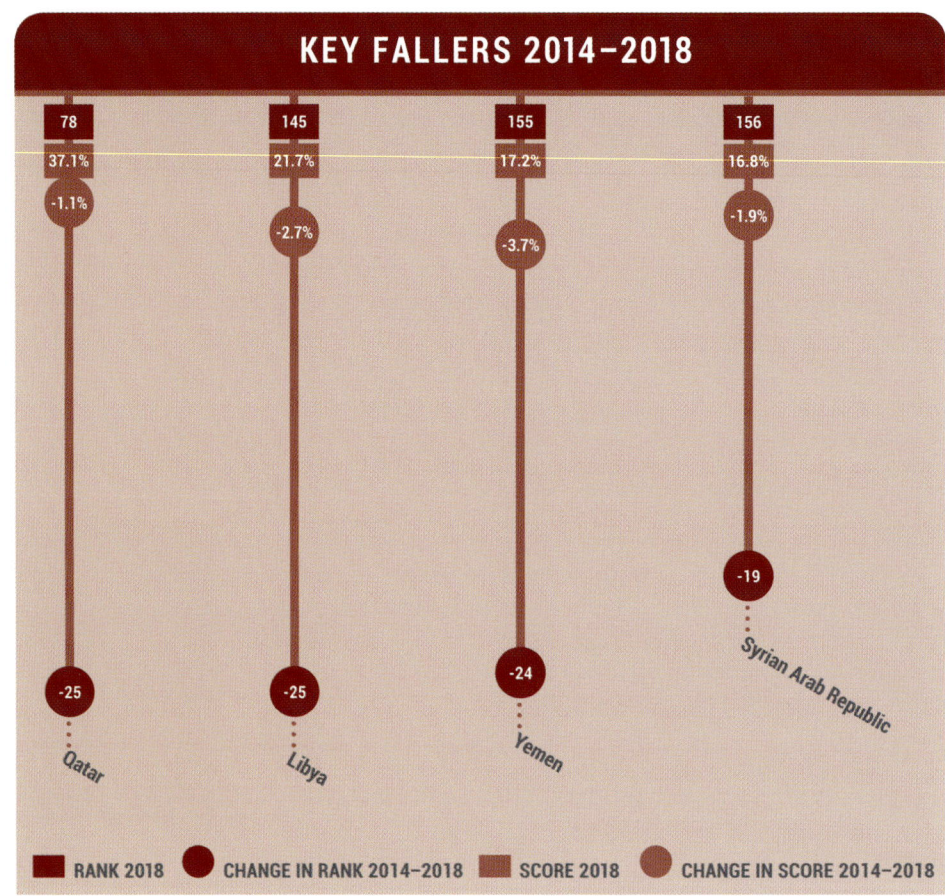

Yemen

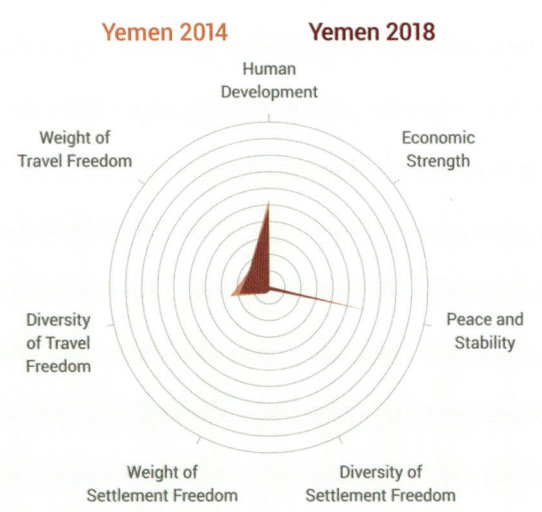

Yemen's extreme destabilization led to its GPI score deteriorating from 2.629 to 3.305. Travel Freedom decreased from 43 to 34 visa-free or visa-on-arrival destinations. As a result, its nationality dropped in value from 20.9% (Low Quality) to 17.2% (Very Low Quality) and is now 155th in the QNI General Ranking.

Libya

Libya's nationality suffered from a significant deterioration in Peace and Stability, with a GPI score of 2.453 in 2014 and 3.262 in 2018. The number of visa-free and visa-on-arrival travel destinations also decreased from 39 such destinations in 2014 to 36 in 2018. Overall, the nationality of Libya lost 2.7 percentage points on the QNI General Ranking and now occupies the 145th position, above only the nationalities of Syria, South Sudan, Afghanistan, and Somalia.

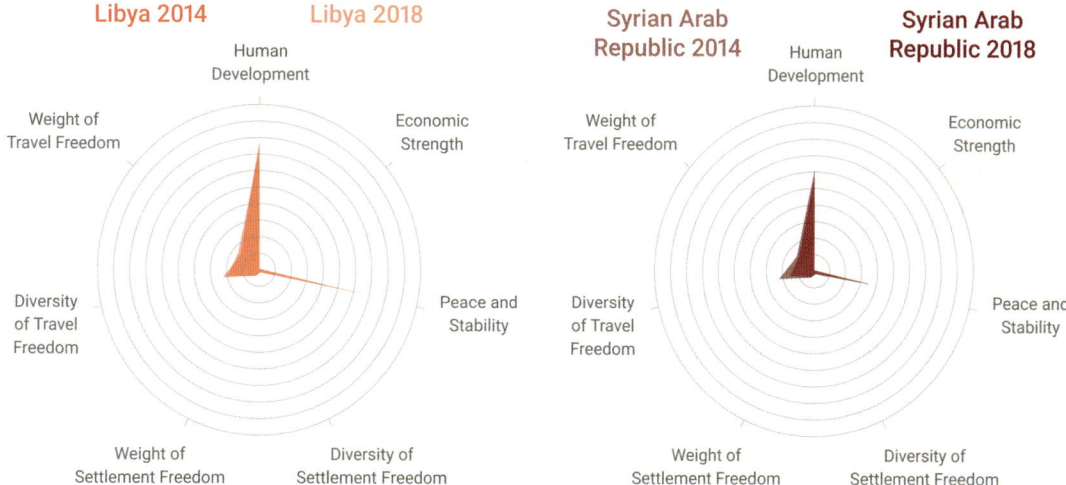

Syrian Arab Republic

The nationality of the Syrian Arab Republic had already lost virtually all of its value by 2014 as a result of the destructive effects of its civil war. Between 2014 and 2018, Peace and Stability has remained at an all-time low. Human Development decreased from 0.550 to 0.536 on the HDI. Travel Freedom of the Syrian nationality is virtually non-existent, with the 39 visa-free and visa-on-arrival travel destinations in 2014 further diminishing to 28 destinations in 2018. Syria's overall value dropped from 18.8% in 2014 to 16.8% in 2018, and the nationality now occupies the 156th position.

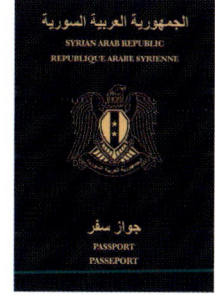

Qatar

Qatar's nationality has lost significant value over the past five years of measurement due to its diplomatic conflict with Saudi Arabia. The GPI measured a decrease in peacefulness from 1.491 in 2014 to 1.869 in 2018, which is a substantial deterioration. While overall Travel Freedom of Qatari nationals increased from 71 to 81 visa-free and visa-on-arrival travel destinations, they lost settlement access to Bahrain, Saudi Arabia, and the United Arab Emirates. As a result, its overall value decreased from 38.2% to 37.1%, and the nationality of Qatar now occupies the 78th position.

Part 4

Regional and Thematic Rankings

18 Europe

Regional Ranking	Nationality	2018 Value
1	France	83.5
2	Netherlands	82.8
2	Germany	82.8
3	Denmark	81.7
4	Sweden	81.5
4	Norway	81.5
5	Iceland	81.4
6	Finland	81.2
7	Italy	80.7
8	United Kingdom	80.3
9	Ireland	80.2
10	Spain	80.0
11	Switzerland	79.8
11	Belgium	79.8
12	Austria	79.7
13	Czech Republic	79.0
13	Portugal	79.0
13	Luxembourg	79.0
14	Liechtenstein	78.9
15	Slovenia	78.6
16	Malta	77.6
17	Hungary	77.5
17	Slovakia	77.5
18	Greece	77.3
19	Estonia	77.1
20	Poland	77.0
20	Lithuania	77.0
20	Latvia	77.0
21	Cyprus	75.3
22	Romania	75.2
23	Bulgaria	75.0
24	Croatia	73.8
25	British overseas territories (Gibraltar)	56.0
26	Jersey	53.3
27	Guernsey	53.2
27	Isle of Man	53.2
28	Monaco	52.5
29	Andorra	51.6
30	San Marino	51.4
31	Serbia	42.1
32	Russian Federation	42.0
33	Montenegro	40.9
34	North Macedonia	39.3

Regional Ranking	Nationality	2018 Value
35	Bosnia and Herzegovina	38.8
36	Albania	38.7
37	Moldova (Republic of)	38.6
38	Ukraine	38.2
39	Turkey	37.7
40	Georgia	37.5
41	Belarus	34.8
42	Armenia	31.7
43	Latvia ('Non-Citizen')	30.8
44	Azerbaijan	30.1
45	Kosovo	25.3
46	British Nationals (Overseas)	25.2
47	British overseas territories	25.1
48	British Overseas citizens	22.8
49	British protected persons	22.6
49	British subjects	22.6

Mean: 60.4% • Median: 75.2%

The nationalities of European countries vary widely in quality, especially taking into account the numerous British statuses other than British citizenship that are of low value. The predominant distinction between European nationalities is that between those associated with Member States of the EU and those associated with non-EU member states. EU nationalities are all in the Very High Quality tier with the exception of the Croatian nationality, which does not yet provide full settlement access in all EU Member States until the end of Croatia's transitional period. The nationalities of non-EU members are predominantly in the Medium and Low Quality tiers. On average, Internal Value is lower than that of nationalities of EU Member States, while they lose more significantly on External Value. This applies in particular to Settlement Freedom, as nationalities of non-EU members have little to no settlement access in other territories compared with those of EU Member States. Travel Freedom, however, is generally lower.

For example, the nationality of Albania comes with settlement access to two territories (Svalbard and Georgia) and 102 visa-free and visa-on-arrival travel destinations. Slovenia, by contrast, has settlement access in 41 territories and visa-free and visa-on-arrival travel access to 170 destinations. Nationals of Croatia, the newest EU Member State, have settlement access to 39 destinations and travel access to 159, while the nationality of Turkey, a candidate for EU membership, grants settlement access only to Georgia and comes with only 110 visa-free and visa-on-arrival travel destinations.

As a result of the sharp distinction between nationalities of EU Member States and those of non-EU members, the mean value of European nationalities (60.3%) is considerably lower than the average value of EU Member State nationalities (75.0%). Compared to other regions, Europe is also unique in having a median that is substantially higher than the mean value, further illustrating the wide variety in quality among European nationalities.

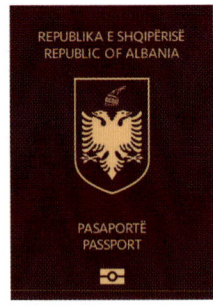
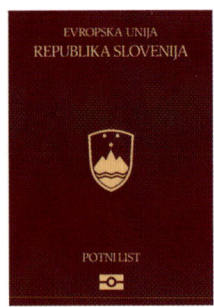
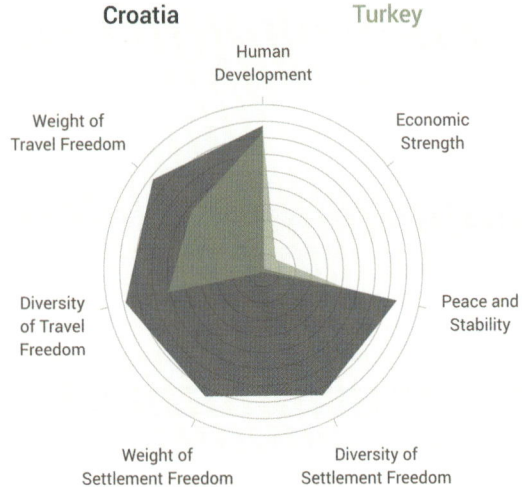
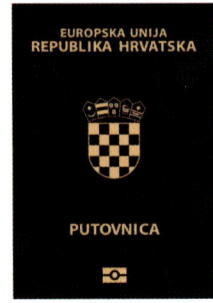

19 Americas

Regional Ranking	Nationality	2018 Value
1	United States	70.0
2	Canada	55.3
3	Chile	55.2
4	Argentina	54.5
5	Brazil	54.3
6	Uruguay	50.5
7	Antigua and Barbuda	47.7
8	Saint Kitts and Nevis	47.5
9	Paraguay	46.8
10	Barbados	46.3
10	Saint Vincent and the Grenadines	46.3
11	Mexico	45.7
11	Grenada	45.7
12	Peru	45.6
13	Bahamas	45.5
13	Costa Rica	45.5
13	Saint Lucia	45.5
14	Venezuela (Bolivarian Republic of)	44.3
15	Commonwealth of Dominica	43.9
16	Panama	43.8
17	Colombia	43.3
17	Trinidad and Tobago	43.3
18	El Salvador	39.7
19	Honduras	39.2
20	Ecuador	39.1
20	Guatemala	39.1
21	Nicaragua	38.5
22	Bolivia (Plurinational State of)	35.8
23	Belize	34.1
24	Guyana	33.6
25	Suriname	33.1
26	Jamaica	32.0
27	Dominican Republic	30.2
28	Cuba	30.0
29	Haiti	23.6

Mean: 52.2% • Median: 44.3%

The nationalities of North and Latin America are on average of Medium Quality, with 16 out of 29 nationalities ranking in the Medium Quality tier. The US nationality stands out clearly with a value of 70.0%, which is almost 15 percentage points higher than the Canadian nationality at second place. The US nationality benefits primarily from a higher degree of Economic Strength and a relatively high degree of Human Development. In addition, US nationals can freely settle in 11 other territories, including Guam, American Samoa, Georgia, and the Dutch Caribbean islands.

In comparison, the Canadian nationality grants less Settlement Freedom, while scoring high on internal factors such as Human Development and Peace and Stability.

In the Latin American region, Chile, Argentina, Brazil, and Uruguay are in the High Quality tier. Their nationalities benefit from freedom of settlement due to economic integration within MERCOSUR. These nationalities also have relatively high Internal Value and a respectable degree of Travel Freedom. Argentinian nationals, for example, have settlement access to 10 foreign territories, and can travel visa-free or by visa-on-arrival to 162 destinations.

The other nationalities of the Americas are of lower quality due to a combination of their more restricted Settlement Freedom and Travel Freedom and generally lower degrees of Internal Value. Hence, the nationality of Bolivia scores lower than that of Argentina on all sub-elements, losing a significant amount of value on Travel Freedom with only 77 visa-free and visa-on-arrival travel destinations.

See also the expert contribution by Diego Acosta Arcarazo on pages 183–190.

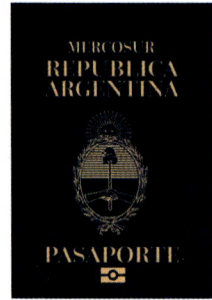

20 Middle East and North Africa

Regional Ranking	Nationality	2018 Value
1	United Arab Emirates	50.3
2	Israel	46.7
3	Kuwait	39.0
4	Qatar	37.1
4	Oman	37.1
5	Saudi Arabia	36.2
6	Bahrain	36.1
7	Israeli Laissez-passer	31.0
8	Tunisia	29.9
9	Morocco	28.1
10	Algeria	27.4
11	Jordan	26.8
12	Iran (Islamic Republic of)	26.2
13	Egypt	25.7
14	Lebanon	25.1
15	Palestinian Territory	23.1
16	Libya	21.7
17	Iraq	19.4
18	Sudan (Republic of the)	18.9
19	Yemen	17.2
20	Syrian Arab Republic	16.8

Mean: 31.0% • Median: 27.4%

In the Middle East and North Africa (MENA) region, the quality of nationalities varies from high-performing passports like those of Israel and the United Arab Emirates on the one hand to practically useless passports like those of Syria and Yemen on the other. With an overall mean value of 29.5% in the Low Quality tier — the MENA region scores only slightly higher than sub-Saharan Africa.

The member states of the Gulf Cooperation Council (GCC) and Israel are the best-scoring nationalities in the region. The GCC entails a free movement for nationals of its members, which means that these nationalities benefit from six or seven Settlement destinations each. Travel Freedom is, on average, lower. Nationals of Saudi Arabia, for example, have visa-free or visa-on-arrival access to 72 travel destinations, while those of Kuwait have such access to 86 destinations.

The nationality of Qatar has lost considerable value in the past few years as a result of the country's diplomatic conflict with Saudi Arabia. As a result, Qatari nationals no longer have Settlement access in Saudi Arabia, Bahrain, and the United Arab Emirates, while also suffering from economic sanctions and a deterioration in Qatar's Peace and Stability value. This decline can also be seen in the comparative round chart of the Qatari nationality in the 'Fallers in 2014–2018' section of this book.

In contrast, the Emirati nationality gained much in value due to its increased Travel Freedom, as discussed in the 'Risers in 2014–2018' section of this book. This nationality is now the region's only High Quality-tier nationality. While the nationality of Israel also comes with a high degree of Travel Freedom and a high level of Human Development, its Peace and Stability suffers from regional tensions, and its Settlement Freedom is limited to Svalbard and Georgia. As a result, the Israeli nationality remains in the Medium Quality tier of the QNI.

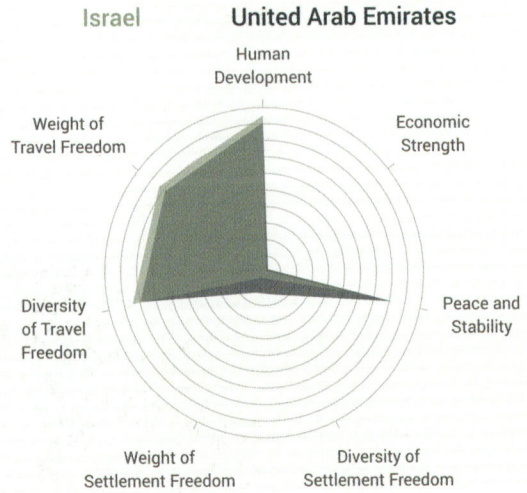

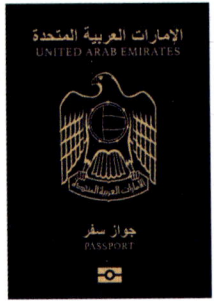

21 Sub-Saharan Africa

Regional Ranking	Nationality	2018 Value
1	Seychelles	46.2
2	Mauritius	45.2
3	South Africa	35.0
4	Cape Verde	34.2
5	Ghana	33.9
6	Botswana	33.0
7	Gambia	32.2
8	Benin	31.8
9	Senegal	31.3
9	Sierra Leone	31.3
10	Togo	30.3
11	Namibia	30.0
11	Côte d'Ivoire	30.0
12	Guinea	29.9
13	Burkina Faso	29.8
14	Guinea-Bissau	28.8
15	Liberia	28.6
16	Nigeria	28.1
17	Mali	27.8
18	Eswatini[1]	27.8
19	Zambia	27.6
20	Niger	27.4
21	Tanzania (United Republic of)	27.0
22	Kenya	26.9
23	Gabon	26.8
24	Lesotho	26.6
25	Malawi	26.4
26	São Tomé and Príncipe	25.8
27	Uganda	25.1
28	Zimbabwe	24.9
29	Equatorial Guinea	24.8
30	Madagascar	24.5
31	Angola	24.2
31	Comoros	24.2
32	Mauritania	24.1
33	Rwanda	23.3
33	Mozambique	23.3
33	Congo (Republic of the)	23.3
34	Cameroon	22.4
35	Djibouti	21.7

1 Formerly Swaziland

Regional Ranking	Nationality	2018 Value
36	Chad	20.7
37	Burundi	20.0
38	Ethiopia	19.9
39	Eritrea	18.8
40	Congo (Democratic Republic of the)	18.0
41	Central African Republic	17.6

Mean: 27.4% • Median: 27.0%

The nationalities of sub-Saharan Africa are generally of low value, with most of them being in the Low Quality tier. The two nationalities clearly standing out are those of Mauritius and the Seychelles. Both countries have a high level of Human Development and Peace and Stability. Moreover, both nationalities come with a respectable degree of Travel Freedom. Citizens of the Seychelles can travel visa-free or by visa-on-arrival to 142 destinations, those of Mauritius to 136 such destinations. As a result, these nationalities are the only two that are firmly established in the Medium Quality tier. The South African nationality has a relatively decent value, also mainly because of Travel Freedom, with access to 100 travel destinations.

The other nationalities of sub-Saharan Africa score significantly lower due to lower scores on most sub-elements. The member states of ECOWAS, an integrated region where the population enjoys free movement, are keeping up with the South African nationality because of their increased Settlement Freedom within the ECOWAS bloc. Accordingly, while Ghana, for example, has only 61 visa-free and visa-on-arrival travel destinations, far behind South Africa's 100 destinations, it compensates by granting its nationals settlement access to 14 foreign territories, while the South African nationality offers only one (Georgia).

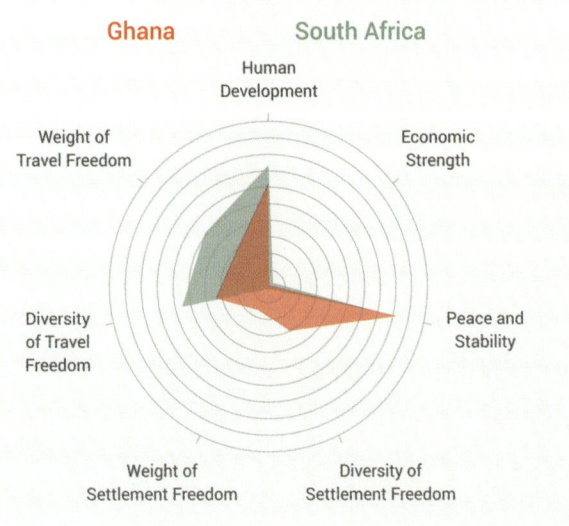
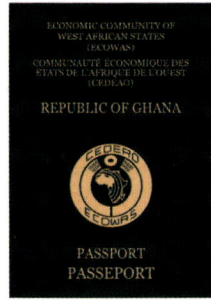

Nationalities of countries such as Comoros and Rwanda entail liabilities in many respects. The Internal Value of these nationalities is weak across all three sub-elements, which is not compensated for by any substantial External Value. Nationals of the Comoros and Rwanda can travel visa-free or by visa-on-arrival to only 50 and 51 travel destinations respectively. In addition, the Comorian nationality gives Settlement access only to Iraq, and the Rwandan nationality entails no Settlement Freedom at all. The result is a poor overall score in the lower regions of the Low Quality tier.

See also the expert contribution by Andreas Krensel on pages 191–198.

  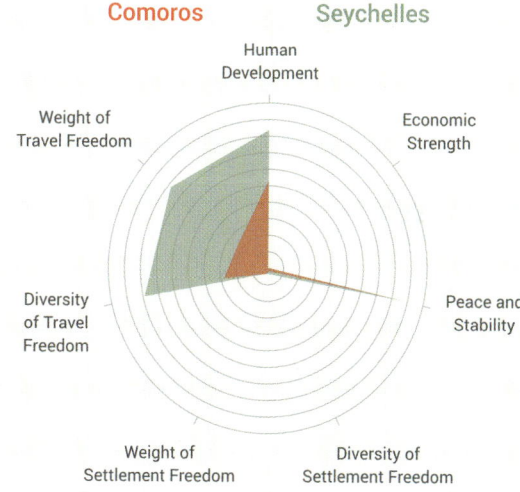

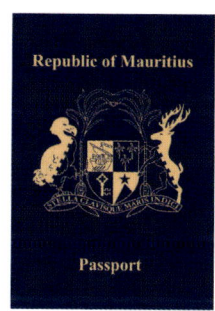 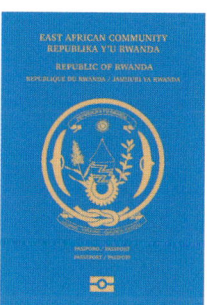 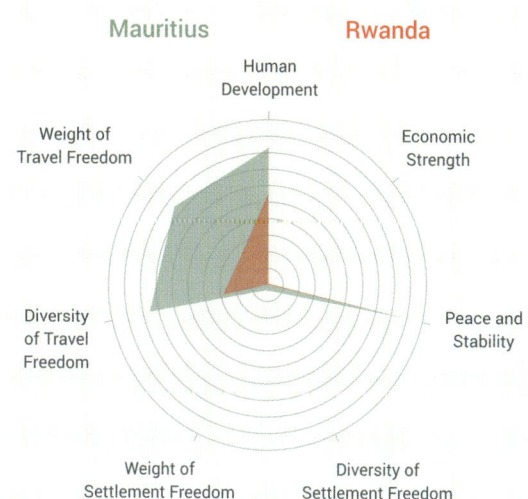

22 Asia and the Pacific

Regional Ranking	Nationality	2018 Value
1	Japan	58.4
2	Australia	55.2
3	Singapore	55.1
4	New Zealand	54.8
5	Korea (Republic of)	54.2
6	Malaysia	51.0
7	Brunei Darussalam	49.2
8	Hong Kong, China (SAR)	48.9
9	Chinese Taipei (Taiwan)	46.1
10	China	44.3
11	Macao	43.8
12	Kazakhstan	35.7
13	Timor-Leste	33.1
14	Maldives	33.0
15	Thailand	32.4
16	India	32.2
17	Indonesia	31.8
18	Kyrgyzstan	30.6
19	Mongolia	29.3
19	Uzbekistan	29.3
20	Papua New Guinea	28.7
21	Tajikistan	27.9
21	Philippines	27.9
22	Bhutan	27.5
23	Viet Nam	26.8
24	Turkmenistan	26.7
25	Sri Lanka	26.2
26	Lao People's Democratic Republic	25.3
27	Cambodia	24.6
28	Bangladesh	23.6
29	Myanmar	23.1
30	Nepal	23.0
31	Pakistan	19.0
32	Afghanistan	15.4

Mean: 35.1% • Median: 31.2%

The nationalities of Asia and the Pacific on average have a Medium Quality value, with a mean value of 35.1%. However, the wide variety in quality is clearly visible by comparing, for example, high-scoring nationalities such as those of Australia and the Republic of Korea and nationalities of extremely poor quality such as those of Bangladesh and Afghanistan.

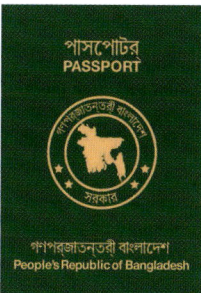
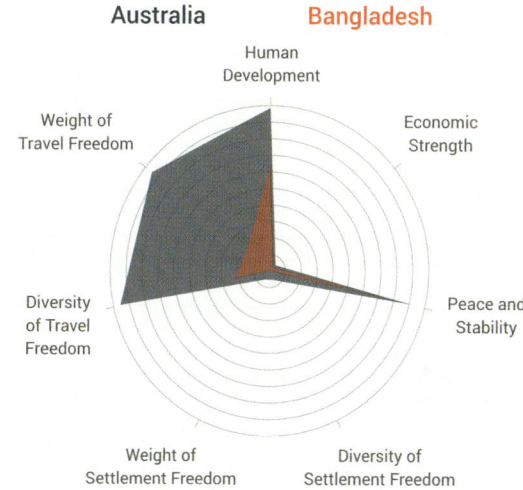

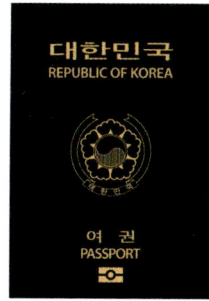

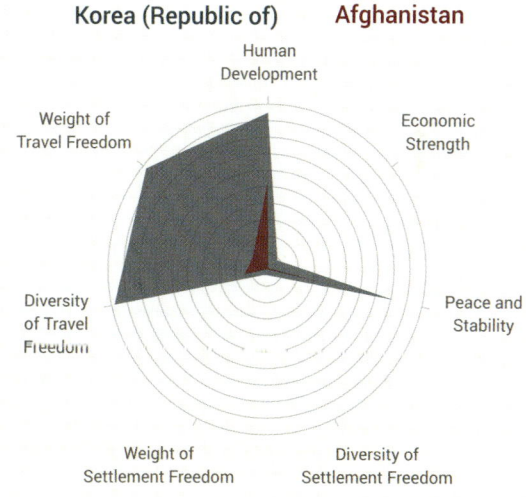

Most nationalities of the East Asian region combine a high degree of Internal Value with considerable Travel Freedom. Nationals of Malaysia, for example, have visa-free and visa-on-arrival access to 168 travel destinations, and those of Hong Kong to 157 such destinations. By contrast, someone from Tajikistan or Laos can travel to only 56 and 49 destinations visa-free or by visa-on-arrival. These lower degrees of Travel Freedom are combined with generally lower levels of Human Development, Economic Strength, and Peace and Stability for most nationalities of Central, South, and Southeast Asia. The nationality of Afghanistan is one of the worst nationalities reported, scoring poorly on all sub-elements even in comparison with its neighboring countries. Notable nationalities in this ranking are, of course, those of China and India, which occupy the 10th and 16th places respectively. These nationalities naturally score high on Economic Strength and perform respectably on Human Development. Both of them do lose some value, however, on Peace and Stability, and even more so on Travel Freedom and Settlement Freedom.

See also the expert contributions by Gerard Prinsen on pages 171–182 and Suryapratim Roy on pages 265–268.

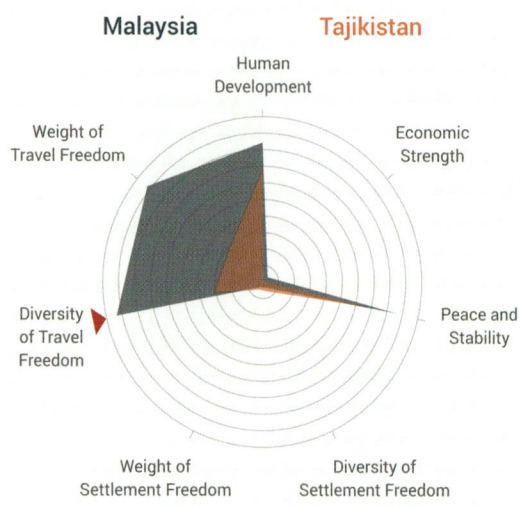

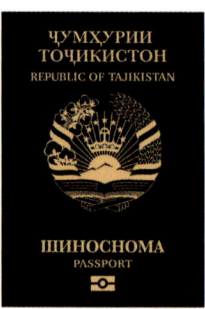
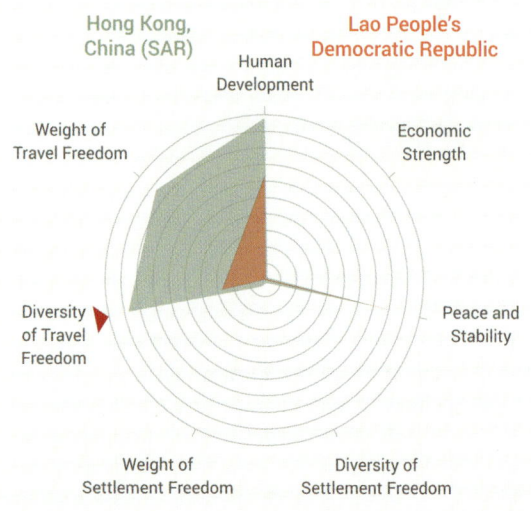

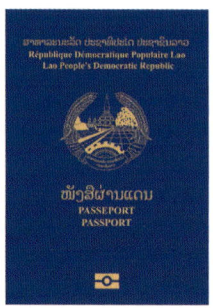

23 European Union

Rank	Nationality	2018 Value
1	France	83.5
2	Netherlands	82.8
2	Germany	82.8
3	Denmark	81.7
4	Sweden	81.5
5	Finland	81.2
6	Italy	80.7
7	United Kingdom	80.3
8	Ireland	80.2
9	Spain	80.0
10	Belgium	79.8
11	Austria	79.7
12	Czech Republic	79.0
12	Portugal	79.0
12	Luxembourg	79.0
13	Slovenia	78.6
14	Malta	77.6
15	Hungary	77.5
15	Slovakia	77.5
16	Greece	77.3
17	Estonia	77.1
18	Poland	77.0
18	Latvia	77.0
18	Lithuania	77.0
19	Cyprus	75.3
20	Romania	75.2
21	Bulgaria	75.0
22	Croatia	73.8
	EU Citizenship	63.6
23	British overseas territories (Gibraltar)	56.0
24	Jersey	53.3
25	Guernsey	53.2
25	Isle of Man	53.2
26	Latvia ('Non-Citizen')	30.8

Mean: 74.0% • Median: 77.6%

The EU, founded in 1957, is a political and economic union currently comprising 28 Member States. It aims at creating an "ever closer union"[21] between the peoples of Europe and has, to that end, achieved extensive and deep economic integration. The EU comprises an internal market in which all obstacles to the free movement of goods, services, persons, and capital are prohibited. Nationals of EU Member States are also EU citizens, which allows them to travel and settle freely in other Member States.

Due to their unprecedented degree of Settlement Freedom, the nationalities of EU Member States have an unmatched value. With the exception of Croatia, which for the duration of the transitional agreements is gradually integrating into the EU internal market, all Member States have nationalities of Very High Quality.

The British statuses included in this sub-ranking are the British overseas territories (Gibraltar) citizenship and the UK citizenships that are acquired by virtue of a connection to the Isle of Man and the Bailiwicks of Jersey and Guernsey. Gibraltarians are EU citizens with full work and settlement rights in all EU Member States. Manxmen and nationals of Jersey and Guernsey are full EU citizens, but UK citizens who acquired that status by virtue of an association with these territories do not enjoy EU free-movement rights on the continent and thus cannot settle in any EU Member State but the UK itself. The status of 'non-citizen' of Latvia has the lowest value in the EU and is not an EU citizenship, strictly speaking, since Latvia never extended EU citizenship to this status.

See also the expert contribution by Dimitry Kochenov on pages 216–221.

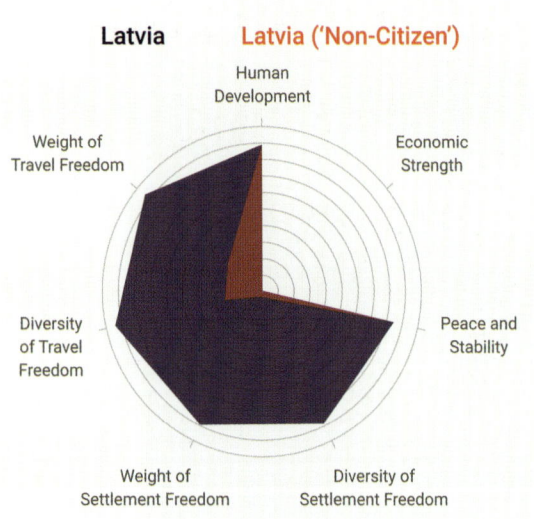
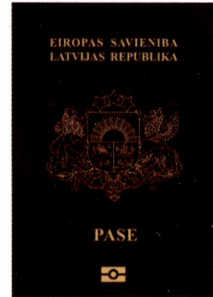
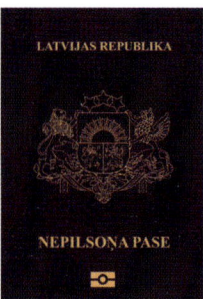
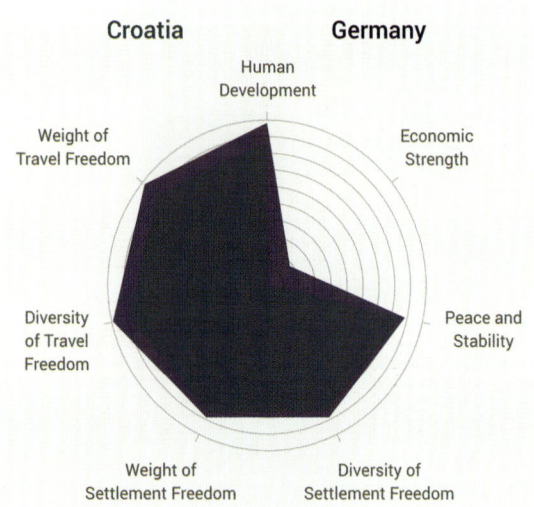
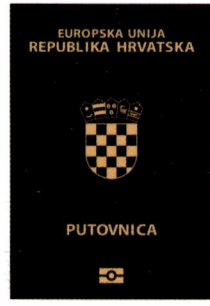

23 European Union • 107

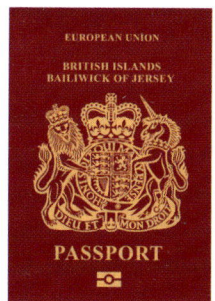

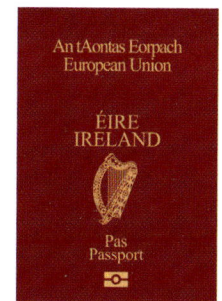

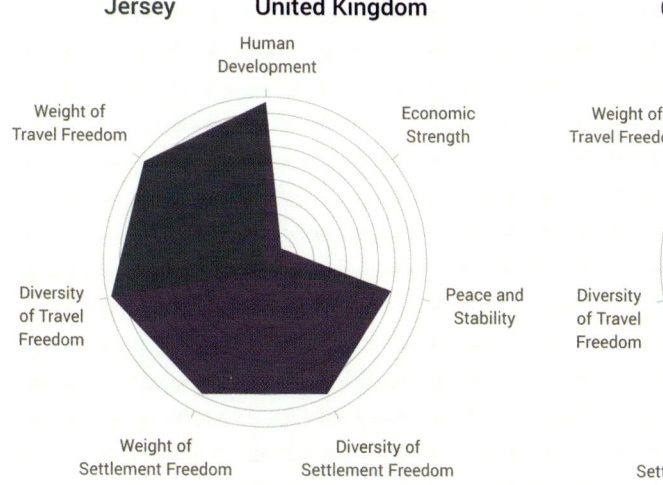
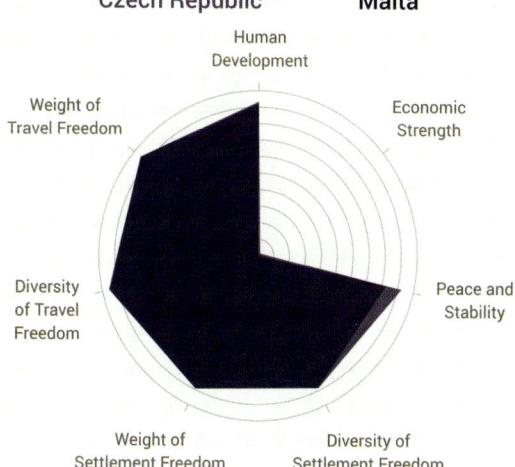
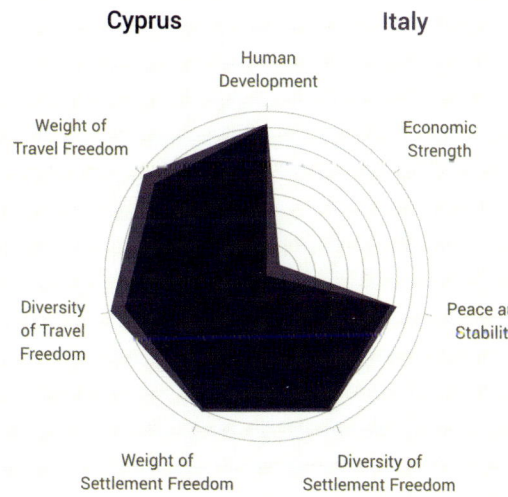
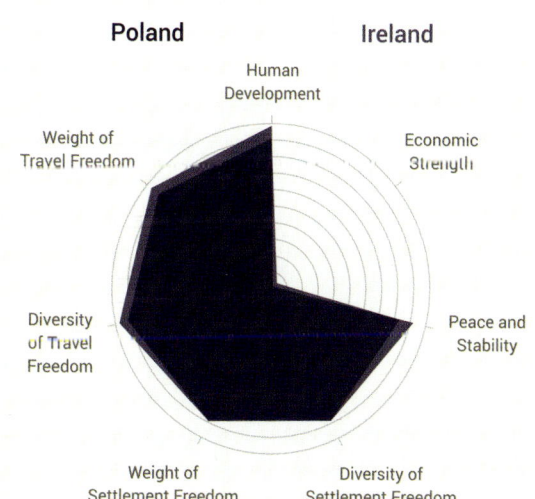

24 Mercado Común del Sur

Rank	Nationality	2018 Value
1	Argentina	54.5
2	Brazil	54.3
3	Uruguay	50.5
4	Paraguay	46.8
5	Venezuela (Bolivarian Republic of)	44.3

Mean: 50.1% • Median: 50.5%

Mercado Común del Sur (MERCOSUR), officially the Southern Common Market, is a regional trade organization that currently consists of five member states: Argentina, Brazil, Paraguay, Uruguay, and Venezuela. Venezuela's membership has been suspended since December 2016 for violations of the rule of law and human rights. MERCOSUR was created in 1991 and aspires to free the movement of goods, services and persons among its members, with the future aim of full economic integration.

The nationalities of MERCOSUR member states are in the High and Medium Quality tiers, benefitting from a substantial degree of economic integration including full settlement access within the bloc.

See also the expert contribution by Diego Acosta Arcarazo on pages 183–190.

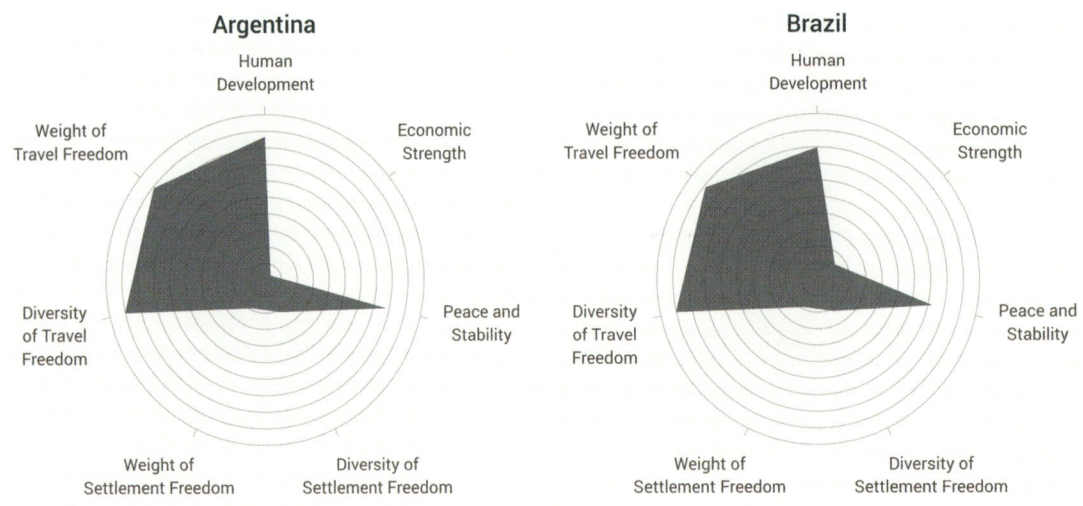

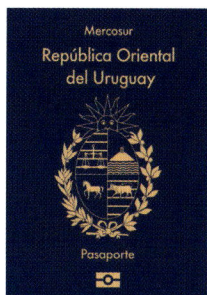
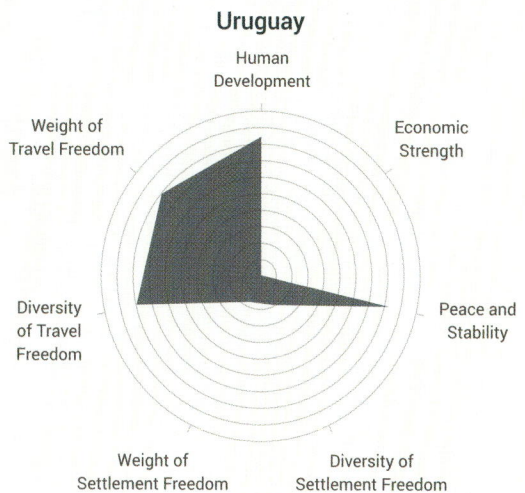

Uruguay

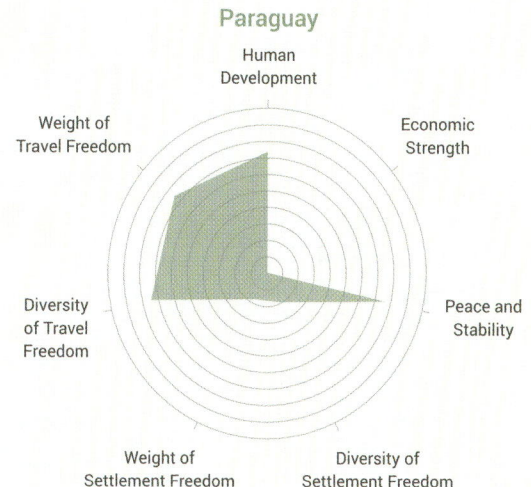

Paraguay

Venezuela

25 Organisation of Eastern Caribbean States

Rank	Nationality	2018 Value
1	Antigua and Barbuda	47.7
2	Saint Kitts and Nevis	47.5
3	Saint Vincent and the Grenadines	46.3
4	Grenada	45.7
5	Saint Lucia	45.5
6	Commonwealth of Dominica	43.9

Mean: 46.1% • Median: 46.0%

The Organisation of Eastern Caribbean States (OECS) was founded on 18 June 1981 with the Treaty of Basseterre. With the ratification of the Economic Union Treaty on 21 January 2011, the OECS is committed to deeper economic integration including free movement of goods, services, persons and capital. Citizens of member states of the OECS enjoy free settlement in the other member states. As a result, the nationalities of the OECS members have relatively high value compared with other nationalities in the region. The mean value (46.1%), for instance, is higher than the mean value of nationalities of the Americas (43.3%). OECS nationalities are still behind the nationalities of Canada, the US, and the member states of MERCOSUR, all of which have considerably more Economic Strength and, mostly, more Travel Freedom. However, compared to other nationalities of the Latin American region, the OECS nationalities are significantly more valuable.

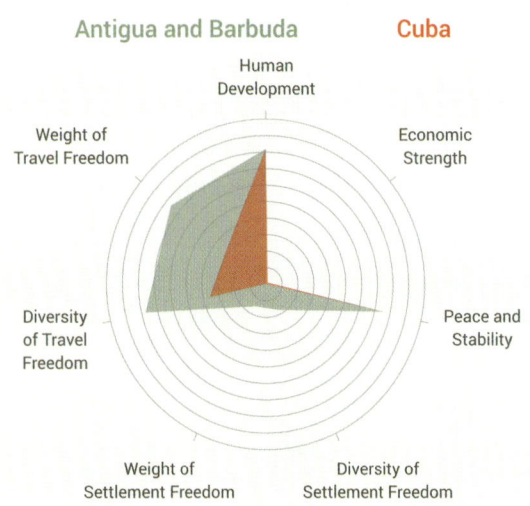
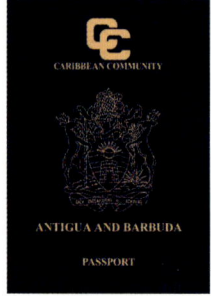
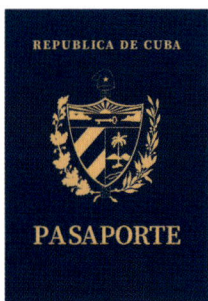

25 Organisation of Eastern Caribbean States • 111

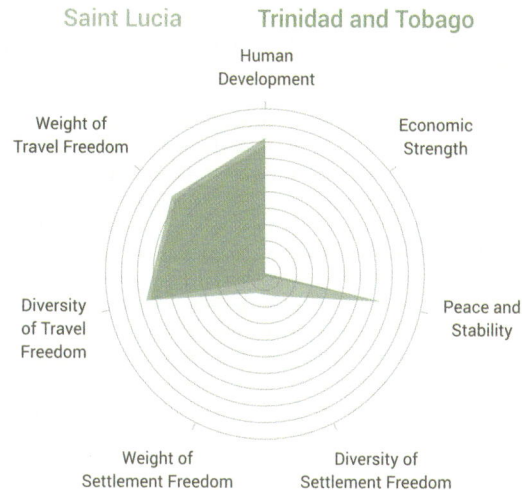
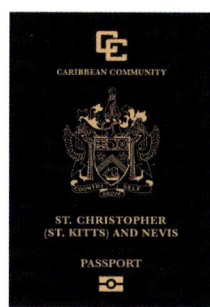
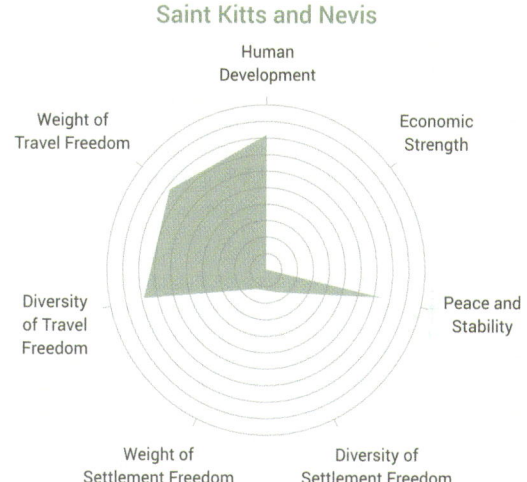

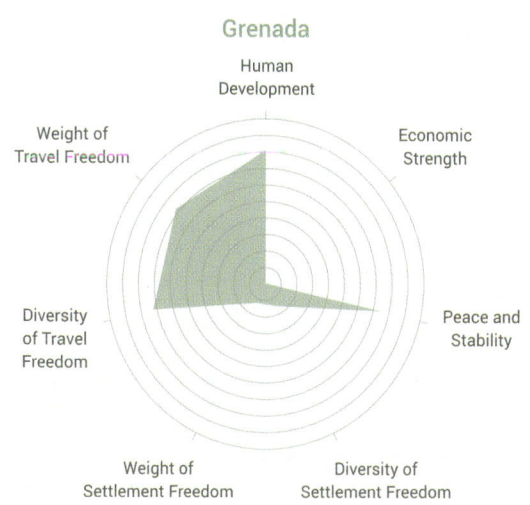

26 Gulf Cooperation Council

Rank	Nationality	2018 Value
1	United Arab Emirates	50.3
2	Kuwait	39.0
3	Qatar	37.1
3	Oman	37.1
4	Saudi Arabia	36.2
5	Bahrain	36.1

Mean: 39.3% • Median: 37.1%

The Gulf Cooperation Council (GCC) is a political and economic union of six Arab countries surrounding the Persian Gulf. The GCC was founded in 1981 and aims to foster cooperation on a number of economic and policy issues, including harmonizing regulation, technological and industrial progress, strengthening ties between nations and developing a common currency.

Nationals of GCC countries enjoy free movement rights and can therefore freely settle in the other member states. However, unlike most other countries, the GCC countries have no clear overlap between inhabitants and nationals: the overwhelming majority of their workforces are non-nationals. Nationals therefore make very little use of their settlement freedom to work in the other GCC countries. Only the nationality of the United Arab Emirates is in the High Quality tier of the QNI, with the others all being in the Medium Quality tier. Relatively low scores on Peace and Stability and Travel Freedom compromise the overall scores of most GCC nationalities as compared to the nationalities of, for instance, European and North American countries.

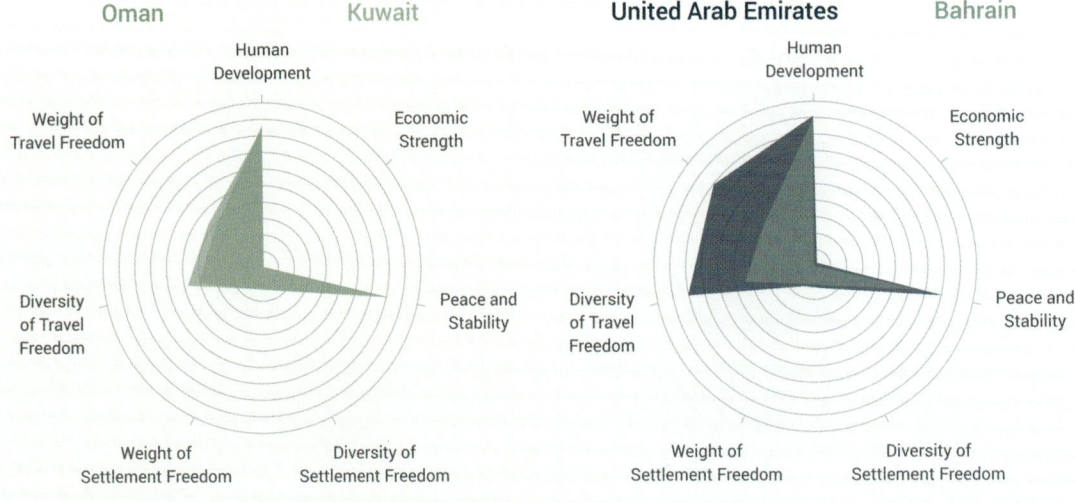

27 Economic Community of West African States

Rank	Nationality	2018 Value
1	Cape Verde	34.2
2	Ghana	33.9
3	Gambia	32.2
4	Benin	31.8
5	Senegal	31.3
5	Sierra Leone	31.3
6	Togo	30.3
7	Côte d'Ivoire	30.0
8	Guinea	29.9
9	Burkina Faso	29.8
10	Guinea-Bissau	28.8
11	Liberia	28.6
12	Nigeria	28.1
13	Mali	27.8
14	Niger	27.4

Mean: 30.4% · Median: 30.0%

The Economic Community of West African States (ECOWAS) is a regional organization in West Africa primarily aimed at creating collective self-sufficiency for its members. It was founded in 1975 and consists of 15 member states. ECOWAS is focused on free trade and the nationals of its members are largely entitled to full access to the other member countries.

All nationalities of the ECOWAS countries are in the Low Quality tier of the QNI. Due to the free movement of persons and workers among them, these nationalities do benefit from a higher level of Settlement Freedom than most other countries in Africa, which also points to their relatively high positions on the sub-Saharan nationalities ranking.

See also the expert contribution by Andreas Krensel on pages 191–198.

28 North Atlantic Treaty Organization

Rank	Nationality	2018 Value
1	France	83.5
2	Netherlands	82.8
2	Germany	82.8
3	Denmark	81.7
4	Norway	81.5
5	Iceland	81.4
6	Italy	80.7
7	United Kingdom	80.3
8	Spain	80.0
9	Belgium	79.8
10	Czech Republic	79.0
10	Portugal	79.0
10	Luxembourg	79.0
11	Slovenia	78.6
12	Hungary	77.5
12	Slovakia	77.5
13	Greece	77.3
14	Estonia	77.1
15	Poland	77.0
15	Lithuania	77.0
15	Latvia	77.0
16	Romania	75.2
17	Bulgaria	75.0
18	Croatia	73.8
19	United States	70.0
20	British overseas territories (Gibraltar)	56.0
21	Canada	55.3
22	Albania	38.7
23	Turkey	37.7
24	Latvia ('Non-Citizen')	30.8
25	British Nationals (Overseas)	25.2
26	British overseas territories	25.1
27	British Overseas citizens	22.8
28	British protected persons	22.6
28	British subjects	22.6

Mean: 65.8% • Median: 77.1%

28 North Atlantic Treaty Organization

The North Atlantic Treaty Organization (NATO) is a post-Second World War intergovernmental military organization based on collective defense. It was set up in 1949 and played a major role in the Cold War rivalry between the US and the Soviet Union. NATO consists of 28 member states, mainly European and North American countries. Most of its members have nationalities in the Very High Quality tier, due to EU Member States' unrivaled Settlement Freedom. The nationality of the US is just behind those of the EU Member States and belongs to the upper part of the High Quality tier; Canada, Albania, and Turkey follow with scores of 55.3%, 38.7%, and 37.7% respectively. The lower scores of Albania and Turkey are the result of their lower scores on most sub-elements, including Peace and Stability and Settlement Freedom.

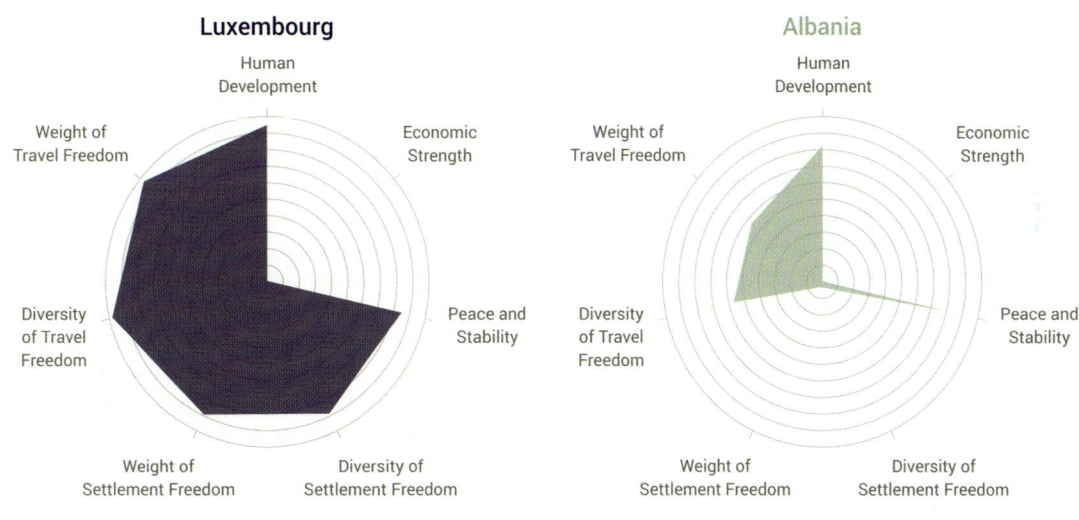

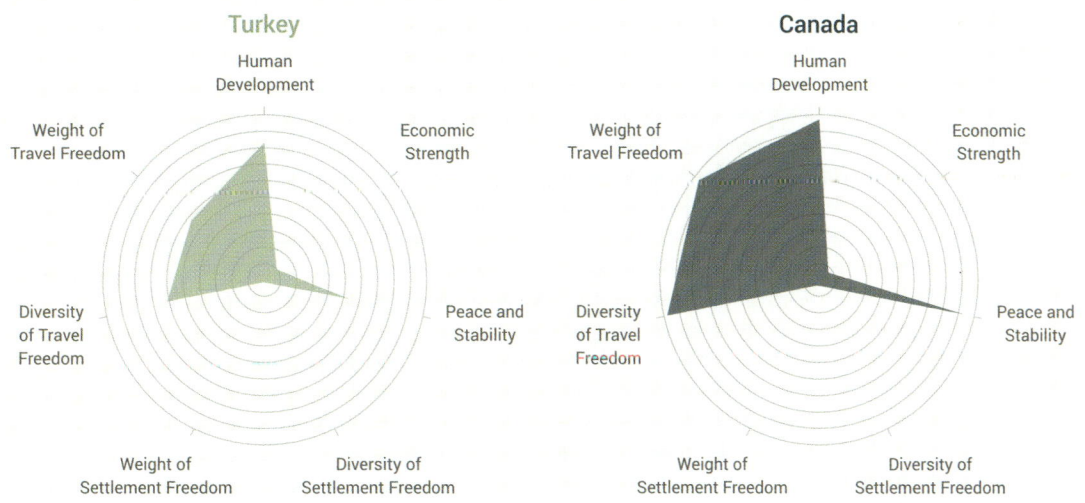

29 Eurasian Economic Union

Rank	Nationality	2018 Value
1	Russian Federation	42.0
2	Kazakhstan	35.7
3	Belarus	34.8
4	Armenia	31.7
5	Kyrgyzstan	30.6

Mean: 35.0%   •   Median: 34.8%

The Eurasian Economic Union (EAEU) is a political and economic union of former Soviet states. The treaty establishing the EAEU was signed on 29 May 2014 and entered into force on 1 January 2015. The EAEU comprises a single market involving the free movement of goods, services, persons, and capital. Due to the free movement provisions of the EAEU Treaty, nationals of the member states have full settlement access to the territories of the other members. Compared to other former Soviet states that are not part of the EAEU, such as Azerbaijan and Turkmenistan, the nationalities of the EAEU members have more Settlement Freedom and a slightly higher overall value.

EAEU nationalities nonetheless remain in the Medium Quality (Russian Federation and Kazakhstan) and Low Quality tiers (Belarus, Armenia, and Kyrgyzstan). These nationalities lose value mainly on Weight of Travel Freedom — visa-free and visa-on-arrival travel destinations typically do not include those in North America and Western Europe — and Peace and Stability.

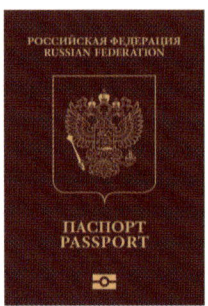

29 Eurasian Economic Union

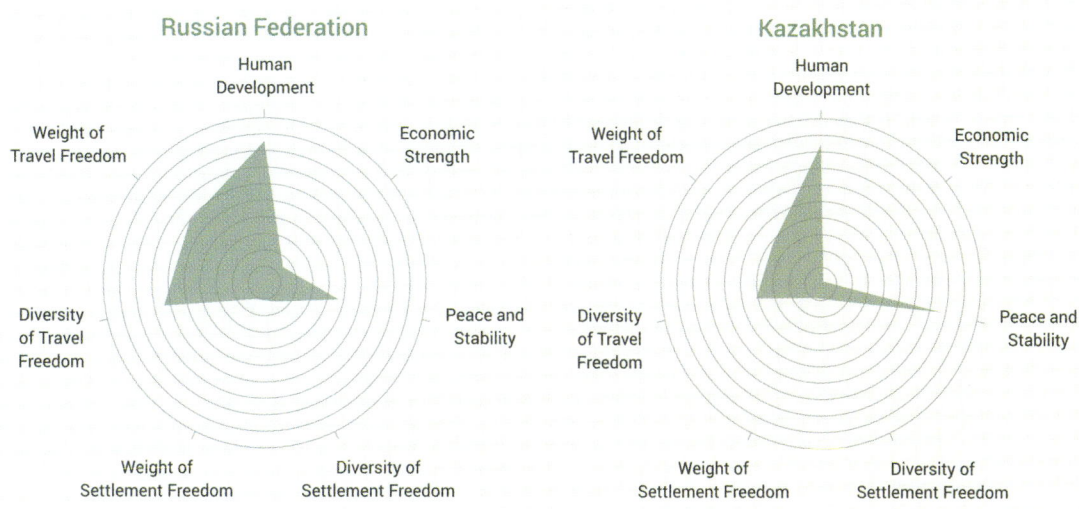

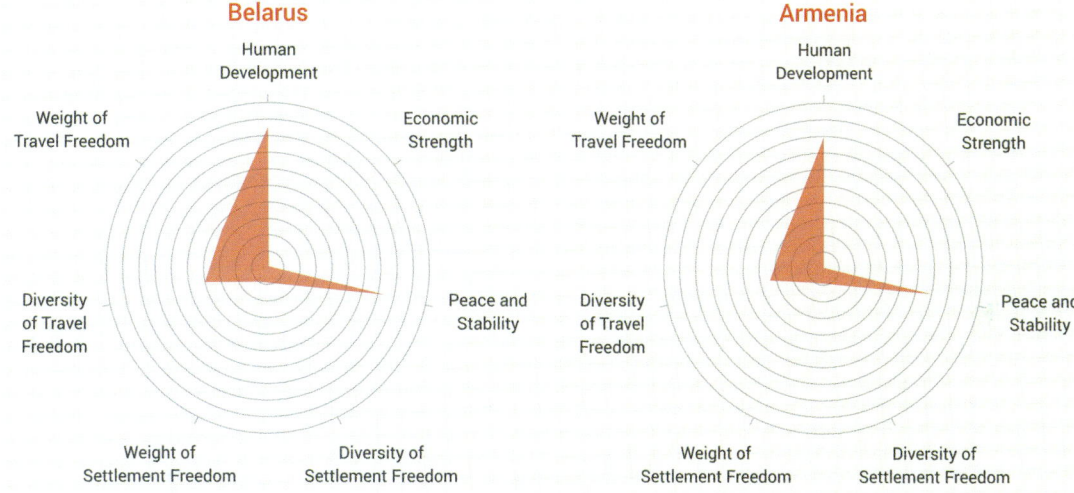

30 Association of Southeast Asian Nations

Rank	Nationality	2018 Value
1	Singapore	55.1
2	Malaysia	51.0
3	Brunei Darussalam	49.2
4	Thailand	32.4
5	Indonesia	31.8
6	Philippines	27.9
7	Viet Nam	26.8
8	Lao People's Democratic Republic	25.3
9	Cambodia	24.6
10	Myanmar	23.1

Mean: 34.7%   •   Median: 29.9%

The Association of Southeast Asian Nations (ASEAN) is a political and economic organization of 10 Southeast Asian countries. It was founded in 1967 and has since then focused on *inter alia* economic cooperation and maintaining regional peace and stability. In 2007 the member states signed the ASEAN Charter, in which they agreed to deepen economic integration to create an 'EU-style community'. While their nationals do not yet enjoy genuine settlement freedom in the other member states, it is the ambition of the ASEAN member states to create full freedom of movement for workers in the near future.

The ASEAN nationalities vary considerably in quality. The nationalities of Singapore and Malaysia are the only ones in the High Quality tier, while that of Brunei Darussalam is closely behind in the upper end of the Medium Quality tier. Unlike the other ASEAN nationalities, which are all in the Low Quality tier, the top three ASEAN nationalities benefit from having stronger economies, a higher level of human development, and greater peacefulness. Moreover, they also outperform the other member states in terms of their External Value, having visa-free or visa-on-arrival Travel Freedom to 150 destinations or more.

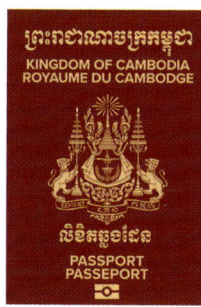
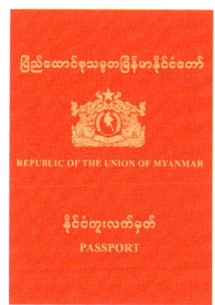

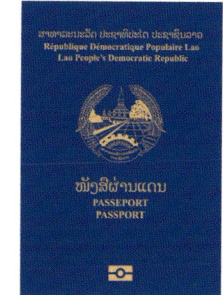
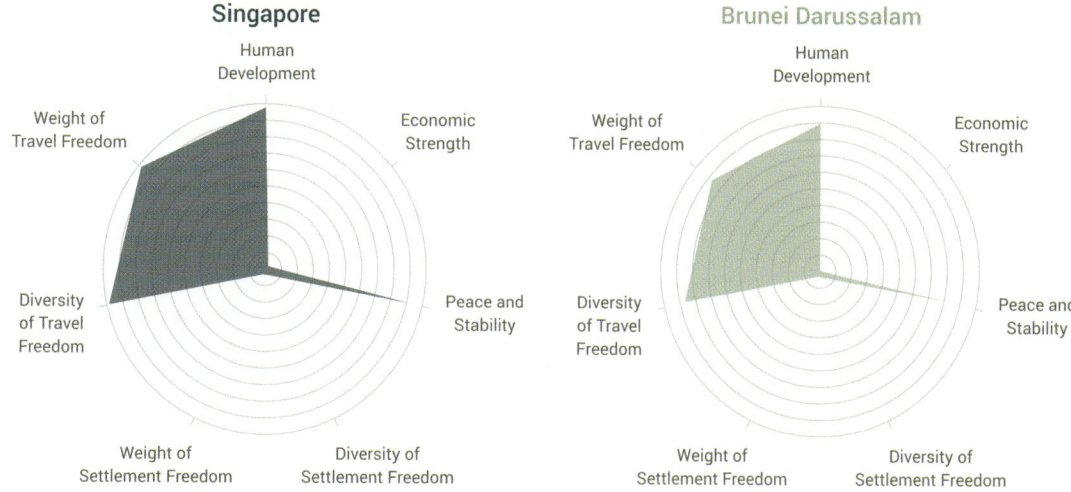
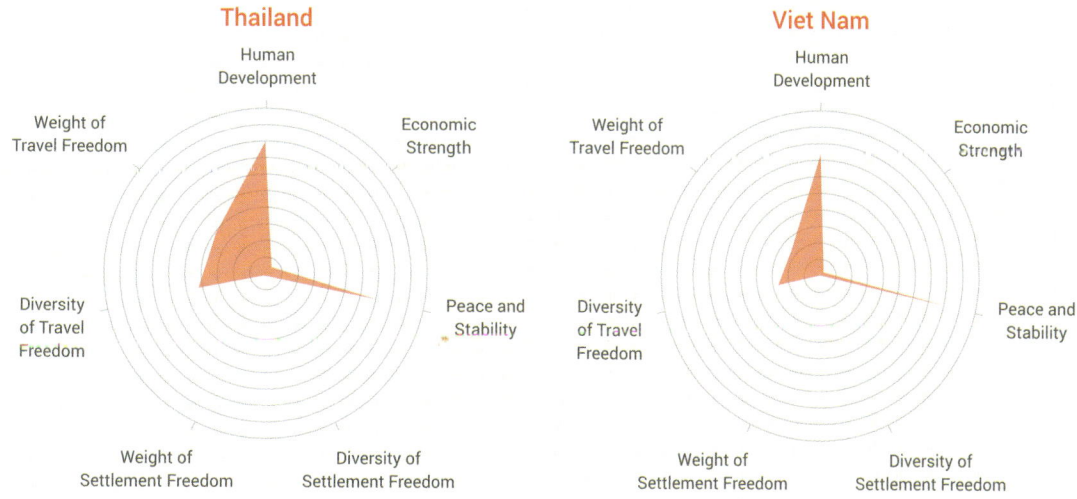

31 Commonwealth of Nations

Rank	Nationality	2018 Value
1	United Kingdom	80.3
2	Malta	77.6
3	Cyprus	75.3
4	British overseas territories (Gibraltar)	56.0
5	Canada	55.3
6	Australia	55.2
7	Singapore	55.1
8	New Zealand	54.8
9	Malaysia	51.0
10	Brunei Darussalam	49.2
11	Antigua and Barbuda	47.7
12	Saint Kitts and Nevis	47.5
13	Barbados	46.3
13	Saint Vincent and the Grenadines	46.3
14	Seychelles	46.2
15	Grenada	45.7
16	Bahamas	45.5
16	Saint Lucia	45.5
17	Mauritius	45.2
18	Dominica	43.9
19	Trinidad and Tobago	43.3
20	Samoa	39.7
21	Tonga	38.7
22	Tuvalu	38.6
23	Vanuatu	37.1
24	Kiribati	36.6
25	Solomon Islands	36.5
26	South Africa	35.0
27	Belize	34.1
28	Ghana	33.9
29	Guyana	33.6
30	Fiji	33.2
31	Botswana	33.0
32	Gambia	32.2
32	India	32.2
33	Nauru	32.0
33	Jamaica	32.0
34	Sierra Leone	31.3
35	Namibia	30.0
36	Papua New Guinea	28.7
37	Nigeria	28.1
38	Eswatini[1]	27.8
39	Zambia	27.6

1 Formerly Swaziland

Rank	Nationality	2018 Value
40	Tanzania (United Republic of)	27.0
41	Kenya	26.9
42	Lesotho	26.6
43	Malawi	26.4
44	Sri Lanka	26.2
45	British Nationals (Overseas)	25.2
46	British overseas territories	25.1
46	Uganda	25.1
47	Bangladesh	23.6
48	Rwanda	23.3
48	Mozambique	23.3
49	British Overseas citizens	22.8
50	British protected persons	22.6
50	British subjects	22.6
51	Cameroon	22.4
52	Pakistan	19.0

Mean: 37.8% • Median: 33.9%

The Commonwealth of Nations is an international organization of 53 member states, mostly former British colonies. Its modern reconstitution dates back to the London Declaration of 1949, according to which all member states would be "freely and equally associated". The Commonwealth aspires towards cooperation between member states for development, democracy and peace. It comprises some of the largest and some of the smallest countries of the world, and the countries of the Commonwealth are home to more than 2 billion citizens.

The nationalities of the Commonwealth of Nations vary widely in their quality. It is the only organization whose member states are associated with nationalities in all five quality tiers of the QNI: from the nationalities of the UK, Cyprus, and Malta in the Very High Quality tier, to the Pakistani nationality in the Very Low Quality tier.

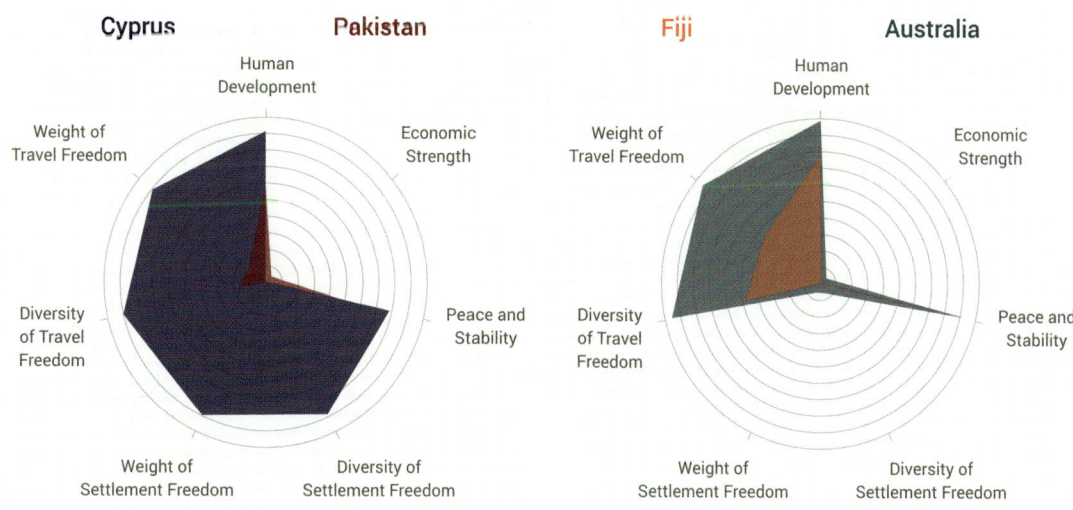

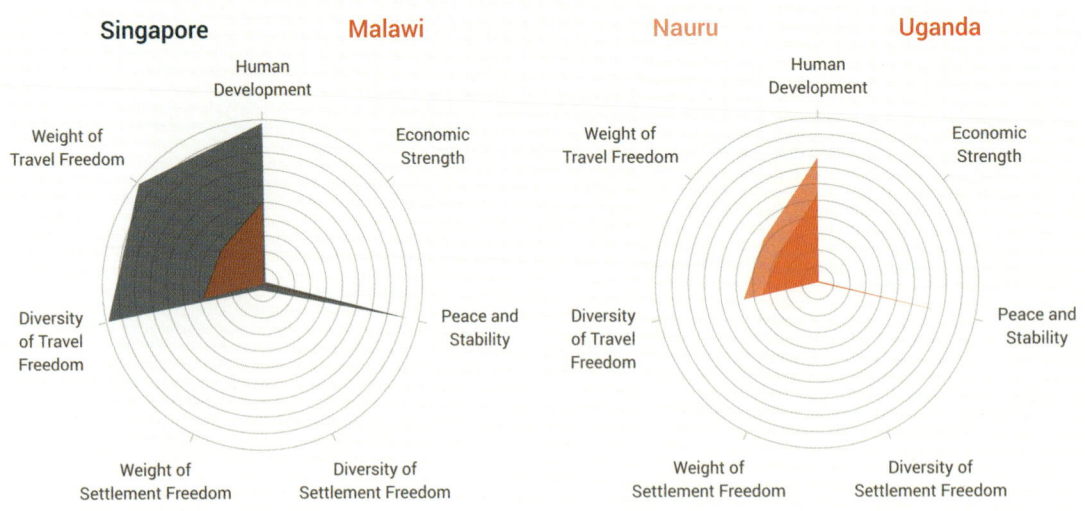

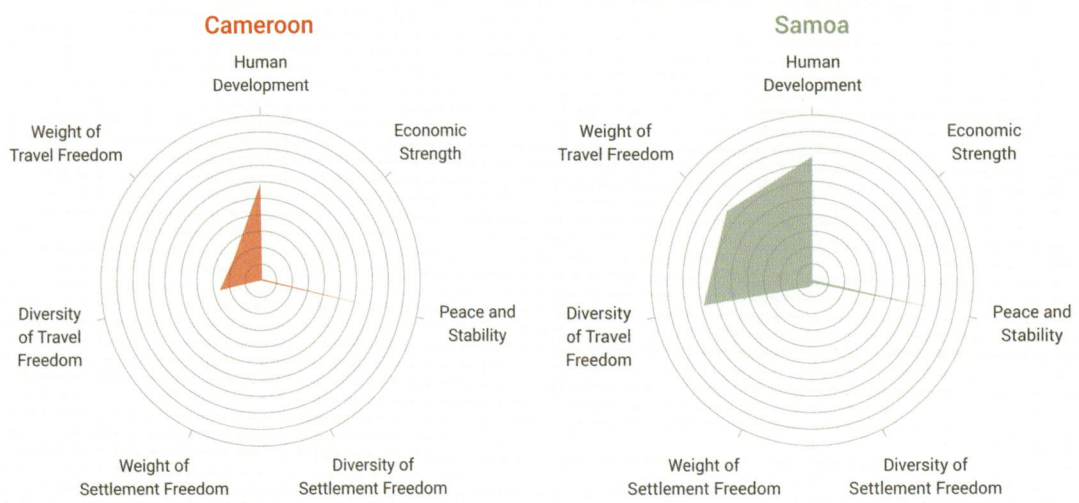

32 Largest Countries by Area

Largest Countries by Land Area	
Rank	**Country**
1	Russian Federation
2	Canada
3	China
4	United States
5	Brazil
6	Australia
7	India
8	Argentina
9	Kazakhstan
10	Algeria

Nationalities of the Largest Countries by Land Area		
Rank	**Nationality**	**2018 Value**
25	United States	70.0
28	Canada	55.3
29	Australia	55.2
32	Argentina	54.5
33	Brazil	54.3
56	China	44.3
62	Russian Federation	42.0
84	Kazakhstan	35.7
95	India	32.2
118	Algeria	27.4

Mean: 47.1% • Median: 49.3%

None of the 10 largest countries by area have nationalities in the Very High Quality tier or in the top 20 of the QNI General Ranking. The nationalities of the US, Canada, Australia, Argentina, and Brazil are in the High Quality tier, while the Chinese, Russian, and Kazakhstani nationalities are of Medium Quality. While they belong to the top 10 of largest countries, the nationalities of India and Algeria are both of Low Quality.

The nationality of the US is considerably more valuable than the other nationalities on this sub-ranking, mainly due to its superior Economic Strength, a high degree of Travel Freedom, and 11 free-settlement destinations. In contrast, nationalities like those of China, the Russian Federation, Kazakhstan, India, and Algeria score more poorly on both Settlement and Travel Freedom. The lower-ranking nationalities in this sub-ranking tier also have generally lower degrees of Human Development and/or Peace and Stability.

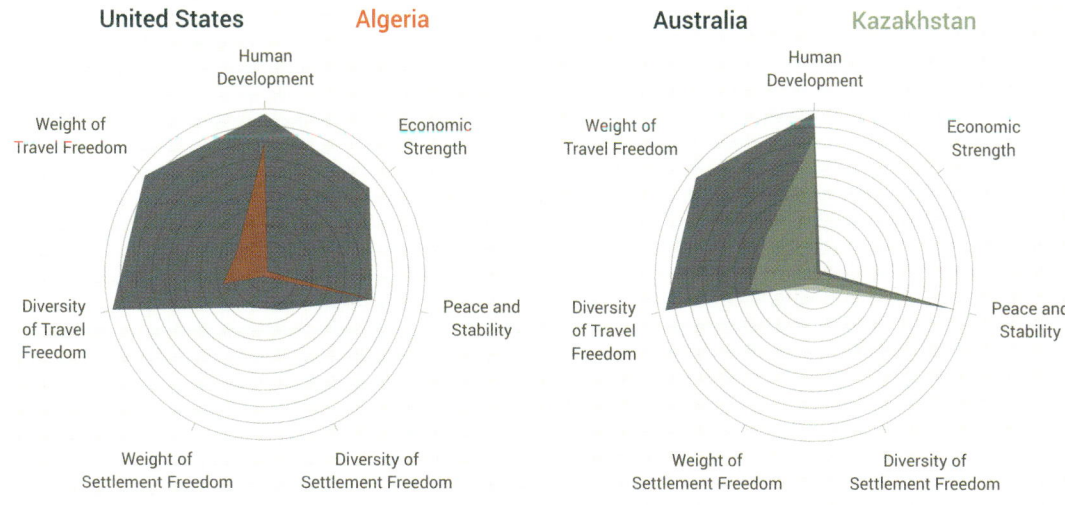

33 Microstates

Rank	Nationality	2018 Value
1	Liechtenstein	78.9
2	Malta	77.6
3	Monaco	52.5
4	Andorra	51.6
5	San Marino	51.4
6	Antigua and Barbuda	47.7
7	Saint Kitts and Nevis	47.5
8	Barbados	46.3
8	Saint Vincent and the Grenadines	46.3
9	Seychelles	46.2
10	Grenada	45.7
11	Saint Lucia	45.5
12	Dominica	43.9
13	Palau	42.7
14	Marshall Islands	41.8
15	Micronesia (Federated States of)	40.2
16	Tonga	38.7
17	Tuvalu	38.6
18	Kiribati	36.6
19	Maldives	33.0
20	Nauru	32.0
21	São Tomé and Príncipe	25.8

Mean: 45.9% · Median: 45.6%

Microstates are usually defined as states with either a very small land area or a very small population or both. The nationalities included in this system of ranking are associated with states that have fewer than 500,000 people *and* have a non-sea area of less than 1,000 square kilometers. These states generally play a marginal role in international relations and have extremely small economies. While their Economic Strength is therefore close to zero, some of these nationalities nonetheless have a remarkable quality. The nationalities of Liechtenstein and Malta benefit greatly from having EU membership, of course, which means that their citizens are given home treatment in all Member States of the EU.

Many other microstates also have respectable nationalities, however, with Andorra, Monaco, and San Marino all having High Quality nationalities, and 14 more sit in the Medium Quality tier. No fewer than 11 microstate nationalities have values that are higher than that of the largest economy in the world, China. At 44.3%, China's value is, in fact, also lower than the mean value of the microstates' nationalities. Many of the Caribbean microstates have monetized the relatively high value of their nationalities by offering citizenship-by-investment.

See also the expert contribution by Christian H. Kälin on pages 161–170.

33 Microstates • 125

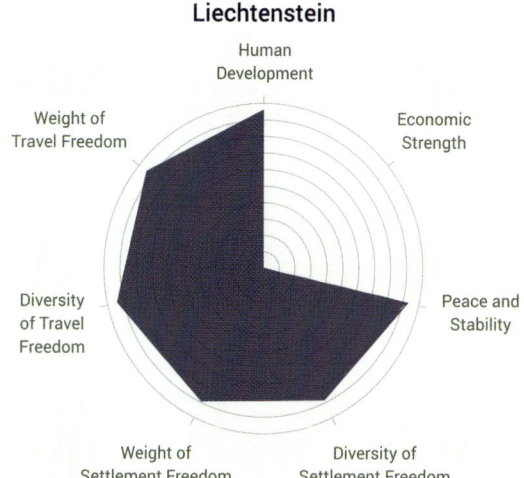

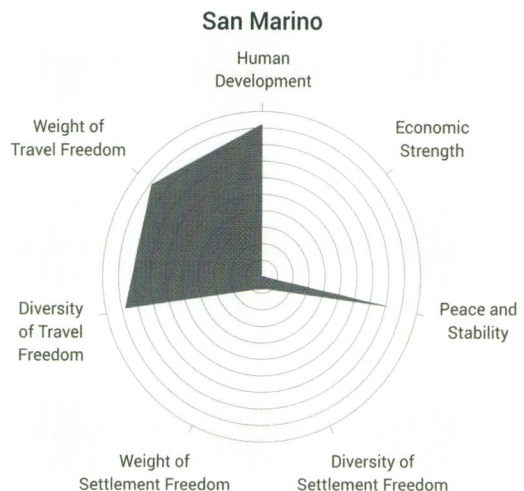

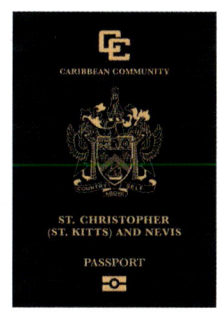
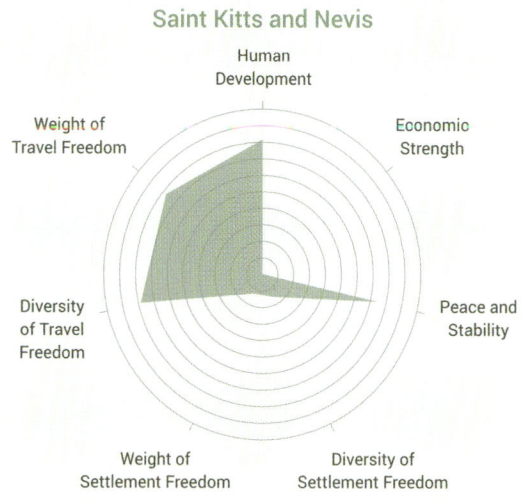

Marshall Islands

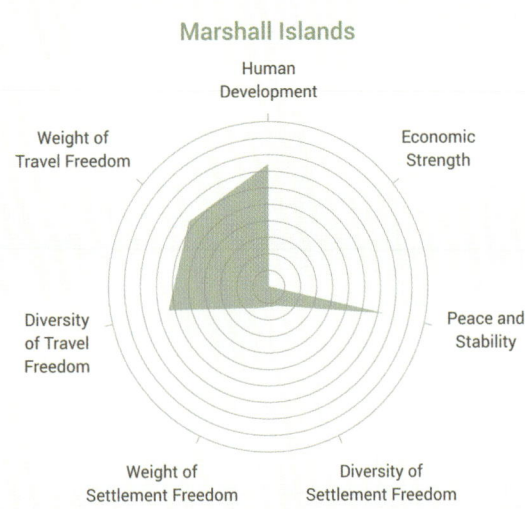

São Tomé and Principe

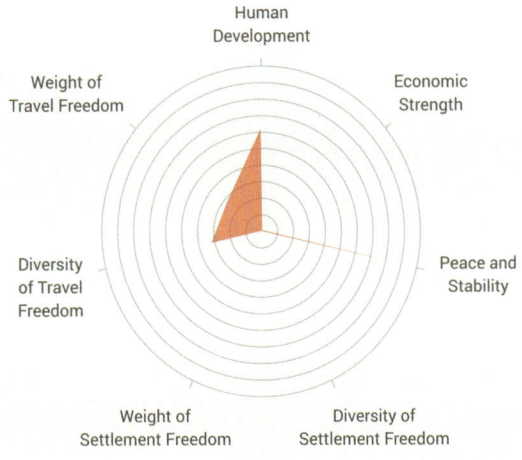

34 Best Countries According to Perception

'Best Countries' in 2018	
Rank	Country
1	Switzerland
2	Canada
3	Germany
4	United Kingdom
5	Japan
6	Sweden
7	Australia
8	United States
9	France
10	Netherlands

Nationalities of the 'Best Countries'		
Rank	Nationality	2018 Value
1	France	83.5
2	Netherlands	82.8
2	Germany	82.8
4	Sweden	81.5
8	United Kingdom	80.3
11	Switzerland	79.8
25	United States	70.0
26	Japan	58.4
28	Canada	55.3
29	Australia	55.2

Mean: 73.0% • Median: 80.1%

The world's 'Best Countries 2018' report is published by *U.S. News & World Report* in cooperation with Y&R's BAV Group and the Wharton School of Business at the University of Pennsylvania. This ranking is based on global perceptions of 21,117 individuals surveyed in 36 countries. Countries were scored on 65 attributes grouped into nine sub-rankings: Adventure, Citizenship, Cultural Influence, Entrepreneurship, Heritage, Movers, Open for Business, Power, and Quality of Life.

The QNI instead is based on an objective methodology that does not take perceptions into account. As we have noted in Part 1 of this edition, the quality of nationality does not always correspond to the quality of the country with which the nationality is associated. Moreover, perceptions of both countries and nationalities can diverge quite significantly from their actual, objective value. To elucidate this divergence between perception and value, the tables above show the top 10 of the 'Best Countries 2018' report and the respective nationalities' score and position on the 2018 QNI General Ranking.

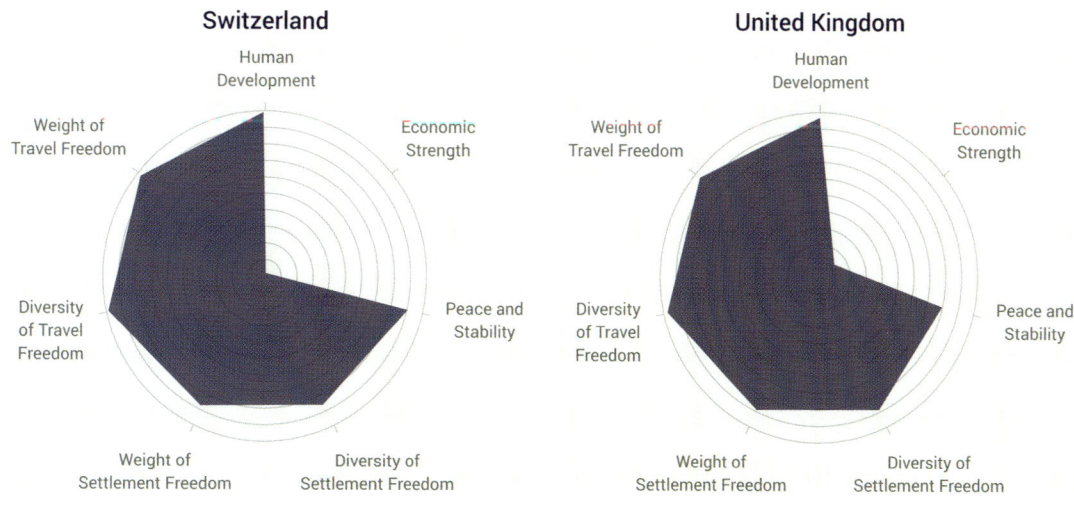

All the top 10 nationalities in the 'Best Countries 2018' report are in the Very High and High Quality tiers and belong to the top 30 of the best nationalities. Nonetheless, considerable difference in value exists among them, the French nationality scoring almost 30 percentage points higher than the Australian nationality. As we can also see, while Canada ranks as the runner-up best country in the 'Best Countries 2018' report, its nationality ranks only 28th in the QNI. Conversely, while France is only the 9th 'best country' according to perception, its nationality is the clear number one in the 2018 QNI General Ranking.

While there is some convergence between perception of countries' quality and the objective quality of their nationalities, it is clear that the QNI's results are considerably different than those of the 'Best Countries 2018' report.

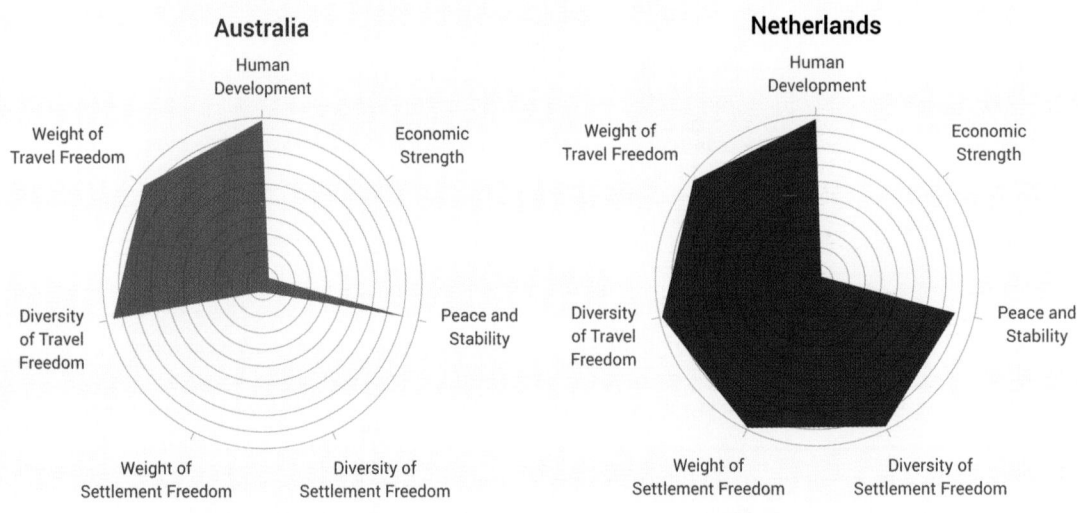

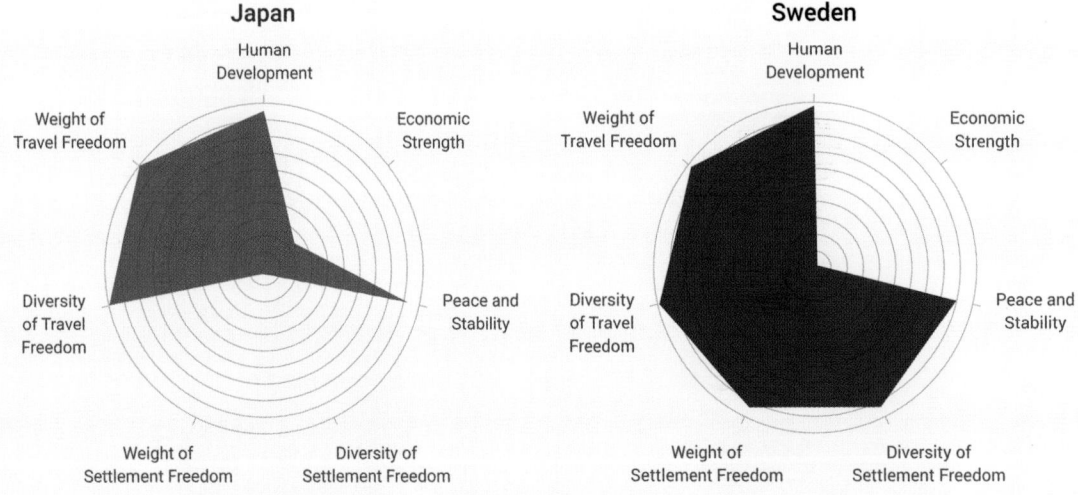

35 Most Powerful Countries According to Perception

'Most Powerful' Countries	
Rank	Country
1	United States
2	Russian Federation
3	China
4	Germany
5	United Kingdom
6	France
7	Japan
8	Israel
9	Saudi Arabia
10	United Arab Emirates

Nationalities of the 'Most Powerful' Countries		
Rank	Nationality	2018 Value
1	France	83.5
2	Germany	82.8
8	United Kingdom	80.3
25	United States	70.0
26	Japan	58.4
42	United Arab Emirates	50.3
48	Israel	46.7
56	China	44.3
62	Russian Federation	42.0
81	Saudi Arabia	36.2
100	Israeli Laissez-passer	31.0

Mean: 56.9% • Median: 50.3%

The 2018 Power Ranking is a sub-ranking of the 'Best Countries 2018' report published by *U.S. News & World Report*, Y&R's BAV Group, and the Wharton School of Business. This ranking is based on global perceptions of 21,117 individuals surveyed in 36 countries. Countries were scored on five attributes relating to a country's power: leadership, economic influence, political influence, strong international alliances, and a strong military.

In Part 1 of this edition we explain that the quality of a nationality does not necessarily correspond to the power of the country with which the nationality is associated. Primary examples are China and the Chinese nationality and Saudi Arabia and the Saudi Arabian nationality. The tables above

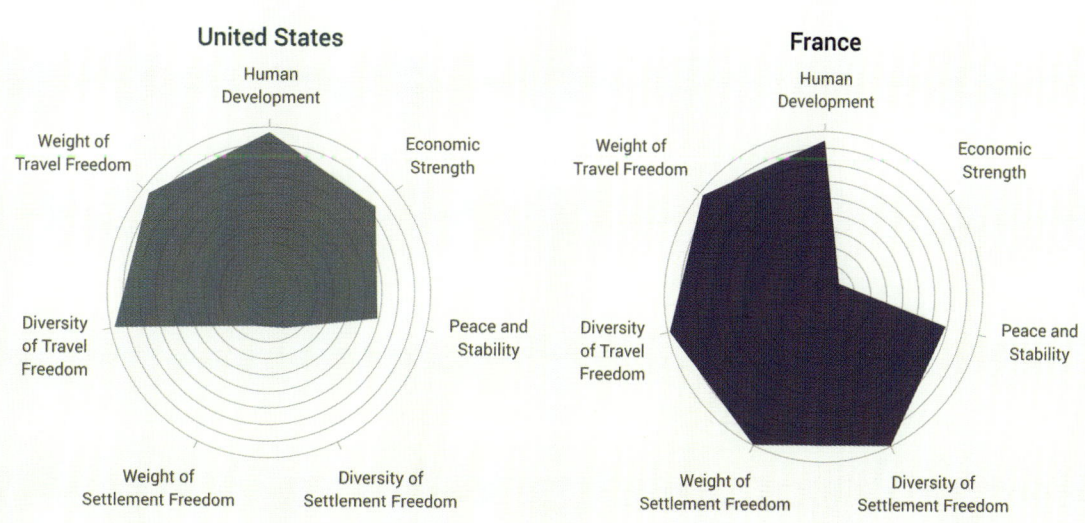

further demonstrate how widely different the top 10 most powerful countries are according to perception and the corresponding nationalities' position in the QNI.

Only three out of the ten most powerful countries have nationalities scoring in the Very High Quality tier of the QNI. While the US nationality ranks at the 25th place, as opposed to the US's 1st spot as the world's most powerful country, the nationalities of the Russian Federation and China score far worse, at the 62nd and 56th places respectively, both in the Medium Quality tier.

Perception of power does not, of course, primarily include 'soft' values like the Human Development of a country. Moreover, the External Value of nationalities — or lack thereof — is not reflected in perceptions of power at all, or at most very weakly, through international alliances. These rankings show how nationalities are to a significant degree disconnected from the perceived power of the countries with which they are associated.

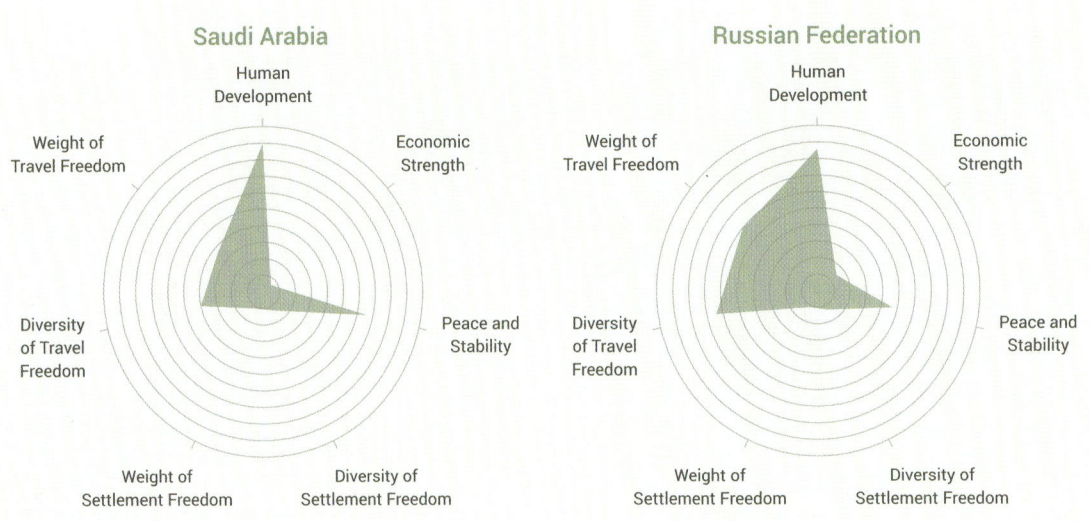

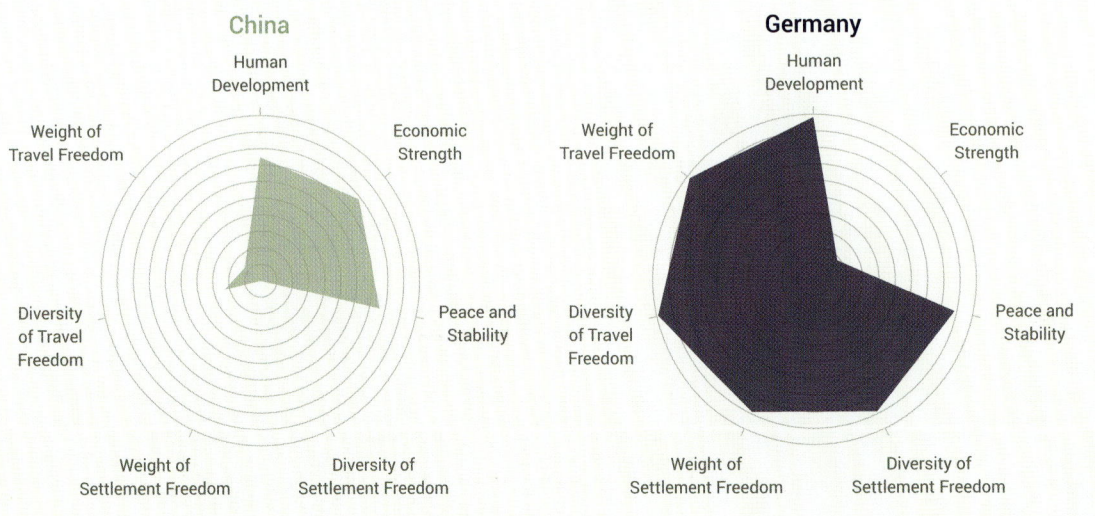

36 Non-Recognized States

\multicolumn{3}{l}{Hypothetical QNI General Ranking 2018 Including Nationalities of Non-Recognized States}
Rank	Nationality	2018 Value
97	Artsakh (Nagorno-Karabakh)	31.9
146	Turkish Republic of Northern Cyprus	21.7
150	South Ossetia	19.7
152	Transnistria (Pridnestrovian Moldavian Republic)	19.1
153	Abkhazia	19.0
160	Sahrawi Arab Democratic Republic	15.9
161	Donetsk People's Republic	15.6
161	Luhansk People's Republic	15.6
164	Somaliland	11.1

Mean: 18.8% • Median: 19.0%

The QNI does not include the nationalities of unrecognized states or states that have very limited recognition. Examples of such statuses are the nationalities of Abkhazia, the Turkish Republic of Northern Cyprus, and Somaliland. These nationalities are not included in the QNI for two reasons.

First, precise data is often lacking, in particular with regard to the Internal sub-elements of the QNI. Unrecognized states are generally not included in the Human Development Index or the Global Peace Index, and their levels of Human Development, Economic Strength, and Peace and Stability are not always easily estimated.

Second, these nationalities often grant only marginal or even non-existent external opportunities. Like their corresponding countries, the passports of many of these nationalities are not recognized by the great majority of other states. Visa-free or visa-on-arrival travel is often extremely limited. More dramatically, these nationalities do not allow their holders to travel to a significant number of destinations at all, with or without a visa. For citizens of Azerbaijan, India, or Iraq, traveling to London or Los Angeles might be difficult practically, but for the holder of an Abkhazian or a Transnistrian passport it is downright impossible. The impossibility of applying for a visa for many countries makes these largely unrecognized nationalities worth substantially less than others. Since the QNI does not take recognition by other states as such into account, applying the methodology to nationalities that are (partly) unrecognized would lead to an inflated value vis-à-vis nationalities that do have nearly universal recognition.

Adding to the complexity, some passports can be used to travel to some countries even though these countries do not formally recognize the conferring state. One of the most notable examples is the recognition of the passport of Chinese Taipei (Taiwan). Taiwan is recognized as an independent state by only 19 UN member states. By contrast, the Taiwanese passport is widely recognized worldwide and can be used to travel to 134 destinations visa-free or by visa-on-arrival, which far exceeds the 66 visa-free or visa-on-arrival destinations of the Chinese nationality. Likewise, while the Turkish Republic of Northern Cyprus is recognized as a state only by Turkey, its passport can be used to travel to the US and the UK among other countries, albeit with prior visa application.

In other words, from the perspective of external opportunities, the value of the nationalities of unrecognized states is often very limited, and lack of international recognition further decreases the value of a nationality because of the impossibility of traveling to certain destinations at all. At the same time, however, the effects of formal non-recognition can be paradoxical insofar as passports of unrecognized states can nonetheless be used as travel documents in practice. Consequently, the status and value of nationalities of unrecognized states remains highly obscure and difficult to quantify, partly because the QNI methodology is not equipped to deal with the significant and sometimes paradoxical effects of non-recognition.

Of course, similar problems occur with some nationalities that are included in the QNI. Think of Israel, for example, which is not recognized by 32 of the 193 UN member states, some of which categorically ban entry by Israeli passport holders to their territories (Saudi Arabia, for example).

  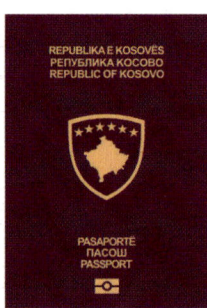

Other notable examples are the Palestinian State (recognized by 136 UN member states) and Kosovo (recognized by 113 UN member states). In measuring the value of the Israeli, Palestinian, and Kosovar nationalities, the QNI abstracts from their partial non-recognition.

Accordingly, we can still try to measure the value of nationalities of overwhelmingly unrecognized status by abstracting from non-recognition as has been done for the Israeli, Palestinian, and Kosovar nationalities. For this purpose, it is necessary to work with estimations and proxies. While these are always suboptimal and likely create some value inflation, the result is still elucidating, particularly because it shows the enormous quality difference between the nationalities of unrecognized states and those of their close neighbors.

Accordingly, we applied the QNI methodology to the nationalities of the following nine largely unrecognized states:

- Abkhazia
- Artsakh (Nagorno-Karabakh)
- Donetsk People's Republic
- Luhansk People's Republic
- Pridnestrovian Moldavian Republic (Transnistria)
- Sahrawi Arab Democratic Republic (SADP)
- Somaliland
- South Ossetia
- Turkish Republic of Northern Cyprus

 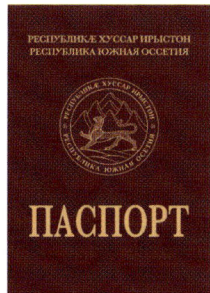 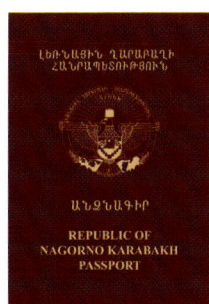 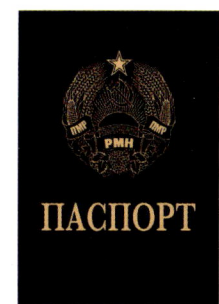
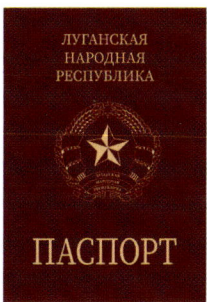 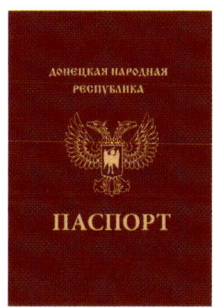 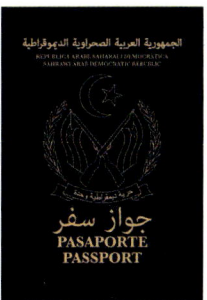 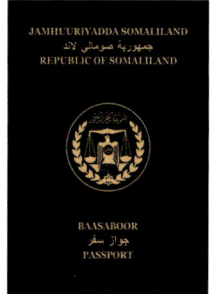

For this measurement, the internal sub-elements have been calculated using reasonable estimations from publicly available data (Economic Strength) and the values of neighboring countries (Human Development, and Peace and Stability). For example, in calculating the value of the nationalities of Abkhazia and South Ossetia, we used the Human Development score of the Georgian nationality, and for the nationality of the Turkish Republic of Northern Cyprus the Human Development score of the Turkish nationality. Similar proxies were applied for Peace and Stability, taking into account regional conflicts and tensions. For example, for Abkhazia and South Ossetia an average of the Peace and Stability scores of Georgia (2.084) and The Russian Federation (3.047) were used, rather than that of Georgia alone. This proxy is based on the assumption that both Abkhazia and South Ossetia are subject to higher regional tensions than Georgia as a whole, which should be reflected in a lower level of Peace and Stability. Estimations of Economic Strength are publicly available, and have been corrected to estimate GDP with power purchasing parity. The external sub-elements have been calculated on the basis of publicly available data, such as visa-waiver agreements, among others, between Abkhazia, South Ossetia, and Transnistria.

Seven of these nine nationalities are in the Very Low Quality tier of the QNI. The Turkish Republic of Northern Cyprus maintains itself in the Low Quality tier because of its settlement access to Turkey and its relatively high level of Human Development and Peace and Stability compared to the other nationalities. The relatively high score of Artsakh's nationality is due to the fact that its citizens are granted not only an Artsakh ID card for internal purposes but also a passport issued by the Republic of Armenia. This is made possible by the law on the main principles of citizenship of the Republic of Nagorno-Karabakh, which allows dual citizenship for nationals of the Artsakh Republic. They can use this passport as a travel document that allows them to enjoy the same external rights as Armenian nationals. This cannot compensate, however, for a profound lack of Travel and Settlement Freedom, which characterizes most other unrecognized nationalities as well. The other seven nationalities are all among the 20 lowest-scoring nationalities in the QNI.

Part 5

Expert Commentary

37 North versus South or Integrated versus Isolated? Notes on the Global Grouping of Nationalities

By Yossi Harpaz

Kälin and Kochenov's Quality of Nationality Index (QNI) offers a high-resolution view of the world's nationalities, highlighting their differential value in terms of economic access, security, and mobility. The most obvious way of looking at the Index is to treat it as a ranked listing that allows us to compare different nationalities and trace the changes in their relative positions over time. There are other ways, however, of thinking about the value of nationality. It is also useful to examine how nationalities cluster into groups that share certain important characteristics. This kind of analysis may help us understand the structure of global inequality, the forces that are shaping it, and the direction that it might take.

The concept of measuring nationalities is new: until recently, comparative data on most aspects of citizenship (for example, political freedom or personal security) was unavailable. Therefore, traditional classifications divided the world into categories of countries, not nationalities. Until the 1990s, the dominant framework for classifying countries was geopolitical; since then, economic classifications have become more prominent.

  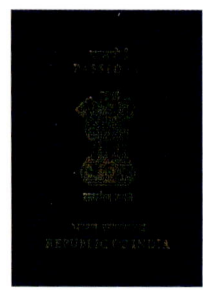

The years following the Second World War saw the formation of an ideological and geopolitical structure that continues to impact our understanding of the world: the division of the globe into first, second, and third worlds. These terms originally referred to a country's political-ideological orientation during the Cold War. The first world included members of NATO and other Western- and capitalist-oriented countries, the second world consisted of communist countries, and the third world included the non-aligned nations of Africa, Asia, and Latin America (Huntington 1996; Wolf-Phillips 1987; Tomlinson 2003). This distinction also had an underlying economic meaning; above all, the third world was associated with low levels of development.

Figure 1. The Three Worlds of the Cold War Period

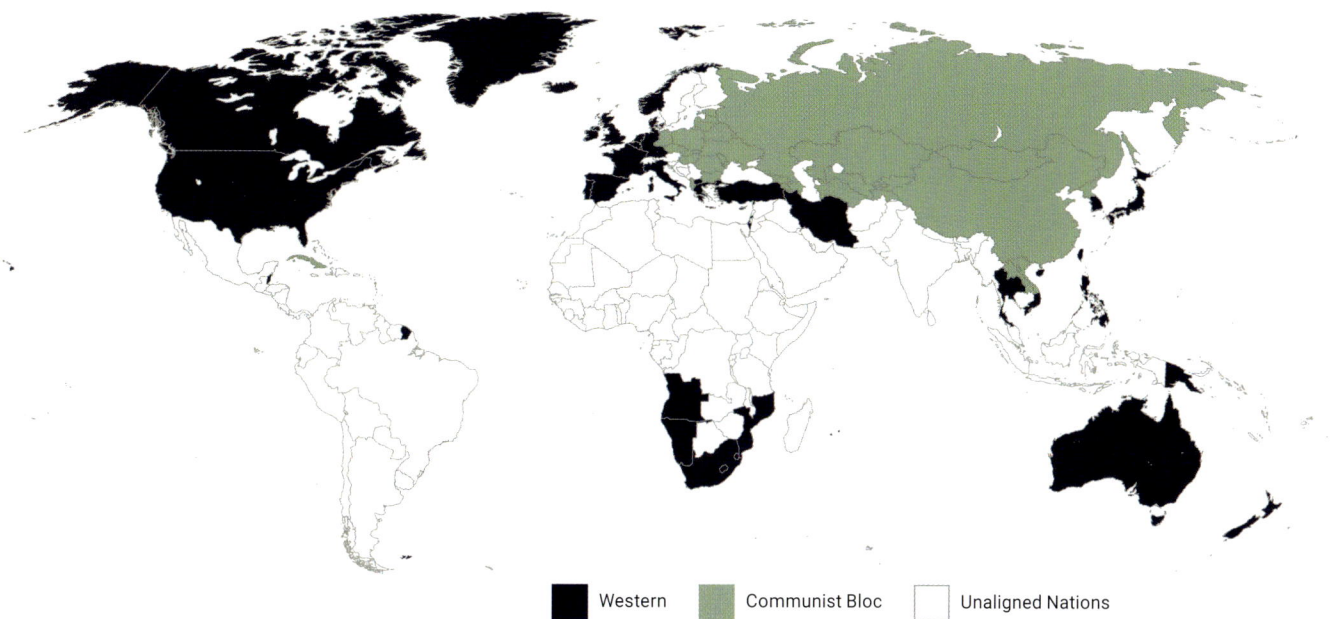

■ Western ■ Communist Bloc □ Unaligned Nations

This geopolitical-ideological division of the world died with the fall of communism in the Soviet Union and Eastern Europe. Since then, scholars have been struggling to define the structure of the global order that replaced it. Two American political scientists, Francis Fukuyama and Samuel Huntington, offered competing visions of the post-Cold War 'brave new world'. Fukuyama (1992) argued that the demise of communism marked "the end of history", a term that he borrowed from the philosopher G.W.F. Hegel. With the Cold War over, liberal democracy was the only ideology left standing, Fukuyama argued. He predicted that after the victory of democracy over its only real competitor, it would continue to spread until no major political-ideological divides remained.

Huntington (1996) agreed with Fukuyama that the era of global ideological conflict was over, but he had a diametrically opposite vision of the future. Instead of converging towards Western-style liberal democracy, Huntington expected the world's countries to diverge ever more strongly along civilizational lines. Huntington divided the world into nine distinct civilizations, the major ones being Greater China, the Islamic world, an Orthodox Christian civilization, and the West (Europe and its overseas offshoots). The essence of his "clash of civilizations" thesis is that as non-Western civilizations develop economically and politically, they will increasingly reject Western dominance, values, and models of governance.

These ways of thinking about global structure — communist versus capitalist countries, an expanding democratic order versus a clash of civilizations — focus on countries and not nationalities, and on ideologies rather than standards of living. They highlight an important issue: if we wish to compare nationalities, we cannot avoid the critical question of values. Do people in Ireland and Iran or Cameroon and Canada share the same vision of the good life? Do they aspire to the same societal goals and accord a similar role to the state in pursuing these goals?

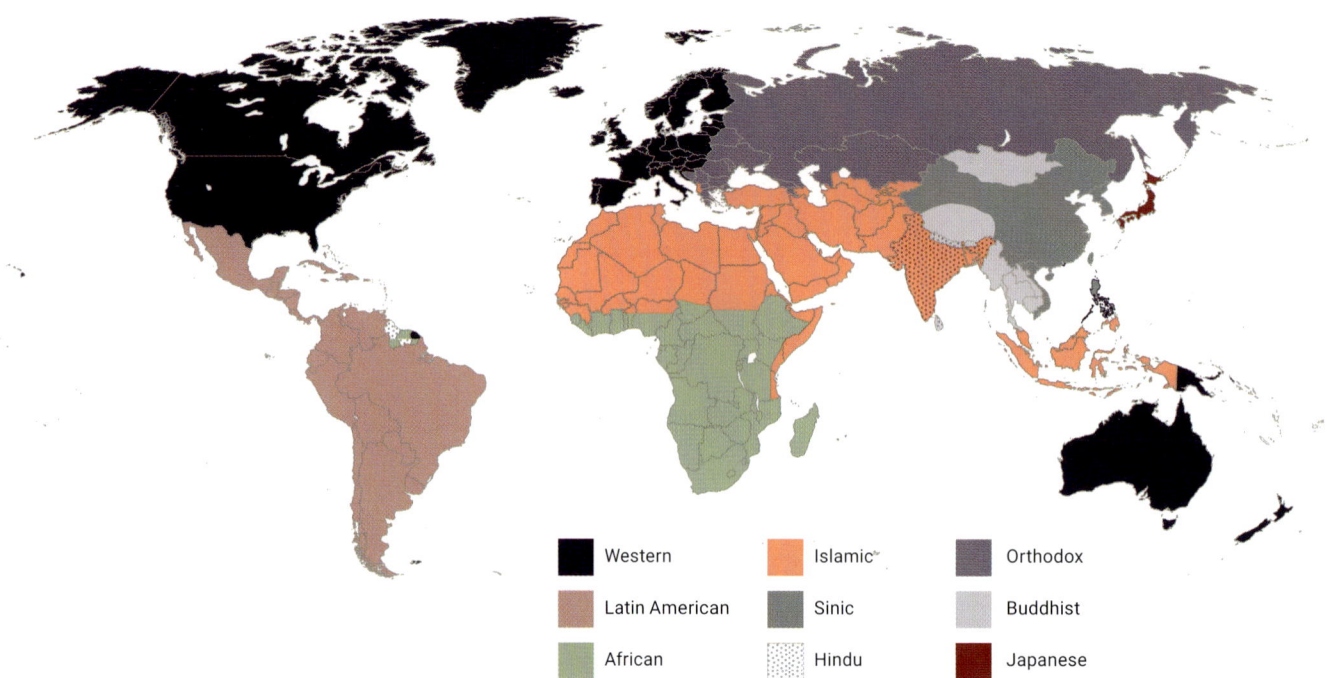

Figure 2. Samuel Huntington's World of Clashing Civilizations

Studies show that publics around the world have different ideals about the societies they wish to live in and the proper role of the state. For example, Pew Center surveys in Egypt, Jordan, and Pakistan indicated that over 90% of respondents believed that the state's laws should follow the principles of Islam or even draw directly on the Koran (Pew Research Center 2012). The opposite approach is found in Sweden, where 80% of surveyed individuals supported a total separation between the state and religion (Sahgal 2018). Another Pew survey inquired about preferred forms of government, and found large gaps among countries in support for and trust in democracy and their government. For example, 48% of Tanzanian respondents said that they had "a lot" of trust in their government compared to under 5% of respondents in Greece, South Korea, or Spain who expressed such faith (Gramlich 2017).

Gaps in values are also found among countries with relatively similar cultural heritages and levels of development. For example, 62% of American respondents rejected the statement "Success in life is determined by forces outside our control", while only 36% agreed, whereas in Germany 72% of respondents agreed with that fatalistic statement, and only 27% disagreed. This reflects the American emphasis on individual striving compared to the greater emphasis on collective responsibility in Western Europe. Given these differences, it is no surprise that a majority of Americans (58%) believed that the state's main role was to provide individuals with freedom to pursue their goals; only 35% believed that the state should primarily guarantee that nobody is in need. In Germany, again, the ratios are reversed: 62% agreed that the state should first of all guarantee everyone's needs and only 36% emphasized individual freedom (Pew Research Center 2011). Correspondingly, income inequality is much higher in the US, with a Gini coefficient score of 0.41 compared to Germany's 0.32 (World Bank n.d.a.). These differences in preferences should be kept in mind when interpreting statistics on countries' economic performance and the scope of citizenship rights. (Of course, these differences in preferences reflect long, historical processes whereby state elites mold public values.)

The assignment of scores and rankings is an act of commensuration that turns qualities into quantities, thereby making them equivalent and comparable (Espeland and Stevens 1998). In the case of citizenship value, it involves the tacit assumption that individuals around the world want the same things from their governments. As the examples above demonstrate, this is not the case. Moreover, measurement and commensuration also change the reality that they purport to represent (Fourcade and Healy 2017). For example, Espeland and Sauder (2007) studied the unintended consequences of the emergence of a national ranking for American law schools; they found that school administrators continually tried to manipulate each component of the score in order to move up the list. States act in a similar manner, engaging in strategic manipulations to improve their position in international rankings (Meyer, Boli, Thomas, and Ramirez 1997). For example, since the OECD instituted its Program for International Student Assessment (PISA) examinations, educational systems in some member countries have begun to prepare schoolchildren specifically for this international exam in order to boost the prestige of the nation (and, perhaps more importantly, the government in power) (Gillis, Polesel, and Wu 2016).

Bearing these caveats in mind, I will now discuss conceptions of global structure that are focused on economic indicators and other measures of the value of nationality. In recent decades, the salience of economic rankings has grown due to the declining importance of ideological and geopolitical divisions as well as the greater availability of data. I will discuss the concepts of global economic hierarchies that divided the world into two, three, and four categories.

The division of the world into two economic categories is common in colloquial usage and in some academic circles, especially among critical social scientists (for example, in anthropology). It consists of a binary division of the world into 'the West and the rest', with a range of different terms: first world versus third world (with the second world forgotten); developed and developing nations; or global North and global South (Dados and Connell 2012). These terms all presuppose two groups of unequal size — a relatively small and privileged elite of Western countries and a large number of less developed countries. The use of binary terms like global North and global South highlights the roles of historical inequality, colonialism, and race in shaping contemporary society. Generally, the first (or northern, or developed, and so on) world mostly consists of former colonial powers, and its population is mostly white; the third world mostly consists of former colonies populated by people of color (Tomlinson 2003). The "global South" category, however, remains too ambiguous and broad to be useful. For example, should Mexico, Kazakhstan, Haiti, and Uganda all be considered third-world or global South nations, even though the per capita income in the former two countries is ten times higher than in the latter two?

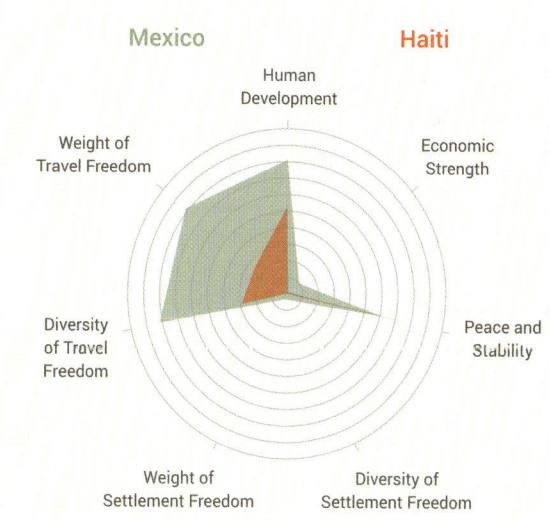

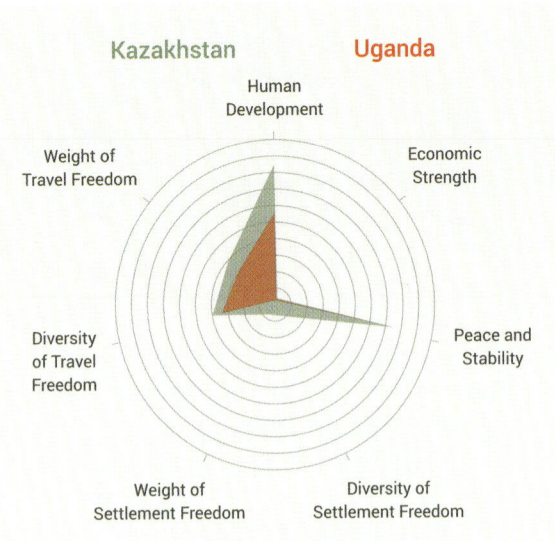

Another influential way of dividing the world, this time into three categories, draws on the Marxist-inspired model of the capitalist world system developed by Immanuel Wallerstein (1974). Wallerstein saw the world as a unified system and applied Marx's concept of a division of labor to it. He argued that the world economy was dominated by a core of rich Western countries (analogous to the bourgeoisie in Marxist theory), while almost all other countries belonged to the global periphery, comparable to Marx's proletariat. He also pointed to a small number of countries, such as Mexico or Turkey, which play an intermediate role in this global division of labor, and which he described as belonging to the semi-periphery. Scholars who follow the world systems approach have not reached a consensus on how to classify countries into regions (see Snyder and Kick 1979; Arrighi 1994; Chase-Dunn and Grimes 1995).

Finally, the World Bank classifies countries into four categories according to objective measures of Gross National Income (GNI) per capita. This categorization defines income thresholds that are updated every year. As of 2019, this classification included 81 high-income economies (with a GNI per capita above USD 12,056), 56 upper-middle-income (USD 3,896 to USD 12,055), 47 low-middle-income (USD 996 to USD 3,895), and 34 low-income economies (USD 995 or less). This classification, one could argue, is not as analytically sophisticated as the ones discussed above: it says nothing about the country's history, cultural identity, or role in capitalist production chains. Its advantage lies in its use of objective, up-to-date data. Such data is indispensable if we wish to understand the structure of the world economy. This is particularly important because the rapid growth of some non-Western regions is creating new economic and political configurations, rendering some of the accepted conceptions of global inequality obsolete.

In recent years, broader and more detailed data about income distributions across the world has become available. Economists and sociologists have used this data to analyze trends in both between-country and within-country income distributions and connect them to phenomena such as international migration and political discontent (Korzeniewicz and Moran 2009; Lakner and Milanovic 2013; Rodrik 2014; Firebaugh 2015). Alongside these detailed economic statistics, numerous international indices rank countries' performance along a range of other indicators, including social development, income inequality, security, democracy, travel freedom, and more. This new data allows us to learn about the lived reality of being a citizen in different countries. In other words, we can analyze and compare not just countries but also nationalities.

Two models were developed to compare nationalities: The QNI developed by Kochenov and Kälin (see Kochenov and Lindeboom 2017), and a model that I constructed and published in an article in the *Journal of Ethnic and Migration Studies* (Harpaz 2019b) and a recently published book, *Citizenship 2.0: Dual Nationality as a Global Asset* (Harpaz 2019a).

Both these models use data to rank nationalities on a number of dimensions, including economic development and security. They also introduce new indices for measuring the external value of countries' nationalities. This latter indicator, the most innovative aspect of the QNI, pertains to the value of a country's citizenship outside its borders. With the advent of globalization, numerous scholars argue, international mobility has become a crucial resource (Beck 2008; Faist 2013; Kim 2018). Zygmunt Bauman has famously argued that "mobility has become the most powerful and most coveted stratifying factor" (Bauman 1998, 9). Therefore, ease of crossing borders and/or settling in another country has become an important measure of the value of a country's citizenship. Below, I will discuss two kinds of classifications that emerge from indices of external citizenship factors: travel freedom and settlement freedom.

When calculating travel freedom, both indices rely on data from the International Air Transport Association (IATA). QNI's Diversity of Travel Freedom ranks the world's nationalities on the basis of the number of countries that their holders may access visa-free or with a visa-on-arrival. A quick look at the ranked list offers few surprises: at the top of the list are nationalities of rich countries in East Asia, North America, and Western and Northern Europe, while the lowest places are occupied by African and South Asian nationalities. We can take the analysis a step further and construct groups of nationalities categorized by their degrees of travel freedom.

A good starting point would be the visa regimes of the two major Western political units: the US and the EU's zone of free movement, the Schengen Area. Owing to their prosperity, security, and prestige (Centeno, Bandelj, and Wherry 2011), these regions are attractive to many millions from all over the world — would-be immigrants, tourists, refugees, smugglers of goods and humans, even terrorists. Easy access to these regions is a scarce resource from which the majority of the world's population is excluded: citizens of most countries must obtain a visa before visiting the EU or the US. By looking at whom these Western blocs let in freely we can identify which nationalities are perceived as trustworthy and which are automatically seen as suspect (Shamir 2005; Hobolth 2014; Mau, Gulzau, Laube, and Zaun 2015).

The US's Visa Waiver Program is highly exclusive. Citizens of about 40 countries may enter the US without a visa, including those from most Western and Central European countries and Australia, Brunei, Canada, Chile, Japan, New Zealand, Singapore, South Korea, and Taiwan. These countries' passports provide the top tier of global mobility. The EU (more specifically, the Schengen free movement zone) is less restrictive. Visa-free access to Europe's Schengen Area is permitted to citizens of all the countries that enjoy a US visa waiver, and to citizens of the US itself, citizens of most Balkan, Caribbean, and Latin American countries, and citizens of Israel, Malaysia, and the UAE. There are approximately 40 countries whose citizens enjoy visa-free access to the EU but not to the US. These nationalities occupy a middle position in terms of travel freedom. Citizens of the roughly 100 countries that make up the rest of the world (including almost all African and Asian nations — among them major powers such as China, India, and the Russian Federation) have no visa-free access to either bloc, placing them in the bottom rung of global travel freedom.

We can divide the world into three tiers of travel freedom based on the visa policies of these core Western regions. The resulting groupings do not quite align with the three worlds of the Cold War era, but neither do they correspond to the binary view of the world that is suggested by the division into global North and global South. In fact, the structure of the world as it emerges from this model is a small elite of privileged nationalities, an equally small middle stratum, and a large mass of lower-tier countries where the large majority of humankind lives.

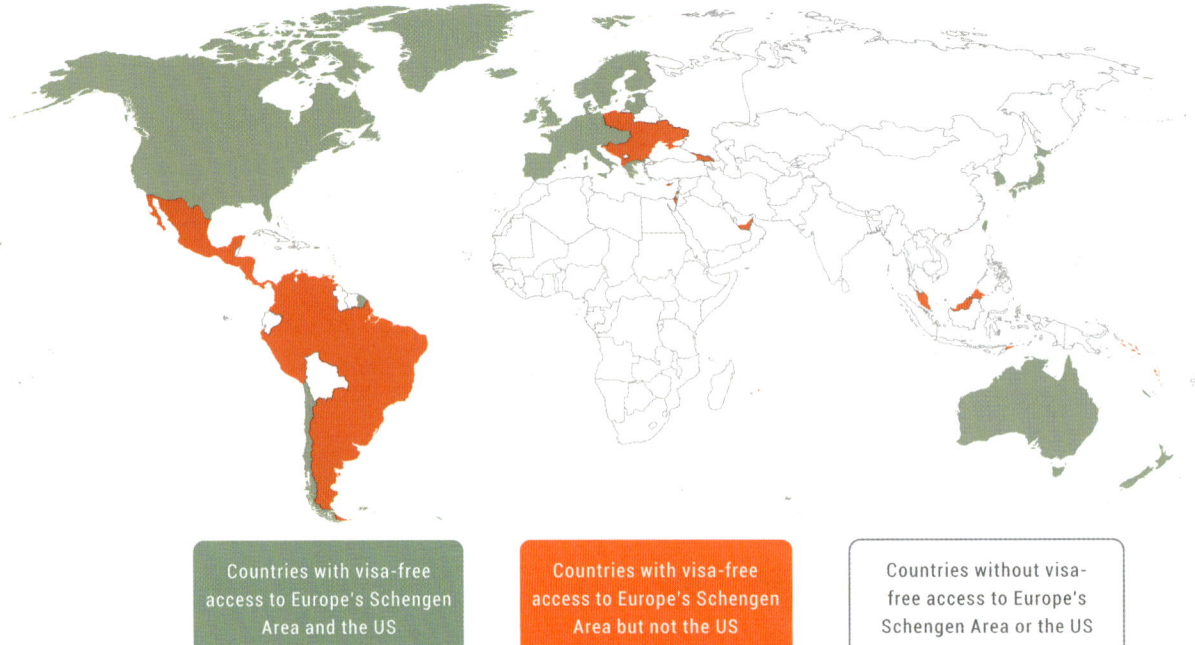

Figure 3. World's Countries by Visa-free Access to the US and the EU

Countries with visa-free access to Europe's Schengen Area and the US

Countries with visa-free access to Europe's Schengen Area but not the US

Countries without visa-free access to Europe's Schengen Area or the US

Note: Europe's Schengen Area (or Schengen Zone) is the EU's zone of free movement. Countries colored in green enjoy visa-free access to both Europe's Schengen Area and the US; those in orange have visa-free access to Europe's Schengen Area but not to the US; and those in white with a grey border have visa-free access to neither.

I explored this global structure and its implications in a recent article (Harpaz 2019b). Combining indicators for the territorial value of citizenship (development, security, and democracy) together with travel freedom (which I measured by counting the number of countries that can be accessed visa-free or with a visa-on-arrival), I constructed a three-tier model of citizenship value. This hierarchy interacts with a new global trend towards the toleration of dual citizenship, which allows individuals to obtain higher-tier citizenship without having to emigrate and/or give up their original citizenship (Harpaz and Mateos 2019). My research shows that patterns of demand and acquisition of dual citizenship are shaped by this global hierarchy. Individuals from middle-tier countries — mostly in Eastern Europe and Latin America — make great efforts to secure a second citizenship from first-tier countries (Harpaz 2019b). For example, when Italy offered dual citizenship to the descendants of Italian emigrants, the vast majority of applications — 780,000 out of 1 million in 1998–2010 — came from Italian descendants in Argentina, Brazil, and other countries in South America. Meanwhile, descendants of Italian emigrants in the US filed only about 25,000 applications (Harpaz 2015, 2019a; see Tintori 2012).

In the book (Harpaz 2019a), I present in-depth studies of three cases where people acquired a second, premium citizenship: Israelis and Serbians who applied for a second passport from EU countries on the basis of their family origin or ethnicity, and Mexicans who strategically gave birth in the US to secure citizenship for their children (Harpaz 2019a). The study's findings demonstrate that people around the world are conscious of the stratification of citizenship and of their place in it, and that they are willing to expend money and effort to move up this hierarchy. This sheds new light on the question of convergence versus pluralism. On the one hand, worldwide demand for Western and EU citizenship seems to support the position that predicts a global convergence in values á la Fukuyama: wealthy citizens of the Russian Federation and China are eager to obtain

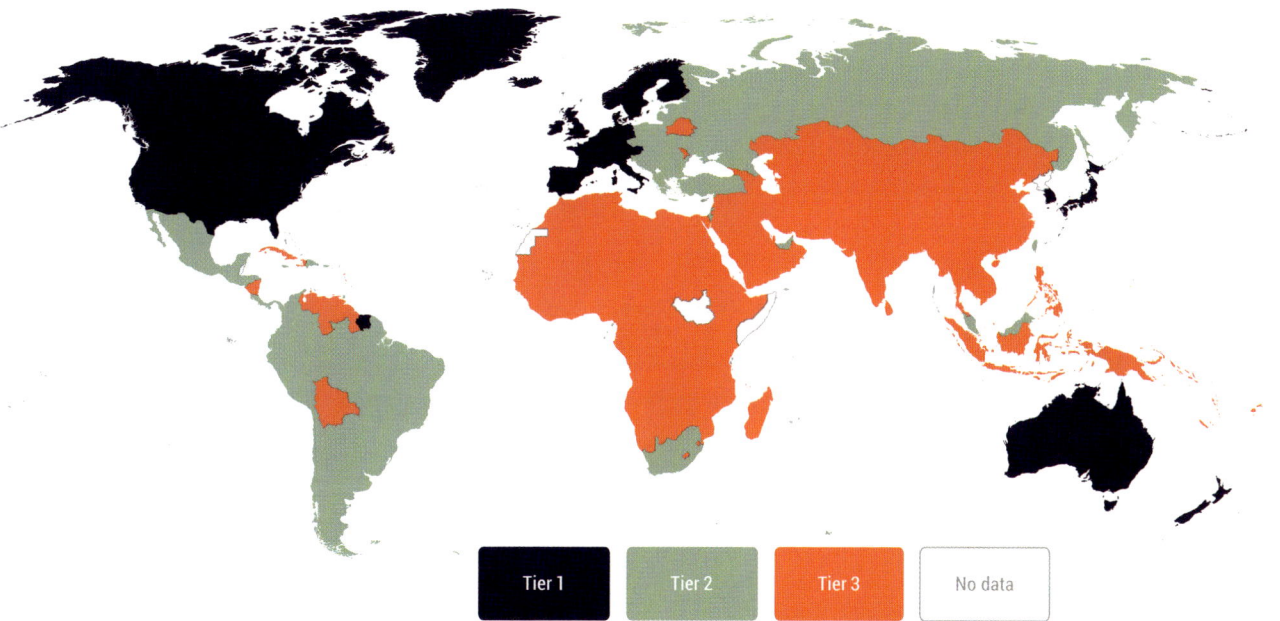

Figure 4. World Map with Citizenship Tiers

Note: This map shows the world's countries according to their tier position. The dark-blue countries are first tier and the orange countries are third tier. Second-tier countries are colored in green. No data was available for North Korea, Somalia, South Sudan, and Western Sahara, all indicated with a grey border.

Western citizenship even as their governments present the West as a rival and competitor (Kroft 2017). On the other hand, strategic dual citizens are typically instrumental about their second nationalities and make a clear distinction between it and their country of origin 'real' citizenship, which they often understand in primordial ethnic terms (Harpaz 2013, 2019a).

The second dimension of external citizenship is settlement freedom. This component of nationality is central to the QNI's ranking. It reflects a novel global development whereby countries provide extensive rights of settlement and employment to citizens of other countries. Typically, this new form of citizenship emerges in regional blocs as a crucial step in their economic and political integration (Kochenov 2017b, 2019a).

The pioneer of settlement freedom is the EU — the world's oldest, biggest, richest, and best-integrated regional bloc. Citizens of EU member countries lead the world in terms of settlement freedom, as their QNI scores attest. Alongside EU nationalities in the global ranking of settlement freedom, however, we find some unexpected contenders: the citizens of nations that are members of the Economic Community of West African States (ECOWAS), as well as other regional unions such as MERCOSUR in South America (see Acosta in this volume), the Gulf Cooperation Council (GCC), and the Eurasian Economic Union (EAEU) (see Nizhnikaŭ in this volume), which includes five post-Soviet countries.

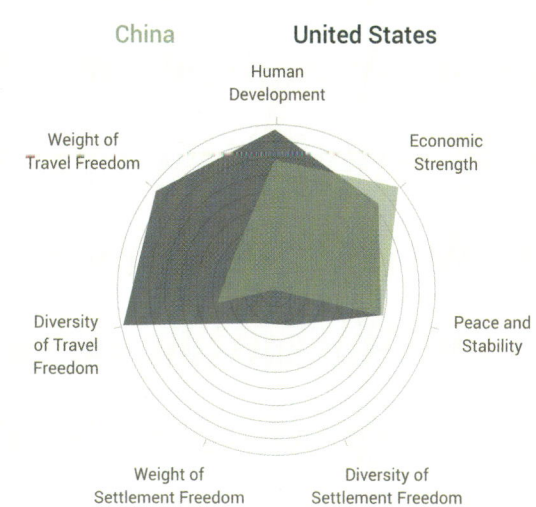

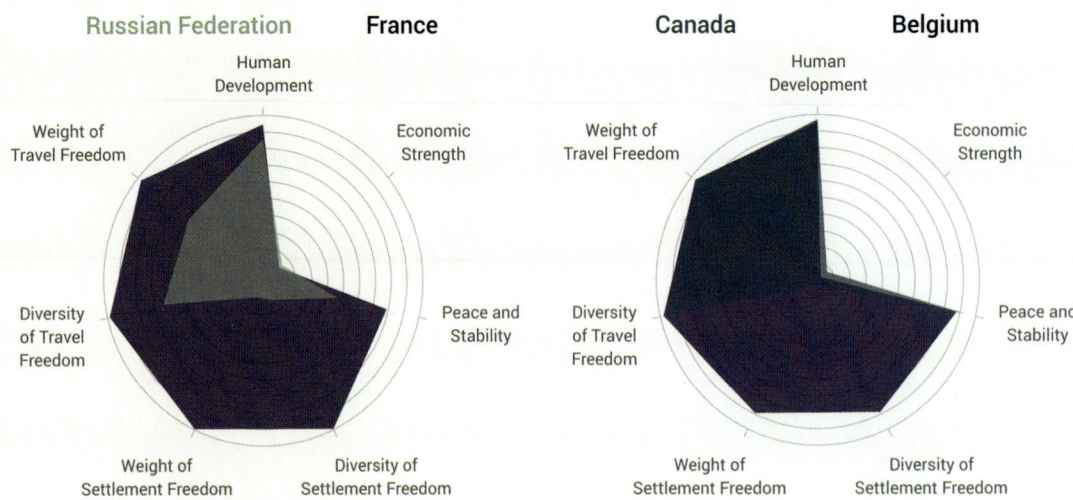

In the same manner that Spanish nationality provides citizenship rights in Belgium or Germany, Brazilian nationality increasingly entails some rights in Argentina, Liberian nationality includes some rights in Nigeria, and Armenian nationality provides rights in the Russian Federation. Currently, these external citizenship rights are not as extensive (or practically useful) as those offered by EU citizenship, but they are continuously growing. In contrast, many countries are not members of any regional union, and their citizens do not enjoy any freedom to settle abroad. This list of 'isolates' is very diverse, ranging from poor countries such as Chad to rich countries such as Canada.

This way of thinking about external citizenship in terms of rights in neighboring countries leads to a ranking and grouping of nationalities that is less centered on the West and thus, in a sense, more democratic. From this perspective, the key distinction is between citizenship in countries that have embarked on the path to regional integration — whether in Africa, Asia, Europe, or South America — and those that have not. If regional unions around the world continue to consolidate and the scope of rights included in them continues to grow, the importance of this component will increase, making region-wide freedom of settlement a key right that individuals may come to expect from their nationality.

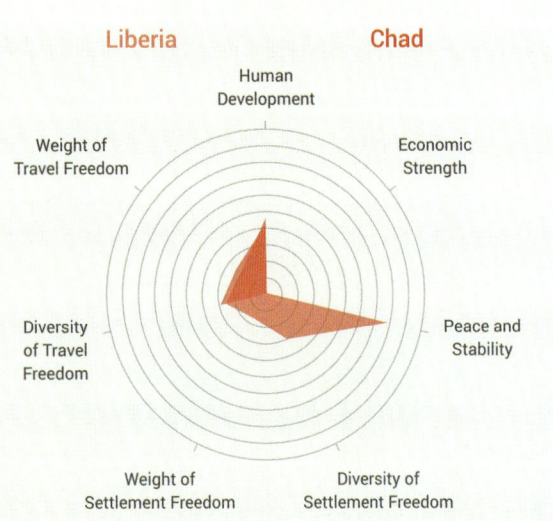

In conclusion, this paper surveyed the key concepts used by scholars and lay people to think about how the nations of the world can be categorized. After the end of the Cold War, the emphasis shifted from ideological and geopolitical groupings to economic clusters. New data now allows us to compare not only countries' economies, but also to compare the values of different nationalities. Focusing on the least studied component of nationality rankings — the external value of citizenship — I have presented two ways of categorizing the world's nationalities. When looking at nationalities through the prism of travel freedom, we find a three-tier hierarchy of passports, with a distinct elite, a small middle tier, and a large bottom tier characterized by severely curtailed mobility rights. In contrast, the settlement freedom perspective suggests a more egalitarian world, where other regions beside the West may unite with the purpose of jointly increasing their citizenship values.

We still do not know what the future holds for nationality: will the benefits of Western citizenship continue to attract millions, creating a converging Western-centric world that moves towards "the end of history"? Or will non-Western countries boost their citizenship value through economic growth and regional cooperation, producing a world where different regional and cultural blocs vie for dominance?

38 Population Density, Wealth, and Refugee Flows: New Perspectives of the Quality of Nationality Index

By Benjamin Hennig and Dimitris Ballas

The map of the Quality of the World's Nationalities in 2018 presented on pages 70 and 71 is based on a conventional approach to visualizing data about countries. Although most people are used to such conventional maps of their countries, which approximate their sizes and shapes according to how they might appear from space or are rendered in the widely used map projections to which we have become accustomed, we would strongly argue that this is not always the best way to visualize human geographical data, such as that depicted by *Kälin and Kochenov's Quality of Nationality Index* (QNI) or its underlying domains. The conventional maps of the QNI show how much land is associated with states that have different qualities of nationality in their territories, but they fail to highlight the number of people that live in each of these countries and therefore give a misleading representation of the respective phenomenon and its spatial distribution across humanity. In addition, within countries, there is a visual bias in favor of sparsely populated areas: urban areas with large populations but small geographic areas are effectively invisible to the map reader.

The QNI maps shown here were created with an innovative use of geographical information systems and novel cartography techniques, and offer an alternative, more flexible way to visualize the world and its people. Geographical regions have been redrawn on the basis of recalculating the area of each small neighborhood in proportion to the number of people who live in it rather than simply its land mass. This kind of visualization differs from traditional maps, putting the visual emphasis on treating all people as equally important rather than what is usually the case, which is highlighting — indeed, overemphasizing — the most sparsely populated rural regions.

The maps of the QNI shown here were created using a gridded cartogram approach (Hennig 2013) that builds on earlier groundbreaking work of mathematician and computer scientist Michael Gastner and physicist Mark Newman (Gastner and Newman 2004). Their so-called density-equalizing cartogram algorithm has been used for a wide range of thematic applications, including the ongoing Worldmapper project (Worldmapper n.d.) and the *Human Atlas of Europe* (Ballas, Dorling, and Hennig 2017), with which the authors of this contribution are involved. The novel gridded cartogram technique involves dividing the whole area to be mapped into a grid of equal-sized cells and then estimating and interpolating the distribution of quantitative data across this raster. The next step is to apply a mathematical technique to resize each cell proportional to the data values within each grid cell area.

Using such a gridded approach with population data, the process results in a contiguous gridded-population cartogram which can also be seen as an equal-population projection, meaning that each new grid cell has an area proportional to the number of people living there, but still touches only its original eight contiguous cells and therefore preserves the physical topology of the 'real' world.

The preservation of topological connections allows the demographic pictures depicted in such gridded population cartograms to be enriched further with additional layers of information, which allows them to be used as base maps for other topics of interest, such as the QNI. In Figure 1, QNI Quality Tiers on a World Map Scaled by Population, we have colored the resized grid cells on the basis of their QNI values. Compared to a conventional map, the new cartogram highlights where and how many people live in different areas, rather than how much land there is in each country.

By following this approach, we can illustrate the underlying inequalities of Quality of Nationality from the perspective of people. In particular, the map highlights that the total number of people who are fortunate to reside in countries with a Very High Quality and High Quality category according to the Index is very small and mostly found in the rich but relatively less densely populated continents of North America and Europe, while vast swaths of the world's population live in countries with Medium, Low, or Very Low Quality nationalities.

When compared to conventional maps, such cartograms are much more effective in highlighting the extent of global inequalities in terms of opportunity, freedom, citizenship value, quality of nationality and, ultimately, quality of life. They put a particular focus on what matters most in this Index: people, who are affected by the quality of the nationalities they possess.

The cartographic method used to create such a cartogram can, in principle, be applied to any quantitative variable with values that add up to a meaningful total for all countries or territories being mapped, just as 'total population' has been used as the quantitative basis for the map above. The index values of the QNI or any of the sub-elements would not be suitable for such transformations, however, due to the specific nature of their data, since they represent only relative or even qualitative data, neither of which is suitable for distorting and visualizing quantitative distributions. The main challenge to using quantitative variables to produce a gridded cartogram is being able to estimate their distribution on the high-resolution grid that provides the basis for the map transformation.

However, there are other suitable variables that relate quite well to the QNI, such as the comparison of population distribution and general QNI, that therefore make similar correlations possible. One striking example for other such visual representations is the total economic output of each country (adding up to the total economic output of the world as a meaningful total that can be compared through the cartogram transformation).

Figure 2, QNI Quality Tiers on a Map Scaled According to the World's GDP, is a map in which the land area in each country has been resized to reflect economic output as measured by its respective GDP output. The GDP output was again interpolated over a regular grid, so that variations within countries also become visible through the individual grid cells.

North America and Western Europe bulge to dominate this world map, while the entire continent of Africa almost disappears. As economic strength is one of the key sub-elements of the QNI, in this map we can see that countries at the highest levels of the QNI are also the countries that

148 • Quality of Nationality Index

Figure 1. QNI Quality Tiers on a World Map Scaled by Population

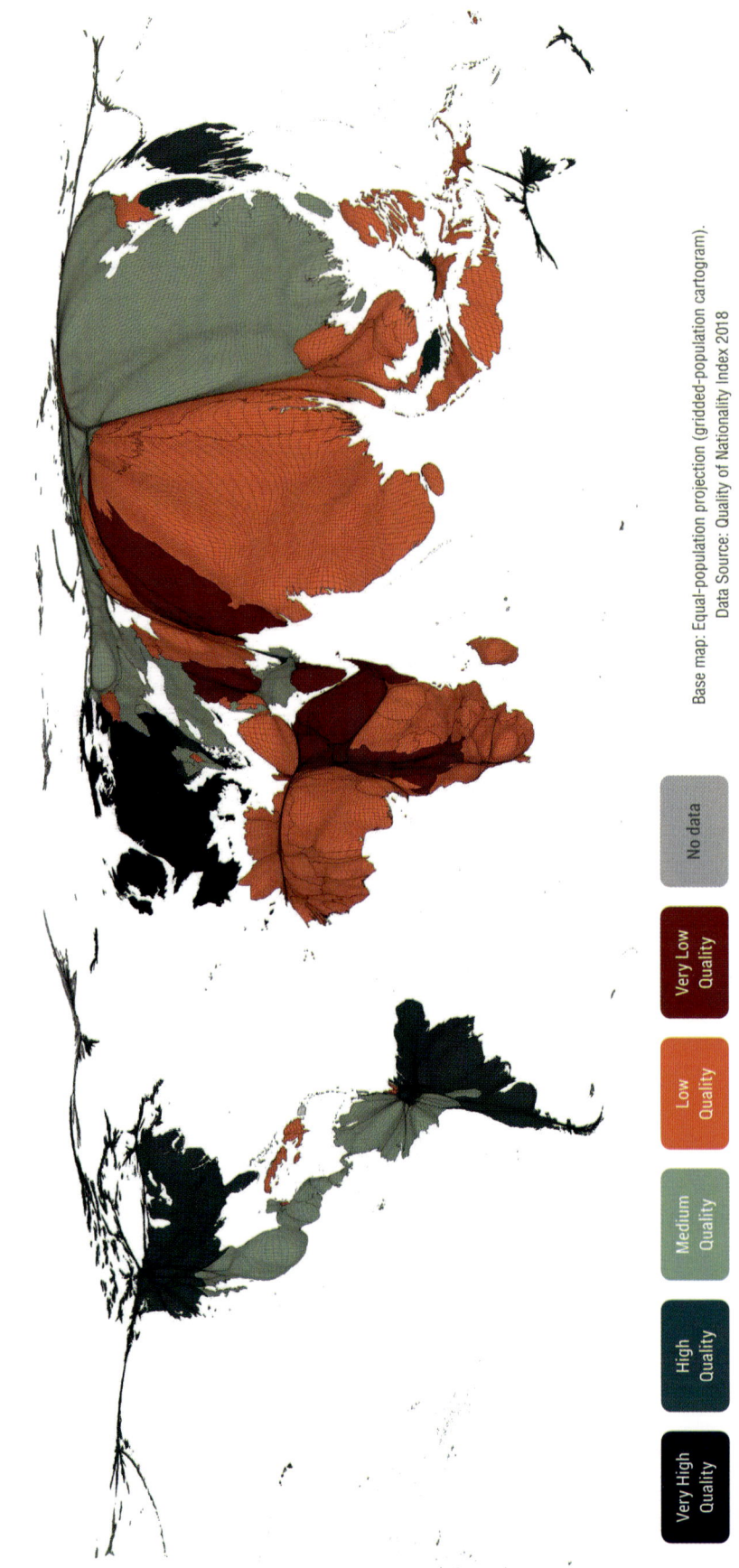

Base map: Equal-population projection (gridded-population cartogram).
Data Source: Quality of Nationality Index 2018

38 Population Density, Wealth, and Refugee Flows • 149

Figure 2. QNI Quality Tiers on a Map Scaled According to the World's GDP

Base map: Equal-economy projection (gridded cartogram of GDP productivity).
Data Source: Quality of Nationality Index 2018

150 • Quality of Nationality Index

Figure 3. QNI Quality Tiers on World Map Scaled According to Refugee Flows

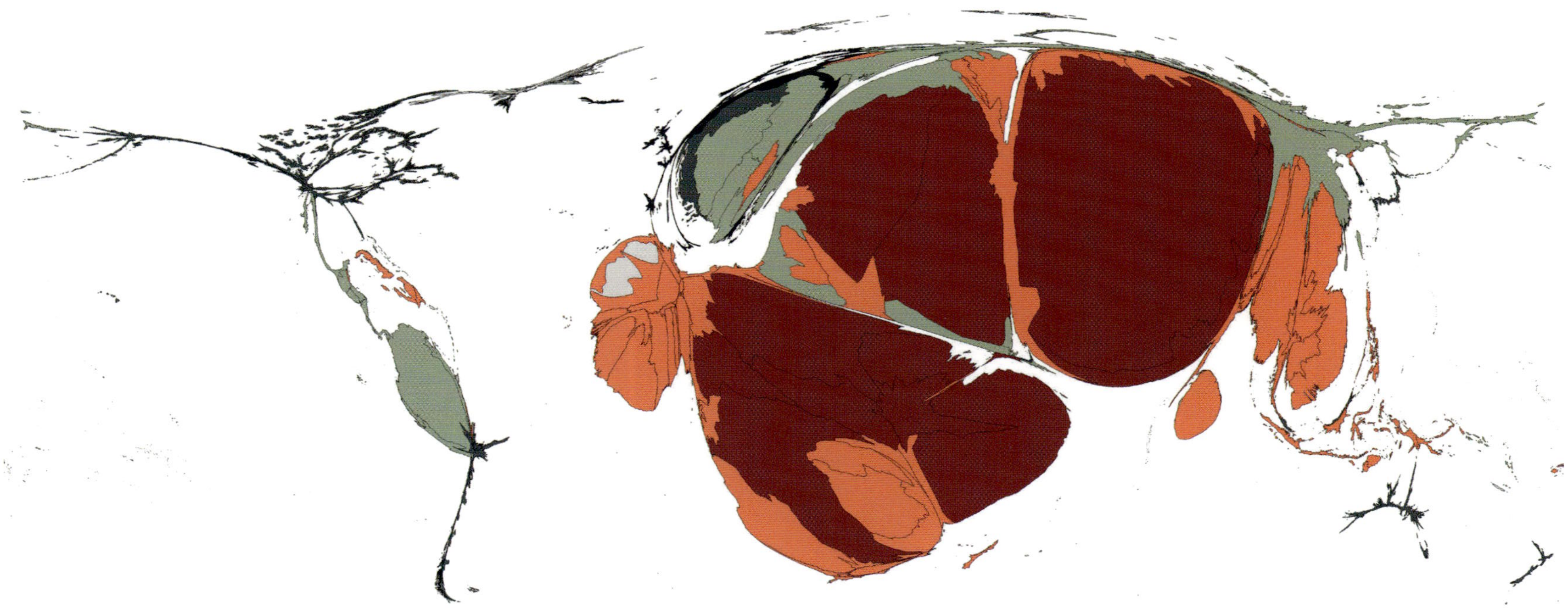

Countries of Origin
Base map: Cartogram where each country is proportional to the number of refugees (origin) between 2000 and 2015

Very High Quality | High Quality | Medium Quality | Low Quality | Very Low Quality | No data

38 Population Density, Wealth, and Refugee Flows • 151

Countries of Destination
Base map: Cartogram where each country is proportional to the number of refugees (destination) between 2000 and 2015

No data
Very Low Quality
Low Quality
Medium Quality
High Quality
Very High Quality

dominate the map. The possibility to also use this 'equal-wealth projection' for other indicators of the QNI provides an interesting perspective to be explored further; it would be a novel way to analyze the spatial patterns of the QNI, similar to the approach using population, above.

The wealth-based visualization shows the strong correlation of mostly high-performing countries in the QNI with those that are the largest in this map, suggesting a strong link between a high GDP and an overall High Quality of Nationality, not only with GDP productivity being an influencing factor in the Index, but also with this strongly affecting the other indicators. Countries with a Low, and even more so those with a Very Low Quality of Nationality, are inconspicuous on this map.

If GDP is such an influential factor, then other global dynamics may also be worth investigating with regard to their correlation with and relation to the QNI. The final case study in this chapter investigates such links in more detail: migration and other types of movement of people are among the most important geopolitical phenomena in recent years. Migration has become a central policy issue in many European countries, the US, and other countries. In some populist arguments the boundaries between migrants and refugees are deliberately blurred, creating rationalizations for more protectionist policies, including curbing migration.

The refugee crises of the past decade have been deployed deliberately to develop a populist narrative that refugees' main motivations for leaving their countries are to be found in factors related to their alleged countries of destination, such as Economic Strength and Human Development, but also peaceful and stable societies, indicators that are the key internal factors also expressed in the QNI.

When taking into account a long-term perspective of global refugee flows and looking at their respective countries of origin and destination between 2000 and 2015 through the lens of the QNI, as shown in Figure 3's two maps, distinct patterns become visible that relativize such assertions often made in contemporary political debates. The two maps show each country resized according to the total number of refugees from their countries of origin and to their countries of destination respectively. Overlaid are the color-coded QNI categories, allowing for a quick reference to the state of the QNI in each of these countries.

The two maps in Figure 3 provide a longer-term view of the origin and destination countries of these vulnerable groups of people. The global movement of refugees is highly dynamic and can change drastically from year to year. These shifts can be accentuated further by media coverage, which in turn influences public perception. Using longer-term and verified data gives us a clearer idea of the movement of people and allows us to see fluctuations in regions that are experiencing ongoing crises.

The maps document the movement of over 170 million people between 2000 and 2015, and the data highlights the changing geopolitical situations and areas of conflict during that period. The main origin continents for refugees were Asia at 52% and Africa at 33%, while Europe was much lower at 6%. Conflicts in countries such as Afghanistan, Iraq, Somalia, and Syria played a large role in the collective fleeing of over 10 million refugees from each of these countries.

The dominance of Low Quality to Very Low Quality QNI values for the nationalities of these countries can mostly be explained through conflicts leading to a decline in their Peace and Stability scores and related effects on other internal factors, so that the emerging patterns here are certainly not surprising.

The destination countries map, however, shows that the majority of refugees flee to destinations close to home, often to neighboring countries. Asian countries make up destinations for 47% of refugees, and African countries follow with 28%. Of the five major destination countries, four of these were adjacent to a conflict region: Iran, Kenya, Pakistan, and Syria. Europe was the destination for just under a fifth of the total global number of refugees between 2000 and 2015. More recently, Germany was the fifth major destination country due, in part, to its recent open-door policy and intake of refugees from 2015 onwards.

The maps show the shifting nature of conflicts and that much can change in only a decade. According to recent figures published by the UNHCR, in the past two decades, the global population of forcibly displaced people has grown significantly, from 33.9 million people in 1997 to 65.6 million people in 2016 alone. The world's forcibly displaced population is now at a record high.

From the perspective of the QNI, the emerging patterns in these maps show how few of the global refugee population are heading towards those countries that promise strong economies, high rates of human development, or peaceful and stable societies, and that geography plays a much bigger role in these population dynamics. Most of those who manage to reach destinations farther away are often those who have been better off, are better educated, or are otherwise more able to overcome such distances. The notion that refugees pose a threat to the quality of life in those societies with a high quality of nationality must be rejected, though, when investigating such global dynamics.

The case studies outlined in this chapter demonstrate how innovative visualizations can create novel insights and new perspectives to understand and further explore the QNI. The juxtaposition of population density and wealth demonstrates how people's opportunities are unequal in different regions of the world. In addition, the example of global refugee flows shows what multifaceted stories the visual exploration of the QNI through cartogram techniques can tell, such as debunking widespread political rhetoric around refugees being attracted by the high quality of nationality in the wealthiest parts of the world.

The explorations outlined here are only the start of seeing how the QNI and other socio-economic dimensions of the planet are connected and interrelated. They provide an accurate view of what it means to live in an interconnected world where nationality is a major contributing element to such dynamics.

39 The Quality of Statelessness

By Katja Swider

Introduction

Kälin and Kochenov's Quality of Nationality Index (QNI) aims to rate nationalities in terms of objective internal and external benefits they offer to their holders. If statelessness is the lack of any nationality,[1] should any instance of statelessness be rated zero in the Index? In other words, is being a stateless person always objectively less beneficial than being a national of any country?

This contribution explores what the methodological frame of the QNI could help reveal about the nature and meaning of the legal status of statelessness, how it compares to the status of nationality, and how it could be addressed through international policies that aim to help stateless persons.

While statelessness is the lack of any specific nationality, it is by no means a lack of states' influence on a person's life. Stateless persons' lives are often extremely 'state-full'. The stateless are physically located within territories of states, and their anomalous legal situation often leads to frequent interactions with state authorities, generating extensive bureaucracy, tailor-made administrative solutions, heightened risk of detention, and so on. States are still in control of stateless persons' access to various rights and benefits, their opportunities to develop and prosper, and their ability to travel and settle. While the relationship between states and their stateless persons is perhaps less straightforward than the relationship between states and their nationals, often less regulated and less homogenous, it is still a relationship of state-controlled access of individuals to QNI indicators. Categories of statelessness can therefore be incorporated into the QNI.

One of the most important contributions of the QNI to scholarship on nationality is the demystification of nationality as inherently and invariably beneficial (see Dimitry Kochenov's contribution to this volume, 2020; Swider 2018). The Index, due to its approach and methodology, allows us to study the wide disparity among nationalities in terms of what opportunities and limitations they carry for their holders (de Groot 1989, 15–17; Gibney 2014).[2] While the UN High Commissioner for Refugees (UNHCR) — the UN agency mandated to address statelessness — focuses on universal possession of nationality as an ideal to strive towards, it largely ignores the issue of *content* of nationality, the possession of which it so eagerly promotes (Kochenov 2019b, 44–45). The QNI allows for an evidence-based questioning of the underlying presumption in contemporary UNHCR policies that every nationality is by definition a solution, and that every instance of statelessness is necessarily a problem. Understanding this evidence can ultimately lead to better-informed policies that aim to protect the vulnerable, or at least to ensure that policies with charitable aims do not unwittingly intensify existing human vulnerabilities and inequalities.

Unless a state heavily discriminates among its nationals (Mantu 2015, 173–78), all holders of its passport will usually enjoy the same internal and external benefits of their status. This allows the QNI to assign a numerical value to the nationality of each state. The situation is somewhat more complex when it comes to the status of a stateless person. A stateless person's access to the internal and external benefits on which the QNI method is based depends on two main factors: the state of residence of the stateless person, and their residence status in that state. A stateless person with a stable permanent residence permit will often enjoy most of the internal benefits of the nationality of that state, but often not so many of the external ones.[3] Stateless persons whose residence is not authorized at all may still enjoy some of the internal benefits (such as peace and stability) but not all (such as the ability to develop professionally or access housing and social services), and none of the external ones. The combination of these two factors — the state of residence and the wide variety of possible residence statuses stateless persons might hold in each state — produces many more possible types of 'statelessness statuses' than there are nationalities worldwide. Indexing the quality of all statelessness statuses might therefore be a more extensive project than indexing the quality of nationalities. Considering that the legal situation of most stateless persons is not well understood or documented, this undertaking may prove altogether unfeasible.

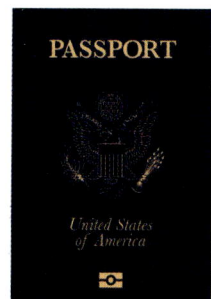

Some types of statelessness (or statelessness-like) statuses, however, can and have been indexed in the QNI already, such as the status of 'non-citizens' of Latvia, analyzed by Aleksejs Dimitrovs in this volume, or some types of UK 'nationalities', which do not offer their holders the right to reside in the UK, and the limited US nationality of American Samoa, mentioned in Gerard Prinsen's chapter. This contribution aims to reflect on peculiarities of indexing the quality of a statelessness status, as a special form of nationality status. First, I briefly discuss the current international legal and policy discourse on statelessness. Second, I consider the example of stateless holders of a German toleration permit. I conclude with a reflection on how the QNI data and method can help shape better-informed policies towards addressing vulnerabilities that result from 'non-nationality' statuses.

Statelessness under International Law

The goal of avoiding and reducing the occurrence of statelessness has a long history in international law (Donner 1994, 154, 202). Before international law was concerned with the wellbeing of vulnerable individuals, states were already trying to cooperate to prevent statelessness as much as possible without compromising their sovereign right to decide who their nationals were.[4] The idea that stateless persons required international assistance evolved alongside the idea of international assistance for refugees. Initially, international law did not draw a clear distinction between the protection needs of these two groups.[5] The first international documents for stateless refugees were the Nansen passports of 1922,

designed initially for the Russian emigrants denationalized in the context of the establishment of the Soviet Union, and later extended on a case-by-case basis to certain other categories of stateless refugees.[6] After the establishment of the UN, discussions intensified on generally applicable international structural mechanisms for protection of refugees and stateless persons, and resulted in the decision to distinguish between refugees, who had a well-founded fear of persecution, and stateless persons, who were not considered as nationals by any state (Hudson 1952; Batchelor 1995, 232–59). Thus, a stateless person may also happen to be a refugee and a refugee can also be stateless — the two labels describe distinct legal phenomena that do not necessarily go hand in hand, and international law has recognized the need for a separate legal regime for stateless persons. However, while the definition of a refugee clarifies the origin of the presumption of vulnerability of refugees based on the existence of a well-founded fear of persecution, the definition of a stateless person does not explain why statelessness is problematic. Statelessness is problematic only if one considers membership in a state to be inherently and invariably beneficial, a presumption challenged by the evidence of the QNI.

Nowadays the two main international treaties on statelessness are the 1954 Convention Relating to the Status of Stateless Persons (the 1954 Convention) and the 1961 Convention on the Reduction of Statelessness (the 1961 Convention), both of which through their content convey that their main intention is to help vulnerable stateless individuals.

The 1954 Convention focuses on the rights that stateless persons have on the territory of the states where they find themselves. The content of this Convention to a large extent mirrors that of the 1951 Convention Relating to the Status of Refugees, however without the non-refoulement principle (Bianchini 2018, 74–113), which is central to the refugee discourse. Depending on the 'level of attachment' of a stateless person to a specific state, different rights are guaranteed (UNHCR 2014a, paras 129–39). For example, the right to identity documents, the right of access to courts, and the right to primary education are guaranteed to all stateless persons on the territory of a state regardless of their residence status. Other rights, such as the right to work and the right to financial assistance, may be made conditional by state parties on stateless persons having authorized and/or habitual residence in the relevant state. Interpretations of which obligations states have vis-à-vis which stateless persons based on this Convention have been the subject of much controversy (van Waas 2008, 215–410; Bianchini 2018, 97–107). In 2014, the UNHCR issued an authoritative interpretation of the 1954 Convention in the form of the *Handbook on Protection of Stateless Persons* (UNHCR 2014a), which helped to increase the functionality of the Convention. Currently the 1954 Convention is ratified by 91 states.[7] The implementation of this Convention is difficult to assess, however, as only a handful of states are operating effective formalized procedures for determining whether an individual is stateless (European Network on Statelessness 2013; European Migration Network 2016, 5–8).

The 1961 Convention contains provisions that oblige states to prevent instances of statelessness by granting nationality to children at birth and by prohibiting loss of nationality that results in statelessness. Interestingly, the 1961 Convention also prohibits voluntary statelessness, unless it interferes with the right to leave one's own country or the right to seek asylum.[8] This Convention thus limits the freedom of individuals to escape an undesirable unbeneficial nationality without having secured an alternative nationality. This raises the question of whether the Convention can be categorized as a human rights instrument at all (Swider 2018, 160–62). Prohibition of voluntary statelessness reveals the patronizing approach of this Convention to the issue of protection of the vulnerable and a naïve understanding of what the possession of a nationality entails. This anomaly is further emphasized by the UNHCR's ambitious campaign to 'End Statelessness in 10 Years', launched in 2014, which promotes universal possession of an unspecified nationality as an attainable solution to all statelessness problems (UNHCR 2014b). The 1961 Convention has been ratified by 73 states.[9] Compliance with the norms of this Convention varies across states and continents, and has been documented and analyzed in a number of studies (Vonk, Vink, and de Groot 2013, 105; Vonk 2014, 387; Manby 2016, 1; Institute on Statelessness and Inclusion 2014, 78–94).

A major shortcoming of the current statelessness protection regime is that neither of the two main statelessness conventions nor any other human rights document guarantees a right to authorized residence for stateless persons in any specific state. Access of stateless persons to the territory of any state cannot by definition happen through the standard channels that require a travel document issued to nationals by their states. At the same time, if a state refuses to admit a stateless person to its territory, or regularize their factual residence, deportation to a country of nationality is also not an option. The UNHCR has interpreted the 1954 Convention as implicitly requiring states to regularize residence of stateless persons on their territory, noting that otherwise fulfilling other Convention obligations to stateless persons is impossible (UNHCR 2014a, 147–52). However, controversies can easily arise, in particular in a migratory context, about which state is obliged to legalize residence of which specific stateless person, thus rendering the effectiveness of the 1954 Convention uncertain.

In theory, stateless persons can hold any immigration status in their host country — as long as access to that status does not specifically require possession of a foreign nationality and the stateless individual complies with other requirements for obtaining that immigration status. Stateless persons may, for example, have a refugee status if they have been determined to have a well-founded fear of persecution, a spousal residence permit if they're a partner of a national or a resident, or a work-related permit if they're employed. They may also reside unauthorized in the country or have an in-between status, such as the German 'toleration' status discussed below. Some countries offer statelessness-specific protection and residence statuses (European Network on Statelessness 2013; European Migration Network 2016, 5–8), granted to stateless persons that fulfill the requirements for that status. This, however, does not mean that every stateless person present on the territory of a state with a statelessness determination procedure will necessarily enjoy authorized residence. Stateless persons may be excluded from the eligibility for a residence status on the basis of the 1954 Convention's exclusion clauses,[10] they may fail to comply with a range of bureaucratic requirements, choose not to apply for the status due to fear of contact with state authorities or may simply be mislabelled as non-stateless by an imperfect statelessness determination process (Bianchini 2018, 157–58; Swider 2018, 108–10).

To sum up, contemporary international legal and policy discourse on statelessness evolves around the ideal of universal possession of nationality, without dwelling on the issue of the content of different nationalities. While possession of a nationality does indeed technically eliminate the statelessness status, not every nationality status can remedy the vulnerabilities associated with statelessness (Gibney 2014). Awareness of the diversity in the quality of nationalities and how those relate to the qualities of various types of statelessness statuses is crucial for constructive rethinking of the current international legal discourse on statelessness.

Stateless Persons with a Toleration Status in Germany

Statelessness in Germany is predominantly a result of migration and refugee flows, a process often characterized by bureaucratic chaos and lack of thorough documentation. There is no clearly elaborated legal status in Germany that is given to individuals solely based on being stateless (Bianchini 2018, 242), and thus stateless persons in Germany can end up in a variety of legal situations depending on the individual circumstances of each person, ranging from undocumented unauthorized residence to stable permanent residence, obtained in the context of refugee claims or an application for any other migratory status.

According to the UNHCR statistics, there were 13,458 stateless persons living in Germany in 2017 (UNHCR n.d.). That number, however, may be higher as cases of statelessness can easily go unidentified due to lack of dedicated procedures for identifying statelessness in Germany (Marambio 2016; Institute on Statelessness and Inclusion and European Network on Statelessness 2017). In 2014, Germany issued 2,319 travel documents to stateless persons, and 1,939 stateless persons were granted refugee protection in 2015 (Marambio 2016; Institute on Statelessness and Inclusion and European Network on Statelessness 2017).

Stateless persons in Germany who do not have a residence permit but whose removal to another state proves impossible for any reason may qualify for the so-called 'toleration' (*Duldung*) status. A person with toleration status is technically not permitted to stay in Germany, and the obligation to leave Germany continues to apply. Toleration status is intended as a temporary measure, for example in cases where deportation attempts have been suspended, but in practice may become a long-term legal situation for individuals who do not fulfill the requirements for an actual residence permit but continue to remain in Germany. This legal status is highly precarious, as toleration permits expire every few months and need to be extended (Bianchini 2018, 243–44, fn. 43). Persons with toleration status have access to some social benefits and limited access to the labor market (Bianchini 2018, 192). The new Integration Act of 2016 expanded the possibilities of persons with toleration status to access education and vocational training and provided for some support for integration into the labor market (Bianchini 2018, 243).[11] Obtaining a stateless person's travel document while holding toleration status is not trivial, as Germany requires stateless persons to be lawfully residing in the country in order to qualify for such a document, and holding toleration status is not considered as a form of lawful residence (Bianchini 2018, 250).

In terms of QNI criteria, the status of a stateless person who finds him- or herself holding toleration status in Germany is undoubtedly of a significantly lower quality than the status of a German national, which is ranked 2nd in the QNI. It is also not as good as any status that permits residence in Germany on a short-term or long-term basis, for example a refugee status or that conferred by a working visa, for which some stateless persons in Germany may qualify depending on their specific individual circumstances. Toleration status is interesting to explore as it offers its holders slightly better opportunities than outright undocumented residence in Germany. In terms of the external criteria of QNI ranking, the toleration status does not entitle its holders to even a travel document — thus, travel or settlement freedom abroad is out of reach entirely. In terms of internal factors, toleration status holders fully benefit from the peace and stability of Germany, but only partially benefit from the economic strength of Germany (as their access to the labor market is restricted), and also only partially from the opportunities for human development (as financial support for education, for example, is limited). It is difficult to assign exact percentages for the extent to which stateless persons with toleration status benefit from the internal welfare in Germany. Indicators such as clean air do not discriminate based on a person's legal status; they are available to everyone present within the state. Similarly, access to education for children and to basic medical care is often widely accessible for everyone. Other indicators, such as an ability to develop professionally and pursue economic ambitions, are structurally discriminatory and unequally accessible to individuals with varying legal statuses. In comparison to the quality of the status of German nationals or quality of the status of foreigners in Germany with authorized residence, the toleration status appears rather unappealing. This, however, is not the only relevant comparative frame. The QNI's methodology allows us to compare the situation of statelessness under the toleration status in Germany to other nationality and statelessness statuses globally. It is undoubtedly true that German nationality is objectively more valuable than the status of statelessness with a toleration permit in Germany. However, is a nationality with a Very Low Quality in the QNI necessarily also objectively better than the status of statelessness with a toleration permit in Germany? Restricted access to top-quality emergency medical care may be more valuable than fully unrestricted access to a barely functional healthcare system. Similarly, full unrestricted access to the labor market of a state with high unemployment rates may be less valuable than a restricted access to Germany's labor market.

It is interesting to compare the case of the stateless German toleration-holders to the very different context of statelessness, that of 'non-citizens' of Latvia, discussed in this volume in the chapter by Aleksejs Dimitrovs. The rights of 'non-citizens' in Latvia are more limited than those of Latvian citizens: the political participation rights of 'non-citizens' are heavily restricted, as is their access to certain types of jobs in the public sector and some property rights related to purchasing land. However, the set of rights to which one is entitled through the status of a 'non-citizen' goes well beyond the minimum requirements of the

1954 Convention, and includes the right to reside permanently in Latvia, to access most state welfare services related to housing, healthcare, education and unemployment benefits, to engage in most economic activities, and so on. In terms of access to other countries, 'non-citizens' of Latvia hold a widely recognized travel document. Their Weight of Travel Freedom (4.13%) is significantly lower than that enjoyed by Latvian citizens (14.09%), citizens of the Russian Federation (8.94%), and Kazakhstani citizens (5.76%). There is thus undisputable discriminatory treatment of 'non-citizens' as compared to citizens, but the human rights situation of the former can hardly be described as "a life without dignity and security" (Türk 2014, 1), as is portrayed in the UNHCR's description of a life without a nationality.

The UNHCR and civil society organizations advocate for access to Latvian citizenship (UNHCR 2010, 5–7; Djackova 2015). Latvian citizenship is, according to the QNI's measurement system, more valuable than the status of a 'non-citizen'. However, the status of a 'non-citizen' is not atrociously bad, either. Depending on the individual circumstances of an affected person — for example, if such a person has no significant travel ambitions and does not aspire the careers that are out of reach to 'non-citizens' — Latvian citizenship might be *subjectively* not as valuable. The wide range of rights that Latvian 'non-citizens' enjoy in Latvia has been found to be a factor in the disinterest among 'non-citizens' to naturalize (Krūma 2013, 408). Indeed, if 'non-citizens' were unable to work, travel, own any property, or access basic human rights in Latvia without becoming citizens, the motivation to obtain citizenship would be higher for many.

Thus, the cases of stateless persons in Germany holding toleration status and of Latvian 'non-citizens', while significantly different from each other in terms of the legal positions of their respective stateless populations in their host countries, both pose challenges to the UNHCR's abstract aspiration to a universal possession of nationality. For both these stateless populations — and, arguably, for any stateless person anywhere — the issue of the elimination of their statelessness status is outweighed by the importance of a number of much more specific questions relating to the subjective and objective value of their statelessness status and the value of any alternative nationality status that may be accessible to them.

Conclusion

The QNI documents the regrettable reality of the 'birthright lottery' whereby individuals are born into nationalities that offer them a very divergent set of opportunities to flourish. The QNI is controversial on several levels. It discusses the uncomfortable truth that nationalities are objectively unequal in value but does not offer a solution to this problem or suggest how nationalities can work towards equality. Even though its creators explicitly state that the inequality of nationalities is something they "do not endorse, but rather observe", conducting purely descriptive research on such fundamental global inequalities without engaging deeply with the normative and prescriptive analysis of the situation may come across as human rights blasphemy. Such research, however, can be empowering to individuals and to agencies that aim to assist vulnerable individuals. It offers a basis for better-informed choices on how to mobilize public and personal resources to harness the opportunities and overcome challenges that result from holding certain nationalities until more structural solutions that deal with global inequalities become available.

This chapter explored the possibility of assigning a Quality of Nationality value to statuses of statelessness in accordance with the QNI methodology. Generally, stateless persons rarely enjoy the external benefits of a nationality, the Latvian 'non-citizens' being a rare exception in this regard. However, stateless persons have varying degrees of access to internal benefits of the states in which they live, depending on their state of habitual residence and their (il)legal residence status in that state. In certain instances, statelessness may be objectively or subjectively more valuable to a specific individual than the alternative of an unwanted nationality (Kochenov 2019b; Bloom 2017, 153–72; Swider 2017; Hanjian 2003). Incorporating awareness of the objective value of nationalities as well as statelessness statuses could help agencies such as the UNHCR to develop policies better equipped to empower vulnerable individuals to improve the quality of their own lives.

40 Citizenship-by-Investment (*Ius Doni*)

By Christian H. Kälin

The concept of citizenship has evolved considerably through the ages. Indeed, it related first to membership in a family, later on in a tribe, and then a city, and currently it's a state (Baker 1928). It should therefore come as no surprise that some authors see "the world as the unit and citizenship in the world-state" (Baker 1928, 124) as the next logical step. While the ideas of a world without borders and universal citizenship (Schneider 2000) go beyond the scope of this work, acquisition and quality of citizenship are nevertheless its focus.

Birth-Based Membership

Citizenship laws reinforce birth-based membership, "advantaging those who have access to the inherited privilege of membership, while disadvantaging those who do not" (Shachar 2013, 145). In particular, citizenship is most often connected with a person's birth (Palandt 2012, 140 et seq.) — either based on the citizenship of the parents (*ius sanguinis* or citizenship by descent) or birthplace (*ius soli*, citizenship by birth or 'birthright citizenship') — Aleinikoff and Klusmeyer 2002 — and in a smaller number of cases, it is derived through naturalization, which represents "acquisition after birth of a citizenship not previously held by the person concerned that requires an application to public authorities and a decision by these" (a definition borrowed from Bauböck and Goodman 2011). Most states base their citizenship laws on a combination of both *ius soli* and *ius sanguinis*; naturalized citizens are usually in the minority among citizens of the state. Both *ius soli* and *ius sanguinis* modes of birth-based membership are the expression of a membership entitlement resulting merely from one's place of birth or generational transfer rather than from any special achievements or allegiances of the individual.

The birth-based membership put into effect by *ius soli* and *ius sanguinis* is rather a bounded membership based on presumption that affiliated members share a sense of common good (Dumbrava 2018). Yet, as rightly pointed out by Kochenov, "[c]itizenship, as a legal status of attachment to public authority, is always distributed uniquely by the authority itself [and] does not depend on any sentiments and feeling of the citizenry" (Kochenov 2017c, 39). Identifying yourself as an American does not make you one (Kochenov 2017c, 39). Being (even accidentally) born on American soil, notwithstanding your feelings, does.

Citizenship and Inequalities

The sad truth is that the citizenships of different states are not equal in terms of their practical value, to which the QNI rankings testify. Yet the legal debate in this respect largely focuses on sovereignty of states and their discretion in the field of citizenship matters. To agree with Kingsbury, there is a certain relationship "of mutual containment" (Kingsbury 1998, 602) between sovereignty and inequality: "[t]he system of sovereignty at least notionally precludes some forms of inequality, while helping to exclude other forms of inequality from real consideration" (Kingsbury 1998, 602). The concept of state sovereignty allows questions in citizenship matters to be treated as the responsibility of states. Thus, "the question of which state would guarantee membership to a particular individual has been seen as largely irrelevant" (Shachar 2009, 8) from the point of view of international law. The issue of inequality has also been left to international law (Kingsbury 1998), which has been primarily concerned, however, with the problem of statelessness. Being a citizen of any state is viewed as more desirable than not enjoying state protection at all (Shachar 2009, 9). However, attempts to resolve the issue of statelessness focus "only on formal equality of status" (Shachar 2009, 9) and not on "rectifying inequalities that correlate with the birthright assignment of membership in 'this or that' particular country" (Shachar 2009, 9).

Yet our nationality has an enormous impact on our life — on our personal and professional development, on the variety and quality of places we visit in our lifetimes, and on the quality of our education, the healthcare we receive, and the air we breathe, to mention only a few aspects where nationality may hugely influence the way we live our lives. The borders within which one happens to be born, and the documents to which one is entitled, are no less arbitrary than other characteristics, such as skin color, gender, or the genetic makeup with which one is endowed (Benhabib 2002, 94–95; Carens 2000; Kochenov 2017c; Paskalev 2018; Shachar 2009). A child born in Laredo, Texas, is able to avail him- or herself of all of the social and economic benefits of the American welfare state as an American citizen and as such can seek employment opportunities throughout the US and enjoy visa-free travel to a wide range of destinations around the world.[1] A child born in the adjacent town of Juarez, Mexico, has significantly fewer choices.[2] Through no acts of their own, the two children will have very different life prospects simply because of their places of birth (Sandel 2010, 230). Allocation of citizenship thus amounts to a 'birthright lottery', to use Shachar's memorable phrase, and "[b]irthright citizenship does more than define the formal boundaries of membership (...) [it] closely correspond[s] to strikingly different prospects for the well-being, security, and freedom of individuals" (Shachar 2009, 8).

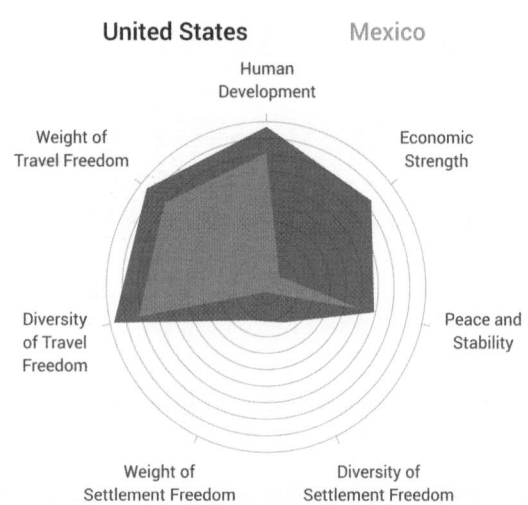

Ius Doni

Since ancient times, states have used their citizenships as sought-after 'goods', using them to reward soldiers and attract talent and investors. Ethnic considerations, ideology, similar histories and languages, special status, or special merit and achievements frequently drive policies in immigration and citizenship law and make some of the grounds on which facilitated naturalization is often allowed. One of the latest trends in the allocation of citizenship is through investment, or *ius doni*.[3] It is difficult if not impossible to imagine that citizenship-by-investment (CBI) programs would flourish in the absence of global disparities and the unequal practical values of citizenship across states. Indeed, the emergence of *ius doni* and the rapid growth of CBI programs and residence-by-investment (RBI) programs aimed at attracting foreign investors can be seen as a result of the discretionary powers of states in the field of immigration and citizenship law on the one hand and a counterbalance to the conservative and exclusionary character of citizenship and opposition to global inequality of citizenship on the other. States have a large amount of discretion in determining who their residents and citizens are and thereby control transnational migration, promote labor market policy requirements, or encourage direct investments and increase direct capital inflows. Furthermore, a new class of 'global citizens' has emerged, and it comprises individuals who have multiple homes and bases, and for whom holding multiple citizenships is the norm (Henley & Partners 2017). Indeed, with their increased mobility and transnational lives, having multiple ties in different countries and even on different continents has become far more commonplace for global citizens. Having multiple social identities and feeling a sense of belonging to more than one state is no longer controversial (Risse 2010, 39).

The acquisition of citizenship through CBI programs is one example of facilitated naturalization based on an applicant's exceptional contribution to a country's economy. Other examples include, for instance, the naturalization of famous artists and sportspeople and the preferential naturalization of foreigners who are considered to have special ties to a state. Residence, language, and test requirements are usually waived in cases of facilitated naturalization. Thus, unlike other immigrants who have to reside in and learn the language of their new countries to some extent, talented footballers and wealthy investors can jump the queue and acquire citizenship relatively quickly, often without residing in the country and learning its language. Such privileged access to citizenship results from a state's interest in naturalizing certain categories of citizens rather than from the latter's keenness to live in or socially integrate into the countries for which they have acquired citizenship. Preferential treatment of such candidates has been possible because of states having wide-ranging discretion in citizenship matters.

While granting citizenship in return for economic contributions took place even in antiquity (Kälin 2019a, 44 et seq.), the first modern CBI program, that of Saint Kitts and Nevis, was introduced in 1984, and the industry has grown through the introduction of similar programs in other countries in more recent years (Kälin 2019a, 186 et seq.). Today, the immigration and citizenship laws of over 100 countries provide for residence or citizenship on the basis of a significant economic contribution. Residence programs secure the investor's residence in the state in which the program is implemented and, after a somewhat lengthy period of time, a citizenship of the host state. CBI options are formulated differently in different states. The majority of states hosting CBI programs require, in adherence to their relevant legal standards, that the monetary inflow is in their domestic (national) interest, without, however, specifically defining this interest. Many programs have poorly defined goals, while others struggle to demonstrate a meaningful economic benefit (Sumption and Hooper 2014, 3). The investment or donation requirements differ from state to state and largely depend on the attractiveness of the host country and on the quality of the passport it has to offer the potential investor.

The QNI offers a solid assessment platform for assessing the general attractiveness of nationalities, taking into account a number of internal and external factors to determine the objective value and rank of each citizenship, such as data on human development, economic strength, and peace and stability and the diversity and quality of unrestricted travel and settlement destinations allowed for by the nationality in question.[4]

Nationalities of Citizenship-by-Investment Countries

Eleven countries were running formal CBI programs in 2018: Antigua and Barbuda, the Commonwealth of Dominica, Cyprus, Grenada, Jordan, Saint Kitts and Nevis, Saint Lucia, Malta, Moldova, Turkey, and Vanuatu. These are countries that have standardized requirements and procedures rather than vaguely defined criteria of 'exceptional contribution' or 'special interest' in their legislations, such as is the case in Austria, Cambodia, Cape Verde, and many others.

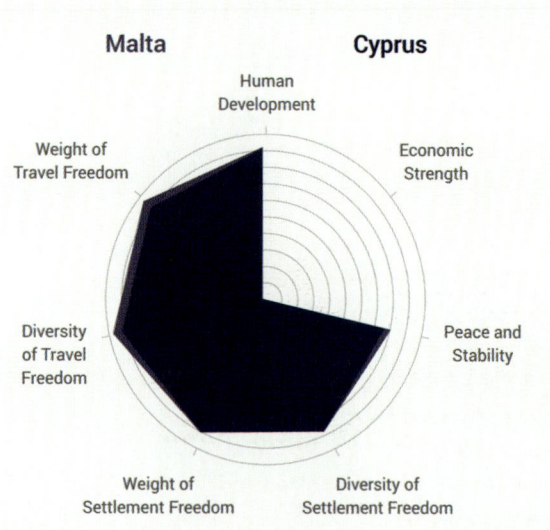

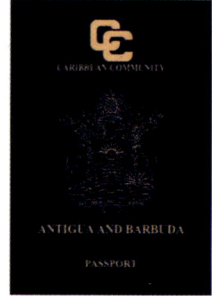

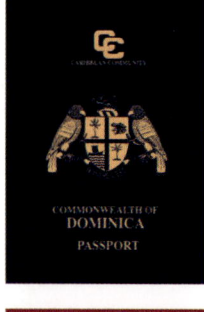

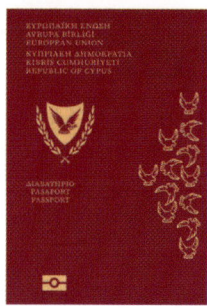

Including Turkey, there were four citizenship programs in Europe in 2018, and Montenegro is expected to begin receiving applications for its program by the end of 2019. Two of the European countries (Cyprus and Malta) are EU Member States and hence confer EU citizenship along with sovereign nation citizenship. EU nationalities are either ranked in the Very High Quality or High Quality tiers of the QNI General Ranking. This is no surprise, as EU citizenship is exceptionally strong: it gives the right of free movement and settlement in one of the world's wealthiest regions and largest economic areas, home to over 500 million people. In 2018, the nationalities of Cyprus and Malta belonged in the Very High Quality tier. Maltese nationality ranked 16th in the QNI General Ranking with 77.6%, increasing in value slightly compared to the previous year (76.9%) and improving its ranking position (23rd in 2017). Cypriot nationality achieved almost the same value as in the previous year (75.3% in 2018 compared to 75.4% in 2017) but ranked better in 2018 in 21st place (25th in 2017). Citizens of both countries could settle and work visa-free in the same number of countries or territories (41), therefore Cypriot and Maltese nationalities shared 7th position in the Settlement Freedom Ranking with 11 other nationalities, achieving 89.5%. Maltese nationality is better positioned in the Travel Freedom Ranking, in 14th place with 95.3%, than Cypriot nationality, which is ranked 26th with 89.6%. Given their Very High Quality nationality and access to the rest of the EU, these two countries also have higher requirements than other countries offering CBI. Cyprus requires investors to donate EUR 75,000 to the Research and Innovation Fund or another certified innovation enterprise, donate EUR 75,000 to the Cyprus Land Development Corporation, and select from committing at least EUR 2 million to the purchase or construction of real estate, the purchase or creation of or participation in businesses or companies that are based and operating in Cyprus, or to participate in alternative investment funds or to purchase financial assets of Cypriot enterprises or organizations licensed by the Securities and Exchange Commission, or a combination of the latter three options. Malta requires a non-refundable contribution to its National Development and Social Fund of at least EUR 650,000 plus participation in approved financial instruments of EUR 150,000 and the purchase of residential real estate with a minimum value of EUR 350,000 or the lease of a residential property with a rental value of at least EUR 16,000 per annum, which must be held for at least five years.[5]

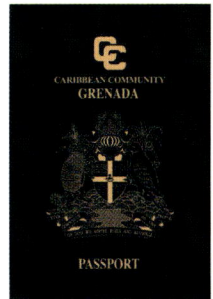

The nationalities of the five Caribbean countries with CBI programs also ranked well in the 2018 QNI General Ranking. All of them fall within the group of Medium Quality nationalities. The nationality of Antigua and Barbuda was the best among the five in 2018, scoring 47.7% and ranking 45th. Slightly weaker was the nationality of Saint Kitts and Nevis, which ranked 46th in 2018 with 47.5%. The Grenadian nationality ranked 52nd with 45.7%, the Saint Lucian nationality was 54th with 45.5%, while the nationality of the Commonwealth of Dominica ranked 57th with 43.9%.

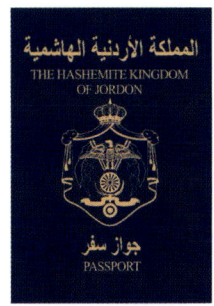

All Caribbean countries are part of the Organisation of Eastern Caribbean States (OECS), which provides mutual freedom of settlement, and of the Caribbean Community (CARICOM), which provides conditional mutual freedom of settlement. They therefore also performed well in the Settlement Freedom Ranking. The Antiguan nationality was again most successful, taking the 25th position with 16.2%, while the nationalities of the remaining four countries shared the 29th position, each with 14.2%. The main advantage of the Antiguan nationality is that it grants free settlement in Georgia, which the other four Caribbean nationalities do not. All five Caribbean nationalities provided a relatively high degree of visa-free or visa-on-arrival travel to their nationals, including to Europe's Schengen Area countries. The nationality of Saint Kitts and Nevis performed best in this respect, occupying 41st place in the Travel Freedom Ranking with

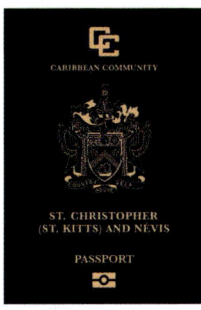

78.2%. It was followed by the Antiguan nationality in 43rd position with 76.9%, the Saint Lucian nationality in 51st position with 73%, the Grenadian nationality in 53rd position with 72.5%, and the nationality of the Commonwealth of Dominica in 58th position with 69.4%.

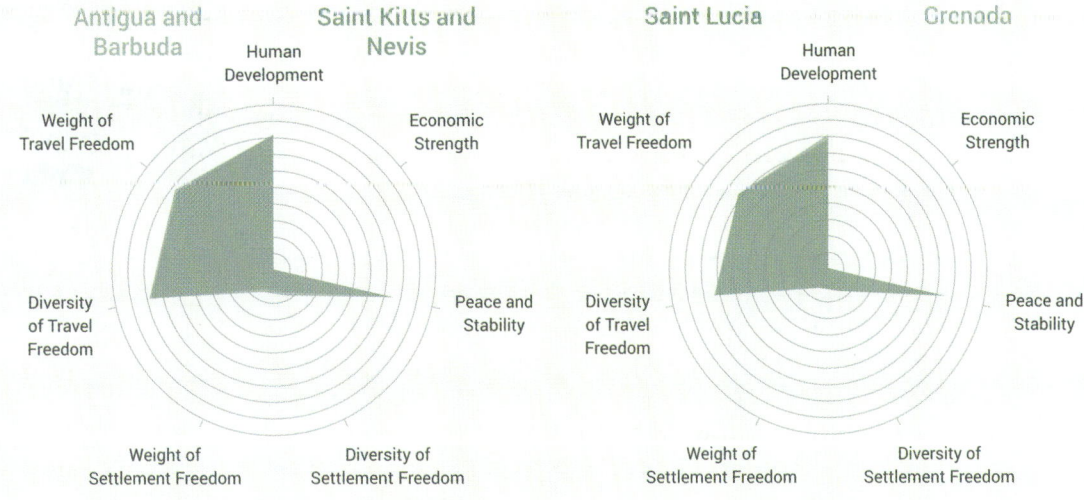

A Caribbean passport can be acquired through making contributions to national development funds or national treasuries (ranging from USD 100,000 to USD 250,000 for a single applicant and more if dependents are included) or through real estate acquisition (starting at USD 200,000), and is thus one of the best options in the world in terms of 'value for money'. Furthermore, the socio-economic benefits that CBI programs brought to these countries are clearly evident. Let us take the examples of the two Caribbean countries with the most successful nationalities: Antigua and Barbuda, and Saint Kitts and Nevis.

Inflows from the Antigua and Barbuda Citizenship-by-Investment Program — created in 2013 — now constitute approximately 15% of the government's annual revenue and are responsible for substantial investments in the construction sector, as well as for the dual-island nation's transition to renewable energy, funding thousands of the electricity-producing solar panels installed on government buildings and land throughout the twin islands. The Antigua and Barbuda Citizenship-by-Investment Program is also essential in generating sovereign equity, which has supported the efforts to rebuild Barbuda after a recent tropical storm devastated the island and forced the evacuation of the entire population. When the International Monetary Fund (IMF) conducted a review of the Antigua and Barbuda economy, it found that the revenue generated by investment migration had significantly boosted public- and private-sector construction, encouraging economic growth and pulling the country out of a deep recession. Furthermore, Antigua and Barbuda was able to pay back its entire debt to the IMF thanks to the income generated by the Antigua and Barbuda Citizenship-by-Investment Program (Henley & Partners 2019; Kälin 2019b).

The Saint Kitts and Nevis Citizenship-by-Investment Program underwent substantial reform in 2007 (Kälin 2019a, 186 et seq.). A non-refundable contribution to the Sugar Industry Diversification Foundation (SIDF) of Saint Kitts and Nevis was required to support the grant of citizenship under pre-determined minimum investment criteria. The SIDF has seen a significant increase in deposits and assets, particularly in the years leading up to 2015, according to the last available data from the IMF (International Monetary Fund 2016). According to the IMF, at the end of 2015 Saint Kitts and Nevis' national development fund had accumulated assets equivalent to 20% of GDP from CBI-related inflows (International Monetary Fund 2016, 42). The CBI budgetary revenues were expected to decline in the following years due to higher levels of competition in the CBI industry worldwide (IMF Country Report 2016, 42) but, interestingly, this was not the case.

The nationalities of the remaining four countries with CBI programs (Jordan, Moldova, Turkey, and Vanuatu) are of different quality. Ranked 73rd with 38.6%, the Moldovan nationality is of Medium Quality, as are the nationalities of Turkey (76th position with 37.7%) and Vanuatu (78th with 37.1%). The nationality of Jordan is of Low Quality, ranking 121st with 26.8%. Not being part of any international or supra-national organization or agreements facilitating the free movement of people, none of these four countries can offer impressive settlement rights to their citizens beyond their borders. Therefore, their nationalities are lower in the Settlement Freedom Ranking. The Moldovan nationality, offering free settlement access to two destinations, is ranked 45th with 4.1%, while the remaining three nationalities of Vanuatu (49th with 2.1%), Turkey (50th with 2.0%), and Jordan (51st with 1.9%) each offer free settlement access to one destination only.

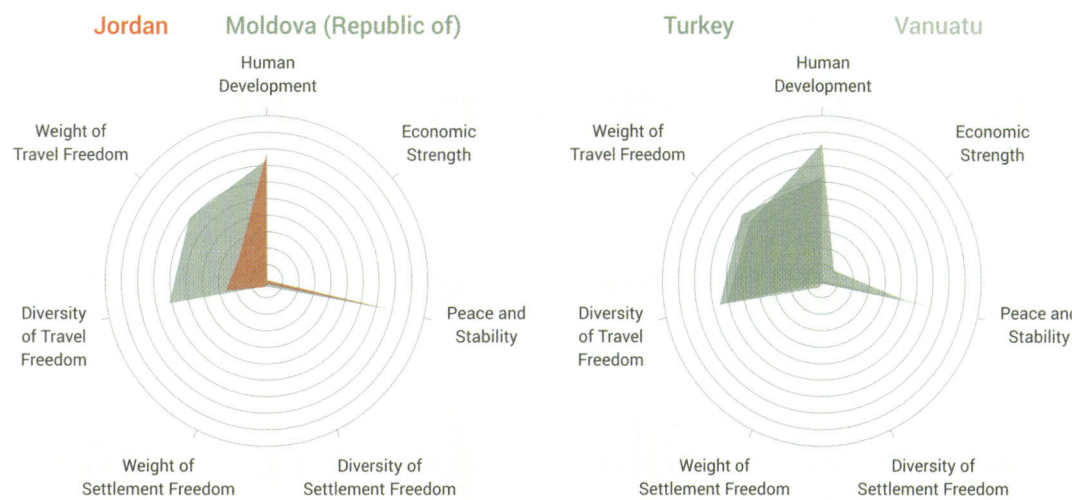

Although it is ranked higher than Jordan, Turkey, and Vanuatu, the Moldovan nationality is also the most affordable of the four, with a required minimum contribution to its Public Investment Fund of USD 100,000 for a single applicant, more if dependents are included. The minimum investment

for acquiring Vanuatu citizenship is USD 150,000 for a single applicant, more if dependents are included. Despite the substantial reduction of the required minimum investment, the Turkish nationality still requires a higher investment than Moldova and Vanuatu, with the minimum investment for real estate being USD 250,000. Jordanian nationality can be acquired through several investment options, but at USD 1 million the minimum investment threshold is set rather high.

Lastly, Montenegro launched its CBI program in October 2019. Montenegrin citizenship will be available to investors who donate at least EUR 100,000 (approximately USD 113,400) and either invest a minimum of EUR 250,000 (approximately USD 283,500) in an undeveloped area of Montenegro or a minimum of EUR 450,000 (approximately USD 510,300) in a developed area of Montenegro. Ranked 64th

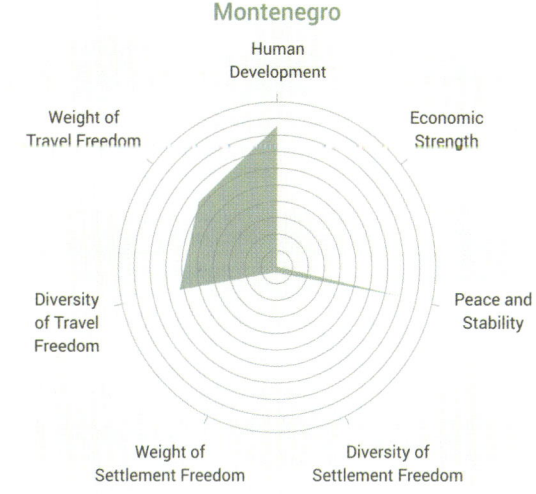

with 40.9% in the QNI General Ranking in 2018, Montenegrin citizenship is of Medium Quality. While this nationality currently offers free settlement to only two destinations and is ranked 44th with 4.1% in the Settlement Freedom Ranking, its value is likely to increase steadily in the future as the country progresses towards EU membership.

Arguments against Citizenship-by-Investment

Socio-economic benefits aside (Surak 2016), acquiring citizenship by means of investment or *ius doni* is often criticized. Strangely, the loudest criticism comes from the EU, which has achieved the most significant break with the tradition of excluding, discriminating against, and segregating different population groups based on their nationalities, hence coming closest to 're-nationalization' if not 'de-nationalization' of the concept of citizenship (Kochenov 2017c).

Notwithstanding this, EU institutions, notably the European Commission and the European Parliament, often express their dissatisfaction with the acquisition of citizenship through investment in general and acquisition of citizenship via the existing CBI programs in particular. Indeed, from complicating the launch of the Malta Individual Investor Program based on (unfounded) claims that "[i]n compliance with the criterion used under public international law, Member States should only award citizenship to persons where there is a 'genuine link' or 'genuine connection' to the country in question" (Reding 2014) to stating concerns that obtaining citizenship through investment schemes "undermines the very concept of European citizenship" (European Parliament 2014, point G) both the European Commission and the European Parliament misrepresented the law and undermined the achievements of the EU. The genuine link is not a requirement in international law but has been engaged merely to resolve diplomatic protection issues in the international arena in cases of multiple citizenship (Spiro 2019b; Sloane 2009, 13; Kälin 2019a; Gauci and Aquilina 2017). Furthermore, the very existence of EU citizenship essentially presupposes rights beyond the Member State conferring the citizenship rather than limiting it to the conferring state's territory. In practice, EU citizenship weakens ties with a Member State, as otherwise the Internal Market would be undermined. The Internal Market and EU citizenship are a success when any considerations of correlation between the citizenship of a Member State (namely, strong ties — or genuine links — with a member state of citizenship) and EU citizenship rights are removed. Article 18 of the Treaty on the Functioning of the European Union (TFEU) established the principle of non-discrimination on the basis of citizenship, which expressly prohibits the Member States from taking into account any ties of EU citizens with their Member States of citizenship or residence. Residence or the exercise of any other rights of EU citizens in any Member State is not conditional on any cultural, linguistic, or other considerations stemming directly from Part II TFEU provisions and are not subject to any restrictions. In fact, EU equality rules, when applied to EU citizens, also cover those who do not have any cultural links with a Member State.[6]

Most recently, the European Commission repeated and deepened the 'genuine link' misinterpretation. It first acknowledged that

> the 'bond of nationality' is traditionally based either on a genuine connection with the people of the country (by descent, origin or marriage) or on a genuine connection with the country, established either by birth in the country or by effective prior residence in the country for a meaningful duration (European Commission 2019, 5).

It then concluded that such an understanding of the bond of nationality "also lies at the basis of Member States' acceptance that Union citizenship and the rights entailed by it under the Treaty on the Functioning of the European Union (TFEU) would accrue automatically to any person becoming one of their citizens" (European Commission 2019, 5). According to the Commission, acquiring citizenship through investment therefore departs from the traditional ways of granting nationality in the Member States and affects EU citizenship (European Commission 2019, 6).

 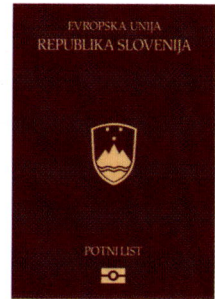

Once again, the European Commission could not be more wrong. While *ius soli* and *ius sanguinis* are indeed traditional forms of granting citizenship, *ius doni* equally has its roots in antiquity (Kälin 2019a, 44 et seq.; Kamen 2013, 79; Osborne 1983, 147 et seq.). Furthermore, while Cyprus and Malta have typical CBI programs (while Bulgaria, which has been also mentioned by the Commission in the report, does not), several others have CBI provisions in their laws, including Austria, France, Italy, and Slovenia, and 20 Member States have residence programs based on investment which, according to the Commission, bear similar risk. Acquisition of citizenship through investment is therefore not as atypical as it is represented by the European Commission. Furthermore, the EU has diminished legal relevance of Member-State nationalities in many areas where EU law applies, led by the principle of non-discrimination on the basis of nationality (Kochenov 2017c), or as put by Joppke, EU citizenship "liberat[ed] the individual from the suffocating grip of nation-states and tam[ed] the latter's demonic potentials that, after all, had forced the idea of 'Europe' back to life after 1945" (Joppke 2018, 13). To claim the opposite makes little sense, as is unfortunately the case with the Commission's reasoning. In particular, while recognizing the *Micheletti* ruling and the fact that EU law prohibits checking of genuine links as well as the right of sovereign countries to

decide on their own naturalization procedures, the Commission concluded that Member States must ensure that genuine links exist. Such a conclusion does not follow but is opposite to the Court's judgment in *Micheletti* (Kochenov 2019c).[7] Furthermore, while noting that "[t]hree Member States operate investor citizenship schemes, where citizenship is granted under less stringent conditions than under ordinary naturalisation regimes, in particular without effective prior residence in the country concerned", the Commission did not seem concerned enough to deal with other ways of facilitated naturalization that do not require residence either. These methods of acquiring citizenship, unlike CBI, represent a large percentage of all naturalizations in Member States. EU citizenships based on investment account for less than 1% of all EU naturalizations (Kochenov 2019c).[8] Other ways of naturalization are therefore likely to be a lot more harmful than acquiring citizenship through investing in states' economies. Furthermore, while every admission to citizenship may be seen as a potential security threat, CBI by no means represents a greater risk than other ways of acquiring citizenship. The residence requirement that the Commission is so insistent on would not lower the risk either — quite the contrary. As rightly noted by Kochenov, many security threats in the EU were caused by first- or second-generation EU citizens rather than by millionaires who 'bought their way' into countries. Indeed, "as long as Maltese billionaires do not stab people at Christmas markets or ram vans into crowds the assumption entertained by the Commission rests unproven" (Kochenov 2019c).

Contrary to the recent views of the Commission, new methods of inclusion are necessary in the contemporary climate of citizenship, and *ius doni*, while certainly not solving global inequalities created by birthright assignment of membership, is an important step forward towards inclusion and further growth of citizenship, as well as towards supporting economies by creating sovereign equity rather than by increasing sovereign debt (Kälin 2019b; Henley & Partners 2019). It is, furthermore, an important "step in the demystification of states and empowerment of individuals" (Joppke 2018, 18). To agree with Joppke, states "have always been strategists in matters of citizenship" (Joppke 2018, 18); however, "[t]he novelty is to see individuals as citizenship strategists" (Joppke 2018, 18). The attempts to advance people's choices regarding how and where to live their lives, as opposed to being bound by the citizenship they are allocated at birth, should be further enhanced rather than supressed.

41 Twenty-Four Shades of Sovereignty and Nationalities in the Pacific Region

By Gerard Prinsen

Introduction

Determining which countries and territories are part of the Pacific region can be a matter of debate, because it is arguably the world's largest region in terms of surface area — occupying about half the globe and encompassing 11 time zones — with rather fluid, or surprising, boundaries. European countries such as France and the UK, at first glance, do not seem to be part of the region, yet the UK is present in the Pacific in the form of the Pitcairn Islands, a British Overseas

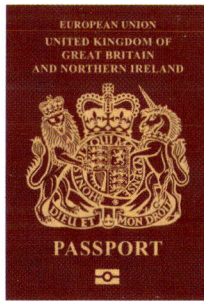
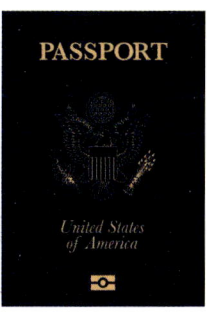
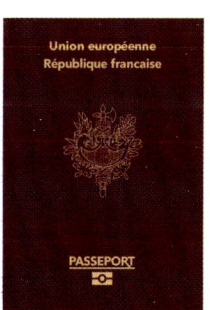

Territory whose Exclusive Economic Zone (EEZ) of 836,000 square kilometers is larger than that of the UK proper. Similarly, three territories in the Pacific are French and their EEZ of nearly seven million square kilometers represents just over half of France's EEZ. The US, on the other hand, would appear to be a Pacific country. Its 50th state, Hawaii, is positioned in the middle of the Pacific Ocean; one inhabited Pacific island territory, American Samoa, is legally classified as an 'unincorporated territory' of the US and another, Guam, as an 'unincorporated organized territory'; and the people of Northern Mariana Islands live in a 'Commonwealth of the United States'. In addition, three Pacific island countries with 'flag independence' and seats in the UN

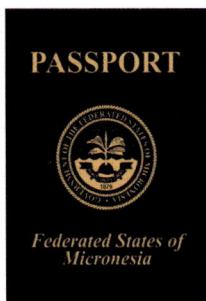  

General Assembly (Bonilla 2015, xiii), the Federated States of Micronesia, the Marshall Islands, and Palau, hold unique Compacts of Free Association with the US. These compacts, among other matters, give the US Navy not only unfettered access to the three countries' territory but also the authority to "deny such access by military forces and personnel of other nations" (US Department of State 2012). Moreover, the US holds legal sway over seven uninhabited Pacific island territories known as 'unincorporated unorganized territories' and controls another uninhabited island as an 'incorporated unorganized territory'. And yet the US does not seem to see itself as a Pacific country; it is not a member of several multi-lateral Pacific bodies, and the US Congress seems to need foreign affairs policies such as the 'Pacific Pivot' to remind itself of its Pacific presence (Manyin, Daggett, Dolven, Lawrence, Martin, O'Rourke, and Vaughn 2012).

Nonetheless, if we concentrate on countries and territories that are entirely located within the Pacific Ocean and have their political and cultural focus predominantly on the Pacific, then the most appropriate list would be the 24 members of the Pacific Islands Forum, the region's pre-eminent intergovernmental body. The US is not a member. The 24 members have a combined population of about 42 million, of which 24 million live in Australia. This leaves most of the remaining 23 members as small or microstates by standards of population. In fact, a majority have populations of fewer than 300,000, some counting no more than a few thousand citizens (Table 1). However, it is worth noting that there are two distinct perspectives on the Pacific. One looks from the outside in and sees small islands in a huge ocean. The other, in contrast, looks from the inside out and sees a sea of many islands connected through migration and kinship (Hau'ofa 1993).

One feature of Pacific nationalities is that they form an array of what Overton, Murray, Prinsen, Avataeao, Ulu, and Wrighton described as "models of semi-autonomy and other sovereignty arrangements ... unique to the world" (Overton et al. 2018, 20). These diverse sovereignty arrangements affect the quality of nationalities. The rather elaborate example in the opening paragraph, of Pacific islands associated with the US, is not a facetious exercise; it is actually a succinct illustration of the many forms sovereignty takes in the Pacific. To begin this contribution, we discuss these various shades of sovereignty and the continuous negotiations over the rights and benefits of the nationalities of several island countries and territories. Next, we look at the consequences of these variations for ranking the nationalities of Pacific countries and territories in the Quality of Nationality Index. Diving yet deeper into Pacific realities, the third section reflects on two factors that particularly affect Settlement Freedom in the Pacific: the non-reciprocity of settlement agreements and the ownership of land. In closing, this contribution looks at potential regional developments that may affect the quality of some Pacific nationalities.

The Shades of Sovereignty and Nationality in the Pacific

When endeavoring to rank the quality of nationalities in the Pacific two challenges emerge. First, there is no clear line dividing Pacific islands into states — defined as 'sovereign territorial entities' earlier in this publication — and non-sovereign territories. Instead, the Pacific region's islands are better understood when placed on a continuum, with sovereign states on one end of the scale and islands integrated into territorial structures of metropolitan centers thousands of miles away on the other. Examples of sovereign states are Fiji, Papua New Guinea, and Tonga. Examples of

  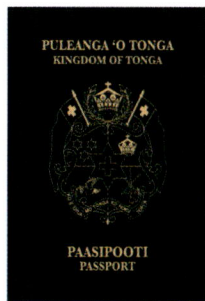

Pacific islands whose nationalities are taken from far-away metropoles are Hawaii (from the US), New Caledonia (from France), and Rapa Nui (from Chile). In between these extreme opposite ends lie islands that have diverse constitutional and legal arrangements that continue to tie them to their former colonial metropoles: France, New Zealand, and the US. These various and diverse 'sub-national island jurisdictions' are not only a defining feature of the Pacific but also have a universal relevance in the global phenomenon of offshoring (Baldacchino 2010).

As a consequence, an assessment of the quality of the nationalities of half of the 24 members of the Pacific Islands Forum is either not possible or needs to be read with caveats. Nine members hold passports of France, New Zealand, or the US, and the quality of the nationalities of these nine members has not been assessed or ranked specifically. Three other members — that is, the ones holding Compacts of Free Association with the US — have been ranked, but their rankings need to be read bearing in mind that their relatively small sizes also mean that the capabilities of their state apparatuses are limited (including with regard to data collection and dissemination), and their rankings are partially based on estimates. In fact, the rankings of eight of the sovereign members in this QNI (Fiji, Kiribati, Nauru, Samoa, the Solomon Islands, Tonga, Tuvalu, and Vanuatu) also need to be read with care for the same reason. These eight island nations were included in the QNI for the first time in 2018; sometimes estimates had to be made here, too.

A few examples illustrate the unique positions nationalities have on the continuum of sovereignties in the Pacific. American Samoa, as a first example, is legally associated with the US as an 'unincorporated territory', and its people hold American passports. However, these passports are imprinted with the message "The bearer of this passport is a United States national and not a United States citizen." These passport-holders have the right to reside in the US, but they cannot vote. They are entitled to enroll in the United States Army (in fact they have the highest per capita rate of military enlistment of any US territory), but they cannot own concealed weapons, are excluded from most government employment opportunities, and cannot sponsor the immigration of family members. The island state of Guam, as another example, is defined as an

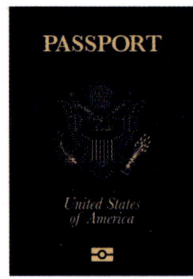

"unincorporated and organized territory of the United States", and its US passport has no residency or employment restrictions, although some civil rights are curtailed.

The Niuean nationality is yet another example. Niue is a self-governing state in free association with New Zealand. People on Niue hold dual citizenship; they are entitled to a New Zealand passport and the associated citizenship entitlements provided they apply for the passport in New Zealand. If they acquire Niuean citizenship in Niue, that document does not automatically transfer into a New Zealand passport, however. Moreover, the arrangement is not mutual and a New Zealand passport does not entitle the holder to rights on Niue that Niuean citizens have. Practically, this not only means restrictions to residency and employment on Niue, but it also means that travelers to Niue must buy return flights unless they prove they are Niuean by birth or by descent.

The second challenge in ranking nationalities for the QNI applies particularly to the half of the 24 Pacific Islands Forum members that retain constitutional and legal arrangements with the former colonial metropoles of France, the US, and New Zealand. These arrangements are generally subject to renegotiations between each individual territory and its respective metropole. While the ranking of all nationalities in the QNI is, of course, subject to change, most of this change is rather gradual. However, a renegotiated constitutional or legal arrangement between these 12 Pacific islands and their metropoles has the definite potential to lead to sharp rises or drops in the quality of these nationalities. Any change will affect the valuations of the internal factors relating to these islands and the external factors regarding the conditions of travel and settlement associated with the metropolitan nationality.

New Caledonia, for example, has had 10 different constitutional arrangements with France since 1946, leading some analysts to speak of a "waltz of statuses" (Leblic 2003, 135). People of New Caledonia hold a French passport, ranked 1st in the QNI since 2017. However, that same passport entails different entitlements within New Caledonia. The latest arrangement, called the Nouméa Agreement of 1998, has led to different employment conditions between, on the one hand, the territory's indigenous population and those on the electoral roll before 1998 and, on the other hand, the people who settled later. Employment in the public sector of French or EU citizens who settled in New Caledonia after 1998 is curtailed by the requirement that they can be hired only if there is no equally qualified indigenous or pre-1998 resident available. Since 2015, this principle has become applicable to employment in the private sector, too. (In contrast, French Polynesia does not have employment restrictions for non-resident citizens.) New Caledonia's independence referendum of November 2018 resulted in a majority vote against separation from France. However, there will be another independence referendum in 2020 and possibly another in 2022. In the course of the next few years, it is quite likely that one or more aspects of the relationship between Paris and New Caledonia will be renegotiated once more. It is important to note that some legal aspects of the current arrangements are already subject to contention (Kochenov 2010b), and whatever will be negotiated in the years ahead, the results will affect the quality of the French nationality within New Caledonia.

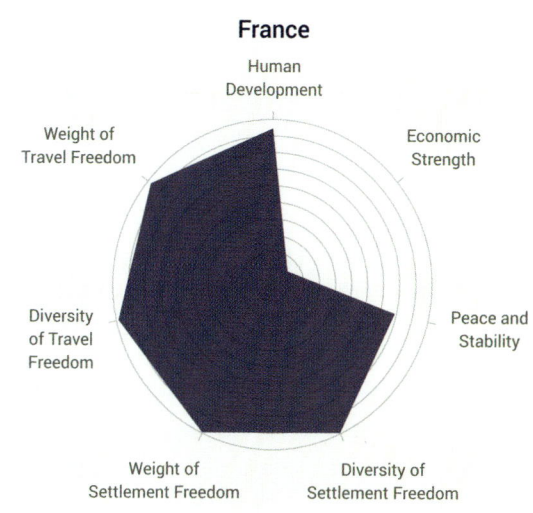

Change is also in the air in Pacific islands associated with the US. Samoans, for example, are increasing pressure on Washington to remove their passport imprint of "The bearer is a United States national but not a United States citizen". A legal challenge to this 'second-class status' (Morrison 2013, 1) is winding its way through the courts and is currently paused after a 2015 United States Court of Appeals ruling against Samoans.[1] In the third metropolitan sphere of the Pacific, there is "the realm of New Zealand ... whose populations are mainly citizens of New Zealand" (Foreign Affairs Defence and Trade Committee 2010, 7). Peoples of the Cook Islands, Niue, and Tokelau hold New Zealand passports with non-reciprocal access; they can settle in New Zealand, but other New Zealand passport holders cannot settle on these islands. In response to a 2010 parliamentary report, a legal review concluded that matters had evolved to a point where there now is "uncertainty and inconsistency when a closer look is taken at the legal documents dealing with citizenship across the Realm" that "could potentially lead to problems" (Perham 2011, 219). In addition, some New Zealand politicians have raised concerns about the "possible use of the Cook Islands and Niue by third country nationals for access to New Zealand contrary to New Zealand interests" (McDonald 2018, 137). At this point in time there is no clear path or leadership for change, but momentum seems to be building.

QNI Ranking of the Nationalities of Pacific Countries and Territories

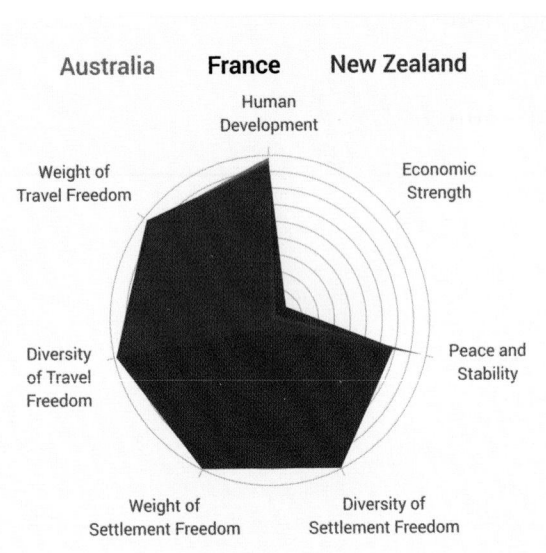

The QNI ranking of the 24 members of the Pacific Islands Forum divides the members into two distinct groups. In one group are the nationalities of Australia, New Zealand, and the six island territories whose people carry the passports of France or New Zealand, with all associated benefits (Table 1). The nationalities of these eight countries and territories rank in the QNI from the mid-50s upward, qualifying as Very High Quality or High Quality. It should be noted that in Table 1 the nationality of territories associated with France and New Zealand have been given the same QNI rankings as their metropoles. This is correct insofar as their passports ensure the same scores for travel and settlement freedom as their metropoles. However, data from these territories for the QNI sub-elements of Human Development, Economic Strength, and Peace and Stability was not always available and estimates had to be made. It is quite possible this means the rankings of these six territories are a few points lower than their metropoles', particularly as their rankings in Human Development and Economic Strength may be somewhat below the rankings of their metropolitan centers.

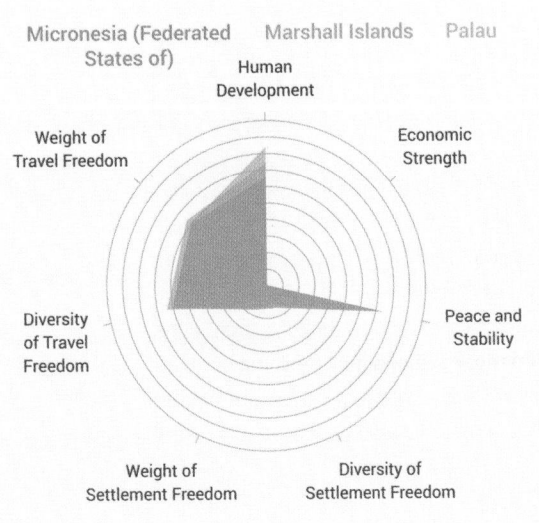

In the other group, the QNI presents a group of 13 Pacific island nations whose nationalities rank in or below the low 40s, placing them in the Very Low Quality or Low Quality tiers (Table 1). At the upper level of this group are the three countries holding Compacts of Free Association with the US. It is worth noting that while people of the Federated States of Micronesia, the Marshall Islands, and Palau travel on their own national passports, their association with the US enables them to enter the US visa-free and engage in employment. However, these three countries' travel and settlement freedoms with regard to other countries varies and is subject to particular arrangements. (For the sake of completeness it needs to be mentioned that the nationalities of the three American territories of American Samoa, Guam, and the Northern Mariana Islands have not been ranked in the QNI; relevant data was not readily available, therefore reliable estimates could not be made. The people of these territories hold American passports but these passports have some restrictions. A major restriction on the passport of American Samoa has already been discussed, but the nationalities of people in the other two territories also have peculiar limitations.)

The gap between the two groups in the QNI General Ranking is a remarkable 15 to 20 points. Rankings are not on a continuum: no Pacific island or territory occupies a position in between. As remarkable as this gap may appear, other comparative research has, in fact, found a similar divide across the globe between small islands that opted to become independent states in the decolonization of the 1960s and 1970s and those that chose to retain a constitutional bond with their former colonial powers. McElroy and Parry, for example, made a longitudinal 1985–2010 comparison of 25 non-self-governing island territories and 30 sovereign island states and found a similar divide. In broad strokes, it seems that non-self-governing islands having about twice the per capita income and half the child mortality rate (McElroy amd Parry 2012). Other research found comparable results (such as Baldacchino and Milne 2009; Dunn 2011). Importantly, closer study of these patterns suggests that non-self-governing islands most often strategically and successfully negotiate benefits with their metropoles. Prinsen and Blaise (2017) reviewed negotiations between 42 non-self-governing islands and their respective metropoles and identified several distinct features of an emerging 'Islandian sovereignty'; Baldacchino (2018) underscored the mutual benefits for metropoles and these islands as an 'autonomy plus' for non-self-governing islands. Against this backdrop, the gap in the QNI General Ranking between the two groups of islands and territories in the Pacific is a confirmation of a wider analysis that small islands tend to benefit more from an association with a metropole than from full independence – including having a higher quality of nationality.

Travel and Settlement Freedom in the Pacific

Unsurprisingly, the nationalities of the Pacific region show a similar distribution over two distinct groups when it comes to travel freedom: the ability to travel visa-free or with a visa-on-arrival for tourism or business purposes. The citizens of the eight countries or territories of the Pacific Islands Forum holding Australian, French, or New Zealand nationalities score highest, as they can travel visa-free to Europe's Schengen Area and to the US, which rank in the highest quality tier of the QNI. The people of the six Pacific islands with American nationalities rank just behind. This leaves a group comprising 10 sovereign Pacific island states, with just over a quarter of the Pacific population, collectively scoring lower on the QNI because they do not enjoy visa-free access to the Europe's Schengen Area and the US.

Policy patterns regarding travel freedom in countries and territories of the Pacific region generally reflect global rules and practices. However, matters in the Pacific get rather more complicated when it comes to settlement freedom. Because this contribution focuses on the Pacific region, it is relevant to take a closer look at issues around settlement freedom in the region itself (that is to say, not those Pacific nationals seeking to settle outside the region). When it comes to settlement freedom in the Pacific, two particular issues stand out: the non-reciprocity of settlement agreements and the ownership of land or real estate. A closer look at these issues will show that for practical settlement purposes in the Pacific region, the devil is in the details.

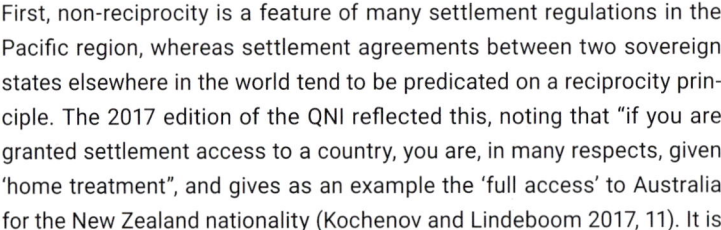First, non-reciprocity is a feature of many settlement regulations in the Pacific region, whereas settlement agreements between two sovereign states elsewhere in the world tend to be predicated on a reciprocity principle. The 2017 edition of the QNI reflected this, noting that "if you are granted settlement access to a country, you are, in many respects, given 'home treatment", and gives as an example the 'full access' to Australia for the New Zealand nationality (Kochenov and Lindeboom 2017, 11). It is true that the two countries have a long-standing 'Trans-Tasman Travel Arrangement' allowing their citizens to move freely between the two countries and to live and work where they choose indefinitely, without the need to apply for prior authority. However, in 2001 Australia unilaterally changed its settlement regulations for New Zealanders, reducing or delaying their access to social security and public services. Since then New Zealanders have not been given 'home treatment'. The Australian parliament's website advertises the resulting non-reciprocity in stark terms: "Australians in New Zealand face fewer restrictions in relation to social security payments than do New Zealanders residing in Australia" (Parliament of Australia 2016, 1). In recent years, several private Australian insurance and banking services followed their government's lead, excluding New Zealanders residing in Australia from benefits, often leaving their customers studying the fine print of contracts too late (Heather, 2015). An advocacy group sees the rights of New Zealanders in Australia gradually being "slowly whittled way" and leaving them as "second-class citizens" (Chenery 2016).

A 'free association' arrangement between two Pacific Islands Forum member states does not preclude non-reciprocity appearing in settlement regulation. The Cook Islands, for example, does not issue its own passports; its free association arrangement with New Zealand means the latter issues passports for all people born in the Cook Islands, and Cook Islanders can freely settle and work in New Zealand as New Zealand citizens, without restrictions. However, people born in New Zealand can acquire a permanent residency in the Cook Islands only if at least one of their parents was a permanent resident of the Cook Islands.[2] Moreover, the number of permanent residents in the Cook Islands is capped by law to a total of 650 people.[3]

A similar non-reciprocal dynamic applies in more instances. The Marshall Islands' Compact of Free Association with the US stipulates that its citizens can take employment and residence in both states.[4] However, actual visa regulations of the Marshall Islands make it nearly impossible for an immigrant to settle on a permanent or regular basis. Obtaining a residence visa essentially requires the immigrant to become a naturalized citizen, for which 11 conditions must be met. Among these are being "able to speak and understand Marshallese" as well as possessing "an understanding and respect for the customs and traditions of the Republic" and having "renounced any other citizenship which he may possess."[5] Moreover, there is an annual cap of persons who can become naturalized citizens of the Marshall Islands. The number "shall not exceed 10, including dependents, in any one calendar year."[6]

The second important issue affecting settlement freedom in the Pacific region is the regulations around the ownership of land or the land on which real estate has been or can be developed. With the exception of large countries such Australia, New Zealand, and Papua New Guinea, the terrestrial areas of most Pacific countries and territories are measured in hundreds of square kilometers, sometimes even fewer than one hundred square kilometers — land is scarce. In addition, in all

 their cultural diversity, one recurring feature of Pacific cultures is that in most countries and territories, 80% to 90% of all land is communally owned and controlled under customary tenure. Freehold land titles are rare, particularly in smaller sovereign Pacific states, and are usually less than 5% of the total area, leaving the remainder as public land in the hands of the state (Keppel, Morrison, Watling, Tuiwawa, and Rounds 2012, 257).

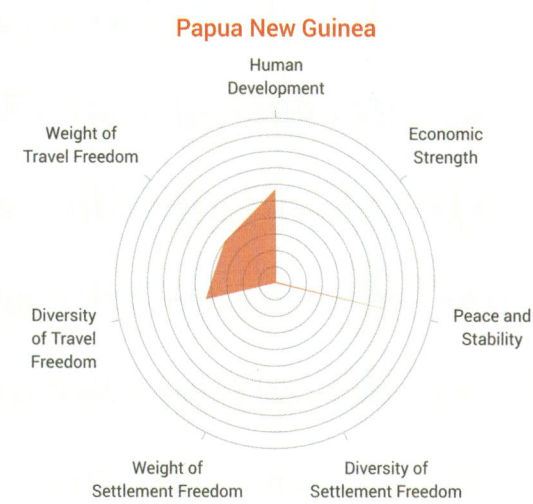

Unwritten customary law distributes land use and inheritance entitlements among families or clans. This results in multi-layered land use rights; usufructuary rights can vary from season to season, or from crop to crop, and in varying ways customary leaders have rights to rearrange existing practices, usages, and compensations to ensure that community members' perceived and changing needs are met (Farran and Paterson 2013). In Australia, New Zealand, and the territories associated with France or the US, the extent of customary land varies, but the principle and practice of customary land exist in all of them. Often, disputes and legal wrangling over colonial dispossession of indigenous land remain or grow as a sensitive and complex issue. French Polynesia, for example, recently established a Land Court to seek solutions to the many hundreds of disputes that have not been resolved for decades (Radio New Zealand 2015).

The rare freehold titles on land that do exist are mostly regulated to exclude sale to non-resident foreigners. While some Pacific countries and territories are gradually and to a very limited extent opening up possibilities for foreign co-ownership of land, major obstacles remain for new residents to start or solidify their settlement by owning land or developing real estate. Two exam-

 ples illustrate this. The sovereign state of Samoa — where about 81% of the land is titled 'customary land' and about 12% is 'freehold land' — has put in place strict controls on the transfer of freehold land to foreign owners, and the Head of State's permission is required for any proposed transfer to companies where more than 25% of the shares are owned by foreigners (Clark Ey Lawyers and Jones Lang LaSalle Real Estate 2014, 2). In another example, the Cook Islands shows very similar restrictions on the purchase of land or

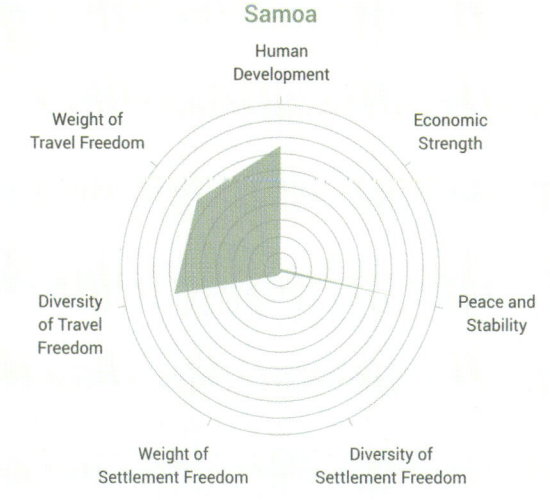

property by foreigners. As a principle, people without a direct Cook Islands family connection cannot purchase land or property. A foreign buyer can circumvent this through the circuitous process of buying an existing local business (foreigners cannot establish a new business in the Cook Islands) and holding it for five years before making an application to buy land or property (Browne Gibson Harvey Lawyers n.d.).

Two Potential Developments That Will Affect Pacific Nationalities in the Next Few Years

Looking forward two to five years, two particular dynamics with regard to the quality of Pacific nationalities are worth highlighting. First, within several countries and territories there are movements afoot that may lead to the territorial fragmentation of some of the current 24 members of the Pacific Islands Forum. If this happens, there will be consequences for the quality of the nationalities should a part of a country or territory secede or go its own way, as well as for the new country or territory that emerges. And it is not unlikely that the quality of neighboring nationalities will also be affected. This risk of fragmentation exists across the board: in sovereign states, in French territories, and in islands associated with the US. Second, and in contrast to these centrifugal forces in some places, it appears that the Pacific region as a whole is undergoing the centripetal forces of increased regional cooperation.

First, we can consider risks of territorial fragmentation in the Pacific. As noted earlier, New Caledonia will probably see two more referendums on its independence. The ultimate result in 2022 will have a significant impact not only in New Caledonia but will also reverberate in French Polynesia, thereby placing two relatively large and wealthy Pacific islands in turmoil. In France's third Pacific territory, Wallis and Futuna, local and customary leaders in Futuna have begun asking openly whether they would not be much better off with a separation from its bigger neighbor, Wallis (Lataste 2015). Elsewhere, the violent unrest and secessionism of the 1990s on the island of Bougainville in Papua New Guinea has resulted in an agreement to hold an independence referendum in 2019. Remarkably, the peace agreement does not oblige the Government of Papua New Guinea to accept the outcome of the referendum, which leaves uncertainty looming over it (Firth 2018, 15). In the Federated States of Micronesia, the State Legislature of Chuuk — one of the four states comprising the Federation — proposed a referendum in 2015 to consider whether Chuuk would be better off if it broke away. After intense debates, the proposed referendum was canceled a few weeks before it was to be held (Mulalap 2016). However, the issue may surface again in the coming years. In all, it is worth noting that many island states are groups of islands brought together by colonial powers for administrative convenience, not by choice of their diverse peoples, who often have distinct histories and cultures.

Second — and on a more positive note for the quality of nationalities in the Pacific region — it can be argued that many of the members of the Pacific Islands Forum see a growing relevance and usefulness of this regional body. The Forum was established in 1971, and its mandate and membership have both expanded significantly since the 2000s. With the recent admission of French Polynesia and New Caledonia as full members, its strategic scope and the technical capabilities of its Secretariat, based in Fiji, are likely to increase further (Leslie and Prinsen 2018). One of its initiatives in 2018 was the development of a 'Pacific business travel card' to ease travel within the region (Secretary-General, Pacific Islands Forum 2018). If this proves to be effective in the next two or three years, the Forum members' Travel Freedom scores on will undoubtedly improve. Another regional body, the Melanesian Spearhead Group, has a more limited geographic

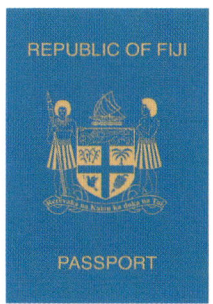  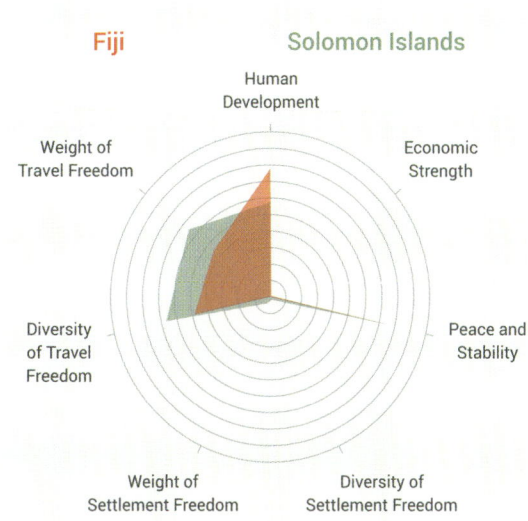

membership (Fiji, Papua New Guinea, Solomon Islands, Vanuatu, and New Caledonia's leading independence party), but its increasing focus on trade cooperation is likely to have positive impacts on the QNI's internal valuation of its members, among the Pacific region's poorest.

Conclusion

 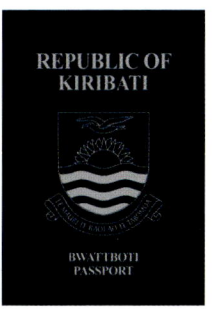 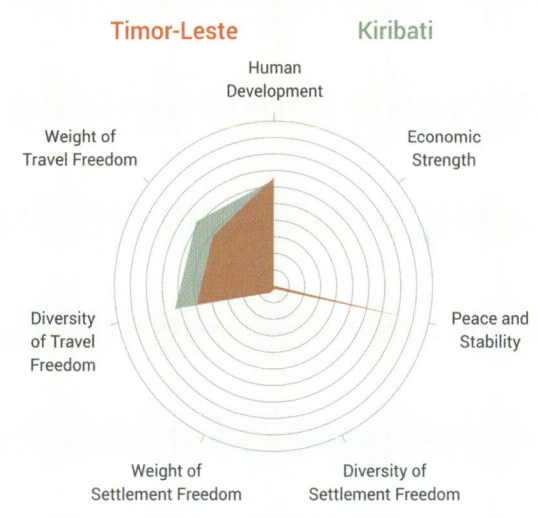

Spanning 11 time zones, the Pacific region is arguably the world's largest geographic region and also its least populated, with only about 42 million inhabitants living in 24 countries and territories. Most of the states are small, with populations of less than 300,000, and half of them maintain an association — in various forms and degrees — with France, New Zealand, or the US. These various forms and degrees mean that sovereignty in the region is not a binary affair; it is best understood as a continuum, or a range of shades, of sovereignty. Nevertheless, the 2018 QNI General Ranking does show a clear division of Pacific countries and territories into two groups based on the quality of their nationalities. A third have Very High Quality or High Quality nationalities, scoring from the mid-50s upward. The other, larger group comprises the nationalities of countries and territories that score in or below the low 40s, leaving a 15- to 20-point divide. The appearance of this divide is consistent with a growing body of research suggesting small islands benefit from a close association with their distant metropoles.

Whereas the Pacific region's dynamics around Travel Freedom are very similar to global patterns, Pacific islands can have unique practices when it comes to Settlement Freedom. In regulatory practices, many islands do not reciprocate residence privileges with other countries, and in many islands purchasing land or real estate is for all intents and purposes limited to people with existing family ties. This, perhaps, illustrates the key conclusion with regard to the quality of nationalities in the Pacific. The QNI provides an excellent first orientation to appreciating the quality of nationalities in the Pacific, both from the perspective of Pacific nationals and from the point of view of people aspiring to become a national. However, most countries and territories have unique arrangements and, moreover, an individual's personal profile is likely to have a significant influence on the real-life quality of a specific nationality — irrespective of whether one considers leaving or settling on an island.

Table 1. Pacific Island Forum (PIF) Members and Associate Members, Population, and 2018 QNI General Ranking

	Members 2016	Population Size 2016	2018 QNI General Ranking				
			VHQ	HQ	MQ	LQ	VLQ
1	Australia	24,125,000	55.2				
2	Papua New Guinea	8,845,000				28.7	
3	New Zealand	4,661,000		54.8			
4	Fiji	899,000				33.2	
5	Solomon Islands	599,000			36.5		
6	French Polynesia*	280,000	(83.5)				
7	New Caledonia*	273,000	(83.5)				
8	Vanuatu	270,000			37.1		
9	Samoa	195,000			39.7		
10	Kiribati	114,000			36.6		
11	Tonga	107,000			38.7		
12	Micronesia	105,000			40.2		
13	Marshall Islands	53,000			41.8		
14	Palau	22,000			42.7		
15	Cook Islands**	17,000		(54.8)			
16	Nauru	11,000				32.0	
17	Tuvalu	11,000			38.6		
18	Niue**	2,000		(54.8)			

	Associate Members 2016	Population Size 2016	2018 QNI General Ranking				
			VHQ	HQ	MQ	LQ	VLQ
19	Timor-Leste	1,167,000				33.1	
20	Guam***	163,000		(Not ranked)			
21	American Samoa***	55,000		(Not ranked)			
22	Northern Mariana Islands***	52,000		(Not ranked)			
23	Wallis and Futuna*	12,000	(83.5)				
24	Tokelau**	1,000		(54.8)			
	Totals (plus 3 unrated)		3	5	9	4	-

* French passport holders, ranking based on France's ranking.
** New Zealand passport holders, ranking based on New Zealand's ranking.
*** Territory associated with the United States, but whose nationality is subject to restrictions.
(…) Not officially ranked in the QNI.

42 Passports, Free Movement, and the State in South America

By Diego Acosta Arcarazo

Introduction

South America consists of twelve states, with four in the High Quality tier of *Kälin and Kochenov's Quality of Nationality Index* (QNI) (Chile in 29th position, Argentina in 32nd, Brazil in 33rd, and Uruguay in 41st), six in the Medium Quality tier (Paraguay in 47th position, Peru in 53rd, Venezuela in 56th, Colombia in 59th, Ecuador in 69th, and Bolivia in 83rd), and two in the Low Quality tier (Guyana in 90th position and Suriname in 92nd). Venezuela, however, deserves special consideration, which I give it below. We must note that due to a lack of data for some indicators, Venezuela remains in a much higher position in the rankings than its present situation warrants. Apart from Venezuela, however, South American countries' rankings have remained fairly stable since 2011; the main exception is Colombia, which has seen a remarkable improvement in its general position, from 102nd to 59th, the result of improved Travel Freedom (by obtaining visa-free travel to Europe's Schengen Area in 2015, for example), a higher level of Settlement Freedom (by implementing the MERCOSUR Residence Agreement, as explained below, for example), and the generally improved economic and political situation in the country (by negotiating a peace agreement with the Fuerzas Armadas Revolucionarias de Colombia [FARC], for example).

With the exception of Guyana and Suriname (which emerged after the Second World War), the South American states are among the oldest states in the world, with 200-year histories. Migration and mobility have been the objects of legislative and political attention since the independence of the former colonies from Spain and Portugal in the early 19th century. From their very early stages, the new states signed bilateral and multi-lateral agreements facilitating free movement and equal treatment of regional nationals. Several of these countries also enshrined constitutional provisions

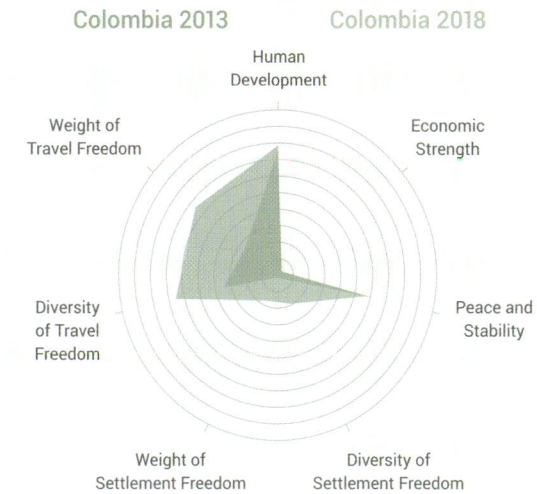

that included principles such as open borders, access to equal rights for foreigners in general, and preferential treatment to naturalize for Hispano-American nationals. Between 1880 and 1930, countries in South America, notably Argentina, Brazil, and Uruguay, were among the recipients of the largest numbers of migrants globally, mainly Europeans. Argentina itself received the second highest number of migrants in the world, topped only by the US, and had the highest number of foreigners as a percentage of the total population (Moya 1998). The 20th century, however, can be largely considered as an era when increasingly restrictive choices to regulate immigration became the norm. These restrictions affected particular groups of individuals more than Latin Americans as such, due to exclusions on grounds of race, ethnicity, or political ideology. With the existence of military regimes in most South American republics in the 1970s, and within a framework of deep suspicion of foreigners, discussions on mobility and open borders almost completely stalled (Acosta 2018).

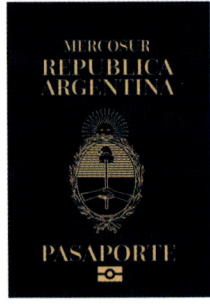

With the return to democracy in all states in South America in the 1980s — the last being Chile in 1990 — three major developments affecting nationality and migration took place. First, the awakening to a new reality: emigration was now the norm in countries that had historically been countries where immigration predominated. As others have also noted, during the 1990s, "emigrant communities came to be viewed as economic footholds in developed economies… [they] were reconceived as a kind of natural resource" due to remittances and the alleviation of unemployment rates in national labor markets (Spiro 2016, 89). The ensuing pressure by emigrant groups led to the acceptance of dual nationality as a normal state of affairs, except in Paraguay. Second, the renaissance of regional organizations and the proliferation of proposals and agreements on free movement of people at the regional level in various fora:

the Andean Community (CAN), MERCOSUR, the now close-to-defunct Union of South American Nations (UNASUR), and the most recent Pacific Alliance. Out of the four, the most important in terms of mobility has been MERCOSUR, whose membership includes six South American countries — Argentina, Brazil, Bolivia (still going through the process of joining), Paraguay, Uruguay, and Venezuela (currently suspended) — and as associate members the remaining six — Chile, Colombia,

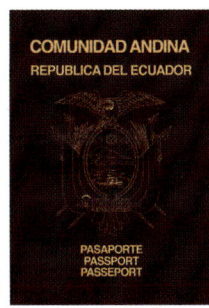
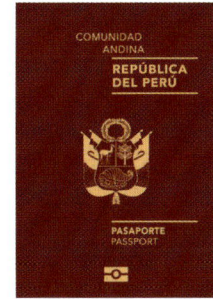

Ecuador, Guyana, Peru, and Suriname. Third, the emergence of a new vocabulary and discourse on mobility emphasizing a rights-based approach, well-represented by the final, non-binding declarations of the annual meetings of the regional process known as the South American Conference on Migration. This new jargon includes concepts such as 'the right to migrate' and 'universal citizenship' and has made its way into some provisions in new migration laws in the region — in Argentina (2004), Uruguay (2008), Bolivia (2013), and Brazil, Ecuador, and Peru (2017). The arrival into power of right-wing governments in countries like Argentina, Brazil, and Chile and the dramatic increase in the number of Venezuelans in the whole region are putting into question some of the advances that took place earlier in the 21st century in terms of the rights of migrants.

In 2018, migration and mobility in Latin America were almost exclusively dominated by the emigration of thousands of Venezuelans to other countries in the region. According to estimates offered by the International Organization for Migration (IOM) in November 2018, the number of refugees and migrants from Venezuela worldwide has already reached 3 million people. 80% of this number now reside elsewhere in Latin America and in the Caribbean, with Colombia (around 1 million), Peru (approximately 600,000), Ecuador (around 250,000), and Argentina and Chile (over 100,000) having received the largest number of Venezuelans (Selee, Bolter, Muñoz-Pogossian, and Hazán 2019). The legal response by the various countries in South America and the value — as well as the difficulty — of holding a Venezuelan passport are analyzed below.

Travel and Settlement Freedom in South America

As the Quality of Nationality Index clearly indicates, having a South American nationality is now more relevant and valuable thanks to the opportunities it brings for visa-free travel among an increasingly larger number of countries but also for settlement in other South American countries. When it comes to the former, most South American nationals — except for Bolivians, Ecuadorians, Guyanese, and Surinamese — are exempted from visa obligations to enter Europe's Schengen Area. Moreover, mobility and settlement have been enhanced among South American states through various regional agreements. Of these, two aspects must be highlighted.

Bolivia (Plurinational State of) — Chile

First, free movement for short stays, usually associated with tourism or business purposes, has been facilitated. With reference to the CAN (which includes Bolivia, Colombia, Ecuador, and Peru), Andean nationals can move between the member states without passports by simply presenting their national identity cards. They may remain in another member state's territory for a period of up to 90 days, with permission renewable for another 90. Andean nationals also enjoy a common passport and consular protection abroad from the authorities of any member state when unrepresented by their own country in the state in which they find themselves. They also enjoy non-discrimination due to nationality in access to the labor market and equal access to social security (Acosta 2018, 173–98). The Pacific Alliance, formed in 2012, numbers among its members not only Chile, Colombia, and Peru, but also the extra-regional country of Mexico. Among this organization's successes are the abolition of visas for short-stay travel between its member countries and a nascent discussion on the free movement of workers. Finally, there are also agreements at the MERCOSUR level concerning travel documents that expand the ability to travel with an identity card rather than a passport to the whole of South America, excluding Guyana and Suriname.[1]

However, the most important legislation in South America is the 2002 MERCOSUR Residence Agreement. Implemented in 2009, the Agreement's main purpose is to facilitate the free movement of intra-regional migrants, and it has transformed the migration regime for South Americans. It provides that any national of a MERCOSUR or associate member state may reside and work for a period of two years in a host state with the only requirements being the absence of a criminal record and proof of nationality. Naturalized citizens in one of the member states need to wait five years before they can move. After two years, the temporary residence permit may be converted into a permanent one if permit holders demonstrate legitimate means of providing for themselves and any family members. It also establishes a number of rights, including the right to work and equal treatment in working conditions, family reunion, and access to education for children.

The motivation behind the MERCOSUR Residence Agreement was to find a solution to irregular migration, not to pave the way for an internal trade market — despite the fact that the latter represented the initial institutional MERCOSUR goal. The agreement's main objective, as declared in the preamble, is to solve the situation of intraregional irregular migration while deepening the regional integration process and implementing a policy of free circulation of people. This difference is crucial to understanding the structure of the agreement itself, because it does not provide for a right of entry but only for a right of residence. In other words, those South Americans who would like to use the agreement often need to prove that they are entering a second member state as tourists (and fulfilling all the requirements to be considered as such). It is only later, once they have entered the country, that they can apply to obtain a residence permit. A residence permit can also be applied for in the country of origin at the consulate of the destination country, although not all countries provide this option.

Its deficiencies and legal shortcomings notwithstanding, the agreement has changed the lives of the estimated 2.6 million South Americans who obtained residence permits from 2009 until 2016 (IOM 2018a). All the countries in South America with the exception of Guyana, Suriname, and Venezuela (and not just the MERCOSUR countries) have ratified the agreement and apply it.

The Special Status of Venezuela

Venezuela, having left the CAN in 2006, joined MERCOSUR as a full member in 2012. Nonetheless, Venezuela never ratified the MERCOSUR Residence Agreement and thus did not apply it to nationals of other MERCOSUR states. In September 2016, the ministries of foreign affairs of Argentina, Brazil, Paraguay, and Uruguay adopted a common Declaration on the Functioning of MERCOSUR and Venezuela's Adhesion Protocol, in which they stated that Venezuela had failed in its obligations to incorporate the MERCOSUR *acquis*, including the agreements on free residence of regional migrants, and announced that, should Venezuela continue in its breach, it would lose its rights as a full member.

Later, in 2017, Venezuela was subject to the mechanism of suspension established in the 1998 MERCOSUR Ushuaia Protocol on Democratic Compromise. According to its provisions, in cases of rupture of the democratic order in a member state, and following a round of consultations with that country, the other member states might suspend its participation in the various regional institutions and the rights and obligations deriving from its MERCOSUR membership. Such measures would cease once the democratic order was re-established in the particular country (Art. 7). This decision, taken on 5 August 2017, established that there had been a rupture of the democratic order in Venezuela, and thus there was a need to trigger the application of the Protocol while minimizing the negative impacts of the decision on Venezuelans themselves. Venezuela's suspension effectively means that other countries implementing the MERCOSUR Residence Agreement are under no obligation to extend its reach to Venezuelans. Any such extension of the agreement is to be based on domestic law and not on the MERCOSUR legal framework.

With this background in mind, the legal responses of South American countries to the arrival of Venezuelans can generally be characterized as open, although with numerous caveats. While most countries in the region are trying to offer residence permits — so as to avoid situations of undocumented residence, which could lead to possible exploitation — typically such permits are applicable to certain categories of Venezuelans only (for example, those arriving after a certain date); are adopted by executive decrees, with little intervention by parliaments; and merely grant temporary residence, thus generating legal uncertainty for the person's future. The value of holding a Venezuelan passport is decreasing.

Depending on their responses, countries can be divided into three categories. First, Bolivia, Guyana, Paraguay, and Suriname have not established any special permits or fast-track procedures for Venezuelans; thus, Venezuelans have the same legal status as any other non-regional foreigner and have no right of residence. To compare the numbers of Venezuelans in each of these four countries is not relevant.

Second, there are those countries that have simply extended the MERCOSUR Residence Agreement to Venezuelans, thus offering them a right to reside upon fulfilling certain conditions (such as a clean criminal record). This is the case in Argentina, where there is a unilateral extension of the law based on humanitarian grounds and reasons of public interest, as allowed by Article 34 of its Migrations Law. In Uruguay, since 2014 Venezuelans and all other South Americans have been able to directly obtain permanent residence thanks to a more generous implementation of the MERCOSUR Residence Agreement.[2] Brazil has also extended the validity of the MERCOSUR Residence Agreement, first temporarily through a ministerial order[3] and later permanently, but only through an administrative act that can be easily revoked.[4] In addition, Venezuelans can opt for a two-year temporary residence permit in Brazil that can be later converted into a permanent one. Ecuador, while not having unilaterally extended the MERCOSUR Residence Agreement, has incorporated into its 2017 Law on Human Mobility the category of the UNASUR temporary residence permit, which all South Americans, including Venezuelans, can opt for. After two years, the permit can be converted into a permanent one.

Third, there are those countries that have created special ad hoc permits for Venezuelans. Chile has established the so-called 'visa of democratic responsibility' allowing Venezuelans to reside in the country with a one-year renewable permit. The visa can be requested only in the two Chilean consulates in Venezuela, however. Colombia has created a special permanence permit offering Venezuelans up to two years residence in the country, but that time does not count towards obtaining Colombian nationality or any other residence. The possibility to apply for the permit has been extended on several occasions, the last time in December 2018, so that those Venezuelans who regularly entered the country with a passport before 17 December 2018 are still entitled to apply and obtain a residence permit.[5] Finally, Peru also has created a temporary two-year residence permit that can be converted into a permanent one. However, the permit can be requested only by Venezuelans who entered the country before 31 October 2018.

Venezuelans and the Passport as Identification

The emergence of the contemporary international passport as an identification document and the "attempt by modern nation-states to assert their exclusive monopoly over the legal means of movement" have been flawlessly delineated by Torpey (1998, 159). In Venezuela the willingness — and desperation — of thousands to leave the country has led to the emergence of a 'paper industry', a term borrowed from Cook-Martin (2013) who coined it to describe the case in Argentina. And as in Argentina in 2001, Venezuelans have tried to obtain European passports, mostly Spanish and Italian, through proving ancestry.

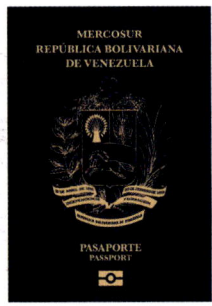

Even more interestingly, after the decision by the Spanish authorities in 2015 to facilitate the acquisition of nationality for the descendants of the Sephardic Jews who were expelled from the Kingdom in 1492[6] without having to renounce their nationalities of origin, around 1,500 Venezuelans have obtained Spanish — and therefore EU — citizenship (Mateo 2018). Venezuelans are second to none but Turkish nationals in making use of this historical reparation route and are thus opening new opportunities for themselves and their families. This represents a unique example of the porosity of the nation as a social construct when political will arises, and how a winning ticket in the 'birthright lottery', to use Shachar's (2009) phrase, can date from centuries ago — if you are lucky enough to have had an ancestor who suffered expulsion at the hands of an overzealous Catholic queen.

Differently from Argentina in 2001, though, the 'paper industry' in Venezuela does not stop with the search for the right document to prove European ancestry. Rather, it also incorporates an elaborate network of corruption that facilitates obtaining the Venezuelan passport itself, elevated to the category of 'sacred object' for those willing to flee. Indeed, as documented by numerous media reports (Castro 2018), obtaining a passport in Venezuela has become a procedure outside normal mechanisms, where those following the established rules have to wait for months or years for the precious document, while those circumventing them deal with 'intermediaries' and pay in US dollars — the amount ranging from USD 700 to USD 5,500 depending on whether the passport is issued for the first time or renewed, and on other variables.

Proving Venezuelan nationality through a passport and in some cases a national identification document has become crucial to accessing alternative residence and rights. Interestingly, not all passports are the same. For example, Argentina has adopted regulations by which Venezuelan passports and national identification documents that have expired less than two years previously can be used to enter the territory and obtain residence.[7] By contrast, those willing to apply for a visa of democratic responsibility in Chile need a passport valid for at least 18 months, a requirement that was previously only six months when the visa was first announced (Ruiz Parra 2018). In Ecuador and Peru, Venezuelans who in principle can enter the countries with national identification documents have been asked to present their passports sporadically since the summer of 2018 (Selee et al. 2019). To complicate matters further, Ecuador introduced a new requirement for Venezuelans on 21 January 2019, by which those entering the country will need to show a clean criminal record certificate of the country of origin or that of residence for the last five years, duly legalized or apostilled.[8] Chile, Ecuador, and Peru have introduced a visa for Venezuelans.

Conclusion

With the adoption of free residency and mobility agreements in South America, nationals of the countries involved obtain a new status that eliminates, in theory, the possibility of being undocumented. Regional migration regimes transform the meaning of citizenship and the relationships between states, their territories, and foreigners. Through regional migration agreements, states renounce their control over the relationship between territory and population since there is a group of non-nationals who obtain rights of entry and/or residence, coupled with other provisions of non-discrimination in terms of access to work, family reunion, or even socio-economic entitlements. Regional migration agreements also tell a different story than the one about the alleged global trend of border closure. Contradicting this accepted narrative, regional migration agreements do open borders, at least for those coming from certain countries. Examples are abundant, South America being one, of nationals who now have better passports that offer more life advancement opportunities in various countries.

Many authors have debated whether South America's free movement regime constitutes an instance of failure or success. Those celebrating its achievements mention that when the MERCOSUR Residence Agreement was adopted in 2002 there were serious doubts that it would be implemented (Alfonso 2012, 51); since then, more than 2.6 million residence permits have been granted. Undoubtedly, South America has made decisive advancements in the direction of a right to reside and receive equal treatment in the territory of a second state. At least two risks are apparent that might affect the value of the passport South American nationals hold, however.

First, developments in Brazil and Chile might follow the already well-trodden path of border closures, and also for regional nationals. Brazil's new pro-torture President has pulled out of the Global Compact for Safe, Orderly and Regular Migration (GCM), which portends a harsher stance on mobility. While the number of foreigners residing in the country is very low (constituting less than 1% of the total population), any restrictive signal by the largest country in the region is likely to have negative consequences for debates in other, neighboring, states. In Chile, another country that opposes the GCM, a draft migration bill — at the time of writing in January 2019 already having been adopted in Congress but subject to debate in front of the Senate — simply ignores the MERCOSUR Residence Agreement even though it has been in operation in Chile since December 2009. Non-application by Chile could, of course, lead to the non-application by other South American countries to Chileans in these states.

Second, the ongoing emigration of Venezuelans to countries in the region will continue, with some projecting that "as many as 5.4 million Venezuelans may be living abroad by the end of 2019" (Selee et al. 2019, 4). There are already thousands of Venezuelans who are in irregular situations in other South American countries (due to administrative delays, documents that cannot be obtained, or lack of information) even if the laws or executive decrees grant them, in theory, a right to reside. The erraticism of migration regulations compounded by the excessive role played by executives therein and their propensity to add layers of bureaucracy makes it difficult to anticipate what new administrative requirements might be put in place that nullify in practice the advantage of holding certain passports, notably that of Venezuela. This is a challenge for ranking nationalities for the QNI.

43 The Quality of African Nationalities

By Andreas Krensel

Geography is key to understanding any area of the world. Africa contains 54 countries and is the world's second largest and second most-populous continent. Currently there are 1.2 billion people living in Africa and 50% of Africans are under the age of 25. This fact is of particular salience with regard to migration, as people tend to migrate in young adulthood.

In 1963, the Organisation of African Unity was formed by its 32 founding states; since then it has changed its name to the African Union (AU) and now encompasses all 54 African states. However, in the last 50 years countries of the AU have not been performing as well as European and South American countries. In 2018 the Quality of Nationality Index (QNI) General Ranking was led by the nationalities of European countries: France, Germany, and the Netherlands. In contrast, most African nationalities continued to be ranked in the lower half of all states included in the Index, and of these, the nationalities of two small African island nations, Seychelles (50th) and Mauritius (55th) score the highest among all African nationalities. Those with large economies rank far lower, such as Nigeria (joint 113th), Kenya (120th), and Ethiopia (148th).

With the formalization in 2013 of Agenda 2063, however, the next half-century appears to be very promising for Africa. A strategic 50-year framework for the socio-economic transformation of the continent, Agenda 2063 builds on and is designed to accelerate the implementation of past and current continental initiatives for growth and sustainable development.

An integral part of Agenda 2063 has been the introduction of an AU passport, which the plan declares is a "call for action to all segments of African society to work together to build a prosperous and united Africa based on shared values and a common destiny."[1] It is hoped that the passport will bring about greater integration

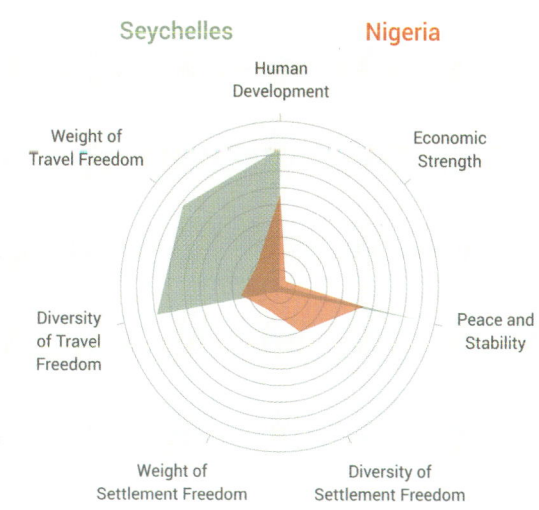

and free movement and help increase trade and economic growth. Launched in July 2016, the AU passport was a bold statement and a potential aid for an underperforming continent, but it is currently available only to heads of state and ministers of foreign affairs of AU member states and to permanent representatives of AU member states based at the AU headquarters in Ethiopia. Even the outgoing president of the AU, Nkosazana Dlamini-Zuma, had to convince the immigration control in her home country of South Africa that her AU passport was a valid document. Initially the plan was to introduce AU passports by 2018, a goal that was never realistic; the roll-out has now been pushed ahead to 2020. Furthermore, recent international developments such as Brexit have shown that not everyone prefers an open market with freedom of movement and migration. Thus, the move to an AU passport will be challenging: many African states are already resistant to migrants and refugees, and some states have been quietly tightening their visa rules.

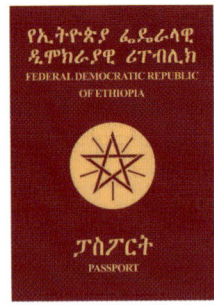

Agenda 2063 also proposed that all member states enable visa-free or visa-on-arrival travel for all other African states by 2018. This might be what people want and might be its future goal, but today's reality looks different, and it will do for some time.

Travel Freedom

With regard to Travel Freedom, the African nationalities' rankings have stagnated, with the nationalities of the Seychelles in 40th place with 78.8% and Mauritius in 45th place with 75.6% again being the positive exceptions.

The next-highest ranked African nationality is that of South Africa, in 80th place with 53.5%. In absolute numbers, South Africans can visit 100 destinations visa-free or with a visa-on-arrival. Other African nationalities are much lower in the rankings.

As mentioned above, Agenda 2063 proposed that all member states should institute visa-free or visa-on-arrival travel for all other African states by 2018. It has long been a reality that holders of passports from most first world countries were issued visas-on-arrival in most African countries, but those countries' own neighbors had to apply for visas before they could travel. The negative impact on business travel and intercontinental trade cannot be overestimated.

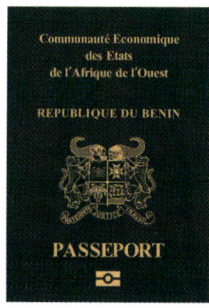
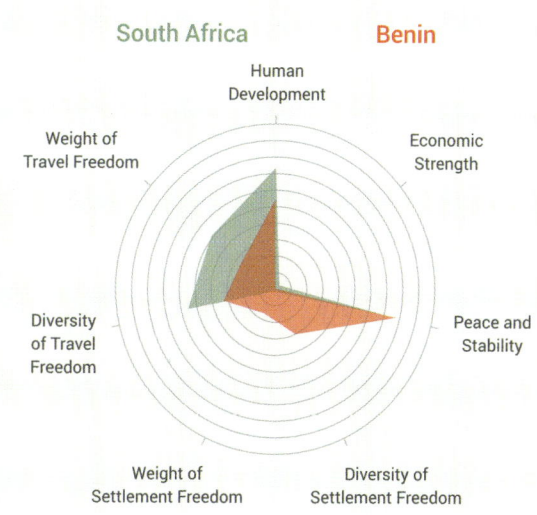

In the past two years there has been some change. For instance, Benin recently became the first francophone country in Africa to offer visa-free access to all African countries, and in March 2018 put new measures in place to improve overall entry access to the country. Since then, non-Africans with a valid passport and yellow fever certificate who wish to visit for less than a week have been able to apply for a special tourist visa-on-arrival for a set fee. Global visitors can now obtain an e-visa for Benin as part of the country's 'Smart Gouv' program to simplify entry and short-stay visa processes. Despite these changes, the Diversity of Travel Freedom score for Benin's nationality has remained almost the same: in 2016 Beninese citizens could visit 58 countries and territories without the need for a visa or visa-on-arrival, and in 2018 that number increased by only one, to 59 countries.

Although the Rwandan nationality enjoyed an increase on the Travel Freedom Ranking from 2014 to 2016, rising from 141st place with 20.3% to 125th place with 26.8%, in 2018 it dropped in both value and rank to 135th place with 25.8%.

The Nigerian nationality has also seen a slight drop in rank and value of Travel Freedom. While in 2016 it was ranked 142nd with 22.2%, in 2018 Nigerian nationality was ranked 147th with 22%.

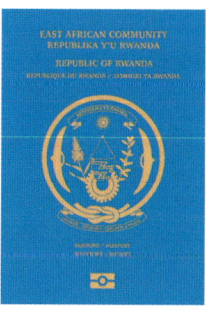
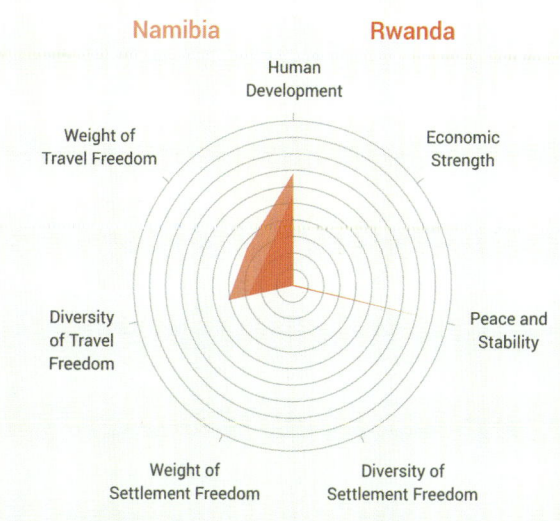

Two countries have loosened their visa policies, namely Ethiopia and Namibia. Namibia moved to liberalize its visa policy in October 2017 with a decision that all Africans were to be issued with visas on arrival as part of a longer-term goal to remove visa requirements altogether. This follows earlier plans to allow citizens of the Southern African Development Community (SADC) to access Namibia visa-free. In

May 2018 Ethiopian Prime Minister Abiy Ahmed announced a decision to liberalize visas for African travelers, which was widely welcomed in African policy and media circles.

Ethiopia has modernized and automated its visa application system, with global travelers able to apply for e-visas. The nationalities of these two countries have seen slight increases in value over the last two years. In 2018, the Namibian nationality increased in value but dropped in rank as compared to 2016, achieving 38.9% and ranking 97th for Travel Freedom as compared to 38.8% and ranking 89th two years previously. Similarly, the Ethiopian nationality increased in value from 19.6% in 2016 to 20.5% in 2018, remaining however in the same position at 151st. When we also consider 2014's rankings, however, both nationalities seem to be following a general upward trend, and therefore the improvement in the Namibian nationality scores cannot be attributed solely to its plans for visa openness.

The two African nationalities that have enjoyed the biggest increases over the past two years are the Seychelles and Mauritius, which currently allow their nationals to travel to the most countries without a visa.

This seems to indicate that the world is not becoming more open to nationals of African countries. The slight increases on the QNI are largely the result of African countries opening their borders to other African nationals, largely thanks to Agenda 2063 and its plan for an all-African passport. The African nationalities with the lowest Travel Freedom scores appear to be in a rut, and it may take considerable time for them to increase their performances significantly.

Countries in Africa face many obstacles and much resistance to opening their borders to fellow African nationals. First, there is already a resistance to immigration in the form of pre-existing visa barriers to other African nationals. For example, Equatorial Guinea requires that citizens from the other 53 sovereign African states acquire visas to visit. Other countries with the same restrictions include the Democratic Republic of the Congo, São Tomé and Príncipe, and Sudan. Second, some countries are averse to allowing entry to more migrants due to their high unemployment rates. In South Africa, for example, there is a widespread perception among some segments of the population, typically those battling high rates of poverty and unemployment, that foreigners are taking too many local jobs. This belief has even led to nationwide xenophobic attacks, most recently in 2015 and 2016. The fundamental underlying reason that many people from other African countries are migrating to South Africa is the economic disparities between countries. For some countries the 'pull factor' of a better economy attracts large numbers of economic migrants.

South Africa, for instance, with its infrastructure and an economy that in 2016 was the second biggest in Africa, entices many Africans who see it as a 'greener pasture', with the result that on the continent South Africa has a relatively high 'pull factor'. This, coupled with high levels of unemployment in the country, has led to South African immigration legislation and policy not being as open as those of other African countries.

South Africa did, however, ease visa requirements for African business travelers and African academics late in 2018, introducing a 10-year visitor visa that grants the holder the right to enter the country multiple times during those 10 years provided that each visit does not exceed 30, 60, or 90 days at a time. Unfortunately, however, in South Africa — as often in the rest of Africa — there is often a difference between what a government minister announces and what the administration does. Most business travelers from such economic powerhouses as Egypt, Ghana, Kenya, Morocco, and Nigeria must still apply for a visa for each trip to South Africa.

An interesting development is the regional integration of West, East, and Central Africa. In West Africa, citizens of ECOWAS member states can enter other member states much more easily and even work for short periods. Similar regional integration is being implemented in the East African Community (EAC) member states. The Central African Economic and Monetary Union has ratified free movement of people as of October 2017, allowing citizens from the six member states — Cameroon, Central African Republic, Chad, Equatorial Guinea, Gabon, and the Republic of the Congo — to travel visa-free. The move is re-energizing integration in the region, with a focus on biometric technology, coordinating security services, and respect for different labor regulations. These countries have all seen improvements in their Travel Freedom scores. Equatorial Guinea

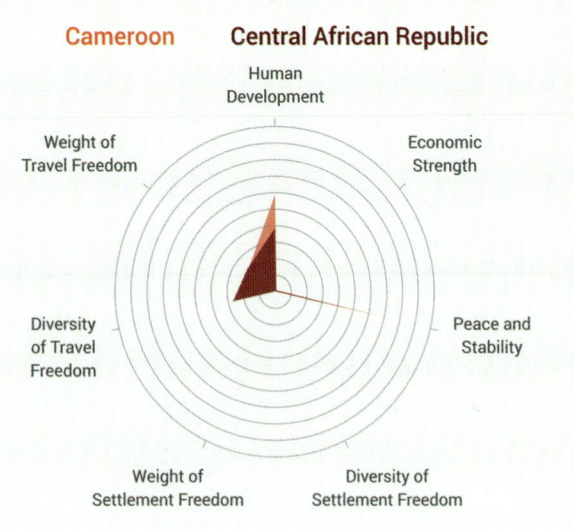
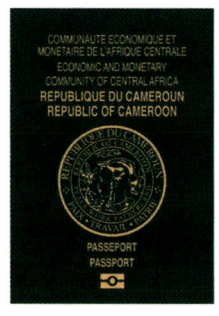

has shown the most significant improvement: in 2016 its nationality was ranked 138th on Travel Freedom with 23.7%; in 2018 this value increased to 25.5% and its rank to the 137th position, a relatively large improvement in the African context.

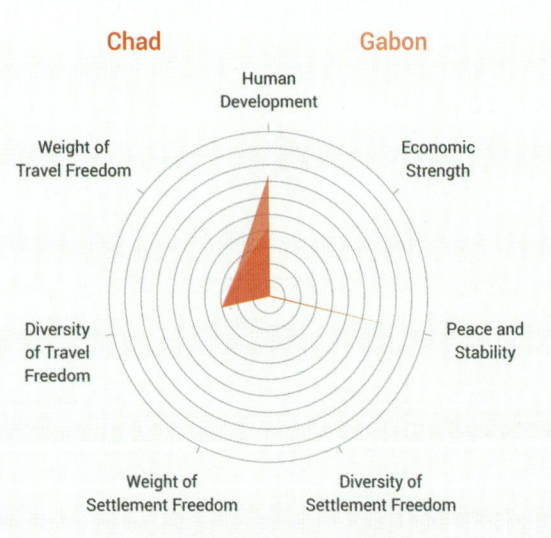
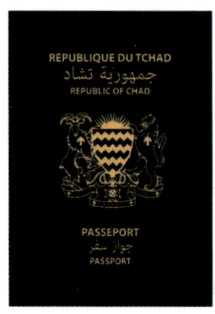

So what lies ahead for visa openness in Africa? The upward trend of African countries liberalizing their visa policies for other Africans seems set to continue as momentum gathers across regional blocs and across the continent as a whole, in line with the Free Movement Protocol.[2]

2018 was a landmark chapter in Africa's integration story. With the establishment of the African Continental Free Trade Area and the commitment to implement the Single African Air Transport Market, closer cooperation and shared investment in Africa's economic growth and sustainable development was again reinforced. Together with ongoing infrastructure improvements and business reforms, visa openness is a valuable tool that will help to bolster integration. (For a detailed analysis, see Krensel 2019.)

Settlement Freedom

When it comes to Settlement Freedom, some African countries have made significant progress, but the majority continue to underperform, and progress is predominantly based on the achievements of regional organizations. Member states of the regional organization ECOWAS are impressively ranked between 13th and 16th place, just behind the EU countries.

 EAC is another positive example of a regional organization, and implementation of the East African Common Market Protocol will lead, among other things, to the free movement of labor. Third-generation ID cards will significantly facilitate the free movement of people in the EAC.

South Africa, on the other hand, has seen a gradual decline in its Settlement Freedom score. Settlement freedom is largely governed by historical relationships between countries, including colonial relationships. Another factor impacting settlement freedom is reciprocity: if one country makes it easy for nationals of other countries to work and settle in its jurisdiction, then other countries may eventually return the favor.

In recent years South Africa has introduced a number of restrictive immigration laws that make it difficult for foreign nationals to settle and work in South Africa, which is also not helped by the excessive bureaucracy.

  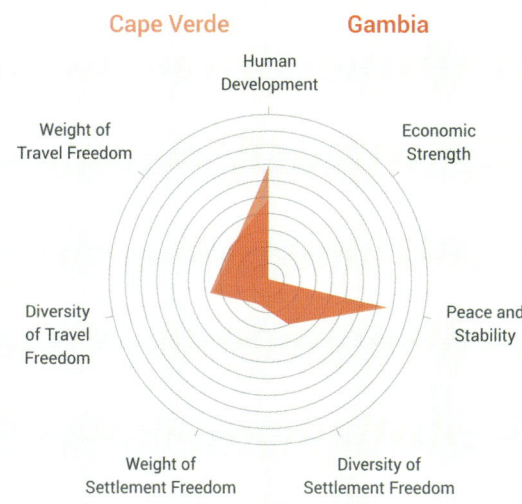

The nationalities of Cape Verde and Gambia outperform the South African nationality significantly on the Settlement Freedom Ranking. Gambia's nationality ranks 14th and Cape Verde's nationality takes 16th position, while South Africa's nationality ranks 50th.

 South Africa's low ranking is due to the fact that among the SADC there is currently no political will to ease freedom of settlement among its member states. Again, the huge economic differences among the SADC states and therefore the 'pull' of South Africa, combined with its very high unemployment rate, make it politically very difficult to implement steps that might lead to a significant improvement in this ranking.

What Will the Future Bring?

In Southern Africa, true freedom of settlement cannot be expected anytime soon. In regions with more or less equal economic development, such as West Africa and East Africa, in my opinion, settlement freedom might be facilitated earlier than in Southern Africa, where the 'push' and 'pull' factors are simply too significant. However, even South Africa is aware of the need to significantly improve business travel within the continent and open its immigration system to accommodate easier access to its labor market for other African workers. The recent "White Paper on International Migration"[3] contains a chapter dedicated to African migration. It has

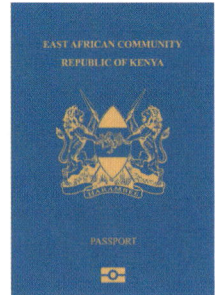

1 Formerly Swaziland

been suggested that Africans applying for long-term South African work visas will be favored over applicants from outside Africa. If South Africa does follow this path, it will also use its political power to ensure its own citizens are granted similar rights in other African countries, which will improve their positions on the Settlement Freedom Ranking.

Conclusion

African nationalities have seen some positive moves in the 2018 QNI General Ranking, with most African nationalities improving relative to nationalities from other continents. The nationalities of Algeria, Kenya, Morocco, and Eswatini (formerly Swaziland) were major risers, each jumping up by five or more spots in 2018. Although these improvements are positive for the continent, the catalysts for these improvements come from within the African continent itself.

The improvements in Travel Freedom predominantly relate to Agenda 2063 and stem from African countries allowing fellow African nationalities to visit without having to obtain visas prior to arrival. African passport holders have not witnessed a significant reduction of visa requirements outside their own continent.

The improvements to Settlement Freedom can be attributed to the benefits of belonging to regional economic communities within Africa. For African nationalities to make true gains on the QNI they should garner support for Africa's efforts from non-African countries and focus on changing any negative opinions of Africa that might exist, a task that will be difficult to accomplish in the short term.

44 Two Sticks, Half a Carrot: External and Domestic Divisions in the Post-Soviet Space

By Ryhor Nizhnikaŭ

Introduction

This contribution presents the quality of nationalities in the post-Soviet space of the Commonwealth of Independent States (CIS),[1] comprising the 12 former Soviet Republics that originally formed the first regional organization in the post-Soviet space. It specifically illustrates the impact of external and domestic pressures that produced the dynamic changes on the quality of nationalities from 2011 to 2018.

After the collapse of the former Soviet Union, the post-Soviet republics made different development, nation-building, and foreign policy choices. Their close economic, political, and security connections gradually diminished despite the Russian Federation's intensified attempts to prevent the erosion of the post-Soviet region (Moshes and Racz 2019). These trends also directly affected the post-Soviet nationalities. The gradual disappearance of post-Soviet intercitizenships among the former Soviet republics and a growing disparity in migration policies, travel, and settlement rights among these countries require a careful investigation of the effects of ongoing disintegration, reintegration, and new integration processes in the region.

By 2011, the CIS nationalities, which are mostly of Low or Medium Quality, evolved into two distinct groups based on their travel and settlement rights. The first one — consisting of Belarus, Georgia, Kazakhstan, Moldova, the Russian Federation, and the Ukraine — enjoyed more rights in general than their South Caucasian and Central Asian counterparts, which comprised the second group. The countries in the first group also had better Internal Value scores, which explain their higher positions in the QNI General Ranking. However, since 2013–2014 the nationalities in the region have realigned along new geopolitical dividing lines, mainly sparked by EU–Russian Federation competition in the region.

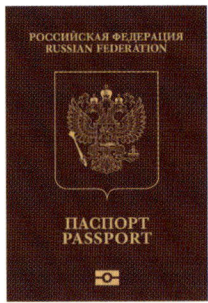
The EU–Russian Federation competition and states' diverse foreign policy strategies pointing towards a "neo-imperial EU" and a "post-imperial Russia" (Torbakov 2013, 173–90) have had a profound effect on the trajectories of the qualities of nationalities in the region, which, since 2018, has been largely divided between two different and competing regional integration processes with opposite sets of benefits and restrictions. As an outcome, visa-free access to the EU was contrasted with a threat of limited access to the Russian Federation's labor market. First, since its inauguration in 2015, the Russian Federation-led Eurasian

 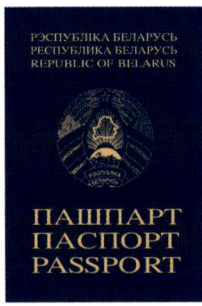 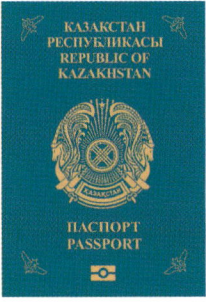 

Economic Union (EAEU), comprising Armenia, Belarus, Kazakhstan, Kyrgyzstan, and the Russian Federation, has offered the free movement of goods, capital, services, and people to its member states. The project revamped integration in the region and created a new intercitizenship based on this integration project, whereby a citizen of Belarus, for example, enjoyed key socio-economic rights in all countries of the Union. The Russian Federation, which was originally a subject of the EU visa facilitation process, transformed access to its territory and labor market into an instrument of power projection applied to maintain its hegemony in the region. It consequently restricted access to non-members, which previously enjoyed de facto and de jure access to the Russian Federation labor market.

Second, the EU offered close co-operation to Georgia, Moldova, and the Ukraine, which proclaimed their Euro-Atlantic aspirations. Aiming at integrating these EU neighbors into its legal and economic space, the EU concluded bilateral political and economic association agreements with three Eastern Partnership countries within the framework of the European Neighbourhood Policy. It also signed Visa Liberalization Action Plans (VLAPs) that granted visa-free travel to Europe's Schengen Area upon completion of a set of reforms. As a major accomplishment, by 2017 citizens of Georgia, Moldova, and the Ukraine were granted visa-free travel to the EU (Ademmer and Delcour 2016, 89–112; Loda 2019, 72–86; Nizhnikaŭ 2018).

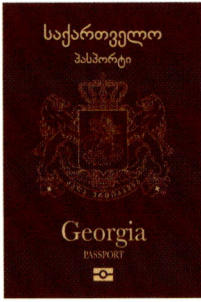  

Today, as an outcome of external developments in the region, Georgians, Moldovans, and Ukrainians can travel to the EU visa-free but have to apply for a patent to work in the Russian Federation. The members of the EAEU face an opposite restriction. The emergence of new regional integration projects accelerated the collapse of post-Soviet intercitizenship (Kochenov 2019a, 19), yet intensified processes that foster new intercitizenships.

Internal developments mattered significantly for the QNI dynamics. The post-Soviet space is a diverse and complex region. The countries differ in their cultures, geographies, demographics, socio-economic development, political institutions, and human capital. They are also at different stages of their state and nation-building processes and have developed different political systems and foreign policy priorities. It is not surprising that the qualities of the CIS nationalities have recorded divergent internal trajectories from 2011 to 2018.

Overall, the domestic developments in the region have led to less stability and prosperity: most of the countries continue to oscillate between defective democracy and authoritarianism; economic growth is rather weak and unsustainable; bilateral and inner conflicts continue to persist; and the South Caucasus remains an area of instability and conflict. On top of that, new major crises emerged in 2014 — the Russo–Ukrainian military conflict after the Euromaidan Revolution, and the annexation of the Crimea — which contributed greatly to instability in the region (Kalinichenko 2016, 334–53).

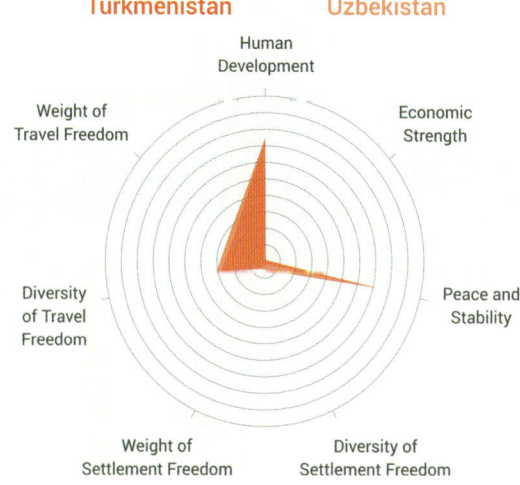

Belarus is the only conflict-free country of the region, yet as the 'social parasites' protests reminded us, its domestic stability is fragile and depends on the Russian Federation's narrowing economic subsidies. In Central Asian countries the ability to access the Russian Federation's labor market remains crucial for their economic and political stability. Two autocracies — Turkmenistan and Uzbekistan — had rather peaceful transitions of power after the deaths of local holders of power. However, the region suffers from weak and corrupt state structures, intra-regional strife, security concerns, and the growing economic presence of China.

Geopolitical competition, domestic developments, and their effects on the quality of nationalities are key developments and challenges, discussed in detail below. In brief, the countries are set on different and irreconcilable trajectories brought about by the presence of two rival transnational projects and persistent divisions of domestic identity, memory, and values.

Competition for Passports and Minds

When Alexander Lukashenko opened up Belarus to the world in February 2017 by allowing five-day visa-free access to the country for the citizens of Canada, the EU, and the US, the Russian Federation's government unexpectedly reinstated passport controls on the officially non-existent border between Belarus and the Russian Federation. Lukashenko, who in 1995 symbolically dug up the signpost on the border between Belarus and the Russian Federation, was furious: "It is not normal to reinstate the border between two friendly and brotherly nations, which we demolished with great difficulty 20 years ago. I do not know, who needs that…. Any [of Russia's] explanations are not valid" (RIA Novosti 2018).

The Russian Federation's border policy towards Belarus, its closest political and military ally, is a show of growing assertiveness in the region sparked by its geopolitical competition with the West. Traditionally both the Russian Federation and the EU promoted their policies towards their shared neighborhood by building political and economic integration and intensifying societal ties. In 2009, the revamped European Neighbourhood Policy offered six post-Soviet states — Armenia, Azerbaijan, Belarus, Georgia, Moldova, and the Ukraine — a new joint initiative, the Eastern Partnership, and the prospect of deeper bilateral political integration in the form of the Association Agreement (AA) and economic integration in the form of the Deep and Comprehensive Free Trade Agreement (DCFTA). Furthermore, the EU visa-liberalization process proposed visa-free travel in exchange for policy and institutional reforms in four blocks that included migration management, public order, and document security. The post-Soviet elites were offered access to the EU market in exchange for economic and political reforms, and the societies were presented with the potential of future economic well-being and visa-free travel to Europe's Schengen Area. Overall, the EU visa-free regime was presented as one of the biggest carrots of the EU's external policy for post-Soviet countries, a major incentive to reform and integrate further with the EU.

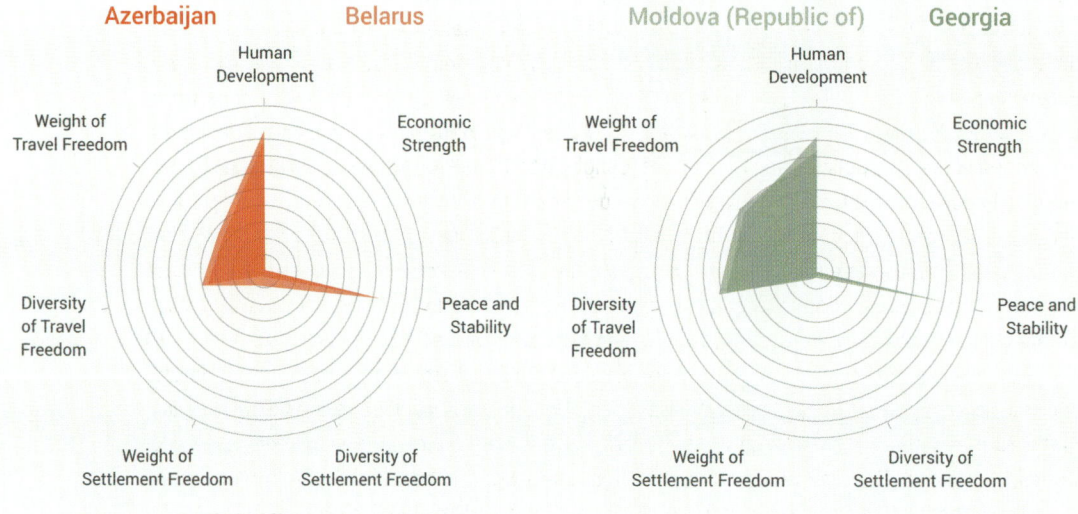

In this regard, Georgia, Moldova, and the Ukraine's significant improvement in their Travel Freedom scores is explained by their achieving visa-free travel to the EU. In 2014, Moldovans were granted the right to reside in Europe's Schengen Area for three months during any 180-day period, which led to an increase in its nationality's External Value score by 7.5 points to 27.2 in 2015. Similarly, the External Value scores of Georgia and the Ukraine's nationalities rose by around 11 points each once their visa-free regimes with the EU were established in 2017. Georgia and the Ukraine nationalities' Travel Freedom scores increased at the same time by around 20 points to 57.0 and 64.7 points respectively, changes that put far behind the nationalities of the other countries in the region, and which continue to lack visa-free access to the developed world.

Whereas the External Value scores of the nationalities of Georgia, Moldova, and the Ukraine increased significantly, the indirect cost was the decline in their Settlement Freedom scores. On the one hand, the 90-day visa-free access to Europe's Schengen Area does not include the right to work. Ukrainian citizens, for example, have limited work rights in the EU and have to apply for work permits. Nevertheless, several EU Member States — the Czech Republic, Hungary, Poland, and Slovakia in particular — have gradually liberalized their labor markets. As a result, the number of Ukrainians who work in the EU has skyrocketed since 2016. Both Polish and Ukrainian officials claim that from one to two million Ukrainians work in Poland (Novoe Vremya 2018). In the third quarter of 2018, Ukrainians comprised 75% of the legal external workforce in Poland, which offers them the right to work for six months without a work permit (Skwirowski 2018).

On the other hand, their access to the Russian Federation's labor market has been reduced. Post-Soviet nationalities have very restricted access to labor markets in general, and the Russian Federation was traditionally a major destination and source of remittances for CIS nationalities. In 2016, Vladimir Putin publicly supported the Ukraine's visa-free regime with the EU, stating that "there shall be no border in Europe", yet the Russian Federation's policies towards the governments of non-EU members and especially Georgia, Moldova, and the Ukraine indicate otherwise.

The Russian Federation has traditionally combined security, economic, people-to-people, and political incentives and pressures to promote its policies. The de jure right to travel to and de facto right to work in the Russian Federation and have access to the higher education it offers there were supposed to maintain its close links with the post-Soviet societies.

The EU's own eastern neighborhood policy clashed with the Russian Federation's traditional vision and interests in the region. The Russian Federation, the regional power with traditionally close political, economic, and cultural ties to the post-Soviet countries, reacted aggressively to the European aspirations of its neighbors and to the new EU policies. Numerous studies discuss, from different theoretical perspectives, how and why the Russian Federation's policies were designed to respond to the EU's policies and their effect (Langbein 2015, 19–42; Ademmer 2017). Led by the Russian Federation, the EAEU served as an institutional response to the EU's regional integration initiatives. In contrast to the AA/DCFTA and VLAP, the EAEU offered economic integration and financial benefits to the elites, and open access to the labor market to the member states. The Treaty on the Eurasian Economic Union introduced a clause stating that from 1 January 2015, employers were allowed to hire the citizens of member states of the EAEU regardless of the existing protection measures of its national labor markets. Furthermore, and in contrast to the EU's external governance approach, the additional advantage for the local elites would be the support of the Russian Federation for incumbent political regimes and their continued hold on power. As a stick, the Russian Federation restricted trade for non-EAEU members and denied them access to its labor market. The Russian Federation tightened its migration laws to prevent granting de facto permanent residence to citizens of countries with visa-free access. As a result, if before

2014 40% of Ukraine's labor migrants traditionally went to the Russian Federation, a number estimated at 1,200,000 in 2012, in 2018 the number fell to hundreds of thousands. According to the Russian Federation's state statistics service, Rosstat, from January to April 2018 only 7,500 Ukrainians entered the Russian Federation's labor market compared to 35,000 from January to April 2016. The number of travel bans increased to 90,000 in 2016 and to 180,000 in 2017 (Rossiyskaya Gazeta 2018).

For non-EAEU nationalities, the Russian Federation has taken two steps to tighten up the residence rules for immigrants from countries with visa-free access who arrive without a work permit. First, the Russian Federation allows foreigners with visa-free access to reside on its territory for a maximum of 90 days within a half-year period. Until 2014, the citizens of CIS countries with visa-free access to the Russian Federation had de facto permanent residence, since they could remain on Russian Federation territory for 90 days without any further time restrictions, which allowed them to return to the Russian Federation the day after any 90-day period without losing the right to legal residence.

Second, in 2015, the mandatory patent system for all foreign laborers from countries with visa-free access to the Russian Federation except those from the EAEU member states was introduced. New rules impose considerable expenses on potential job seekers. It obliges workers from CIS countries to obtain work patents within 30 days of arriving in the Russian Federation. To obtain work patents, applicants are required to register with the Migration Service, undergo a special medical examination, buy insurance, receive an identification tax number, and pass a special exam testing their knowledge of the Russian language, the history of the Russian Federation and Soviet Union, and the Russian Federation's legislation. A fee is charged for each of these official requirements, which often adds up to an overall cost of approximately EUR 200 for each work period, and can rise to as much as EUR 450 when indirect fees are also considered. Additionally, workers have to pay a monthly fee that differs by region. In Moscow the monthly fee for 2019 is set at RUR 5,000 (EUR 70) per month, whereas in Yakutia it is twice as much.

Overall, 1.7 million patents were issued across Russia. Yet, arriving in the country and applying for a work patent is not a guarantee of employment. The official statistics for Moscow show that out of the million workers from the CIS region member states who applied for work patents in Moscow in 2017, only 323,000 work patent applications were satisfied.

The Russian Federation's new policies have a direct effect on the quality of nationalities in the CIS. While travel is visa-free among most CIS countries with some notable exceptions (as, for example, the restrictions placed on Georgians in the Russian Federation), the variation in Settlement Freedom scores is significant. Today the Russian Federation provides unrestricted labor access exclusively for members of the Customs Union/EAEU — that is, Belarus (since 2011), Kazakhstan (since 2012), Armenia (2014), and Kyrgyzstan (2015). In contrast, for example, the Ukrainian nationality's Settlement Freedom score halved in 2016; from a score of 7.9% in 2014 it dropped to 4.1% in 2017 and remained at 4.1% in 2018.

Finally, in addition to competition between the EU and the Russian Federation, conflicting bilateral relations also put constraints on travel. For instance, since 1991, travel between Tajikistan and Uzbekistan has been restricted due to border, transit, water, and energy disputes. Only in 2018 did these parties agree to visa-free travel for up to 30 days. Travel has been mutually impeded between Armenia and Azerbaijan since the Nagorno–Karabakh conflict. In a similar way, after the annexation of Crimea and the beginning of the conflict in the Eastern Ukraine, the Ukraine has imposed entry restrictions for Russian men aged 16 to 60, who are required to provide additional documents to enter the country. In January 2018 the Ukraine introduced biometric border control requirements for Russian citizens, and in November 2018 it imposed a full travel ban on Russian men aged 16 to 60.

The nationalities of unrecognized states in the post-Soviet space face significant restrictions, often having de facto or de jure recognition from the Russian Federation only. In such cases the Russian Federation's policies towards these nationalities vary significantly. For example, only South Ossetians have de jure access to the Russian Federation's market, based on the intergovernmental agreement, On Alliance and Integration, signed in 2015. Moreover, South Ossetians run in elections to serve in Russian Federation legislative bodies and work in its state bodies (Kremlin.ru 2015). The documents of Georgia's other breakaway region, Abkhazia, Moldova's separatist region of Transnistria, and the Ukraine's occupied territories of Donetsk and Luhansk, do not grant the right to settle in

the Russian Federation. Yet Abkhazia's passport allows visa-free travel to the Russian Federation according to the intergovernmental agreement signed in 2009 (Lindeboom 2018, 60–61). In 2017, the Russian Federation recognized the passports of Ukraine's breakaway regions and allowed their holders to travel to the country visa-free (Kremlin.ru 2017). Furthermore, while outright majorities of Transnistrians and South Ossetians possess Russian Federation passports today, the inhabitants of Nagorno-Karabakh automatically receive Armenian passports.

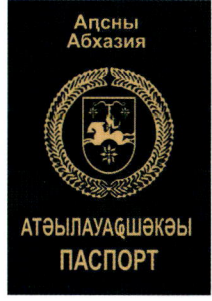
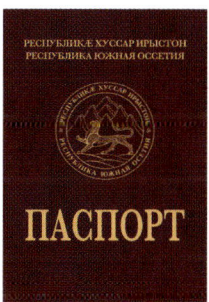
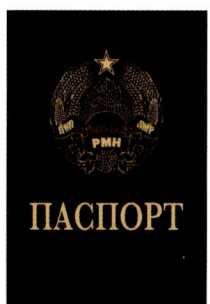
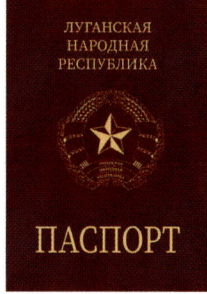
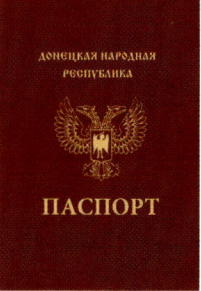

Growing Domestic Disequilibrium

The CIS countries differ significantly in prosperity and human development among themselves and with their Central and Eastern European neighbors. The diverging trajectories of domestic political and economic development in post-Soviet countries present several conundrums. After the collapse of the Soviet Union, Belarus and the Ukraine's human capital and industrial potential offered equally good starting conditions to those of Lithuania or Poland. In 1991, Belarus had a level of per capita GDP similar to Poland and Estonia. However, by the 2010s Poland's per capita GDP had already more than doubled since 1991, whereas the Ukraine still struggles to reach its 1991 level. Today Belarus, Moldova, and the Ukraine 'compete' for the status of the poorest European country. Nevertheless, all three are better off economically than Central Asian countries.

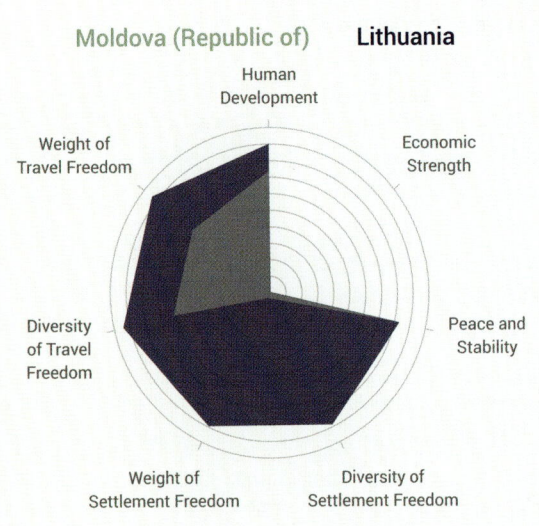

Post-Soviet republics have a dismal record of persisting "crony capitalism, authoritarianism and bad governance" (Gel'man 2015). Their chronic inability to break out of this vicious circle has been the subject of many discussions in the literature. Their political and economic underdevelopment are often attributed to the quality of their political and economic institutions, state capacity, elite preferences, and societal values. The post-Soviet countries possess extractive institutions and have limited access to organizations and resources. Bennich-Björkman summarizes the literature's findings and highlights two key systemic features of the post-Soviet states: the prevalence of personal over institutional ties and a monolithic — rather than differentiated — governance (Bennich-Björkman 2017, 53).

Studies point to neopatrimonial, inefficient, and unaccountable states that are often captured by narrow elite groups, creating fertile ground for backwardness, underdevelopment, corruption, and the region's growing disparity with developed countries. With regard to migration, numerous loopholes caused by obsolete laws and dysfunctional management systems have enabled migrants to the Russian Federation or the Ukraine to prolong their residence automatically after the first 90 days. A significant number of foreign workers have been employed in this way in countries such as Kazakhstan and the Russian Federation. External developments have, in part, made fixing disorganized state institutions, improving regulations on work permits, and tackling illegal labor migration a necessity.

The Russian Federation's attempt to legalize at least a part of this illegal workforce resulted in additional restrictions on employment (as occurred in the Russian Federation itself), as Georgia, Moldova, and the Ukraine reorganized their asylum policies, migration management, and border control and ensured the stricter enforcement of rules as required by the bilaterally agreed VLAPs (EU Commission 2017).

The issue of post-Soviet states being weak and corrupt is compounded by the existence of conflicting nation-building projects in 'unexpected nations' that divide societies along lines of identity and of language, religion, and ethno-regionalism, with contesting views on the past, present, and future. Nationalist anti-migration protests in the late 2000s played a role in the redesigning of the Russian Federation's state migration policy. If ethnic and linguistic cleavages are slowly decreasing in some countries, identity-memory divisions persist. To further complicate the situation, societal groups often possess fluid double identities reflecting their affinity to supra-national identities (such as those of the EU, the Russian Federation, or Turkey). In the Ukraine, Belarus, and Moldova, societal groups attach themselves to Russia or the EU, Romania, Turkey, or Poland (on the Ukraine see Melnykovska, Schweickert, and Kostiuchenko 2011, 1055–72).

Civil societies in post-Soviet states are weak, suppressed, and somewhat passive. In general, state-society relations are distorted, often based on redistributive societal contracts and pervasive corruption. The post-Soviet region records the highest level of corruption in the 35 countries surveyed by the European Bank of Reconstruction and Development (EBRD). In 2016, an EBRD survey showed that eight out of 10 countries with the highest perceived level of corruption are from the region, ranging from 65% of respondents in Azerbaijan, who "usually" or "always" made unofficial payments when interacting with the authorities in their official capacities, to over 20% of respondents in Moldova, Tajikistan, and the Ukraine.

The inequality levels are also alarming. In the Ukraine, in 2018, the energy oligarch Rinat Ahmetov reportedly controlled 30% of the country's GDP, while in 2017 around 7 million Ukrainian households needed state subsidies to pay their utilities bills.

General similarities notwithstanding, large variations among regimes and states in the region can be observed, such as in the different degrees of openness and plurality among the defective democracies and authoritarian states, the varying levels of societal development, and of human capital (Hale 2015; Bennich-Björkman 2017, 51–68). Notwithstanding the situations in Azerbaijan, Belarus, and the authoritarian Central Asian republics, in-decay yet stable political systems in Armenia, Georgia, Moldova, and the Ukraine underwent several readjustments following popular uprisings.

The foregoing discussion highlights the overall instability of domestic political and economic institutions and the growing societal dissatisfaction with elites and the change of direction in the region. The economic recession and hardships of the 2010s were preceded by an economic boom and improving well-being in the 2000s. For example, in 2006, the ERBD's Life in Transition survey recorded fairly high satisfaction with the economic and political situations in Belarus, Moldova, and the Russian Federation. The GDPs of Belarus, Georgia, the Russian Federation, and the Ukraine grew by 5% to 7% annually. In Belarus, the average salary increased from USD 100 per month in 1997 to USD 420 in June 2008, the eve of the financial crisis.

Economic growth and the rise in living standards contributed to the growth of social capital and gradual societal modernization. Though variations across the region remained, new technologies, migration, and growing access to travel and information all became widespread. The number of internet users increased significantly in the region. If web access was scarce in the early 2000s, by October 2018 the internet was being used on a daily basis by 57% of Russians (Levada 2018b); in Belarus, 84% of the population aged 15 to 74 were using the internet on a daily basis. Access to higher education widened, and people were better prepared to pay for university studies. In Belarus, official statistics indicated that 19% of the population had a university degree in 2015 compared to 14% in 1999.

In the 2010s the trend reversed. Severe economic challenges, recessions, and subsequently slow economic growth greatly affected these societies. Except for the Russian Federation, the region's national economies are comparatively small or medium-sized. EBRD estimated that in the 2010s, up to 50% of households were affected by economic difficulties. Corruption, socio-economic challenges, and unemployment remain key concerns for the public (see International Republican Institute polls). As a result, life satisfaction has declined across almost all demographic groups except for those in Central Asian countries and is lower on average than the Central and Eastern European region by up to 17% (as in the Ukraine). In 2010, just over 29% of Ukrainian respondents were satisfied with life, the third-lowest result in the transition region. Life satisfaction and the level of optimism dropped further in 2016 across the region (EBRD 2016, 29). In October 2018, a majority of Russians could not afford to make even short-term plans (Levada 2018a). Trust in public institutions and authorities has plummeted and remains low.

These trends have caused tensions between the elites and the rest of society, with mass protests in post-Soviet countries across the region, from the 'stolen billion' protests in Moldova in the autumn of 2015 to the 'social parasites' protests in Belarus in the spring of 2017. Altogether, societal modernization and growing dissatisfaction with the socio-economic situation and with elites has led to the rise in popular demands for better lives, economic well-being, and services, including access to visa-free travel to the EU. If, in the beginning, the visa-free reforms were a tool to mobilize the public and civil society to put extra pressure on their governments, after the completion of reforms they became a tool for leaving the country. In 2015, during the second stage of Ukraine's VLAP, surveys showed that Ukrainians wanted to put more pressure on authorities to implement the reforms required by the EU (30%) and strengthen sanctions for non-compliance by suspending financial support (22%) (GfK New Europe 2015). In 2017, the official number of Ukrainians working in Poland was one million, and Poland has gradually become the major source of labor for Central and Eastern Europe.

Finally, the post-Soviet nationalities not only lag behind developed countries in human development and economic prosperity, they also face higher security risks. Most states lack stability and peace and numerous conflicts remain frozen and unresolved in the region. Abkhazia, Nagorno-Karabakh, South Ossetia, and Transnitria are just a few examples of areas with unresolved conflicts.

Conclusion

The CIS nationalities, greatly impacted by geopolitical competition and domestic challenges, are in the Low or Medium Quality tiers of the QNI. In general, the settlement policies in the CIS region are characterized by a significant level of protection of their national labor markets, but policies vary, depending on the regime, from all-free-to-work countries such as Georgia to fully restricted Turkmenistan. The rest of the CIS countries, however, have special quotas for their foreign labor forces and oblige potential foreign workers to obtain patents to settle. The overall tendency in the region between 2011 and 2018 has been to improve regulatory access to national labor markets.

The External Value scores of most nationalities in the CIS region have increased to some extent since 2011. Georgian, Moldovan, Russian, and Ukrainian nationalities are the leaders in the region, while Armenian, Belarusian, and Kazakh nationalities lag. The overall increase in External Value scores can be attributed to growing regional integration tendencies in the post-Soviet space. In 2015, the Settlement Freedom scores of the nationalities of countries outside the Russian Federation-led integration projects decreased to some extent due to the growing tendency of Kazakhstan and the Russian Federation — the biggest destination countries — to protect their national labor markets from the nationalities of non-members of the EAEU. Moldova was the only exception because of being admitted to the visa-free regime by the EU.

Among the CIS countries, the Russian nationality enjoys the best place on the QNI General Ranking (62nd) and the highest positions in the Travel Freedom and Settlement Freedom Rankings (72nd and 33rd respectively). Its Settlement Freedom score in particular has grown, from 8.2% in 2011 to 12.2% in 2018, accompanied by the steady increase in its Travel Freedom score during the same period (from 42.7% to 61.9%) thanks to the conclusion of the bilateral visa-free agreements made during that time with a number of countries such as Gambia and Paraguay.

Similar trends are observed with other EAEU nationalities' rankings, in particular those of Belarus (98th on the Travel Freedom Ranking) and Kazakhstan (95th on the Travel Freedom Ranking), which grant each other's citizens the right to settle. Belarusian nationality predictably followed the Russian nationality due to its high Internal Value score, while its Settlement Value score remained stagnant, then decreased slightly, from 10.6% in 2011 to 10.3% in 2018. This can be explained by the fact that while Belarusians' right to settle in some post-Soviet countries was attained before the activization of regional integration processes, Belarus showed a lack of interest in other initiatives, such as visa liberalization with the EU. The Moldovan nationality, in 81st position on the External Value Ranking, and that of the Ukraine, in 73rd position, whose External Value scores skyrocketed after visa liberalization plans were completed, overtook the Belarusian nationality, which is in 106th position, and currently follow the Russian nationality which is in 70th position on the External Value Ranking. Although the Ukrainian nationality improved its position on the QNI General Ranking in 2018, the Russian Federation's decision to review its right of settlement for non-EAEU citizens — and the war in the Eastern Ukraine — explain its 75th position, compared to the 73rd place of the Moldovan nationality. The nationalities of the South Caucasian republics show similar tendencies on the QNI General Ranking: the Armenian nationality (98th) is closer to the Belarusian (86th) and Kazakh nationalities (84th), while the Georgian nationality (77th) is closer to the Ukrainian (75th).

The nationalities of Central Asian republics are in the second group of CIS countries based on their External Value scores. They have been similarly affected by the Russian Federation's new policies, which led to some deterioration in External Value scores in the Tajikistani (124th), Uzbekistani (124th), and Turkmen (140th) nationalities. The Central Asian republics were also affected by the decision of Kazakhstan — which has more than a million citizens of Kyrgyzstan, Tajikistan, and Uzbekistan registered in the country — to grant work permits to citizens of visa-free countries only if they are providing household services to individuals.

Finally, the developments in the region in the last decade point not only to the ultimate collapse of the post-Soviet web of intercitizenships, but also to the gradual appearance of new ones — a trend that will be important to observe in the years to come.

45 Post-Yugoslav Nationalities

By Elena Basheska

The citizenship law of Yugoslavia, evolving along with the federation,[1] served different purposes. These have been well captured by Igor Štiks: from a tool of integration in the Kingdom of Yugoslavia to a tool of reunification and co-operation in the Federal People's Republic of Yugoslavia (FPRY)/Socialist Federal Republic of Yugoslavia (SFRY), the citizenship law became a tool of fragmentation in post-Yugoslav states in the 1990s (Štiks 2010). Indeed, the first citizenship law of Yugoslavia, which was enacted in 1928 (and applied retroactively from 1918), aimed at national unity and the creation of the Yugoslav nation. As put by Malešević, 1928 law "established a single, unitary, state citizenship which corresponded with the then dominant idea that the new state consisted of a single nation composed of the three 'tribes' — Serbs, Croats, and Slovenes" (Malešević 2017). Yugoslav citizens were all persons who had the citizenship of the Kingdom of Serbia, Kingdom of Montenegro, or the Kingdom of Croatia and Slavonia on the day of unification (1 December 1918) and those whose citizenship has been regulated by peace agreements (Štiks 2015, 33). Every citizen had to have ties (or 'home belonging') to one of the municipalities. As with the majority of other federations in the world at the time, the dual character of the FPRY/SFRY nationality was explicit, with all Yugoslav citizens being registered as republican citizens at the republican level. Every citizen of a republic was automatically a citizen of the federation. The 1976 Law on Citizenship regulated the acquisition and termination of citizenship but transferred important responsibilities of the citizenship legislation from the federal to the republican level, including the registration of citizens, the termination of federal citizenship, and the responsibility of republican supreme courts to preside over citizenship matters (Štiks 2010).

Since Yugoslavs had full access to all the republics and could, in principle, choose their republican citizenship depending on their residence, the dual character of SFRY citizenship had hardly any practical meaning for them. Furthermore, the SFRY passport has been described as "one of the most convenient in the world, as it was one of the few with which a person could travel freely through both the East and West" during the Cold War (Van Dijk, Gray, Savranskaya, Suri, and Zhai 2008, 898).

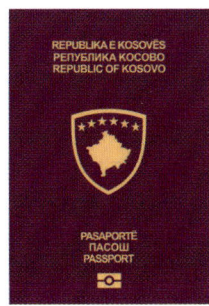

Acquisition of Citizenship in Post-Yugoslav Countries

The post-Yugoslav period, especially the years that immediately followed the dissolution of Yugoslavia, has been characterized by building ethnic citizenship in independent post-Yugoslavian states, which has entailed numerous problematic aspects for citizens of other former-Yugoslav countries who found themselves caught in alien states almost overnight.[2] After the dissolution of Yugoslavia, a number of nationalities emerged from the newly independent states. Currently, there are seven nationalities from the post-Yugoslav countries that are assessed for the purposes of the QNI: those of the six former socialist republics and that of Kosovo. The status of Kosovo, which proclaimed its independence in 2008, is still disputed by a large number of states. Indeed, 48% of the UN member states have not recognized Kosovo as an independent state, including five EU Member States (Cyprus, Greece, Romania, Slovakia, and Spain). The QNI has assessed the nationality of Kosovo without prejudice as to the status of the new-born state. Similarly, this article discusses the nationality of Kosovo in the context of post-Yugoslav nationalities.

All post-Yugoslav countries have adopted *ius sanguinis* and a combination of *ius sanguinis* and *ius soli* as main methods of acquisition of citizenship (Džankić 2012; Krasniqi 2015; Medved 2012; Ragazzi, Štiks, and Koska, 2013; Rava 2013; Sarajlić 2013; Spaskovska 2012). Pure *ius soli* is rather exceptionally used, to prevent statelessness. Citizenship in post-Yugoslav countries is generally granted to all children born in the country to at least one citizen parent (combining *ius sanguinis* and *ius soli*). In (now officially) North Macedonia,[4] there is an additional condition required for automatic acquisition of citizenship at birth: children should not acquire other nationalities.[5] That said, children that had become Macedonians (now citizens of North Macedonia) at birth are then allowed to acquire other citizenships. Children who are born to citizens abroad can receive citizenship from the respective post-Yugoslav countries of which their parents are citizens either automatically or through registration (*ius sanguinis*). Strict *ius soli* applies in general only to children of unknown parents, children with parents of unknown citizenship, and stateless children born on the territory of the respective state.

Acquisition of citizenship after birth is not automatic but is based on lawful residence, ethnic ties, or special contribution to the state. The residence requirement differs in post-Yugoslav states. Kosovo,[6] Montenegro,[7] and Slovenia[8] require ten years of residence, Bosnia and Herzegovina,[9] Croatia,[10] and North Macedonia[11] require eight years, and Serbia requires three years of residence.[12] However, facilitated naturalization is practiced in all seven post-Yugoslav countries, making the way to citizenship easier for certain groups of applicants, including foreign spouses, ethnic descendants, and foreigners who have contributed to the states in various ways. For instance, Article 10(3) of the Citizenship Act of Kosovo stipulates that naturalization requirements (including residence) need not be fulfilled if a grant of citizenship "is in the special economic, social, sports, cultural, scientific, political or professional interest of the Republic of Kosovo." There are similar legal provisions in the Macedonian Citizenship Act (Article 14) and the Montenegrin Citizenship Act (Article 12). The Bosnian Citizenship Act (Article 11) allows for naturalization of people who are considered to be particularly useful for the country even if they do not satisfy all citizenship conditions. Article 12 of the Croatian Citizenship Act allows for the citizenship of people and their spouses where not all citizenship criteria have been fulfilled if granting citizenship would be of a particular interest to the country, as does the Serbian Citizenship Act (Article 19). In Slovenia, foreigners may obtain citizenship if it is in the interest of the country, provided that they has been living in Slovenia uninterruptedly for at least a year prior to applying (Article 13 of the Citizenship Act of Slovenia).

All post-Yugoslav countries allow dual nationality in certain circumstances, at least. Kosovo is most flexible in this respect by unconditionally recognizing and respecting dual citizenship (Krasniqi 2013; Krasniqi 2015, 13). Such wide acceptance is largely due to the political context in which Kosovo emerged as a newly independent state. As noted by Krasniqi, "Serbia's refusal to recognise Kosovo's independence has transformed the country into a territory of overlapping sovereignties" (Krasniqi 2015, 1). The members of the Serbian minority in Kosovo have kept their Serbian citizenship either as their only citizenship or in addition to their new Kosovan citizenship, and some ethnic Albanians have kept their Serbian citizenship in addition to their Kosovan citizenship. Croatia,[13] North Macedonia,[14] and Serbia[15] require applicants who wish to naturalize in their countries through residence to renounce their existing citizenships. Bosnia and Herzegovina[16] and Montenegro[17] allow dual citizenship in general if there is a bilateral agreement with the applicant's country of nationality. Each of them has concluded such agreements with very few countries: Bosnia and Herzegovina has such an agreement with Croatia, Serbia, and Sweden; Montenegro has concluded only one such agreement, with North Macedonia. Slovenia, in principle, does not allow retention of other citizenships to those who wish to acquire Slovenian citizenship through naturalization and satisfy all other criteria.[18] However, EU citizens of Member States with reciprocal agreements on dual citizenship with Slovenia are not required to renounce their existing citizenship when naturalizing in Slovenia.[19]

Qualities of Post-Yugoslav Nationalities

Unlike Yugoslavia, where possessing the citizenship of a particular republic had no significance at all for the people living in the different republics given the federative character of the Yugoslav citizenship as a strong protector of citizens' rights, the qualities of the seven nationalities of the post-Yugoslav countries are different. These can be generally divided into two groups: post-Yugoslav EU nationalities (Croatian and Slovenian nationalities) and post-Yugoslav non-EU national-

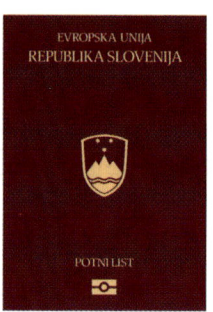

ities (Bosnian and Herzegovinian, Kosovan, Macedonian, Montenegrin, and Serbian nationalities). EU membership certainly boosts the quality of nationalities of Member States by allowing freedom of movement on the territory of the entire Union and beyond, in two other countries of the European Economic Area (EEA), Iceland, and Norway, and also in Switzerland.

Both Slovenia and Croatia have benefited from strong nationalities due to their EU memberships. In other words, the supranational entity, if not federative, significantly contributed to the improvement of Slovenia's and Croatia's nationalities. In terms of the QNI, Slovenian nationality is of Very High Quality, being ranked 15th in the QNI General Ranking with 78.6%, while Croatian nationality is of High Quality in 24th position with 73.8%. Both nationalities have high External Value due to their exceptional performances in both the Settlement Freedom and Travel Freedom Rankings. Thus Slovenians can feel equally at home in 41 countries and territories outside Slovenia (Slovenian nationality shares the 7th place with 11 other EU nationalities and Liechtenstein in the Settlement Freedom Ranking), and can travel visa-free or with a visa-on-arrival to 170 destinations (Slovenian nationality shares 16th place with the Hungarian nationality in the Travel Freedom Ranking),

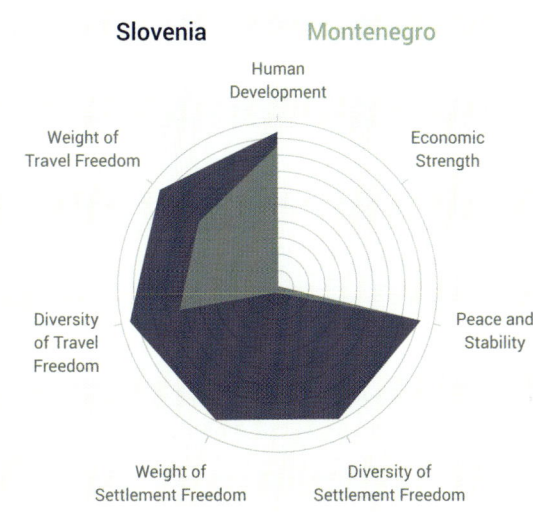

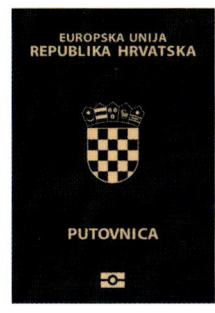 

while Croats have full access to 39 countries and territories outside their home country (their nationality ranks 12th in Settlement Freedom) and can travel visa-free or with a visa-on-arrival to 159 destinations (their nationality is 30th in the Travel Freedom Ranking). At the time of writing, the US has neither removed visa restrictions for Croats nor taken any genuine step towards visa liberalization, in violation of US–EU reciprocity. The value of Croatian nationality improved quite significantly with the most recent removal of settlement restrictions by Malta, the Netherlands, Slovenia, and the UK. Only Austria out of all other EU Member States kept settlement restrictions for Croatian nationals after the end of the second stage of the seven-year transitional period in 2018. Restrictions also apply to Croatian nationals who wish to settle in Switzerland due to the transitional period which is set to end in 2021.[19] Thus, further improvement of the Croatian nationality should be expected in the future with the removal of settlement restrictions by Austria[20] and Switzerland.

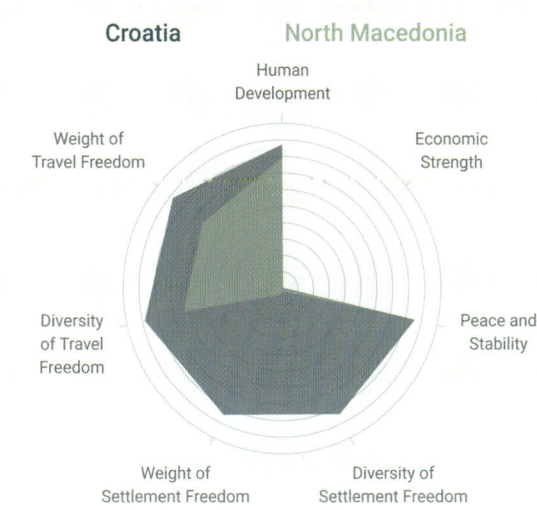

Other post-Yugoslav countries will not join the EU anytime soon, and their nationalities are not expected to improve significantly on either the Settlement Freedom or the Travel Freedom Ranking. Their progress towards EU membership is not the same, however. Starting with accession talks in June 2012, Montenegro has made the best progress on the path to EU membership, and is followed by Serbia, which started its accession talks in January 2014. Blocked for almost 10 years by neighboring Greece since the first recommendation of the European Commission to open EU negotiations, the now North Macedonia has changed its name in the hope of finally unblocking the process (Basheska 2015) and expects to open its accession talks in the near future. Albeit moving at different speeds, towards the EU, all three countries should see improvements in the value of their nationalities once they do join the EU. Finally, the potential candidate countries of Bosnia and Herzegovina and Kosovo are at the 'back of the queue' and have a very long way to go to meet the accession criteria.

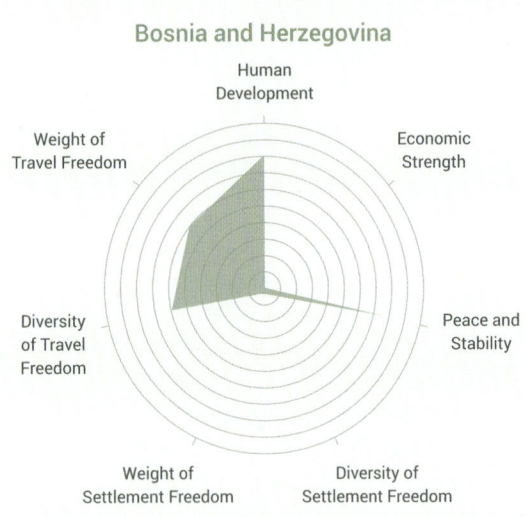

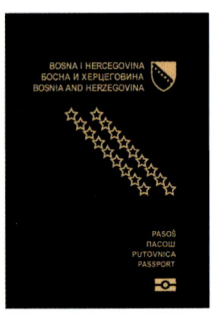

The nationalities of non-EU post-Yugoslav countries are of Medium Quality except for Kosovan nationality, which is in the Low Quality tier in 128th position in the QNI General Ranking with 25.3%. The Serbian nationality is 61st in the QNI General Ranking with 42.1%, Montenegrin is 64th with 40.9%, Macedonian is 67th with 39.3%, and the Bosnian nationality is ranked 71st with 38.8%. In general, non-EU post-Yugoslav countries have weak economies and are fragile in terms of Peace and Stability because of the political instability and numerous ethnic tensions in the region. Furthermore, none of these nationalities allows full access to more than two other states and territories. Thus, Bosnian, Montenegrin, and Serbian nationalities share the 44th position (out of 52) in the Settlement Freedom Ranking along with 21 other nationalities, Macedonian nationality is ranked 49th along with 19 other nationalities, and Kosovan nationality is ranked last in 52nd position along with 47 other nationalities, having 0% and no free settlement access to any country.

All non-EU post-Yugoslav nationalities except for the Kosovan nationality allow visa-free travel to Europe's Schengen Area, which makes the quality of Kosovan nationality the worst among all post-Yugoslav countries. Although the European Commission confirmed in 2018 that Kosovo has fulfilled all the required criteria for visa liberalization, and the European Parliament approved the proposal to amend the regulation listing countries and territories whose nationals need visas for entering Europe's Schengen Area, to date the decision for visa liberalization has not been made by the Council of the EU, and there is no clear indication as to when this may happen (Ivković 2018). The value of Kosovan nationality will increase significantly once Schengen visa restrictions are removed, however.

Belonging to federations and supranational unions usually boosts the quality of nationalities of member states, to which the former Yugoslav nationality and EU citizenship both testify. In summary, since the days of the 'Red Passport', which was considered valuable both in the East and in the West, the quality of the nationalities of post-Yugoslav countries have come to vary significantly. Countries that have become member states of the supranational union (that is, EU Member States) have experienced significant improvement in the quality of their nationalities compared to their value in the period before their EU accession. For instance, until Croatia joined the EU on 1 July 2013 its nationality had a quality comparable to most nationalities of other non-EU post-Yugoslav countries that were ranked in the Medium Quality tier. Thus, in 2013 the nationality of Croatia was ranked 48th in the QNI General Ranking with 43.3%, only nine places above Serbian nationality (57th with 38.1%) and ten places above Montenegrin nationality (58th with 37.4%). The following year, only one year after Croatia joined the EU, the quality of its nationality improved significantly, climbing to the 29th position in the QNI General Ranking with 54.2%, and moving up to the High Quality tier for the first time. It has steadily improved in subsequent years and is now very close to being ranked in the top, Very High Quality tier, which may well be achieved by the Croatian nationality once Austria and Switzerland remove their settlement restrictions for Croatian citizens.

Unlike Croatian and Slovenian nationalities, which benefited significantly from their EU membership, non-EU post-Yugoslav nationalities achieved less impressive scores, and no significant progress is expected in the near future. Except for the possible removal of Schengen visa restrictions for Kosovan nationals and the concomitant improvement of Kosovan nationality, 2019 is not expected to bring notable changes to the qualities of post-Yugoslav nationalities. This teaches us an important lesson: the quality of nationality is not a constant category but follows a country's changes in circumstances. Federations are formed and dissolved, states join and exit unions, or they are torn apart by wars, and economies rise and fall over time. All these factors and many more determine the quality of our nationality. The quality of nationality is therefore anything but permanent and can quickly improve or deteriorate. Indeed, who would have thought that Kosovans, once enjoying great privileges as Yugoslav nationals, would today be worse off than Kenyans and Zambians in terms of the quality of their nationality? Or that British citizens would be applying for Irish citizenship in droves in the face of the UK's exit from the EU? While the example of Croatian nationality shows that nationalities can quickly improve, the nationalities of non-EU post-Yugoslav countries provide excellent examples of the swift deterioration of nationalities. Quality of nationalities must, therefore, not be taken for granted.

46 Citizenship of the European Union and Brexit

By Dimitry Kochenov

Although the EU is not a state, like a state it boasts a citizenship, established more than 20 years ago by the Treaty of Maastricht and derived from the nationalities of the 28 (at the time of writing) Member States of the Union (Kochenov 2009). This citizenship allows the EU to distinguish between 'European citizens' and foreigners, called 'third-country nationals' in contemporary Eurospeak. This distinction, although seemingly clear, is more a symbolic one, since the nationals of the countries in the European Economic Area (EEA) (Icelanders, Liechtensteiners, and Norwegians) and Swiss citizens enjoy almost as many rights as EU citizens despite not being EU citizens (Maresceau 2011a; Maresceau 2011b). The majority of the world's other nationalities are strictly excluded from EU-level rights. In fact, the very territory of rights, which is the unified EU's internal market plus Switzerland and the EEA, does not exist for such third-country nationals, since admission for residence and employment 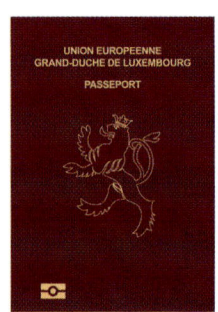 is regulated by EU Member States at the national level, leading to the accusation that the EU is building an *apartheid européen* (Balibar 2001, 190–191). Indeed, while just as, say, Swiss or  French citizens can reside for any number of years and accept offers of employment anywhere in the EU based on the status of their citizenship alone, a 'true' third-country national — an American, an Indian, or a citizen of the Russian Federation, for example — will need to meet the stringent conditions of the national immigration law of one of the EU Member States to settle. And once those conditions are met, the permission to work and reside will usually apply *solely* to the territory of the state issuing the permission, not to the EU as a whole (the exceptions to this rule are truly few) (Kochenov and Van den Brink 2015). By way of comparison, imagine the situation of New Jersey officials gluing a residence and work permit into your Indian passport only to have the New York or Pennsylvania authorities arresting and deporting you on suspicion of residing in their states or engaging in gainful activities across an unmarked boundary between the states. This is exactly how the EU deals with its guests.

Those who are lucky enough to be citizens, however, get a superbly attractive deal, which includes virtually unlimited — that is, unless you are destitute and incapable of working (O'Brien 2017, 509; Schiek 2017, 360–61) — access to residence and work across the EEA, the EU, Switzerland, and in many EU Member States' overseas possessions, including the Canary Islands, French Guyana, and La Réunion. More than 30 of the countries and territories open to EU citizens are world leaders in the Human Development Index and offer extremely high economic potential and significant cultural, linguistic, and social diversity. Some come with generous social security and medical-care systems and have been largely at peace with each other since the end of the Second World War. As a result of this 'EU citizenship boost' added to the nationalities of the Member States, the EU is unprecedented in its concentration of the highest-quality nationalities in the world, and Europe emerges by this measure as the gold standard for all the other continents. This is exactly why the UK leaving the EU without negotiating access to EU citizenship rights, which would be similar to those enjoyed by Norwegian or Swiss citizens, would have disastrous consequences, as discussed in detail in the last section of this contribution.

By law, every national of each of the EU's (still) 28 Member States is a citizen of the EU. And since EU citizens enjoy an array of crucially important rights in the territories of all the Union Member States, including those of residence, work, and non-discrimination, and since membership also confers some political rights, including participation in European Parliament elections and municipal elections in any of the Member States where they choose to reside, the status of EU citizenship is undeniably valuable.

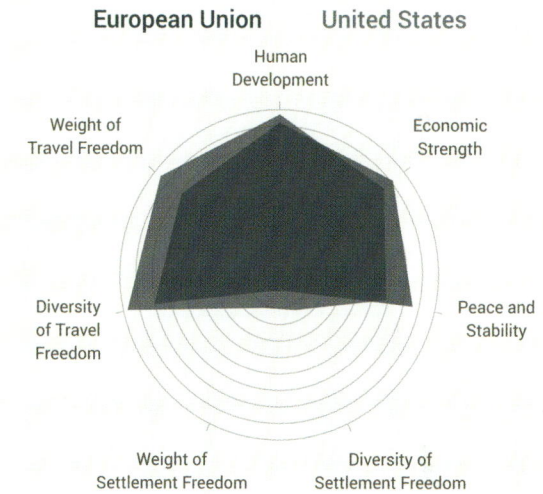

As the biggest economy in the world, boasting very high levels of human development, the EU can legitimately be expected to have one of the best nationalities in the world. And it does. EU citizenship has steadily occupied one of the leading places among the High Quality nationalities in the QNI ranking, consistently ranking alongside the US nationality, and thus above Australia's, Canada's, and Japan's. Only nationalities of the countries in the EEA that are not included in the EU and the Swiss nationality, which enjoy full access to EU territory for settlement and work without any prior authorizations, score higher than the EU's and the US's citizenships. Indeed, if all the individual EU nationalities are excluded from the QNI (since they are component parts of EU citizenship, just as citizenships of, say, Utah and Vermont are parts of the package of US citizenship),[1] as illustrated in Table 1, EU citizenship is ranked in the top 10 in the world, consistently occupying the 6th place, below only Norway, Iceland, Switzerland, Liechtenstein, and the US.

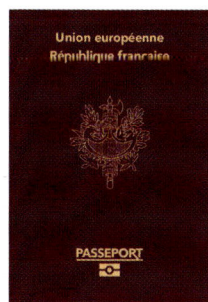 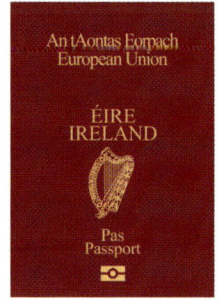

Table 1. QNI Ranking of the World's Top 10 Nationalities with Individual EU Member States Excluded

	Nationality	2018
1	Norway	81.5
2	Iceland	81.4
3	Switzerland	79.8
4	Liechtenstein	78.9
5	US	70.0
6	EU	63.6
7	Japan	58.4
8	Canada	55.3
9	Australia	55.2
10	Chile	55.2

	Nationality	2017
1	Norway	82.0
2	Iceland	81.5
3	Switzerland	80.2
4	Liechtenstein	79.2
5	US	70.9
6	EU	63.8
7	Japan	58.3
8	Australia	55.7
9	Chile	55.5
10	Canada	55.2

	Nationality	2016
1	Norway	81.9
2	Iceland	81.3
3	Switzerland	80.3
4	Liechtenstein	79.2
5	US	71.2
6	EU	64.9
7	Japan	58.6
8	Australia	55.8
9	New Zealand	55.5
10	Chile	54.9

	Nationality	2015
1	Norway	81.6
2	Iceland	80.8
3	Switzerland	79.8
4	Liechtenstein	78.7
5	US	67.2
6	EU	64.5
7	Japan	58.1
8	Singapore	54.4
9	New Zealand	54.2
10	Australia	54.0

	Nationality	2014
1	Norway	81.4
2	Iceland	80.5
3	Switzerland	80.2
4	Liechtenstein	79.0
5	US	65.4
6	EU	65.3
7	Japan	59.2
8	Australia	55.0
9	Chile	54.8
10	Singapore	54.8

Europeans travel on standardized EU-model burgundy-colored passports. (Only Croatia, the latecomer to the feast, has not yet upgraded its blue travel documents, but will eventually, in due course, follow EU soft law on this.) EU passports, which display all their information in the EU's 24 official languages, are inscribed with "The European Union" in the respective language(s) above the name of the Member State that issued the passport.

Unlike other international organizations around the world that mandate their members to issue similar-looking passports, like CARICOM, for instance, the EU Member States' passports are actually symbols of a robust legal status hiding behind their burgundy covers (O'Leary 1996; Shaw 2007). While the internal rights of the holders of such EU passports are far-reaching, as mentioned above, EU citizenship status is also of crucial external significance, and not just for the rights of EU citizens outside the EU to receive protection and services from the consulates of any EU Member State in the countries where their own nationality is not represented (Vigni 2017); if a Maltese national loses her passport in Gabon, for example, the French consulate there will issue a replacement document to enable her to return to the EU. It goes without saying that this right is of huge importance, in particular for those EU citizens coming from small Member States not boasting worldwide networks of diplomatic and consular offices. Any EU citizen's right to receive protection abroad will thus be of much greater importance to a Lithuanian or Maltese EU national than to a French or German EU National.

The status's external importance goes much further. The majority of EU Member States have agreed that the EU, not the individual Member States, will be responsible for the visa regime and visa-free arrangements applicable to foreigners coming to the EU. This has far-reaching implications: the EU is absolutely prohibited by its own law from tolerating any discrimination against its own citizens who are traveling on the documents issued by different Member States in the context of visa-free entry to all the countries of the world enjoying visa-free access to Europe. In fact, the law is crystal clear: any country whose citizens have been granted visa-free travel to the EU will see that visa-free status revoked if it treats EU passports issued by different Member States differently. For example, if Canada were to allow a German visa-free entry but require that a Czech or Romanian apply for a visa, in an attempt to

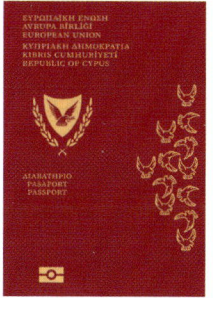

deal with such discrimination the EU would be obliged by its own law to introduce visas for all Canadians traveling *anywhere* in Europe's border-less Schengen Area, which includes 22 EU countries and a number of allied states and semi-independent territories, such as the EEA, the Faroe Islands, Greenland, and Switzerland (Smith-Spark 2018). Only one country in the world has refused to cooperate with the EU on this matter — the US — while Australia and Canada, to give just two examples, changed their visa requirements to preserve visa-free access to the EU for their nationals. The dispute with the US is ongoing: at the time of writing it was discriminating against EU passports issued by Bulgaria, Croatia, Cyprus, Poland, and Romania, not allowing the holders of these documents to enter US territory under ESTA, the automated Electronic System for Travel Authorization that determines the eligibility of visitors to travel to the US under its visa waiver program. The worst-case scenario here, as was concluded by the European Parliament at the beginning of 2017, will be the introduction of entry visas for US citizens for travel to Europe's Schengen Area, a move that will undoubtedly affect the quality of both EU and US citizenships in a sharply negative manner, but is virtually unavoidable as long as the US discriminates against EU citizens who have acquired the status by virtue of a nationality connection with different EU Member States. One can only wonder how effective such blunt pressure could be in developing the relationship with President Trump's White House, which is already confrontational. This is probably the reason why the European Commission has so far been effective in fending off the European Parliament's pressure to introduce visas. In doing so the European Commission was both rational and delinquent, and the Parliament has on numerous occasions threatened to sue.

The QNI looks at the average values of the Weight and Diversity of Travel Freedom enjoyed by all the nationalities of the EU (fully excluding intra-EU travel and settlement rights, which are inherent in the status) to come up with the Quality figure for the EU nationality. This explains why EU nationality occupies a lower place on the QNI rankings than the nationalities of many of the individual EU Member States, such as for instance the Estonian, Finnish, and French nationalities. The discrepancy between the French and the general EU nationality is even better explained by looking, specifically, at Settlement Freedom: since EU nationality works in the entire EU territory, the internal ability to settle across EU Member States enjoyed by all EU nationals is not taken into account as an external component of the quality of EU nationality. This is logical, since when the QNI ranks the nationalities of federal states such as Brazil, India, or the US, the ability to travel and settle between individual states within those federations is not taken into account outside of the scope of the factors contributing to the internal quality of the given nationality. The EU is no different for the purposes of the QNI's methodology. This explains even better the fact that the quality of EU nationality is lower than that of some of the EU's component parts — that is, its Member States. To return to the same example, French nationality benefits from the added external value of the settlement rights that all French nationals enjoy in other Member States of the EU, while EU nationality confers settlement rights in only a handful of countries outside of the EU, such as in Georgia, Iceland, Norway, and Switzerland.

All in all, the QNI makes it absolutely clear that the qualities of EU and US nationalities have remained constant at a relatively similar high level. Importantly, both nationalities are attached to extremely important economies and enjoy a lot of preferential treatment around the world through asymmetrical travel access for short-term tourist and business travel: just like Americans, Europeans are not required to apply for visas in advance to visit the majority of countries in the world, although in this regard some discrepancies exist between the two nationalities: US citizens require visas to travel to Brazil and Iran, for instance, while these destinations are visa-free for Europeans. Where the EU and the US *are* similar is in that there are plenty of countries around the world whose own citizens cannot visit the US or Europe's Schengen Area without a visa but that would not apply reciprocity to EU and US citizens, reflecting the power balance in the contemporary world and reconfirming Yossi Harpaz's analysis of the key nationality groupings (see Harpaz in this volume).

In a way, even though EU nationality ranks below that of the US in the QNI, it is also somewhat undervalued, since the value of US nationality is assessed on the assumption that the EU is a combination of 28 Member States. Should the value be reassessed, replacing visa-free travel to 28 EU states with visa-free travel to just one 'state' (that of the EU) — which would be most logical for the purposes of our thought experiment — the gap between the quality of the US and EU nationalities would greatly increase.

The last issue to mention in the context of EU citizenship is the implications of its loss for any state that withdraws from the Union. The opinions in the literature regarding whether the hypothetical withdrawal from the EU is at all legal, moral, or desirable vary greatly (Kostakopoulou 2018; Worster 2018; van den Brink and Kochenov 2019), but lawyers and politicians are in agreement that the withdrawal of a country from the EU means the loss of EU citizenship by the nationals of the country withdrawing. In the context of Brexit, the future relationship between the UK and the EU thus becomes key in determining the quality of UK nationality. If all the perks of additional EU-level rights are lost, and UK citizens come to be downgraded in terms of rights to the level enjoyed by, say, Moroccans or Belarusians in the EU, the situation will be radically different compared to the choice of a 'Norwegian' or a 'Swiss' model of the future relationship, which, as we have seen, implies the safeguarding of almost all the rights of EU citizenship except for voting in European Parliament elections and in EU Member State municipal elections. As I have demonstrated elsewhere, both the Moroccan option and the Swiss option are possible (Kochenov 2017a).

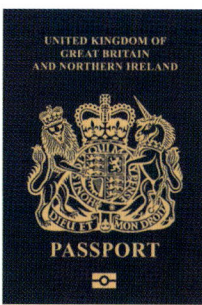
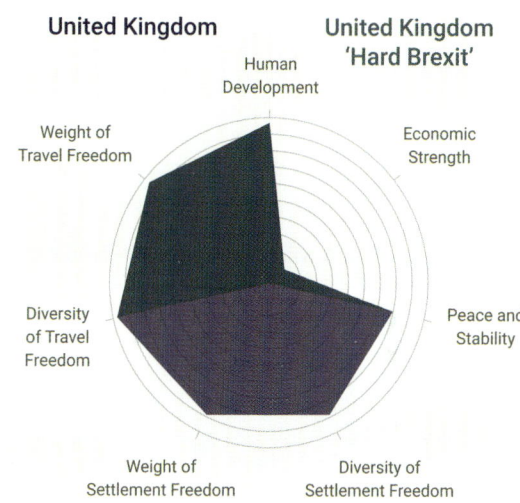

A 'hard Brexit' will result in the UK having a nationality that does not grant settlement and work rights in 27 leading states in terms of HDI and economic strength, thus greatly diminishing the quality of UK nationality. Research shows that the quality of such a crippled UK nationality — even presuming no economic loss for the UK resulting from leaving the EU (an impossibility given the strong economic ties between the UK and the continent) and focusing solely on the external, rather than internal, components of nationality quality — will be in free fall, losing its value very sharply, outpacing by far the countries in the middle of bitter political and armed conflicts and those divided societies whose nationalities are at the 'forefront of failing to perform', such as Libya, Syria, and the Ukraine. This is a sober facts-based warning for Prime Minister Boris Johnson, facts that are no doubt very well known to the populists in power in the UK. The UK is about to establish a world record in terms of profoundly undermining the quality of its nationality without going through a violent conflict, which will cause it to fall from the top tier of Very High Quality nationalities to at best the High Quality tier and, depending on the extent of the economic downturn that Brexit will cause, possibly even to the Medium Quality tier, changing neighbors in the ranking from the likes of Switzerland and Germany to the likes of China and the Russian Federation, nationalities that have never ranked high in the QNI. The *moralité* is simple: EU citizenship is an extremely valuable resource. The decision to give it up — and by doing so diminishing citizens' scope of opportunities — should not be taken lightly.

47 Canadian Nationality: The Value of Belonging

By Jacquelyn D. Veraldi

Introduction

A Canadian national has the right to settle in the 10th-highest scoring destination included in *Kälin and Kochenov's Quality of Nationality Index* (QNI), that is to say Canada itself, a nation that does not grant access to any other group of individuals purely on the basis of their nationality. Indeed, the Canadian nationality fares well in terms of its internal measurements, entitling its possessors to build their lives in a country where there is the promise of enjoying a high quality of life. This contribution, however, seeks to assess Canadian nationality from the perspective of global mobility and to examine, among other things, what it has required from those who have not won the *jus soli* 'birthright lottery' (Shachar 2009) to obtain this status,[1] and what opportunities for such status-holders lie outside the destination to which Canadian citizenship status is attached. In this regard, the Canadian nationality has several distinguishing elements, which are examined in more detail below.

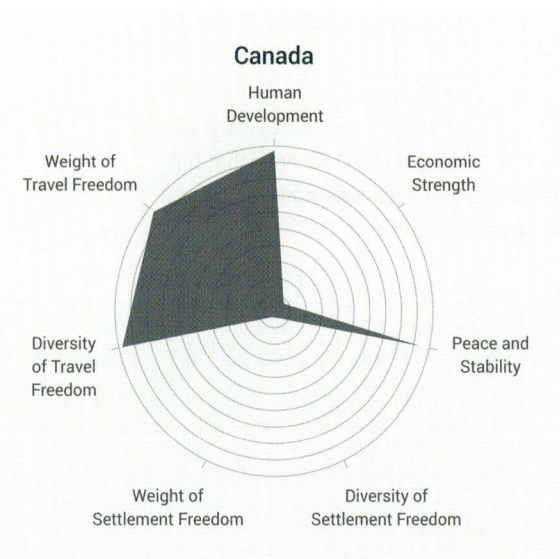

Canadian nationality is relatively recent — the Dominion of Canada was formed in 1867 only — and its enjoyment has been based on legislation crafted from a starting point of exclusion. The first peoples to be excluded from this citizenship (and formerly British subjecthood) status were the Canadian Indigenous peoples, followed by those hoping to migrate to Canada and one day be eligible for Canadian citizenship but were deemed undesirable by the gatekeepers of entry. This policy of exclusion based on nationality, ethnicity, financial standing, and health sought to strike a balance between the country's economic considerations and the perceived undesirability of the majority of the world's inhabitants. A further demonstration of Canada's preference for potential immigrants perceived as economically valuable — and therefore worthier of permanent residence and naturalization — was the invention of the modern points system and the Immigrant Investor Program (IIP). What can be enjoyed by those defined as belonging — that is, the beneficiaries of Canadian nationality status obtained via birth or the selective process preceding naturalization eligibility — is equally noteworthy. Indeed, a Canadian citizen has settlement access to one of the most exclusive, high-scoring QNI destinations, while at the same time having far fewer settlement options than the majority of the world's nationalities attached to other high-value territories. This places the Canadian nationality in 28th position in the 2018 QNI General Ranking, a rather neutral position in terms of its value, neither particularly awful nor spectacular.

The Historical Delineation of Canadian Nationality

The Canadian Indigenous Peoples: Citizens or 'Indians'?

While nationality laws can often be used as tools to exclude territorial outsiders, government authorities in Canada first experimented in the legislative realm to define the rights of the original inhabitants of the territory, its Indigenous peoples. A well-known dark period in Canadian history was marked by the systematic discrimination by settlers against Indigenous Canadians, which was predictably extended to the country's citizenship laws. In the mid-19th century, with an objective to "assimilate the Indians of Canada" (Cannon 2006, 40),[2] the *Gradual Civilization Act* — the precursor to the 1876 *Indian Act* — outlined the conditions an Indigenous man had to meet to be enfranchised, which at that time was the same as becoming a citizen (Milloy 1999, 18; Cairns 2011). The Catch-22 for equality was the surrendering of 'Indian status'[3] (Milloy 1999, 18). When, finally, in 1946, the Indigenous peoples of Canada were defined as citizens in the *Canadian Citizenship Act*, the official justification for their continued disenfranchisement then changed from lack of citizenship status to issues of taxation: only the Indigenous peoples who waived their right to exemption from taxation would be eligible to vote (Bartlett 1979, 191). This electoral disqualification of Indigenous Canadians was only removed entirely in 1960, possibly due to the policy's spectacular failure — of the 60,000 Indigenous persons on reserves only 122 made use of it (Bartlett 1979, 188–91). Today, an Indigenous person who qualifies under the *Indian Act* may possess both Indian status[3] and Canadian citizenship. However, the government continues to insist on enforcing a single Canadian identity for travel purposes, illustrated, for example, by the controversies surrounding the Haudenosaunee passport issued by the Iroquois Confederacy, specifically in the federal government's insistence that foreign countries not accept this document and the penalization of individuals attempting to return to Canada on the basis of it (Marques 2011, 388–90; Corntassel 2012, 87).

Similar to the Canadian government's historical attempts to exclude Indigenous peoples from Canadian citizenship, legislative efforts to exclude groups from abroad that were also disliked by the European settlers became commonplace, but through the use of different tools: immigration law and policy.

The Role of Canadian Immigration Policy in Shaping the Citizenry

It is particularly important to consider Canadian immigration policy in light of the fundamental role it has played in shaping the citizenry of this former colony. Indeed, Canada has long been referred to as the "land of immigrants" (Woodcock 1989, 1), but authorities have not always been particularly welcoming when selecting eligible eventual citizens. In its early days after Canada became a self-governing dominion, when leisure travel occurred only rarely, the common assumption was that those entering the country intended to 'land' and would one day form part of the citizenry.[4] To this day the Canadian naturalization rate is quite high: over 90% of those who arrived before 2000 have naturalized (Griffith 2018). While full-fledged Canadian nationality did not materialize until the 1946 *Canadian Citizenship Act*, authorities carefully determined who could land by using their competence in immigration matters acquired in 1867[5] to determine the future citizenry's demographics.

Since the first *Immigration Act* of 1869, immigration policy balanced a 'White Canada' (Ward 2002) ideal with economic concerns. This was seen, for instance, in the case of the 'head tax' imposed on Chinese immigrants when their labor was no longer needed for the railway; the *Chinese Immigration Act* banned Chinese nationals almost entirely in 1923 (Abu-Laban 1999, 71). Also based on racial discrimination was the 'continuous journey' rule implemented to reject what were fellow British subjects from India,[6] highlighted by refused entry in 1914 of the *Komagata Maru*, a chartered ship that brought nearly 400 East Indians to Canada in defiance of discriminatory Canadian law (Munshi 2017, 65–69). Jews aboard the *MS St. Louis* were similarly refused entry in 1939, an incident identified as a "symbol of Canada's exclusionary immigration policy" in this period (Klein 2012, xviii). These three groups are but a few examples of those who have been precluded from the possibility of building their lives in Canada and one day obtaining Canadian citizenship by virtue of the country's explicit policies of exclusion.[7]

Only the pressure of business interests after the Second World War made Canada open its doors once more during the post-war economic boom, when it welcomed select northern and western Europeans and later Jewish and eastern-European displaced persons, with preference nevertheless given to Baltic 'Nordic types' (Troper 1993, 259–61). The 1962 Immigration Regulations were the first step toward eliminating the 'White Canada' policy (Knowles 2007, 187); preference was still maintained, however, for a category of family members allowed to 'land' from specified countries.[8] After a brief period of openness to refugees, a 1992 amendment during an economic slump heavily restricted their entry while at the same time making it easier for economic migrants to enter (Troper 1993, 280; Drumbl 1994).

A similar pattern of balancing Canada's economic interests against its desire to exclude in its immigration policy, inevitably shaping the demographic composition of Canada, has also been seen in relation to other groups regarded as undesirable (Niles 2018). Since Canada's inception, the prohibition of those deemed likely to become 'public charges' has been a powerful tool to keep the financially worse-off and those in ill health out.[9] Individuals with economic promise have often been exempted, however. This was seen early on, in 1919, with a literacy test intended to filter out the uneducated; nevertheless, the test emphasized that "otherwise desirable and admissible" illiterates who were farmers and domestic workers from select western and northern European countries would be allowed to land (McLean 2004, 19) and eventually obtain 'Canadian domicile' and hence eligibility for citizenship. Candidates from an otherwise inadmissible class thus became less undesirable if they served an economically useful purpose.

The far-from-exhaustive inadmissibility clauses set out in the current *Immigration and Refugee Protection Act* (IRPA) are, similarly to those of its 1978 predecessor, "flexible enough to be restrictive or open, as the government of the day sees fit" (Wood 1978, 564). Applicants are inadmissible on grounds of security, human or international rights violations, criminality, health status — including if they "might reasonably be expected to cause excessive demand on health or social services" — or for financial reasons if they are, or will be, unable or unwilling to support themselves and their dependents.[10] An entire family seeking permanent residence can be denied if one member, accompanying or not, is deemed inadmissible,[11] thereby making them ineligible for Canadian citizenship via naturalization. This was seen in the case of a York University professor whose entire family was denied permanent residence because of his son's health condition, a decision that was overturned at the discretion of the immigration minister on humanitarian and compassionate grounds only after an appeal and much campaigning (Capurri 2018).

Overall, it is apparent that, historically, Canadian immigration policy — a significant determinant in shaping the Canadian citizenry — has been exclusionary on the basis of nationality, ethnicity, wealth, and health, becoming more open only in times of economic necessity or prosperity.

The Continued Economic Focus: The Points System and IIPs

The 1967 immigration regulations introduced the first points-based immigration system in the world,[12] ensuring that the foreign nationals deemed the most economically valuable would have the greatest opportunity among immigrants to one day be eligible for naturalization. While these rules have been described as "totally non-discriminatory" (Hawkins 1988, 52), in reality they sought to filter out a great number of 'unskilled' and 'poorly educated' potential future citizens from the formerly broad family-sponsorship route (Triadafilopoulos 2013, 29). The class of individuals that could be 'nominated' for residence by family members were thus subject to economically focused criteria like those for independent applicants, where points were accumulated in several categories, with education and training being the most heavily weighted. The current *Immigration and Refugee Protection Regulations* (IRPR) divide applicants into the economic, family, and refugee classes.[13]

Under Prime Minister Justin Trudeau, the economic/family/refugee migrant ratio has remained largely the same as in previous years. In 2017, 55.6% of permanent residents were of the economic class, while family members and refugees accounted for 28.8% and 15.6% respectively (Hussen 2018, 15). Despite the Trudeau government's welcoming rhetoric to all migrants, the "reality is growing evidence of [an] econocentric [Harper] policy, both discursively and in actuality" (Dobrowolsky 2017, 211). Evidently, the economically focused policy shaping the demographics of Canada's citizenry will be more accessible to foreign nationals coming from higher-income countries and/or classes, such as those performing particularly well in the QNI's Economic Strength indicator. The policy's gender-related implications are also noteworthy: for principal applicants admitted under the economic class a male-female gap of 12% remains. This number is skewed by the fact that women make up 94% of the caregiver category — the only one of the three economic categories requiring previous Canadian work experience — while representing only 36% of principal applicants admitted as skilled workers and 22% admitted as federal and Quebec business immigrants (Hussen 2018, 17–19).[14] By placing an emphasis on education and skilled-work experience, the points system has the effect of disadvantaging both individuals of low financial means and women, such that the former are largely excluded from meeting this category's requirements and the latter most frequently come in as 'dependents' if at all (Abu-Laban 1999, 77), decreasing their opportunities to one day naturalize and become Canadian citizens.

Previously, a federal IIP also existed. This 1986 IIP provided a path to permanent residency and citizenship eligibility in exchange for putting hundreds of thousands of dollars in specified funds, making Canada the first major destination to offer this type of scheme (Shachar 2018, 5). The program was paused in 1994 (DeRosa 1995, 360, 388) and ended in June 2014 after it was shown to provide little economic benefit to the country (Shachar 2018, 5; Ley 2003). It was perceived as problematic that investors often maintained few links to Canada, reported below-average incomes, and paid fewer taxes (Cohen 2017, 19; Ley 2003, 434–35). In 2015, the Harper government launched a similar program, aiming to attract 'ultra-high-net-worth' individuals willing to make a non-guaranteed investment of CAD 2 million, to be locked in for 15 years, in exchange for permanent residence (Cohen 2017, 9–10). Despite assertions that it would "greatly benefit the Canadian economy" (Government of Canada 2015) the program was an utter failure, having hoped to collect CAD 120 million from 60 individuals but receiving only seven applications (Bagley 2016, 930). Such a result was not unforeseeable given the Canadian nationality's foreign settlement limitations discussed in the following section, not to mention the existence of other residence and citizenship investment programs for destinations and nationalities of higher value as rated by the QNI. Because Canada grants each of its provinces the power to determine immigration policies suited to their particular labor markets and economic needs,[15] with particular powers reserved for Quebec, the latter has maintained its own IIP. This has not come without complications, since the program requires only that investors *intend* to live in Quebec in exchange for Canadian permanent residence, which may leave other provinces with their healthcare bills and increasing real estate costs (House of Commons 2013); the future of the Quebec IIP remains uncertain.

In sum, Canadian law and policy continue to give considerable preference to economic factors in determining who will become a permanent resident and one day become eligible for Canadian nationality, often leaving some of the world's most vulnerable people particularly disadvantaged by ensuring that they will never enjoy the status of 'Canadian citizen' while giving the greatest opportunity to the world's economic elite.

Canadian Nationality: Of What Value?

The QNI data supports the idea that Canada deserves its reputation as a high-value destination: of the internal indicators measured, it is tied for the third-highest Human Development Index score, ranks 7th in Peace and Prosperity, and 17th in Economic Strength — a significant score given the country's population of 37 million. However, the positive global perception of Canada and its citizens widely reported in the media bears practically no relation to the formal willingness of other countries to receive Canadian nationals or to its nationality, which is not particularly valuable in terms of the opportunities granted to its holders seeking to build their lives elsewhere. This is reflected in Canada's underwhelming position of 28th in the QNI General Ranking and even more so in its 44th rank in Settlement Freedom, where it scores 4.1 out of 100. Canadians have temporary visa-free or visa-on-arrival travel to roughly 175 destinations, a highly diverse range, but one that is in no way exceptional: over two dozen other nationalities have access to the same number or more.[16] And the ability of Canadians to settle and take up life in another country without restrictions is nearly non-existent: just Svalbard and Georgia are options, and these destinations are by no means uniquely available to Canadians.

Thus, while Canada as a destination with a high quality of life is less accessible for every other nationality in the world, if Canadians possessing only Canadian nationality want to settle elsewhere they must go through the typical legal hurdles encountered by other nationalities that also have few or no restriction-free settlement opportunities abroad. Of course, it may often be easier for Canadian nationals to overcome these hurdles because of the opportunities they enjoy within their own country. For instance, given this nationality's strong performance in internal determinants of quality, Canadians may be more likely to possess the financial means or skills necessary to apply for visas for destinations of interest than nationals of lower-income countries faced with the same legal barriers. Nevertheless, the position of the Canadian nationality within the QNI demonstrates that it is hardly remarkable in terms of formal barriers to settlement abroad. It also demonstrates the importance of measuring citizens' opportunities on the basis of more than internal indicators: by making use of their extensive settlement opportunities, nationals with freedom of movement in the EU from countries with lower overall quality-of-life scores than Canada's may still be better placed to move abroad and improve their own quality of life, as demonstrated by the higher QNI General Ranking of every nationality with such access; for Canadians wishing to settle abroad, by this measure their nationality is largely unhelpful.

Conclusion

This contribution has sought to draw attention to several elements that together tell the somewhat peculiar story of Canadian nationality. Since Canada's inception, authorities have gone to great lengths to mold the Canadian citizenry via legislative exclusion by laying down conditions to be met for Canadian citizenship status eligibility and enjoyment of the benefits of Canada as a high-value destination — otherwise not available without restriction. Such exclusion was applied first to the Indigenous peoples of Canada and subsequently to those perceived as 'undesirable' based on nationality, ethnicity, wealth, and physical or mental fitness. Discrimination was the rule in determining who could land and one day become eligible for Canadian nationality; exceptions were made where the economic prosperity of the country depended on it. The continued economic focus in determining who can eventually naturalize has been reflected by the creation of the points and IIP systems. In terms of its quality, the Canadian nationality's greatest strength may lie in the right of its holders to settle in a high-value destination, which is to say Canada itself. Depending on whether an individual wishes to stay in Canada or settle abroad, the utility of Canadian nationality to its bearer will differ accordingly.

48 Mexican Nationality

By Pablo Mateos

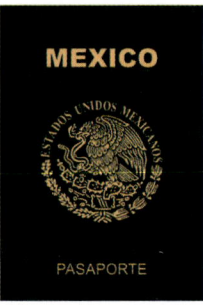

Mexico is a country with nearly 120 million inhabitants, 99.2% of whom are native-born and hence full citizens, thanks to automatic *ius soli* provisions. Moreover, there are 11.6 million Mexican-born people living in the US, comprising a total citizenship population of about 131.6 million Mexican-born people residing in North America. Furthermore, there are 12.6 million US-born persons living in the US or Mexico with at least one Mexican-born parent. This group includes Mexican nationals by birth, since Mexican nationality is automatically assigned to children of the Mexican native-born. Finally, there are another 11.8 million people living in the US who claim other Mexican heritage (third generation or beyond), and who may soon be entitled to Mexican nationality thanks to a constitutional reform being discussed for the last few years in the Mexican Senate and Congress (Mateos 2017). If successful, this constitutional reform would introduce unlimited *ius sanguinis* transmission of Mexican citizenship over generations, as the Italian model does. All in all, there could soon be 156 million Mexican nationals on both sides of the 3,000-kilometer Mexico–US border (all figures, US Census Bureau 2015). The magnitude of these numbers explains why Mexico's nationality policy is increasingly relevant in North America and cannot be disentangled from the population of the US or from the migration policies of its powerful northern neighbor.

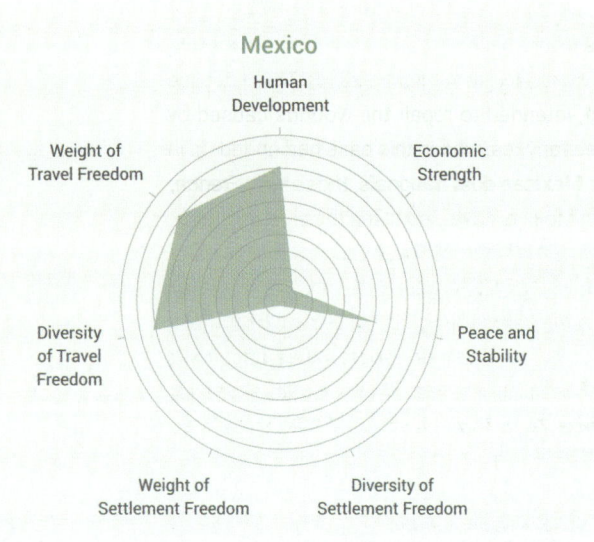

The recent shift towards a renewed interest in Mexican citizenship can be traced back to 12 December 1996, when the Mexican Congress approved a constitutional reform known as 'non-forfeiture' (*no pérdida*) of Mexican nationality (Secretaría de Relaciones Exteriores 2009), together with a new nationality law that for the first time in history allowed dual nationality for Mexican nationals. That Congress chose such a symbolic date to pass this legislation — the Day of the Virgin of Guadalupe (*Día de la Virgen de Guadalupe*), one of the most important symbols of Mexican nationalism — was a strong signal of the intentions behind this reform and that it was a tool of diaspora politics, aiming to embrace the large Mexican-born population living in the US and to facilitate the political integration of its members into both countries. This new law, which entered into force in 1998, has allowed de facto Mexican dual nationality for Mexicans and eased the naturalization requirements for the acquisition of Mexican citizenship by removing the need to renounce one's birth citizenship (Mateos 2018).

The naturalization route to becoming a Mexican by residence is open to foreign nationals with work permits who live in Mexico. The residence period is typically five years of legal permanent residence. This period is reduced to two years for those born in Ibero-American countries (including all of Spanish-speaking Latin America), Brazil, Portugal, or Spain, and for the spouses or parents of Mexican nationals (Camara de Diputados 1998). The two years' residence period preferentially required of Ibero-Americans for naturalization is typically reciprocal, and so Mexican nationals can naturalize after two years of residence in 22 countries, including in the EU Member States of Spain and Portugal. This is another intrinsic value embedded within Mexican citizenship.

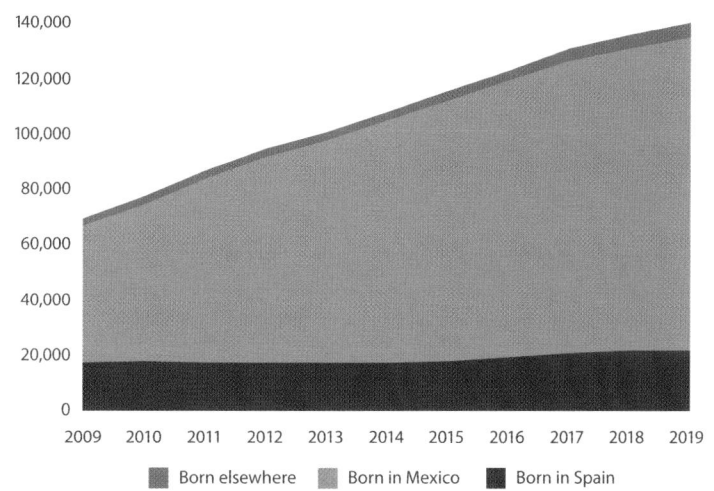

Figure 1. Birthplace of Spanish Citizens living in Mexico (2009–2019)

Furthermore, over the last decade a renewed global interest in obtaining EU passports through the ancestry route has been particularly popular in Latin America, a continent historically settled by European migrants in the late 19th century and the first half of the 20th century. As of 2018 there were 135,955 Spaniards who were born and continue to live in Mexico, an increase of 100% since 2009, when such data was first collected (Instituto Nacional de Estadística 2018). This increase is mostly due to Spain's 2008 Historic Memory Act, intended to repair the wounds caused by the Spanish Civil War and embrace that war's refugee families, who in this case had ended up in Mexico (Izquierdo Escribano and Chao 2015). Other Mexican dual nationals, those with French, German, Greek, and Italian passports who are living in Mexico, have also taken the ancestry route to EU citizenship. Through over 90 interviews with these dual Euro-Mexican nationals, I gathered evidence about their main motivations for seeking EU citizenship: to increase their global mobility options and travel visa-free or with a visa-on-arrival to the neighboring US; to seize opportunities for short periods of education, work, or business; to improve career opportunities (including intracompany transfers and freelance work); and, in the case of older Mexicans, to reconnect with part of their family histories, repair memories of exile, or foster a sense of belonging to an ancestral community (Mateos 2018).

Mexican nationality is ranked 52nd with a value of 45.7 in *Kälin and Kochenov's Quality of Nationality Index* (QNI) 2018 General Ranking. This places Mexico in the Medium Quality tier, but behind other

Latin American countries such as Chile, Argentina, Brazil, and Uruguay, here listed in their ranking order. This is most likely because of the issues of violence and lack of good governance that Mexico has experienced over the past 13 years, which are some of the internal factors that are looked at to calculate the QNI. These national-level indicators perhaps ignore the stark contrasts in the political and security situations among geographical regions and between socio-economic classes. Middle- to high-income families living in the main urban areas and prosperous economic regions enjoy a far superior quality of life than Mexican citizens in less affluent areas, and the more affluent areas are attracting foreign investment, expatriates, and retirees.

The External Factors in the Index are more positive, however, since Mexico enjoys a high ranking in Travel Freedom Ranking at 35th; on the Diversity of Settlement Freedom scale Mexico is in the bottom half of countries but not among the bottom quartile. In fact, between 2015 and 2018, Mexico's Travel Freedom Ranking improved dramatically, from 49th to 35th.

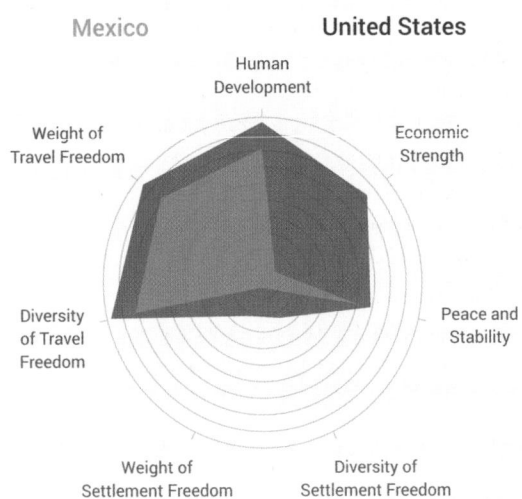

Overall, a Mexican passport allows visa-free or visa-on-arrival travel to Europe's Schengen Area and the whole of the EU/EEA, the rest of Latin America, and other developed countries such as Japan, New Zealand, and, most importantly, Canada, which at the end of 2016 lifted a visa restriction on Mexicans that had been in effect for seven years. This was due to the introduction of Canada's electronic pre-approval system prior to flight departure, a tool that in fact distinguishes Mexicans by using certain profiling rules. As more countries move to implement electronic pre-approval systems, it is very likely that formal visa requirements for Mexican nationals will be lifted for even more destination countries.

Furthermore, the qualitative value of a Mexican passport is also important in the context of the US. During the research interviews I carried out at Mexican consulates in the US, I found that a common reason for dual US–Mexican nationals to apply for a Mexican passport was to be able to travel more freely than would be permitted on their US passports to places such as Cuba and Russia, or Iran, the Middle East, and Muslim countries elsewhere in the world. The other two reasons are to be able to inherit or acquire property in Mexico, which is very difficult for foreigners (and in coastal and border regions, completely forbidden) and to be able to attend Mexican universities. Given the strong devaluation of the Mexican peso against the US dollar over the last five years and the rising costs of US universities, Mexico has become even more attractive for immigrants from the US and Canada seeking a second home, affordable retirement, high-quality and more affordable graduate education, and, for entrepreneurs in the tech industry, close proximity to Silicon Valley.

With regard to this last point, it is interesting to observe a sharp increase in the number of skilled foreign workers employed by American, German, Indian, and even Russian software companies in Mexico, especially in the Guadalajara technology hub (which is just a three-and-a-half-hour flight away from San Francisco). As the US under the Trump administration places ever more stringent restrictions on skilled immigration, the value of Mexican nationality, which provides access to a base from which to work and conduct business with the US, will most likely increase.

It is now common in Mexico to see IT and engineering employees from Chile, China, Egypt, India, Pakistan, the Russian Federation, Turkey, and other countries supplying the global IT workforce (Selee 2018). These are highly skilled individuals, typically with valid US tourist visas but for whom their companies cannot get US work permits because of the limited number of those visas available. Their companies can get them Mexican work visas, however; by setting up bases in Mexico they can attend meetings with customers and contractors in the US and easily follow up on business from the Mexican side of the border. We could even witness a situation similar to that of the late 19th to early 20th centuries, when a US immigration ban aimed at Asian countries led to large populations of Chinese and Japanese nationals stuck on the Mexican side of the US border (Durand 2014).

In the long term, this trend will encourage more interest in the value of Mexican permanent residence and eventually Mexican citizenship. As Mexican nationals, employees of multinational companies would find it much easier to obtain US tourist visas linked to their companies, and even North American Free Trade Agreement (NAFTA)/United States-Mexico-Canada Agreement (USMCA) three-year work visas, also known as non-immigrant NAFTA Professional or TN visas.

In 2018 NAFTA was revoked by the US and replaced by a new agreement, the USMCA. Neither of these trade agreements include visa-free labor mobility clauses. However, the quota-free system of preferential US temporary visas (that is, TN visas) for Mexican nationals performing skilled jobs in certain professions or for businesspeople who make investments in the US enabled thousands of wealthy Mexicans to escape the critical period of drug-cartel violence of 2006–2012. Mexico is also a signatory to other free-trade agreements with ease-of-travel and settlement provisions, such as the Pacific Alliance signed in 2011 with Chile, Colombia, and Peru, and other agreements with Asian nations. As a result of various trade agreements, for instance, Mexican nationals do not need tourist visas to travel to Japan, Korea, New Zealand, and all of Latin America and Western Europe.

In the Trump era of American politics, Mexican nationals have faced new challenges in North America on both sides of the border. We have seen a substantial growth of documented Mexico–US migration flows characterized by more skilled and educated migrants and many fewer undocumented migrants than in previous decades.

As the US collects more and more data on foreign nationals, the worldwide value of Mexican nationality will increasingly depend on personal factors such as income, education, assets, business, career history, ancestry, dual citizenship, and — more worryingly — on phenotype. My personal take is that we are seeing the end of an era in which the value of a nationality meant a universal bundle of rights covering all citizens, inside and outside of their countries of citizenship. Slowly but steadily we are witnessing the unbundling of citizenship rights into person-level profiling, facilitated by the arrival of Foucauldian-style biopolitics, through new state technologies of biopower and discipline. Over the next few years we will see many more of these technologies deployed along the Mexico–US border and in international airports. The dangers of these developments are related to the possibility of the unbundling of Mexican citizenship into poorer and richer Mexicans, or darker-skinned and lighter-skinned Mexicans, at least in terms of mobility rights.

49 French Nationality

By Sébastien Platon

Acquisition and Loss of French Nationality

The analysis of nationality law is always instructive. Beyond the technicalities of conditions and procedures, it reveals a lot about a country's culture, history, and conception of 'belonging'. French nationality law is no exception. Rules about the acquisition of French nationality reveal some aspects of French history and the country's challenges in the 19th and 20th centuries whereas the rules, debates, and practices with regard to the loss of French nationality reveal more recent concerns, in particular in the context of terrorism.

French law on the matter of the acquisition of French nationality distinguishes between acquiring the nationality 'by birth' (called 'attribution') or after birth, termed 'by acquisition'.

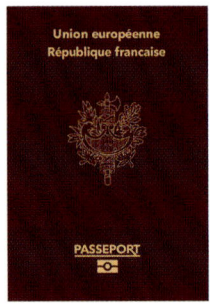

With regard to acquisition by birth, French nationality law is a mix of *jus soli* and *jus sanguinis*. Some scholars argue that the *jus solis* was introduced into French nationality law as a way of coping with birth-rate issues back in the 19th century, especially for military purposes in the aftermath of the 1870 Franco–Prussian War (Bonnet 1974, 8, 153–54, 159–60). Niboyet, a celebrated French private international law professor practicing at the beginning of the 20th century, is often quoted for his observation that "the shadow of the recruitment office looms over [French nationality-law] texts" (Niboyet 1938, t. I, 54). Others argue that the relationship between *jus solis* and military service in France is more complex. Brubaker, for example, argues that the introduction of *jus solis* in France in its 1889 Nationality Act was both a way to ease the resentment of French nationals disgruntled by the fact that second- or third-generation immigrants were exempted from military duties and a manifestation of the republican ideology of assimilationism (Brubaker 1998, 85 et seq.). Be that as it may, the French legal system of nationality displays features of both *jus sanguinis* and *jus soli*. For example, children are French at birth when at least one of their parents is French regardless of where the children themselves were born (*jus sanguinis*).[1] However, French nationality is also granted at birth to children who are born in France provided either that one of their parents was born in France[2] (double *jus soli*) or that the children have no other nationality.[3] Furthermore, people who are born in France to non-French parents acquire French nationality automatically and without any formality when they reach the legal age of majority (currently 18 years old) provided that they reside in France when they reach that age and that they have been continuously residing in France for at least five years from the age of 11 (simple *jus soli*). However, such people can claim French nationality through their parents, earlier, from the age of 13 onwards (in this case, after continuously residing in France from the age of eight), or by themselves from the age of 16 onwards.[4]

People can also become French after birth, either automatically by declaration or by naturalization.

There are several cases in which people can acquire French nationality automatically after birth. This is notably the case for underage children when one of their parents acquires French nationality, provided that children reside continuously with the parent in question, this condition being adapted in cases of divorce.[5]

This is to be distinguished from the situations of some persons, who have a *right* to French nationality and can acquire it by a simple declaration. Unlike in cases of naturalization, the French authorities cannot refuse such applications for 'nationality by declaration'. The government can refuse the acquisition of French nationality only if it gives reasons, which can be based only on a very limited number of grounds as set out in French law. This system of acquisition by declaration applies, for example, to children who have been adopted by a French national or placed in the care of a French national or the French child welfare office for a certain period;[6] persons who have behaved as and who have been treated as French nationals by the public and by the administration for at least 10 years;[7] and elderly immigrants who have resided in France for at least 25 years and who have a direct French descendant.[8] The acquisition of nationality by marriage, after a certain period, is technically one of these forms of acquisition by declaration. However, because there is also a suspicion of possible marriages of convenience, this form of acquisition is subject to numerous conditions, some of them vague enough to allow the administration a degree of discretion, notably the option to conduct an interview, the purpose of which is to make sure spouses have lived together continuously since the date of their wedding and have, since that date, had a material and 'emotional' [*sic*] relationship.[9]

Finally, a person can be given French nationality by naturalization. In this case, the administration may refuse to grant nationality even if all the conditions are fulfilled. To apply for naturalization, applicants must be of legal age,[10] reside legally in France,[11] be professionally and culturally integrated into the French community,[12] and have good morals,[13] which includes not having been convicted of one of the crimes which would prevent them from acquiring French nationality.

French nationals who have at least one other nationality can either ask to renounce their French nationality[14] or lose it as the consequence of a decision of the French public authorities. The latter possibility contrasts with the traditions of other republics. For example, in *Afroyim v. Rusk*, the US Supreme Court ruled that citizens of the US may not be deprived of their citizenship involuntarily.[15]

There is a distinction under French law between 'loss', strictly speaking, and 'deprivation' of nationality. Deprivation of nationality is a form of punishment applicable to nationals deemed 'unworthy' of French nationality. Historically, this form of loss of nationality for unworthiness was first applied in the context of the abolition of slavery. According to Art. 8 of the 1848 Decree on the abolition of slavery, any French citizen in France or abroad who owned, bought, or sold slaves or participated in slave trafficking, directly or indirectly, would be deprived of French nationality. Nowadays, deprivation of French nationality is usually the consequence of having been convicted of certain serious crimes, notably terrorism, misbehavior in the case of public officials, or avoidance of national service obligations. However, if French nationals have acted for the benefit of foreign states against the interests of France and in a manner incompatible with French nationality, they can be deprived of French nationality without having been convicted.[16] In any case, people can be

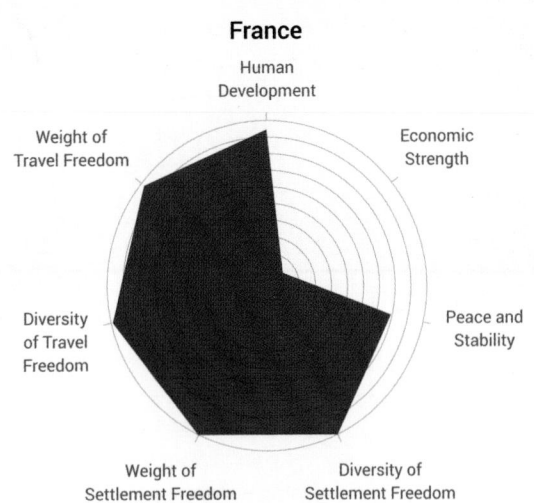

deprived of their French nationality only within 10 years of first acquiring it and no later than 10 years following the events that would legally justify them being deprived of nationality.[17]

It is worth noting that only people who have acquired French nationality after birth can be deprived of their nationality, which means that French legislation contains an intrinsic difference in the treatment of French nationals by birth and French nationals by acquisition. The French Constitutional Council stated in 1996[18] and confirmed more recently in 2015[19] that despite the fact that French nationals by birth and French nationals by acquisition are in the same situation — which in principle prohibits any difference in how they are treated — the French legislation on deprivation of nationality is not contrary to the constitutional principle of equality considering the importance of fighting against terrorism, the gravity of acts of terrorism, and the limited period (10 years) during which such deprivation may occur. This reasoning is rather questionable and has been heavily criticized by scholars (Julien-Laferrière and Teitgen-Colly 1997, 86; Lagarde 2004). In particular it is rather unclear how the 'gravity' of terrorism justifies the difference in treatment of French nationals by birth and French nationals by acquisition. In any case, it does not concern crimes other than terrorism, for which the issue of constitutionality remains open. Deprivations of nationality are rare,[20] however, especially on grounds other than terrorism,[21] which makes it unlikely (although not impossible) that the Constitutional Council will ever be called on to decide whether or not the other grounds of deprivation of nationality are compatible with the French Constitution.

In recent years, successive governments have tried to 'weaponize' (Lepoutre 2015, 118) the deprivation of nationality as an instrument to fight against insecurity and especially against terrorism, usually as a reaction subsequent to a dramatic event. In 1996, terrorism was added as a ground for deprivation following the 1995 Paris attacks.[22] In 2010, after gunshots were fired at police officers in Grenoble in a period of civil unrest, the French president at the time, Nicolas Sarkozy, suggested in a speech to extend deprivation of nationality to any person who wilfully endangers the life of a police officer (Rakotoarison 2010) but he never implemented this. In 2015, after the more recent attacks in Paris, the French president at the time, François Hollande, tried to amend the French Constitution so that parliament could pass a bill allowing the French authorities to deprive French-born nationals of their nationality[23] even though it was far from certain that such a constitutional amendment was necessary since such a bill would probably not have violated the Constitution. In addition to other criticisms, it was argued by some that the project was targeting French nationals born in France of foreign parents and that it would add to an ethnic conception of nationality incompatible with the republican liberal tradition of France (Geisser 2015, 10 et seq.). After tense debates in parliament and among the general public, President Hollande dropped the project (Willsher 2016).

One may wonder, however, if there is not already, hidden in French law, an unspoken system of deprivation of nationality for French nationals by birth. In some cases, French nationals who have another nationality can lose their French nationality, regardless of whether they are French by birth or by acquisition. For example, if a French national has never resided in France and has neither behaved like nor been treated as a French national by the public and by the administration for 50 years, a judgment can declare that this person has lost their nationality.[24] Unlike deprivation, this loss, strictly speaking, is not exactly a form of punishment. It is, rather, supposed to be a statement of the 'fact' that a French national has ceased to behave like a French national. However, in some cases, the loss of nationality may seem like a form of punishment. In particular, French nationals can lose their nationality by governmental decree if they behave like nationals of other countries of which they are nationals[25] or if they have not renounced serving foreign states or international organizations of which France is not a member despite being ordered to do so by the French government.[26] In such cases, the distinction between the grounds for deprivation and those for loss appear blurred. Some scholars (Lepoutre 2016) consider this to be a form of 'unnamed deprivation of nationality'; it was applied after the Second World War and until the end of the 1960s to Nazi collaborators, Italian fascists, and Soviet communists[27] with multiple nationalities, even though they were French by birth.

French Nationality and French Overseas Territories

The French nationality is better than any other nationality, ranked 1st and scoring 83.5% in *Kälin and Kochenov's Quality of Nationality Index* (QNI) General Ranking for 2018. French nationality allows visa-free or visa-on-arrival travel to 177 destinations, which is a lot, yet it is ranked 5th in Travel Freedom in the 2018 QNI, scoring 98.3% along with the Danish, Italian Spanish, and Swedish nationalities and lagging behind the nationalities of Japan (ranked 1st and scoring 100%), Germany (ranked 2nd and scoring 98.8%), Singapore (ranked 3rd and scoring 98.6%), and Finland (ranked 4th and scoring 98.4%). To understand how France has taken the 1st position in the General Ranking of the QNI, we have to take French overseas territories into consideration.

Remnants of the French colonial empire, the overseas territories form part of France, and French nationality rules apply to them. This was not always the case, however, and France's history as a colonial empire was characterized by discriminatory statuses based on race and religion, especially in Algeria. In 1865, under the Second Empire, the *senatus-consulte* (an Act of the Senate) on the status of persons and naturalization in Algeria stated that "The Muslim native is French; nevertheless he will continue to be governed by Muslim law" (Article 1) and that "The Israelite native is French; nevertheless he continues to be governed by his personal status [that is, the 'Mosaic' status]" (Article 2). A native "may, at his request, be admitted to enjoy the rights of a French citizen; in this case he is governed by the civil and political laws of France." This sort of 'naturalization' (even though the 'natives' were *already* supposed to be French) was at the discretion of the French administration, and it meant people giving up their personal status. This distinction between nationality and applicable law, based formally on religion (but more deeply on race) led to a distinction between nationality and citizenship, since 'natives' were not allowed to vote (Blévis 2001, 557; Sahia Cherchari 2004, 741). This discriminatory act was repealed for the 'Israelite natives' as early as 1870, when the Crémieux Decree granted them full French citizenship. However, it was only in 1946 that the Lamine Guèye Law granted French citizenship to "all nationals of the Overseas Territories (Algeria included)," and therefore to 'Muslim natives'. Yet, even after that, voters in Algeria voted in two different colleges until 1958, depending on whether they had common-law civil status or local civil status. Moreover, after Algeria's independence in 1962, Algerians of 'civil status under local law', or 'Muslim', were considered 'refugees' in France and not 'returnees' such as those of common-law civil status (Stora 1992, 20). An *ordonnance* (piece of delegated legislation) of 21 July 1962 deprived them of French nationality unless they subscribed to a "recognitive declaration of nationality" in France before 22 March 1967.

Overseas territories, even though they are part of France, are not part of the territory of the EU, which means that EU law does not apply fully to them. This has several consequences.

First, according to Article 138 of the 1990 Convention implementing the Schengen Agreement, the provisions of the Convention apply only to the European territory of the French Republic. Overseas territories are therefore allowed to carry out identity checks at their borders, and Schengen visas are not valid for these territories, which crucially hinders movement of persons between French overseas territories and their neighbors and therefore hinders regional cooperation.

Second, under EU law, French overseas territories are divided into two categories: the outermost regions (French Guiana, Guadeloupe, Martinique, Réunion, Saint Martin,[28] and, since 1 January 2014, Mayotte[29]) and the overseas countries and territories (French Polynesia, French Southern and Antarctic Territories, New Caledonia and Dependencies, Saint Pierre and Miquelon, Wallis and Futuna Islands,[30] and, since 1 January 2012, Saint-Barthélemy[31]). EU law applies to the out-

ermost regions, but the Council, upon a proposal from the Commission and after consulting the European Parliament, can adopt specific measures aimed, in particular, at laying down the conditions under which the EU Treaties apply to those regions.[32] By contrast, overseas countries and territories are 'associated' with the EU[33] but do not form part of it. This association is the subject of arrangements defined in Part Four of the Treaty on the Functioning of the European Union, with the result that, failing express reference, the general provisions of the Treaty do not apply to these countries and territories.[34] The purpose of this association is to promote the economic and social development of the overseas countries and territories and to establish close economic relations between them and the EU as a whole.[35] As a result of the association, the right to free movement of EU citizens does not *fully* apply to these territories. Particularly, freedom of movement for workers does not apply in overseas countries and territories because the measures required by the treaties to make this freedom applicable to these territories[36] have never been adopted. To be more precise, "the functioning of EU citizens' free movement rights in the OCTs [overseas countries and territories] is atypical since only one-directional movement is covered: that from the OCT to the EU proper" (Kochenov 2010c, 230, 243). On the one hand, the inhabitants of these territories do enjoy the right to free movement in other EU Member States based on EU law as long as they have the nationality of a Member State of the EU[37] (usually France). On the other hand, however, non-French EU citizens permanently residing outside the French overseas countries and territories cannot rely on EU law should they wish to move overseas, whereas French nationals can rely on French law to do just that. Therefore, EU citizens are not as free to enter and live in French overseas countries and territories as French nationals, giving French nationals an advantage in terms of free movement and right of settlement. Thus the French nationality allows free settlement in 46 destinations, three more destinations than most other EU nationalities, which explains its 1st position and 100% score in the Settlement Freedom Ranking.

The situation of New Caledonia deserves special attention. In response to its growing pro-independence movement, which led to a period of secessionist unrest in the 1980s, New Caledonia has been given a high degree of autonomy, with a broad set of competences, including taxes, 'customary civil status',[38] civil procedure, trade with third countries, and access to employment for foreigners.[39] It has a congress[40] that can pass laws, called 'laws of the land',[41] which can be brought before the Constitutional Council for constitutional review[42] according to a procedure that resembles the constitutional review of the Acts of the French parliament.[43] It has an executive branch called 'government'.[44] Some authors consider that this special status for New Caledonia makes France a quasi-federal state, albeit with only one unit (Goesel-Le Bihan 1998, 32 et seq.).

With regard to questions of nationality and the QNI, two elements are noteworthy. First, under the Nouméa Accord, signed in 1998 following a period of secessionist unrest in the 1980s and approved in a referendum, there is a special New Caledonian citizenship. Every French national who has been residing in New Caledonia since 8 November 1998 or who is the child of at least one New Caledonian citizen is a New Caledonian citizen.[45] It should be noted that this 'regional' citizenship is a sub-status within French nationality — unlike, notably, British overseas territories' citizenship, which is different from British citizenship, notwithstanding the fact that all British overseas territories citizens (apart from those solely connected with the Sovereign Base Areas of Cyprus) were granted British citizenship on 21 May 2002.[46] New Caledonian citizens *are* (and remain) French nationals, and are also, therefore, EU citizens. New Caledonian citizens enjoy special rights. In particular only New Caledonian citizens can participate in provincial and congressional elections; to be more precise, the conditions for being a New Caledonian citizen are exactly the same as the conditions needed to be able to participate in provincial and congressional elections.[47] More importantly, perhaps, New Caledonia can adopt measures aimed at favoring employment for its citizens and persons who have resided long enough in the territory.[48] This special status therefore has the potential to create a form of privilege for at least *some* French nationals.

Second, again under the Nouméa Accord, New Caledonia held a referendum on independence on 4 November 2018, which was rejected by 56.7% of the voters. This, however, did not close the case. According to the Nouméa Accord, as implemented by the Constitutional Bylaw no. 99–209, a second referendum could occur within the next two years if a third of the Congress demands it.[49] Since the results of the November 2018 referendum show that a significant proportion of voters are still in favor of it, the prospect of independence is not unrealistic. New Caledonia could then become an independent state in years to come.

50 Nationality of the Kingdom of the Netherlands

By Jeremy Bierbach

Although it is regarded as a single state on the international scene, the Kingdom of the Netherlands, based on its Charter (*het Statuut van het Koninkrijk der Nederlanden*), is a monarchy composed of four component countries (*landen*) in Europe and the Caribbean Sea — Aruba, Curaçao, the Netherlands, and Sint Maarten — with their own legislatures, executives,

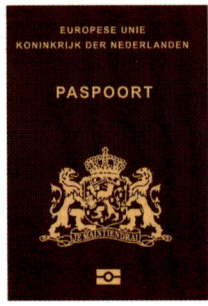

and at least partially autonomous judiciaries. Until the last major revision of the Charter in 2010, Curaçao and Sint Maarten (the southern half of the island on which the northern half, Saint Martin, is an integral part of France), together with the other Caribbean islands of Bonaire, Saba, and Sint Eustatius, composed the country of the Netherlands Antilles. At the same time as Curaçao and Sint Maarten became autonomous countries, Bonaire, Saba, and Sint Eustatius became special municipal entities of the Netherlands, the component country of the Kingdom whose territory had previously been limited to Europe.

Aside from the King, who is monarch over the Kingdom as a whole and over the four separate countries (Art. 2(1) Charter), a key tie binding the citizens of all four countries is that they have a common nationality: the status of *Nederlander* (Netherlands national), which is not subdivided in any way.

In the days of the Dutch colonial empire, the people of the then Antilles, along with the people of the former colonies of Suriname and the Dutch East Indies, were classified by statutes enacted in 1910 and 1927 as '*Nederlandse onderdanen niet-Nederlanders*' or 'non-Dutch subjects of the Netherlands', with no rights of settlement or political participation in the metropole. However, subsequent to the independence of Indonesia, the statute on Netherlands nationality, which previously applied only to persons indigenous to the European Netherlands, was amended in 1951 to effectively grant full Netherlands nationality to the people of the Antilles and Suriname. By the same statute, the people indigenous to Netherlands New Guinea were classified as the last remaining non-Dutch colonial subjects, and they would remain so until the transfer of sovereignty over that territory to Indonesia in 1962 (de Groot and Tratnik 2010, 47–8).[1]

With the independence of Suriname in 1975, Netherlands nationals living in Suriname with a closer connection to Suriname automatically became nationals of Suriname and lost their Netherlands nationality, while Netherlands nationals from Suriname who lived in the European Netherlands retained their Netherlands nationality and did not become nationals of Suriname (Id., 49–50). This development split many families into holders of two different nationalities, only one of which was theoretically entitled to the rights attached to freedom of movement in the European Economic Community (EEC), which gave rise to the first decision of the European Court of Justice concerning 'reverse discrimination' in the EEC.[2]

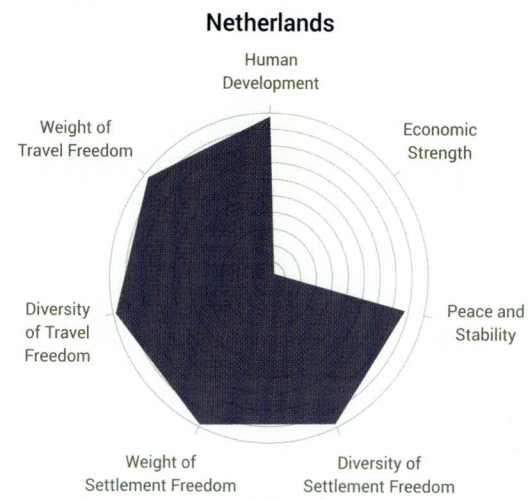

All bearers of this nationality are also citizens of the EU, despite the fact that neither the countries of Aruba, Curaçao, and Sint Maarten, nor the Caribbean special municipal entities of the Netherlands are themselves part of the territory of the EU: they are classified as Overseas Countries and Territories (OCT) of the EU.

Freedoms of Movement and Residence Entailed in Netherlands Nationality

A passport from the Kingdom of the Netherlands ranks highly for diversity and heft of travel freedom, which contributes to its high ranking in *Kälin and Kochenov's Quality of Nationality Index* (QNI) at 2nd place, tied with Germany.

But more importantly, as EU citizens, all bearers of Netherlands nationality, those from both Europe and the Caribbean, can make full use of the freedom of movement and residence in the territory of the EU provided for by Article 21(1) of the Treaty on the Functioning of the European Union (TFEU) — and, based on other treaties, in the EEA and Switzerland — an even stronger contributing factor to the ranking of Netherlands nationality on the Index as 2nd. For that matter, all Netherlands nationals enjoy the right to vote for and be elected to the European Parliament, in light of the *Eman and Sevinger* decision of the European Court of Justice: Netherlands nationals resident in the Caribbean countries could no longer be excluded from the franchise due to the enfranchisement outside the Kingdom of Netherlands of nationals formerly resident in the (European) Netherlands.[3]

The Charter of the Kingdom of the Netherlands does not however provide for an unrestricted right of freedom of movement and residence for Netherlands nationals within the Kingdom, and indeed implicitly allows each of the countries to maintain admission and expulsion procedures for Netherlands nationals. (Art. 3(1)(f) Charter provides for the heretofore unused possibility of regulating this matter in Kingdom law.) Nevertheless, only the Caribbean countries in the Kingdom and the special municipal entities of the Netherlands in the Caribbean maintain formal restrictions on settlement (which in Aruba are substantially more restrictive than in Curaçao, Sint Maarten, and the special entities, especially when it comes to the right to work)[4] for longer than six months for Netherlands nationals hailing from elsewhere in the Kingdom.

In a somewhat surreal development, furthermore, an outright alien who is a citizen of the US now has immigration rights in the Caribbean countries equal to those of Netherlands nationals hailing from the European part of the Netherlands, based on a 2014 judgment of the Joint Court of Justice of Aruba, Curaçao, Sint Maarten, and of Bonaire, Sint Eustatius, and Saba[5] interpreting the 1956 Treaty of Friendship, Commerce and Navigation between the Kingdom of the Netherlands and the US (the so-called 'Dutch–American Friendship Treaty'), of which Protocol provision 3 provides

> 3. With respect to Article II, paragraph 1, and the first sentence of Article VIII, paragraph 1, nationals of the United States of America shall be accorded in any Part of the Kingdom of the Netherlands outside Europe the treatment accorded therein to Netherlands nationals not born in that Part..

This means that the Caribbean countries of the Kingdom of the Netherlands have been counted in the Index as possible settlement destinations for nationals of the US and the Netherlands but *not* for EU citizens other than Netherlands nationals, who are arguably subject to the full restrictions of ordinary immigration law in the Caribbean countries.

For a striking example of the patchwork quilt created by the interplay of EU law, Kingdom law, the Dutch–American Friendship Treaty, and local law, one need only look at the tiny island of Sint Maarten/Saint Martin. Saint Martin, as an integral part of France, is part of the EU, albeit as one of the so-called Outermost Regions, and freedom of movement for all EU citizens applies on its territory, including for Netherlands nationals from Sint Maarten, other Caribbean countries in the Kingdom, and the European Netherlands. Sint Maarten, on the other hand, is not part of the EU and offers no freedom of movement for EU citizens, including French citizens from Saint Martin.[6] Rights of residence in Sint Maarten are significantly facilitated for Netherlands nationals from elsewhere and for US citizens.[7] Nevertheless, those rights of residence are still more restrictive than the rights of residence guaranteed to Netherlands nationals not from the former Antilles who wish to settle in France (including Saint Martin) based on the EU's Citizenship Directive 2004/38 of the European Parliament and of the Council (known as the Citizenship Rights Directive), which also stipulates that economically inactive EU citizens must have sufficient resources, but does not require them to prove that they have housing and no criminal record.

The Netherlands (that is, in Europe) does not maintain any restrictions, formal or otherwise, on the admission and settlement of Netherlands nationals from the Caribbean. Nevertheless, such restrictions have been proposed from time to time since the turn of the 21st century. In 2005, the then minister of alien affairs and immigration from the right-liberal VVD party (or *Volkspartij voor Vrijheid en Democratie*), Rita Verdonk, expressed a desire[8] to be able to expel Antillean and Aruban 'problem youths' from the European Netherlands, which was followed by three successive governments of the Netherlands pursuing negotiations with those countries (and their successors) to enact a Kingdom statute (*Rijkswet*) regulating movement and residence. In 2011, however, a subsequent government of the Netherlands indicated that in the face of resistance from Curaçao (certainly not the only Caribbean country to express its displeasure), it was no longer going to pursue the previous governments' efforts.[9]

An additional hallmark of Verdonk's term of office as minister was introducing the bill that became the Civic Integration Act (*Wet inburgering*). In its current form this statute gives certain classes of non-EU-citizen immigrants in the Netherlands a deadline to pass an exam testing their knowledge of the Dutch language and Dutch society, and their ability to look for work in the Netherlands, or otherwise be fined. Verdonk's original bill, however, aimed to subject to the integration requirement also Netherlands nationals who either were naturalized or came from the Caribbean countries. That provision was deleted from the bill after the Council of State, in its role as a legislative advisor, advised against it, noting in particular that such an obligation for Netherlands nationals would introduce a form of reverse discrimination against Netherlands nationals relative to EU citizens from other Member States that was difficult to justify given that EU citizens from other Member States would be exempt, because any such requirements were likely to be construed as barriers to freedom of movement. Moreover, it would introduce a form of discrimination against one kind of Netherlands national relative to others. Most strikingly, in fact, the Council noted that any Netherlands nationals who had made use of freedom of movement in the EU before settling in the Netherlands would have to be exempt due to being protected by EU free-movement law: "A Netherlands national hailing from Sint Maarten, for instance, who would [otherwise] be subject to the integration requirement, would be […] exempt if before coming to the Netherlands, he had lived on the French part of the island, while that would not be the case for a Netherlands national who had moved directly from Sint Maarten to the Netherlands."[10]

In 2013, a VVD[11] member of the States General (the bicameral parliament) of the Netherlands, André Bosman, introduced a private member's bill for a Netherlands-only statute regulating the admission and residence of Netherlands nationals from Aruba, Curaçao, and Sint Maarten[12] to lukewarm support from the government; the bill was rejected in 2016 by the House of Representatives, the lower chamber of parliament.

Supporters of restrictions on settlement of Netherlands nationals from the Caribbean countries[13] in the European Netherlands, such as Bosman, cite formal equality within the Kingdom[14] as a guiding principle: that is, if the Caribbean countries can introduce restrictions, why can't the Netherlands do it? However, others point out (van der Wal and Heringa 2005, 223–4), including by reference to a 2000 decision from the Supreme Court of the Netherlands,[15] that the Caribbean countries' restrictions are justified in light of the inherently asymmetrical situation of those countries. They have relatively tiny populations (currently 105,264 for Aruba, 161,014 for Curaçao, and 41,109 for Sint Maarten, compared to more than 17 million for the Netherlands) and very limited resources and housing stock that would not be able to absorb an unrestricted influx of Netherlands nationals from Europe.

Moreover, most of the people in the Dutch Caribbean countries are people of color, largely descended from the populations of the former colonial empire of the Netherlands, including people who were enslaved and indentured to work on plantations. Any restriction on settlement of Netherlands nationals previously resident in those countries would inevitably be suspect as a form of indirect discrimination based on national origin, according to the largely negative legislative advice issued by the Council of State of the Netherlands.[16] It noted that one particular provision of the bill that called for restrictions on Netherlands nationals born outside the Kingdom but descended from a parent from one of its Caribbean countries clearly constituted direct discrimination based on national origin.

Recent Legislative Developments in Netherlands Nationality Law

Netherlands nationality law is governed by a Kingdom statute, the Kingdom Act on Nationality (*Rijkswet op het Nederlanderschap*), which is equally valid in all four countries. However, there is a clear asymmetry in the Kingdom's legislative process, in that the primary locus of legislative activity is the Netherlands, in the lower chamber (House of Representatives) of its parliament; after a bill for a Kingdom statute has been introduced there, the legislatures of the Caribbean countries are given the opportunity to review the bill (art. 15(1) and 16 Charter) and their Ministers Plenipotentiary in the Netherlands or special delegates sent by their legislatures are given the opportunity to participate in the debate and propose amendments (art. 17 Charter). If any of the Ministers Plenipotentiary or special delegates expresses opposition to the bill before the final vote, it can pass only by a three-fifths majority (art. 18 Charter). However, the parliamentary record of recent legislative activity on the Kingdom Act of Nationality shows no record of any of the Caribbean countries exercising its right of opposition,[17] meaning we can interpret the legislative activity on Netherlands nationality law as largely a function of politics in the Netherlands.

Of the two most recent legislative initiatives to change the Kingdom Act on Nationality, which were undertaken by the previous government of the Netherlands (the second chaired by VVD leader and current Prime Minister Mark Rutte), one was defeated and one passed. The first bill,[18] proposed to lengthen the residence requirement for most aliens wishing to apply for naturalization (art. 8(1)(c)) from five years of continuous legal residence in the Kingdom to seven years, and also to abolish the current provision of the Act (art. 8(2)) that states that aliens married to Dutch nationals outside the Kingdom are able to apply for naturalization as long as they are not living in their countries of nationality (art. 9(1)(c)) after three years of cohabitation with their spouses. After passing the House of Representatives, however (with a number of amendments), the bill was defeated in the Senate, the upper chamber of parliament, due to the last-minute opposition of 50PLUS, the senior citizens' party, which was concerned about its effects on the ability of Dutch pensioners abroad to be able to bring their foreign spouses back to the Netherlands.[19]

The other bill introduced by that government[20] aimed to allow the minister of security and justice, in consultation with the Kingdom government council, to revoke the Netherlands nationality of persons deemed to be involved in organizations designated as terrorist organizations. The bill attracted criticism, however, because based on the Convention on the Reduction of Statelessness and its implementation in the Kingdom Act, such a revocation could not be applied against Netherlands nationals without any additional nationalities, since that would leave them stateless. This meant that the bill would affect only Netherlands nationals with additional nationalities, most prominently those with additional nationalities by descent that cannot be renounced, even voluntarily (such as that of Morocco), leading to at least indirect discrimination on the basis of national origin. Moreover, the schedule of qualifying terrorist organizations published by the government included only Islamist organizations such as Al Qaeda and the Islamic State (IS), and excluded other terrorist organizations such as the Armed Revolutionary Forces of Columbia (FARC), the Kurdistan Workers Party (PKK), and the Tamil Tigers (de Groot 2016). Nevertheless, the bill was enacted into law (with the added sub-paragraph art. 14(4) in the Kingdom Act) after passing the Senate on 7 February 2017. (At the time of writing, the Legal Affairs Committee of the Council of Europe has adopted a draft resolution condemning the deprivation of nationality as an anti-terror measure.)[21]

Pending Legislative and Judicial Developments in Netherlands Nationality Law

All of the pending legislative and judicial developments in Netherlands nationality law concern the statutory restrictions on dual nationality for Netherlands nationals. The Netherlands has historically been one of the most restrictive member states in the EU when it comes to allowing dual nationality, although in the 21st century it has become slightly less restrictive than Austria or Germany, for example. Ever since the enactment of the first separate nationality statute of the Kingdom of the Netherlands in 1892, the *Wet op het Nederlanderschap en ingezetenschap* (replaced by the first version of the current Kingdom Act in 1985), some combination of three modes of enforcing limits on dual nationality has generally been in force:

1) Automatic loss of Netherlands nationality by a Netherlands national voluntarily obtaining a foreign nationality (currently art. 15(1)(a) of the Act)

2) Automatic loss of Netherlands nationality by a Netherlands national who possesses an additional nationality (usually by birth), has reached the age of majority, and who lives outside the Kingdom (in the revision of the law that entered into force in 2003: outside the Kingdom *and* the territory of the EU) for 10 years without being in the public or international service of one of the countries in the Kingdom and without having completed some administrative procedure prescribed by the statute involving the expression of a desire to retain Netherlands nationality (currently art. 15(1)(c) of the Act; currently, the administrative procedure prescribed by art. 15(4) of the Act is to have a passport, identity card, or certificate of Dutch nationality issued by an embassy or consulate)

3) A legal obligation for naturalized Netherlands nationals to be willing to do everything in their power to relinquish their original nationalities, if possible (currently art. 9(1)(b) of the Act), or otherwise have their Netherlands nationality revoked (currently art. 15(1)(d) of the Act).

By and large, political support for restrictions on dual nationality has generally been strong in the Netherlands, to the extent that it is perceived as a phenomenon relating to immigrants to the Netherlands and their descendants.[22] In anti-immigrant discourse, possession of a second nationality is sometimes made out to be a sign of a weaker tie of loyalty to the Netherlands, and indeed right-wing politicians in parliament have sometimes made a point out of certain members of government having additional nationalities (Agca and Kaya 2015, 73–4). Nonetheless, the restrictions outlined in the first and third points have already been relaxed significantly since a revision of the Act in 2003 stipulated (as the most prominent exemptions) that a Netherlands national married to[23] a person of the nationality they are acquiring would not automatically lose their Netherlands nationality upon voluntarily acquiring that foreign nationality, and likewise that a foreign national married to[24] a Netherlands national would be exempt from revocation of their Netherlands nationality for not doing everything in their power to relinquish their original nationality upon becoming a naturalized Netherlands national.

Strikingly, it was the entry into force of the revision of the Act on 1 April 2003 that may also have sparked public discussion of a possible abolition or amelioration of the mode of loss of Netherlands nationality outlined above in the second point. Because the statutory condition for loss by non-residence, to be defined as residence outside the Kingdom and the territory of the EU, was revised at that time, it reset the 10-year clock for all Netherlands nationals with additional nationalities outside the Kingdom and the EU who had not already lost their nationality due to the previous condition, which was 10 years' residence in one's other country of nationality. This meant that on 1 April 2013 there was a considerable wave of loss of Netherlands nationality on the part of dual nationals abroad who had not been sufficiently informed of their need to have a new passport, identity card, or certificate of Netherlands nationality issued by a consulate of the Netherlands within those 10 years to prevent loss. Largely in response to the victims of this phenomenon, but also in response to the complaints of Netherlands nationals abroad not married to foreign nationals who had inadvertently lost their Netherlands nationality by being naturalized in their countries of residence to gain more economic rights, the national ombudsman issued a report in 2016 (National Ombudsman of the Netherlands 2016) condemning the Government of the Netherlands for insufficiently informing Netherlands nationals abroad about the circumstances under which they could lose their nationality and for not enacting legislation making it easier for them to get their nationality back once it had been lost.

Four individuals who had all lost their Netherlands nationality (and therefore their EU citizenship) through 10 years' non-residence appealed their respective losses all the way to the jurisdictional division of the Council of State, the Netherlands' highest responsible administrative court. They cited Article 20 of the TFEU, providing for the right to EU citizenship for Member State nationals as interpreted by the Court of Justice of the European Union in its *Rottmann*[25] decision, which stipulated that any loss of Member State citizenship entailing loss of EU citizenship was a matter of concern for EU law, and was subject to review against the EU law's principle of proportionality. The Council of State made a preliminary reference to the Court of Justice,[26] asking if EU law precluded such an automatic loss by a period of non-residence, to be able to decide on the appeals of the four individuals. At the time of writing, the decision of the Court is still forthcoming,[27] although Advocate General Mengozzi has already issued an Opinion[28] that art. 20 TFEU does not preclude such a loss on the part of adults, while it does preclude such a loss on the part of minor children who lost their Netherlands nationality (and therefore their EU citizenship) through no fault of their own but as a consequence of their parents' loss through non-residence. If the Court decided to follow the line of the Opinion, then in combination with another recent development in EU law, the *Chavez-Vilchez* decision of the Court of Justice,[29] that would mean that the expatriated parents could possibly obtain a right of residence in the Netherlands with their Netherlands-national children. This would be conditional on the children being still so dependent on their parents that without the parents' presence to take care of them, the children would be effectively deprived of the most essential of their rights of EU citizenship in the Netherlands based on art. 20 TFEU.[30]

Finally, years of lobbying by Netherlands nationals abroad, particularly in the US, to be allowed to retain their Netherlands nationality upon being naturalized has borne political fruit.[31] The progressive-liberal '*Democraten 66*' or D66 party had for some time included the relaxation of restrictions on dual nationality as a plank in its party platform; when it became one of the parties in the current four-party coalition formed on 10 October 2017 in the third government chaired by Prime Minister Rutte, it ensured that the coalition accord would include a commitment to the modernization of Netherlands nationality law. (Arguably, another source of this change, of course, was the looming exit of the UK from the EU and the large number of Netherlands nationals in the UK and British citizens in the Netherlands clamoring to be able to obtain the opposite nationality without automatic loss or an obligation of relinquishment, respectively.) The coalition accord announced that a bill would be introduced to "expand the possibility of possessing multiple nationalities for arriving first generations of immigrants and emigrants. At the same time, for successive generations, there will be an obligatory moment to choose that will genuinely lead to the possession of no more than one nationality."[32]

So far, the government has informed parliament[33] only that it is currently working on a bill for "considerable adaptations" in the Kingdom Act on Nationality, in which the Court's decision in *Tjebbes* will be taken into account, without giving any further details beyond the text of the coalition accord.

51 Bulgarian Nationality: Dire Straits?

By Kamen Shoilev

Annina: "We come from Bulgaria. Oh, things are very bad there, Monsieur. The devil has the people by the throat. So, Jan and I, we ... we do not want our children to grow up in such a country."
Rick: "Yes, I'll bet."[1]

Casablanca, 1942

The dialogue above from the wartime blockbuster *Casablanca*, set in 1941, must have been at least somewhat credible to both its scriptwriters and its audience. If in 1941 the Bulgarian citizenry were in the grip of evil to the point that they did not wish their children to grow up in Bulgaria, surely a Quality of Nationality value for Bulgaria in the hypothetical 1942 edition of *Kälin and Kochenov's Quality of Nationality Index* (QNI) would have been diabolically low?

How far has the quality of Bulgaria's nationality come in the 20th and early 21st centuries? Was *Casablanca* taking artistic license or were things quite so dire?

In 1942, Bulgaria was still feeling relatively limited war-related socio-economic pain. It had avoided the substantial loss of life and had yet to lose substantial assets. But, in 1943 Allied bombings destroyed swaths of its cities, including Sofia, to penalize Bulgaria for being an Axis satellite.

1943 also witnessed a widespread Bulgarian popular and political mobilization to resist German demands that Jewish Bulgarians be deported. This mobilization succeeded remarkably and indigenous Jewish deportation was thwarted. One reason for the success may have been the close identification of Bulgarian Jews with the national in-group (Reicher 2006). A current of solidarity was shown to be part of the national psyche and this period has itself since been woven into how Bulgarians historicize themselves, with the associated intangible benefit to being Bulgarian.

Economically, things were less rosy. Immediately prior to the war, Bulgaria's economy had become entwined with that of Germany, with which 68% of trade was conducted. In line with the latter's gradual asphyxiation, Bulgaria reversed the gains in GDP it had made from 1935 to 1940.

Modern Bulgarian Developmental History

Since the creation of the modern Bulgarian state in 1878, Bulgaria's GDP ranking in Europe had mostly languished at the bottom of the European-league table. Although data for the period is sparse, and estimates tend to be based on proxies — such as the number of post offices in operation — most reports suggest that Bulgaria was poorer than Russia, then richer, then poorer again, mostly richer than Portugal, and initially richer than Serbia and the countries of the former Yugoslavia (Broadberry and Klein 2012).

In headline terms, GDP had grown from around GK$ 800 in 1990s international dollars at Liberation in 1878 to around GK$ 1,500 towards the end of the Second World War, by no means a spectacular gain. Economic development was characterized by extensive growth before 1920 in which the overrepresented agricultural sector was growing mainly in line with the expansion of the population and available agricultural labor, so that growth in GDP per head was static before a reorientation in the 1920s and 1930s in which both capital and equipment accumulated, and began in later decades to form the basis for an intensification of agriculture and an acceleration of overall growth. In essence Bulgaria remained a peripheral economy; its extraction from the Ottoman Empire had not placed it in the economic brackets of Central or Northern Europe.

More positively, from a human development perspective, in the first 50 years of its independence (that is, to 1922) — in the space of roughly three generations — Bulgaria achieved almost complete literacy, saw increasing urbanization and a drop in the fertility rate to modern levels (Ivanov and Tooze 2007).

The holders of Bulgarian passports in the first half of the 20th century were not considered unwelcome in the desirable places of the period, just somewhat exotic. Bulgaria was increasingly successful at providing higher education at home but it also sent students abroad to Western Europe and the US, and in the 1930s began exporting its specialized itinerant laborers (such as market gardeners) as its own agricultural sector turned to higher value-added items such as vegetables and tobacco. Despite the earlier substantial population increases, there was no mass emigration from Bulgaria as there had been from Greece or Italy, although some Bulgarians did settle in the New World (Ivanov and Tooze 2007).

See-Sawing Settlement and Travel Freedoms

The end of the Second World War caused a number of population ripples. A famous Bulgarian emigrant of the 1940s was the puerile King Simeon II, who settled in Spain. More typical were those displaced for their political convictions or escaping the depredations of the war and the immediate post-war period, such as Carl Djerassi of contraceptive-pill-invention fame, whose Jewish family had found a safe haven in Sofia in the 1930s and 1940s but had resettled in the US by the height of hostilities. The Jewish population of Bulgaria, which had largely survived the war, enthusiastically embraced settlement in Israel, and some 40,000 Bulgarian citizens made that journey.

Once a Communist government had become entrenched, by 1950, emigration became rare and generally illicit other than in government service and within the Communist sphere. In line with other Soviet Bloc states, Bulgaria imposed exit visas and harassed the left-behind family members of unauthorized emigrants. This was, however, mirrored by an open-arms policy in the West that measured the political success of its model by how attractive it was to dissident migrants from the Soviet Bloc.

Accordingly, as elsewhere in the Bloc, external settlement freedom was very high, provided one forewent the prospects of returning.

Bulgaria rapidly industrialized and made further strides in public health and education, quickly urbanizing, and by 1989 growing its economy to about USD 6,000 in 1990s dollars (placing it on a par with countries such as East Germany). Its commitment to a model of Soviet soft power projection and internationalism meant that it opened itself to African and Asian students and others for whom it became attractive as a destination for settlement.

At several junctures in this period Bulgaria sent out or accepted waves of migrants. In the 1950s and 1980s, many of those who identified as ethnic Turks left for Turkey.

Politically persecuted left-wing refugees from Greece arrived in the 1960s and 1970s and quasi-indentured laborers from Viet Nam arrived in the 1980s. The former naturalized, while the latter mostly did not before they repatriated in the tumult of the early 1990s.

The relative migratory quiescence of Bulgarian nationals themselves changed abruptly in and around 1989 when Communism fell and, alongside it, the country's internal restrictions on emigration. Yet that was when the magnetically attractive Western European and American destinations were placed behind the barrier of high visa refusal rates. It took until 2001 before Bulgarians gained access to visa-free short-term travel in Europe's Schengen Area, and it was only several years after the country's 2007 accession to the EU that an increasing sense of normality replaced the neurosis previously associated with travel and with being treated as undesirables at international borders.

Bulgaria as a Magnet for Migrants

Since its accession to the EU in January 2007, Bulgaria's citizenship has gradually — and then suddenly — acquired a cachet it did not previously have. It has become distinctly desirable to hold a Bulgarian passport. This may have been sensed earliest by those from countries in Bulgaria's vicinity endowed with fewer opportunities, such as Macedonia (now North Macedonia), Moldova, and the Ukraine. In the early 2000s, as about a million Bulgarians emigrated, a smaller but substantial number of Albanian, then Macedonian, Moldovan, and Ukrainian citizens became migrants in the opposite direction (though often without physically moving to Bulgaria but instead making use of the status elsewhere), typically relying on Bulgaria's liberal citizenship-on-the-basis-of-origin route to naturalize. Some 123,000 new Bulgarians and their family members were naturalized on this basis from 2001 to 2018.

More recently, non-Bulgarian-origin routes to qualification for citizenship have received increasing attention, and Bulgaria is one of the top three EU destinations offering a citizenship-by-investment route to naturalization, with some 400 applications to date.

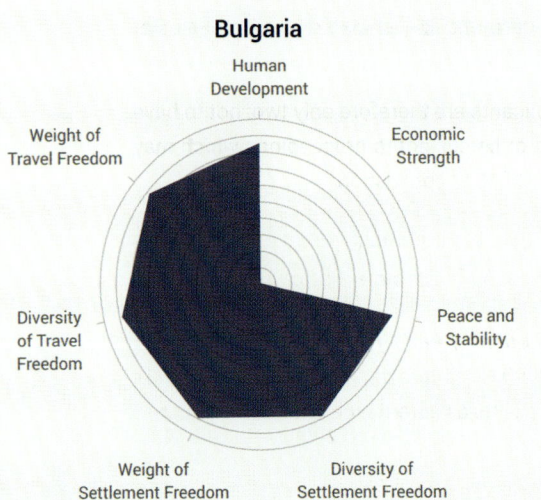

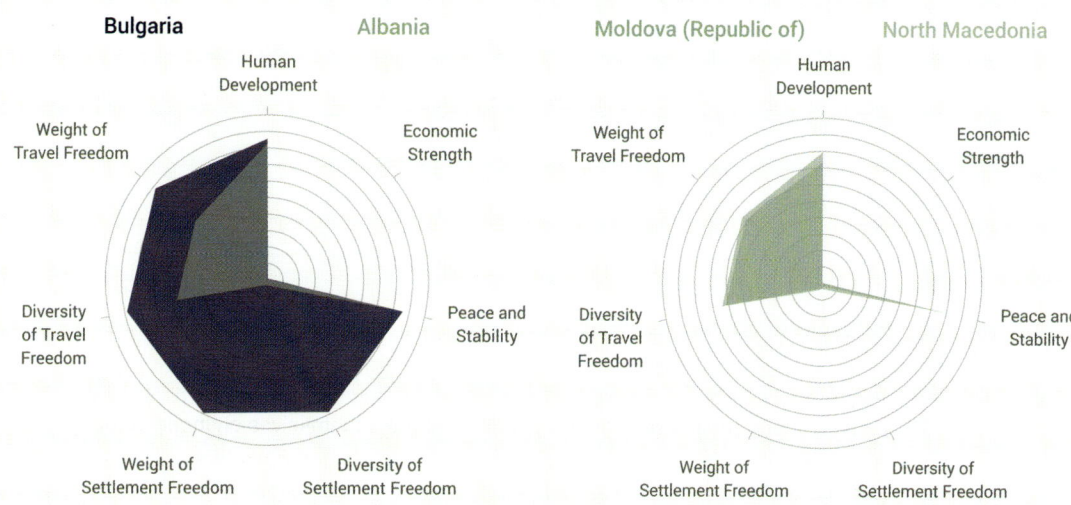

Bulgaria's Citizenship-on-the-Basis-of-Origin

Between 1989 and the present day, Bulgaria's population has shrunk by some 30%. In line with its demographic contraction and with a widespread historical interpretation according to which diasporic Bulgarian populations were owed a right of return to the homeland (while lands on which they resided were no longer capable of being conceivably reintegrated into the modern state), Bulgaria legislated with a perhaps uniquely liberal attitude towards the naturalization of citizens on the basis of origin.

The naturalization of persons 'of Bulgarian origin' is governed by Section 15 of the Bulgarian Citizenship Act of 1999. This functions as a means of lowering the standard requirements set out in Section 12 of the Act, which itself is the general enabling provision. A set of requirements that normally apply to naturalizations are thus not applied to persons of Bulgarian origin:

- The requirement for minimum residence in Bulgaria
- The need for an applicant to have an income or occupation affording him or her a basic standard of living in Bulgaria
- The need to demonstrate competence in the Bulgarian language
- The requirement for applicants to be free of their current citizenships or to be so free as at the date of naturalization

The residual requirements that still apply to such applicants are therefore only two: not to have been convicted of a crime requiring intent in Bulgaria or be subject to proceedings which may lead to such a conviction; and to have attained the age of 18 at application.

The definition of a person of Bulgarian origin is contained in Section 2.1 of the Additional Provisions of the Act. This is said to be a person of whom "at least one ancestor is a Bulgarian."

In normal Bulgarian legal language the category of 'ancestor' is entirely open-ended, and there is no indication that the legislature intended otherwise with respect to naturalization on the basis of origin. The category of ancestor is in use in such contexts as inheritance law and may indeed include all superior blood and adoptive relations.[2]

Definitions of Bulgarian-ness

The Act does not itself define 'Bulgarian'. A number of possibilities present themselves, for example that a Bulgarian ancestor is a Bulgarian citizen or subject; a person of Bulgarian ethnicity; a person who lived in historically Bulgarian lands; a speaker of the Bulgarian language; or a combination of some or all of the above. Each of these possibilities entails a different universe of qualifying contemporary descendants.

For instance, since being a Bulgarian subject or citizen is generally understood to have coincided with modern Bulgarian statehood, using ancestor citizenship as a sole qualifying basis might exclude a large number of likely intended beneficiaries of the Act. Examples would be descendants of diaspora Bulgarians in Transylvania and Russia who migrated in the 18th and early 19th centuries, before the establishment of modern Bulgaria, and who therefore did not acquire citizenship or subjecthood.

Using ethnicity as a singular criterion of belonging is also potentially problematic given that domestic equality law, the Constitution, and Article 14 of the European Court of Human Rights, all prohibit discrimination on the basis of ethnicity. Practically, too, modern Bulgarian citizenry is far from mono-ethnically Bulgarian: there are recognized communities of Roma, Russians, Turks, and so on, and individuals who in recent censuses have jokingly or otherwise declared self-identification as Inuit or Jedi. A criterion of ethnicity as a sole test of Bulgarian origin would therefore also be underinclusive and unwieldy.

Although a mixture of criteria is not specifically instructed legislatively, this may be what has been adopted in practice, and properly so. To start with, a steady stream of judicial pronouncements from appellate administrative courts has found that ethnicity is indeed a matter of self-identification and thus not a singular, reliable test of who is a Bulgarian pursuant to Section 2.1 of the Act. At the same time, the courts have found that having a Bulgarian ancestor who was a Bulgarian citizen or subject is a robust test.

The role of challenger in this line of cases has been played by an executive agency of the Bulgarian government, the Agency for Bulgarians Abroad (ABA), whose remit includes both outreach to diasporic Bulgarians and the more mundane business of issuing documents certifying Bulgarian origin. Through what is likely a form of regulatory capture, ABA has been aligned with a more nationalist position, which sees the function of Section 15 of the Act as narrowly protective of ethnic Bulgarians abroad and supposedly at home, in particular by restricting the numbers of Turkish (and sometimes Israeli) citizens whose ancestors were Bulgarian citizens from claiming Bulgarian origin for the purposes of naturalization.

The ABA has therefore at times refused to recognize Bulgarian origin in such cases. The administrative courts (to whom the ABA's decisions are generally subject) have, however, built a consistent body of case law in which they have struck down such refusals. This sometimes results in standoffs through repeated cycles of refusal to certify origin followed by repeated quashing of the refusals.

A more recent problem for the ABA, one that dates to 2018, is the uncovering of a scheme in which payments were allegedly demanded with the ostensible promise of securing issuances of certificates of origin. These caused domestic outrage and fears of international (and particularly EU-facing) embarrassment. In this narrative, Bulgaria is seen as an unsecured back door to EU citizenship in which an overly wide basis for qualifying as a Bulgarian is combined with an unsecured bureaucratic process.

In reality, the process of establishing Bulgarian origin may be most stymied by the absence of clear evidentiary pathways. Comprehensive and well-preserved pre-20th century records of the people resident in households on Bulgarian lands are absent, nor were ethnic Bulgarians abroad always registered as such. Non-state systems of record-keeping are equally incomplete; unlike in other European societies, the national Bulgarian Church was unable to maintain a system such as parish records, for instance. Perhaps one solution (scientifically valid only insofar as Bulgarian origin could be equated with genetic belonging) would be the adoption of allele distribution analysis (based on haplotyping, for example — for instance, if it could be established that those resident on Bulgarian territory share certain genomic features, irrespective of ethnicity), but it is difficult to imagine the current ABA correctly validating and adopting the use of scientific tools.

The proof of earlier originating Bulgarian-ness may have potentially wide-reaching and politically explosive effects. In our understanding from work on a previous matter, one line of the descendants of the medieval Bulgarian czars may be the forebears of approximately a quarter of the population of Quebec (adding some 2 million potential new Quebecker-Bulgarians).

However, as is common enough, popular concern lags behind the crest of real-world phenomena. Just as increasingly well-off Bulgarians are becoming particular about allowing others to join them in citizenship, the number of applicants appears to have tapered off as the pool of potential candidates is becoming exhausted.

What does Bulgaria's Current QNI *Feel* Like?

Externally, being a Bulgarian citizen is increasingly appreciated as valuable. Bulgarian passport in hand, one could visit 159 countries and territories in 2018 without the substantial advance planning, cost, or complex pre-clearance involved in visa applications. More generally, the Bulgarian nationality found itself among the best nationalities in 2018, in the Very High Quality tier of nationalities with 75%, and ranked at 23rd.

A small number of irritants remain. Within Europe, Bulgaria's borders are much more obvious to those crossing them, as the country is not part of Europe's Schengen Area. This tends to affect Bulgarian citizens themselves (who are more likely to cross such borders) disproportionately but, on the one hand, does not appear to be a considerable practical or psychological inconvenience, and on the other, the distinction may soon be eliminated by either the entry of Bulgaria into the Schengen Area or the system's diminution (or both).

As above, largely due to Bulgaria's EU membership, it is now possible to travel to an unprecedently high number of countries visa-free or with a visa-on-arrival, and this is a privilege which Bulgarians use with gusto for a range of purposes: from tourism in Bali and Rio de Janeiro to extended surfing-and-working holidays in the Caribbean while tending to online businesses. Bulgarian nationality was ranked 29th on the Travel Freedom Ranking with 88.6%, along with the Romanian nationality. In this respect, the last major real and symbolic barrier to overcome is visa-free travel to the US. Given Bulgaria's close alliance with the US, this barrier looks bound to be dismantled when the Washington pendulum next swings in a liberalizing direction. Bulgarian nationality also benefited tremendously from the country's EU membership with regard to Settlement Freedom.

In 2018, Bulgarians could freely settle in 41 countries and territories, including all EU Member States. Bulgarian nationality shared the 6th position on the Settlement Freedom Ranking with Romanian and British overseas territories (Gibraltar) nationalities, achieving 89.6%.

Internally, the quality of being a Bulgarian is also increasingly valued by citizens and non-citizen residents or potential residents alike. There has been a shift in perception of Bulgaria as its presence has established itself. The benefits of Bulgarian citizenship are now apparent to wider groups of foreigners and its own citizens. Bulgaria is appreciated for the friendliness of its business environment (including its low corporate and personal income tax levels and its increasingly complete integration into the EU market and regulatory frameworks); for its remaining, underexplored (if not quite frontier-level) opportunities; and for the relaxed and less hurried lifestyle it offers or, indeed, demands.

For this reason, a steady trickle of previously ambitious emigrant Bulgarians have returned from Western Europe to exchange their participation in the rat race for a quiet life, while peripatetic global citizens (from Americans to Israelis to Syrians) are setting up 'shops' of various sizes in what they see mostly as a low-regulation paradise. Sadly, at least some of this idealization is based on illusion.

Despite rising slightly closer towards average European numbers, Bulgaria's per capita GDP remains below half of the EU average level, and following a partly botched transition, the country remains the EU's poorest, lagging behind Poland and eastern Germany. As the low-hanging business opportunities are picked off and the desire to catch up with the old EU becomes passé, Bulgaria's business landscape has acquired a somewhat mundane and second-rate air. Against a drastically shrinking labor force, future economic growth can come from either a radical liberalization of immigration (to which the secular trends appear inimical) or from an escape from the middle-income trap and a significant upgrade of educational attainment, stock of knowledge, and accumulations of capital and technology, which for the moment appear elusive, except for some dynamism in the IT sector.

The country has shown resilience, shifting from a peripheral agricultural kingdom to an austere and dusty communist republic, and then through the wide-eyed, part-Wild West, part-gangsterish era of the 1990s into the hipster-lite suburban kleptocracy of today. There may be still more reinvention to experience, which will be most needed and mostly welcome.

52 'Non-Citizens' of Latvia

By Aleksejs Dimitrovs

The Latvian nationality ranks 20th in *Kälin and Kochenov's Quality of Nationality Index* (QNI) 2018 General Ranking, scoring 77% and, as such, being in the Very High Quality tier. Contrary to that, the status of 'non-citizen' of Latvia ranks 101st with only 30.8%, that is, merely Low Quality.

The legal history of the status of a 'non-citizen' of Latvia, which is hugely inferior to full Latvian citizenship, is closely intertwined with the recent past of the state itself. On 15 October 1991 the Latvian Supreme Council (interim parliament) passed the decision *On the Renewal of the Rights of the Citizens of the Republic of Latvia and on the Fundamental Principles of Naturalization*,[1] which was based on the concept of the continuity of the citizenship of the Republic of Latvia that existed before the Soviet occupation.[2]

The doctrine of continuity is enshrined in the 1990 *Declaration On the Restoration of Independence of the Republic of Latvia*.[3] As the Constitutional Court put it,

> If a state, independence of which has been illegally terminated, restores its statehood, it can under the doctrine of continuity recognize itself as the same State which had been illegally terminated. In this case it is necessary that the state itself establishes its continuity and acts in accordance with the claims of this doctrine both in international relations and domestic policy, and it is also necessary that such self-assessment of the state is accepted by the international community.... A State may be said to be the 'same' State (with the consequence that the same legal rules, including conventional rules, continue to apply) where it is continuous in the sense defined or where after temporary suppression, an entity with substantially the same constituent features is re-established and its claim to continuity is accepted.[4]

As a result, only those persons who had been citizens of independent Latvia in 1940 and their descendants had their citizenship restored.[5] This approach was confirmed by the *Citizenship Law* of 1994.[6]

The legal status of persons who were not recognized as citizens of Latvia remained unclear until 1995 when the *Law on the Status of Former USSR Citizens Who Do Not Have the Citizenship of Latvia or of Any Other State*[7] was adopted. The Law introduced a special legal status of 'non-citizen',[8] granted to those who enjoyed registered domicile in Latvia on 1 July 1992 and who did not have citizenship of Latvia or any other country (except for some retired USSR army officers and members of their families).[9]

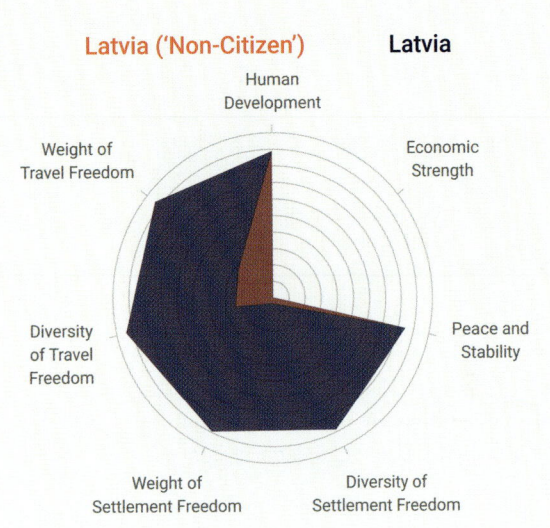

According to the clarification by the Latvian Constitutional Court, 'non-citizens' "can be regarded neither as the citizens, nor as aliens and stateless persons".[10] Latvian and international courts clarified that this status amounts to a permanent legal bond between the Latvian Republic and its 'non-citizens', thus excluding statelessness.[11]

This status is now held by more than 224,000[12] people belonging to ethnic minorities (Office for Citizenship and Migration Affairs 2019) — a large share of the population of a tiny state (10.7%) — and this situation is permanent: 'non-citizens' are born every day.[13] Efforts to amend the Citizenship Law in 2017 to allow children of 'non-citizen' parents automatically have Latvian citizenship failed.[14] Moreover, Latvian law in some cases allows foreign national parents to register their child as a 'non-citizen'.[15]

'Non-citizens' have rights akin to citizens. These include, for example, the right to reside in Latvia without visas or residence permits,[16] the right to work without a work permit,[17] and so on. Some rights and opportunities are reserved, however, only for 'full' citizens. These include political rights (such as the right to participate in elections[18] and the right to establish political parties),[19] the right to hold certain government positions, and social and economic rights (land property rights in some territories,[20] public and private sector careers in some professions,[21] and pensions for work periods accrued during the Soviet period outside Latvia if the period is not covered by an international agreement).[22] As of August 2016, there were as many as 84 differences in rights between citizens and 'non-citizens', mainly relating to careers in the public sector.[23] The absolute majority persists to this day. In particular, the citizens of Latvia can go without visas to 113 states and territories, while 'non-citizens' to only 47. (One of them – Russia – provides a visa-free entry for those born before February 1992 and for minors.)

The huge discrepancy between Latvian citizenship and the status of 'non-citizen' of Latvia is due to their unequal external values: while the Latvian nationality ranks among the best nationalities on the External Value Ranking, taking the 20th position, the 'non-citizen' of Latvia status ranks towards the bottom of the scale, taking the 137th position with 14.9%. Similar discrepancies can be observed with both External Value components, Travel Freedom and Settlement Freedom, which reflect diversity and weight of travel and settlement destinations. In particular, Latvian nationality is at the top of the Travel Freedom Ranking in 18th position with 94.2%, while the 'non-citizen' of Latvia status ranks 135th with 25.8%. Furthermore, while Latvian nationality is in 7th position with 89.5% on the Settlement Freedom Ranking, the 'non-citizen' of Latvia status ranks 44th with 4.1%. This should not be surprising because unlike Latvian citizens, 'non-citizens' of Latvia are not EU citizens, which means that they have no rights at all to settle and work in other EU Member States or in Iceland, Norway, or Switzerland; in terms of the sphere of rights they are effectively locked inside the territory of the tiny Latvian republic (Kochenov and Dimitrovs 2016).

Such a discrepancy between those possessing the two statuses of legal attachment to the Latvian state — that is, that of Latvian citizenship and that of 'non-citizen' of Latvia — could not but give rise to questions concerning possible discrimination. In September 2008 the Latvian Ombudsman completed an investigation into the differences in rights between citizens and 'non-citizens'.[24] The Ombudsman found that some restrictions on 'non-citizens' were not proportional, such as the ban on 'non-citizens' from working as advocates or patent attorneys,[25] from receiving the highest level of clearance for security work,[26] or from being heads or members of the board in the investigative agencies.[27] He also found a disproportionate restriction to the legal limitations on acquiring land property in cities by 'non-citizens'.[28] The Ombudsman recommended verifying whether restrictions concerning those rights guaranteed for EU citizens but denied to 'non-citizens' were justified.[29] Such verification has never taken place in practice, however, since the new Ombudsman elected in March 2011 declared that the principle of equality required a differential treatment towards persons in legally different situations, finding that the difference in rights between citizens and 'non-citizens' was not of a discriminatory nature, since the legal status of 'non-citizens' is not comparable with that of citizens.[30]

53 Georgian Nationality

By Laure Delcour

Georgia, a post-Soviet country, has developed the most welcoming migration policy in the world, combined with an extremely liberal visa regime (Delcour 2013; Brouillette 2018). Yet this open policy is in sharp contrast to the way in which Georgian citizens have long been treated worldwide. Since 2012, Georgia has consistently remained in the lower half of the nationalities ranked in *Kälin and Kochenov's Quality of Nationality Index* (QNI); its position, however, has significantly improved since 2017.

During the early to mid-2010s, Georgia was ranked from the 92nd to the 100th position of the QNI General Ranking, rising only slightly in value between 2012 (27.9%) and 2016 (31.2%), while staying in the same position at 101st. Among post-Soviet countries, only four Central Asia republics (Kyrgyzstan, Tajikistan, Turkmenistan from 2012 onwards, and Uzbekistan after 2013) were ranked behind Georgia, while Kazakhstan consistently did better. In addition, in 2016 all the other countries included in the EU's European Neighbourhood Policy (ENP)/Eastern Partnership (EaP) — except Azerbaijan — were better positioned in the QNI. This despite the fact that Georgia enjoyed closer relations with the EU than some of them, for instance Armenia and Belarus. In 2014, simultaneously with Moldova and the Ukraine, the country signed both an Association Agreement (AA) and a Deep and Comprehensive Free Trade Agreement (DCFTA) with the EU, significantly enhancing the prospects of Georgia's political and economic integration with the EU. Three years later, the introduction by the EU of a visa-free regime for Georgian citizens resulted in a significant leap forward in Georgia's QNI ranking. In 2017, Georgia moved up 22 positions in the Index (from 101st to 79th), thereby achieving the second largest gain (after the Ukraine) in the QNI. Georgia is ranked in 77th position in the 2018 QNI General Ranking.

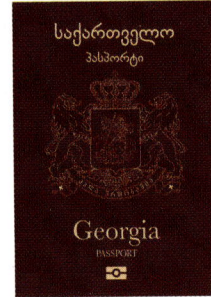

Georgia's position has improved by all QNI indicators. In 2016, the country was part of the group of states that rank last in terms of Settlement Freedom in the QNI and, in fact, was the only post-Soviet country belonging to this group. Most other post-Soviet states did substantially better, for instance the members of the Eurasian Economic Union (Armenia, Kazakhstan, the Russian Federation, and, to a lesser extent, Belarus), which enjoy freedom of movement between themselves, but also countries that do not belong to any regional integration organizations, like Azerbaijan and Uzbekistan. In terms of Travel Freedom, Georgia ranked between the 98th and 104th positions from 2011 to 2015. By 2017 its position had substantially improved. Georgian citizens can now travel freely (that is, without a visa or with a visa-on-arrival) to 114 countries compared to 67 countries in 2016. The diversity of these countries has sharply increased. The destinations to which Georgian citizens can freely travel are located mostly in Europe (the Schengen Area and some other European states, such as Montenegro and Serbia), the post-Soviet space (with the major exception of the Russian Federation), Central and South America, and, for a few of them, Asia (such as Turkey and India, which requires an e-tourist visa), and Africa (with, for example, e-visas required for Kenya and Rwanda).

Georgia's foreign policy course since the collapse of the Soviet Union carries substantial explanatory weight to account for the country's poor performance in terms of quality of nationality until 2017. Since the early 1990s, Georgia has been extremely reluctant to engage in any of the regional cooperation or integration schemes of which other post-Soviet states are members. It joined the Commonwealth of Independent States (CIS) in December 1993 in the wake of the conflict with Abkhazia, yet withdrew from the CIS's Council of Defence Ministers in 2006 and decided to fully withdraw from the organization after the August 2008 conflict with the Russian Federation. Georgia has never joined any of the other regional initiatives set up by the Russian Federation; for instance, while signing the Collective Security Treaty in 1994, it refrained from renewing its participation in 1999 and did not become a member of the Collective Security Treaty Organization when the latter was created. Like Turkmenistan (albeit for different reasons), Georgia has therefore remained absent (or at best marginal) in any of the post-Soviet cooperation attempts. This detachment from the post-Soviet space has gone hand in hand with increasingly strained relations with the Russian Federation, first over the conflict in Abkhazia in the early 1990s and then over the first conflict in Chechnya from the middle to the end of the 1990s (Serrano 2007; Gvalia, Lebanidze, and Iashvili 2011, 41; Oskanian 2016).

Against this background, mobility and migration were among the first levers used by the Russian Federation to exert pressure over Georgia. In the context of the war in Chechnya, the Russian Federation unilaterally introduced a visa obligation on Georgian citizens in December 2000 (Utkin, 2017). Thus, Georgia and Turkmenistan are the only post-Soviet countries besides the Baltic States that have experienced a visa regime from the Russian Federation. After the Rose Revolution, the sharp deterioration of Georgia's relations with the Russian Federation and the new government's clear prioritization of accession to NATO and the EU (Gvalia et al. 2015; Oskanian 2016) only exacerbated retaliatory actions on the part of the Russian Federation. Huge numbers of Georgian migrants living in the Russian Federation were expelled in the wake of the 2006 diplomatic crisis, and conditions for obtaining Russian visas became significantly tougher for Georgians after the 2008 conflict, not least because of the rupture of diplomatic relations between the two countries.

Georgia's unresolved conflicts (and the Russian Federation's role in them) are yet another factor that explains the country's weak QNI performance. After the violent conflicts that erupted in the early 1990s, Georgia de facto lost control over the two breakaway regions of Abkhazia and South Ossetia, which have been supported by the Russian Federation ever since. In this context, both freedom of movement and citizenship have increasingly become sources of contention between Georgia, its secessionist entities, and the Russian Federation. The latter has used visas and passports as levers to further detach Abkhazia and South Ossetia from Georgia. For instance, the visa obligation introduced in 2000 for Georgian citizens did not apply to the citizens of the breakaway regions, which benefited from a simplified border-crossing procedure. Crucially, the Russian Federation's 'passportization' policy (that is, the delivery of Russian passports to citizens of Abkhazia and South Ossetia[1] combined with the allocation of Russian pensions) further undermined the attractiveness of Georgian passports. It further disconnected the links between state, population, and territory and thereby produced exceptional spaces within the territory of Georgia (Artman 2013), where the distribution of Russian passports to non-Russian extraterritorial populations contributed to reigniting the conflict.[2] While being in clear breach of international law and remaining isolated on the international arena, the Russian Federation's decision to recognize the independence of Abkhazia and South Ossetia in the wake of the 2008 war resulted in further alienating these territories from Georgia. For instance, the Treaty of Alliance and Integration signed between the Russia Federation and South Ossetia in 2014 (in force since March 2015) facilitated the acquisition of Russian nationality for South Ossetian denizens.[3] Combined with other provisions merging key administrations of the secessionist entity with those of the Russian Federation, this was clearly meant to obstruct any attempts by Georgia to restore its territorial integrity and citizenship over the breakaway regions (German 2016, 160). In Abkhazia, the majority of Georgian residents in the district of Gali hold Georgian citizenship, which (as a result of decisions made by the de facto Abkhazian authorities) prevents them from having Abkhaz documents as well.[4] This is perhaps the best illustration of the limitations encountered by Georgian passport holders, as these Georgian citizens face obstacles to travel from the breakaway region to Tbilisi and other parts of Georgia.

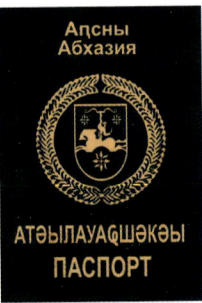
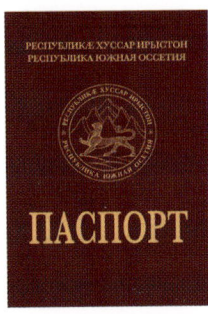

While the strained relations with the Russian Federation are crucial to understanding Georgia's poor performance in the QNI between 2012 and 2017, the enhanced perspectives offered by the EU in terms of mobility explain the country's improved ranking since 2017. The EU's decision to lift the obligation of a Schengen visa for Georgian citizens (agreed upon in February 2017 and effective as of 28 March 2017)[5] was long-awaited in Georgia. In fact, a visa-free regime should have been introduced already in 2016. However, the EU delayed the process in a context marked by the growing reluctance of the EU's Member States to offer enhanced mobility to new countries after the experience of visa liberalization with the Western Balkans, which was followed by a drastic rise in asylum applications lodged by citizens from the Western Balkans in some EU Member States (Delcour 2018). This reluctance only grew against the background of the sharp increase in migration flows to the EU in the mid-2010s. In essence, Georgia met all the EU's requirements for a visa-free regime in 2015, and on 9 March 2016, considering that the country had met all benchmarks in all four blocks of conditions (document security, illegal migration, public order, and security and external relations), the European Commission recommended lifting the visa obligation for Georgian citizens holding biometric passports. However, the process was marred because of the resistance of EU Member States (primarily Germany, followed by France and Italy), fueled by the refugee crisis and the general sentiment around migration in the EU. The Council of Ministers therefore demanded the introduction of a suspension mechanism (allowing the temporary suspension of the visa-free regime in the event of abuse or breaches to the conditions set by the EU) prior to granting visa liberalization. However, this demand triggered disagreements with the European Parliament, which co-decides with the Council but holds more liberal views on visa-free travel with neighboring countries. The Member States and the Parliament finally agreed on the simultaneous entry into force of both mechanisms on 13 December 2016, and the European Parliament voted in favor of visa liberalization for Georgia by an overwhelming majority on 3 February 2017. The Parliament's and Council's votes on the suspension mechanism followed later in February, thus paving the way to visa-free travel to the EU for Georgian holders of biometric passports.

The concerns raised by the EU about the implementation of the Visa Liberalization Action Plan (VLAP) in 2015–2016 have only increased since the obligation of Schengen visas was lifted, thereby leading to discussions about a possible use of the suspension mechanism against Georgia (schengenvisainfo.com 2018). While detections of irregular border crossings remain very low for Georgian citizens between 2016 and 2017 (85 for 2017), refusals of entry increased by approximately 200%, with 2,655 refusals recorded in 2017 compared to 810 in 2016 (European Commission 2018a). The main concern raised by the EU and its Member States relates to the increasing number of asylum applications, with 11,755 applications submitted in 2017 compared to 8,700 in 2016, an increase of approximately 35% (Ibid.). In the third quarter of 2018, some 3,720 Georgians lodged a request for asylum in EU countries. While this figure amounts to only 4% of the total number of asylum-seekers in the EU, it represents an increase of 67% over the third quarter of 2017. Only a very minor proportion of Georgian asylum-seekers are granted asylum in the EU (5.48% for 2017). It should be noted, however, that the number of asylum seekers has decreased since the first quarter of 2018, when a peak of 5,020 requests for asylum were lodged, and that number seems to have stabilized to around 3,700 requests per quarter. (All above figures, Eurostat 2018.) This reflects the first outcomes of the information campaigns organized in Georgia to raise awareness on the rules and functioning of the visa liberalization process. Georgia's ability to implement its commitments as part of the EU's visa liberalization process will therefore be critical to ensuring the continuity of the visa-free regime, and thus to maintaining its ranking in the QNI.

The limited travel and residence freedom still available to Georgian citizens is in sharp contrast to their country's own liberal approach to migrants entering Georgia. This contrast was especially stark in the early 2010s and persists — even if much attenuated — since 2017. For most of Georgia's post-Soviet existence, debates on migration, while discussed and politicized in the country, have failed to translate into a comprehensive migration agenda (Makaryan and Chobanyan 2014, 54). As a consequence, migration remained largely unregulated, and the country had no strategic policy document in the migration arena. This 'laissez-faire' was only reinforced by the Georgian authorities' preferences for an open-door policy; in the wake of the Rose Revolution, migration came to be seen as a pillar of the authorities' economic strategy, which primarily sought to attract foreign investment and to create a favorable business environment (Delcour 2013; Brouillette 2018). The legal framework then pursued a very liberal approach to visa categories, visa issuance, and the employment of foreigners. For instance, the 2006 Law on Aliens and Stateless Persons clearly prioritized the facilitation of mobility and the protection of foreigners over the fight against irregular migration. The law introduced only two visa categories ('ordinary' and 'students'). In addition, the country did not require visas for citizens from a number of countries worldwide. Nationals from over 100 countries could enter Georgia and stay there for up to one year without a visa, and those persons who entered the country legally were not required to have work permits in order to work.

This approach to migration increasingly collided with the EU's demand for increased regulation of migration flows as part of the ENP/EaP. The ENP Action Plan agreed upon with the EU in 2006 placed emphasis on border management and the prevention and control of irregular migration (EU–Georgia European Neighbourhood Policy Action Plan 2006). Under the Eastern Partnership, visa policy follows a "phased approach, leading to visa liberalisation under specific conditions and with accompanying measures" (European Commission 2008, 6). Thus, EU demands became most stringent as part of the visa facilitation and liberalization processes. In the wake of the 2008 conflict with the Russian Federation, the EU explicitly linked its offer of a visa facilitation agreement to the conclusion of a readmission agreement, a key EU instrument to curb irregular migration (Trauner and Kruse 2008). The next steps of the visa liberalization process[6] highlight an extensive reliance upon ex-ante conditionality. Under the Eastern Partnership, VLAPs are divided into two phases: an adoption phase, during which partner countries have to approximate their legal frameworks with the EU's requirements, and an implementation phase, which requires approximated legislation to be properly enforced. For each phase, evaluation missions are conducted to assess the fulfillment of benchmarks in all four blocks of conditions. Owing to the weak degree of regulation of visa, residence, and work permits, however, Georgia did not comply with EU demands as part of the visa liberalization process. As a result of both increased EU conditionality under the VLAP granted to Georgia in early 2013 (Fix, Gawrich, Kakachia, and Leukavets 2019) and the new authorities' more flexible approach to EU demands, Georgia shifted toward a stricter regulation of migration flows (Brouillette 2018). Yet the law On the Legal Status of Foreigners and Stateless Persons that entered into force on 1 September 2014 was sharply criticized as a disincentive for tourism or for applying for residence to work, study, or reside in the country (Delcour 2017). While clear-cut visa categories remain in force in line with EU requirements, the Georgian parliament adopted a package of amendments to the law in May 2015 that reintroduces 360-day visa-free stays for citizens and permanent residents of 94 countries listed in a governmental decree. This demonstrates how deeply entrenched the liberal approach to migration is in Georgian society (Ademmer and Delcour 2016).

While hinging critically upon the persistence of a visa-free regime with the EU, Georgia's QNI ranking is also connected to the potential of the Russian Federation to decide to ease travel conditions for Georgian citizens. As a result of the slow normalization of economic and cultural relations between Georgia and the Russian Federation since Mikheil Saakashvili left power, in December 2015 President Putin suggested lifting visa obligations for Georgian citizens traveling to Russia

(Ademmer and Delcour 2016). As a first step toward visa liberalization, the Russian Federation's ministry of foreign affairs decided a few days later to facilitate the visa regime for Georgian citizens. This includes in particular the possibility to issue multiple-entry visas for business, educational, humanitarian, private, and work purposes. In 2018, the opening of a Russian visa center in Tbilisi further facilitated the procedure for visa applications.[7] The elimination of the obligation of Russian visas remains a distant prospect, however, in light of both the absence of diplomatic relations between the two countries and the Russian Federation's increasing stranglehold over the two Georgian breakaway regions of Abkhazia and South Ossetia.

54 Israel: Citizenship, Residence, Taxation: A View from Practice

By Eli Gervits

As in most other states, in Israel there exists a Law of Citizenship[1] that regulates the acquisition of Israeli citizenship for those who "were not born into Israeli citizenship".[2] The overwhelming majority of Israeli citizens, if not citizens by birth, have received their citizenship under the provisions of the Law of Return.[3]

Acknowledging the history of persecution, the founders of the State of Israel proclaimed upon its establishment the renewal of the Jewish State in the Land of Israel, "which would open the gates of the homeland wide to every Jew". The Law of Return grants every *oleh* (Jew immigrating to Israel) the right to become a citizen. The Supreme Court called the Law of Return "one of the most important laws of Israel",[4] "a part of the non-written Israeli Constitution",[5] and "the cornerstone of the State of Israel".[6] It grants certain categories of individuals connected to Judaism by bonds of blood or marriage the immediate right to Israeli citizenship, without a protracted many-year period of naturalization or the requirement of taking exams.

One Citizenship, Two Passports

Israel appears to be the only country in the world to provide two different types of ordinary travel documents to its citizens without distinguishing between different classes of citizenship. Two passports are issued in this respect by the State of Israel: an ordinary international passport (Hebrew: *darkon*) and the Israeli Laissez-passer. The latter is issued in exceptional circumstances, including to:

- Israeli citizens who have stayed more than 10 years abroad without visiting the motherland; and
- Israeli citizens who have lost or destroyed two or more passports within a period of 10 years.

In addition, until recently, citizens who had just acquired Israeli citizenship status by virtue of the Law of Return were also granted the Israeli Laissez-passer and could apply for the ordinary international passport only after the passage of one year from their repatriation date. On 28 July 2017, however, an amendment to the Law on Passports came into force.[7] According to the law's new amendment, new repatriates are now able to obtain their first ordinary international passport without having to wait out the statutory one year in Israel from their date of repatriation.

Although they are associated with the same citizenship, the ordinary Israeli passport and the Laissez-passer passport have been given diverging values in Kälin and Kochenov's Quality of Nationality Index (QNI). This discrepancy is the result of differences in Travel Freedom and Settlement Freedom. The ordinary Israeli passport grants visa-free or visa-on-arrival travel access to 159 destinations, while the Laissez-passer passport permits visa-free or visa-on-arrival travel access to only 57 destinations. While both passports grant settlement access to Svalbard, only the ordinary international passport allows Israeli citizens to settle in Georgia. At the time of writing, the Ministry of Internal Affairs is trying to further secure visa-free entry for Israelis to more destinations.

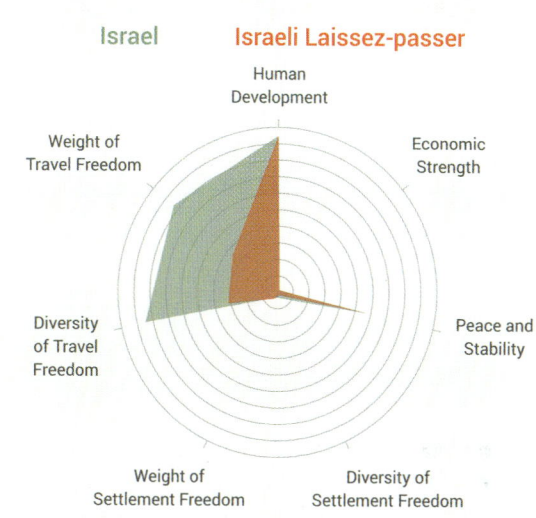

Overall, the Israeli nationality is ranked 48th in the 2018 QNI General Ranking, scoring 46.7%. By contrast, the Israeli Laissez-passer passport is ranked 100th with a value of 31.0%. As a result of the amendment to the Law on Passports, however, the appreciably lower value of the Laissez-passer passport no longer has implications for recently repatriated Israelis.

Jewishness under the Law of Return

As the concept of 'Jewishness' is central to the Law of Return, to better understand the functioning of this law it is important to first define 'Jewishness'.[8] Jewishness is inherited through the female line in a family. That is to say, a Jew is a person whose mother is a Jew, or whose mother's mother is a Jew, or any of whose maternal ancestors are Jews.[9] Of course, no evidence from the beginning of the world is required by consuls. The Law of Return regulates neither method nor depth of evidence to prove the existence of Jewish roots, leaving it to the discretion of consuls.

In this regard, however, applicants' (or their ancestors') Jewishness must be supported by documents. Within the post-Soviet territory, consulates give priority to original documents, not to duplicates, and documents that were issued in the Soviet era are preferred to those issued by the Russian Federation.[10] The former is related to consulates holding their ability to distinguish between authentic and fake documents in high regard, while the latter is associated with them having less confidence in modern administrative issuance systems than the Soviet system. No 'necessary and sufficient' list of documents exists, but examples of weighty documents are birth certificates, internal passports, military cards, personal files from places of work or study, and copies of house registers of tenants insofar as they contain information about the applicant's Jewishness. In the absence of original documents, applicants can provide the documents of indirect relatives (brothers and sisters of a parent, for example) or family documents from archives or the Red Cross.

The Law of Return endows Jews, their children, grandchildren, and spouses of three mentioned categories with the right to Israeli citizenship without any required period of residence in Israel prior to the acquisition of the status. Thus, not only Jews (children of a Jewish mother) are entitled to Israeli citizenship but also some categories of the non-Jewish, namely those whose fathers or grandfathers are Jewish. These categories are not considered Jews under Jewish religious canon, but they do have the right to repatriate.[11] It is also important to underline that spouses of persons 'with Jewish blood in their veins' will possess Israeli citizenship under the same conditions and time frameworks as their Jewish spouses, even without their own blood ties to Jewishness.[12]

Dual Citizenship and (Non-)Residence

Israel does not demand that new repatriates reject their current citizenships. Israeli citizenship can be received immediately upon arrival and without a prolonged period of residence, unlike that required by many countries for naturalization. This practice produces the result that for many fresh citizens of Israel (who did not acquire their citizenship by birth) the status of a citizen precedes the status of a resident. For example, applicants for US citizenship are obliged to endure a stepped process that can take many years and in a framework where many requirements — including having to actually stay within the territory of the US — have to be met.[13] In Israel, provided that they have passed all required procedures in special departments of Israeli consulates abroad, individuals who apply for Israeli citizenship based on their 'Jewish roots' de facto receive the citizenship upon arrival. Thus, in today's world, where many high-net-worth individuals (HNWIs) live with no strict territorial anchors, many newly fledged Israelis receive their citizenship without obtaining the status of a resident (and most importantly for this discussion, without the status of a 'tax resident').[14]

Taxation of New Repatriates

One of the most attractive advantages of Israeli citizenship for new repatriates is the 10-year vacation on taxes for sources of incomes located abroad.[15] Taxation in Israel is personal, and usually Israeli tax residents must pay their taxes[16] in Israel for their incomes obtained from anywhere in the world.[17] However, another set of rules is applicable to new Israeli citizens with respect to global non-Israeli income and the obligation to pay taxes. First of all, as mentioned above, individuals who acquire Israeli citizenship do not automatically become Israeli tax residents.[18] If individuals' 'centers-of-life' remain outside Israel after they acquire Israeli citizenship, and if they spend fewer than 183 days per year in Israel, the Israel Tax Authority does not consider them to be Israeli tax residents.[19] Moreover, if individuals spend more than half the year outside Israel, there is no reason for the Israel Tax Authority to examine their centers-of-life since such an examination will not lead to the collecting of taxes within the 10-year period.

The second bulwark protecting new repatriates against the payment of Israeli taxes on global revenues — the cherry on the cake — is that it takes 10 years for new Israeli citizens to become Israeli taxpayers (if they ever do).[20] Within this 10-year period, they will not be subjected to taxation for most sources of their revenue earned outside Israel.[21] At present this 10-year period comprises not only the exemption from taxation itself but also exemption from reporting related to incomes. The Organization for Security and Co-operation in Europe is pressing Israel with a demand that all new citizens report their sources of worldwide income, a legal initiative that has been blocked for many years in the Israeli parliament by a lobby of Russian repatriates.

Thus, new repatriates who have received Israeli citizenship and who have become Israeli tax residents are able to structure their global revenues so that their incomes are collected in offshore holding companies[22] and pay dividends to themselves without paying income tax in any country in the world.

55 China and India

By Suryapratim Roy

China and India have been in the international spotlight for the last two decades primarily because of their robust economic growth and cross-border financial flows. According to the latest World Bank estimates of GDP growth, China's annual growth rate is a remarkable 6.9% and India's is 6.7%. The is reflected in the Economic Strength internal factor in *Kälin and Kochenov's Quality of Nationality Index* (QNI), which constitutes 15% of the QNI General Ranking. Economic Strength may have myriad indirect effects on the other sub-factors of the QNI; such indirect effects are not evident from China and India's cumulative rankings, however, and in the case of India they are probably modest: Chinese nationality shares the 56th position in the QNI General Ranking with Venezuelan nationality, and Indian nationality shares the 95th position with Gambian nationality. These rankings may be attributed to the fact that little progress has been made in relation to other factors in the QNI.

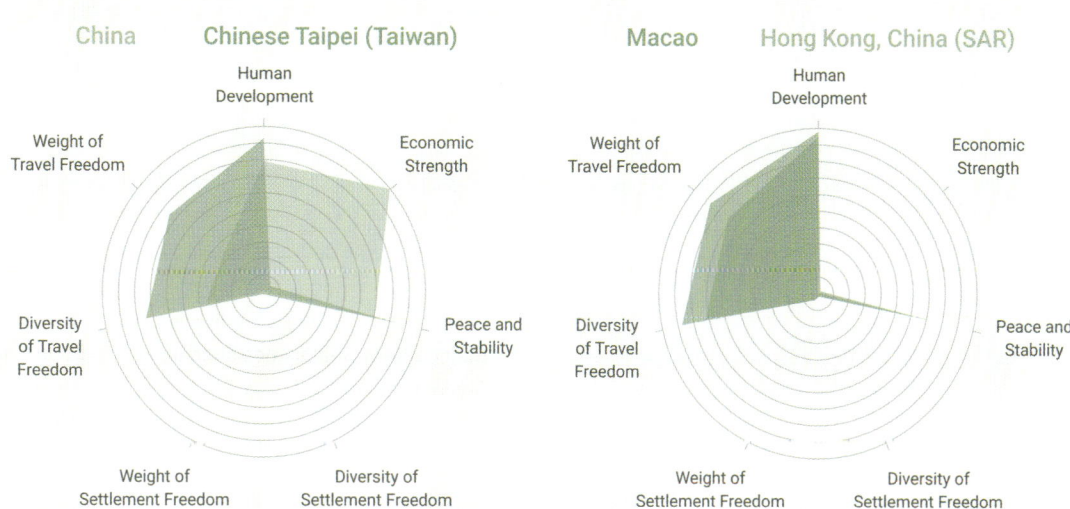

The other things China and India have in common are their vast sizes and the internal diversity of their populations — both countries encompass several metaphorical nationalities, and with regard to China this metaphor assumes a literal quality — several passports are issued within the Chinese territory corresponding to different statuses of citizenship as defined in Chinese law. Importantly, these nationalities are not ranked equally in the QNI. In fact, the 'Chinese nationality' mentioned above refers to the nationality of the People's Republic of China (PRC) and does not include the

nationalities of Hong Kong, Macao, or Taiwan. All three of these latter nationalities rank higher than PRC nationality on the QNI General Ranking: 44th position for the nationality of Hong Kong, 51st for the Taiwanese, and 58th for the nationality of Macao. To be clear, a Taiwanese passport is a passport issued by the Republic of China and is distinct from a PRC passport. Permanent residents of Hong Kong and Macao are eligible for PRC Special Administrative Region (SAR) passports issued under the Basic Laws of the Hong Kong and Macao SARs respectively; in these two territories, the rules and regulations governing residence and citizenship must adhere to the constitution of the PRC. In comparison, since its independence and after its break from Pakistan and Bangladesh, India has issued a single passport for all its citizens.

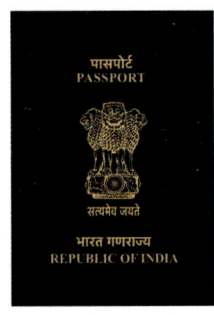

The nationalities of both India and the PRC demonstrate minor improvements in their QNI General Ranking scores between 2011 and 2018. This is due to improvements in the Internal Values of the two nationalities; the External Values (namely, Travel Freedom and Settlement Freedom) have remained mostly unchanged. Despite similarities in both Economic Strength and Peace and Stability, the comparatively higher Internal Value of Chinese nationality than that of Indian nationality may be attributed to its position on the Human Development Index (HDI), where PRC nationality is ranked 86th, while India is in 130th place. In contrast, Hong Kong is in 7th place in the HDI rankings. (Taiwan and Macao are not ranked separately.) The relatively high scores for Economic Strength and Human Development of Hong Kong, Macao, and Taiwan also enhance the weighted Travel and Settlement Freedoms of the nationalities that provide access to them. Travel Freedom also increased with the PRC's relaxation of visa restrictions on Taiwanese citizens in July 2015 and the introduction of entry and exit permits for Taiwan issued to citizens of the PRC. Historically, there have been tensions regarding the autonomy of Hong Kong, Macao, and Taiwan on the one hand and attempts at PRC unification on the other. This has resulted in some cooperative freedoms with regard to travel and settlement between the PRC and Hong Kong and Macao. Such cooperative freedoms are bested by the Travel Freedom enjoyed by Taiwan. The period between 2011 and 2015 was particularly significant for Taiwan because

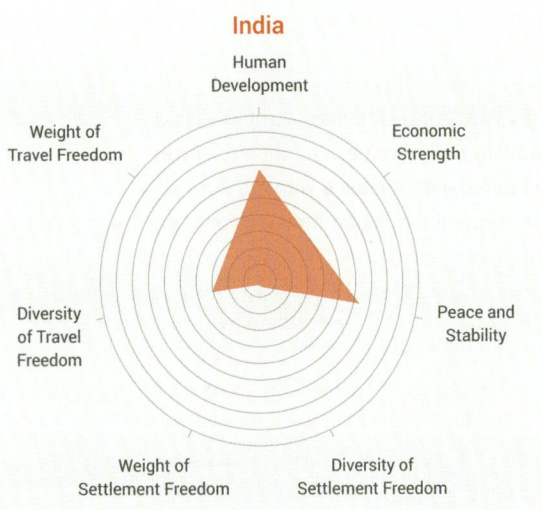

of a visa-exemption policy for short-term access to Europe's Schengen Area, resulting in a gain of 12.6 in the QNI General Ranking of its nationality. The PRC and Hong Kong nationalities witnessed rises in their Travel Freedoms between 2015 and 2016 (a rise of 8.2% on the Travel Freedom scale for PRC nationality and 4.9% for Hong Kong) that may be attributed to the cooperative arrangements with Taiwan. However, the positions of these nationalities dropped slightly in the QNI General Ranking between 2015 and 2016, the Chinese nationality dropping from the 61st to the 65th position and the Hong Kong nationality dropping from 45th to 46th. This is not because of any major adverse events, but instead to improvements in the ranking of other nationalities that have made favorable travel and residence arrangements with countries in Europe's Schengen Area.

In contrast, India continues to restrict entry of its neighbors other than citizens of Bhutan and Nepal. In fact, Indian nationality grants visa-free or visa-on-arrival access to 55 countries and territories only, a number easily surpassed by nationalities of smaller economies (such as the Bulgarian one, for instance, which affords visa-free or visa-on-arrival access to 159 destinations). There has been some improvement in the position of Indian nationality over the last few years, however, due to the introduction in 2013 of its fast-track e-Tourist and e-Business visas to several countries. Since then, there has been a gradual expansion of the list of countries eligible for fast-track e-Tourist and e-Business visas, and in January 2019 the country introduced multiple-entry visas. This has been a much-needed improvement, as reciprocity is an important marker in easing the process of international travel, and the difficulty in accessing India may be a contributing factor to the difficulty that Indians experience in accessing other countries. E-visas, however, are restricted to short-term visits and are not useful for making inroads into the Indian labor market.

On the matter of access to markets, the only sub-element where Indian nationality performs marginally better than the nationalities of the PRC, Hong Kong, Macao, and Taiwan is Settlement Freedom, where Indian nationality is ranked at 47th. (The nationalities of Hong Kong, Macao, and Taiwan share 49th place, and PRC nationality is ranked 52nd on the Settlement Freedom and 104th on the Travel Freedom Ranking scale.) This is due to the access of Indian citizens to Nepal, but since Nepalese nationality does not score well on weighted Settlement Freedom, this advantage is marginal. The QNI clearly indicates that holders of most South and Southeast Asian nationalities are not welcome to settle in other countries despite their recent economic performance and so-called 'cultural soft power'. Thus, increased international migration flows from the PRC and India are relatively high despite Travel and Settlement Freedoms.

As is evident in other segments of this report, the way a country is positioned within regional blocs has an impact on the value of its nationality in the QNI. By virtue of their being Member States of the EU, for example, some countries acquire a substantially higher value in relation to Travel and Settlement Freedoms, and the association of some post-Soviet republics with the Russian Federation has had various impacts on the values of their nationalities. In comparison, however, there are relatively few advantages regarding settlement freedoms that India and China can derive from the blocs in which they find themselves. This may be understood as being due both to their post-colonial arrangements and the arrangements among these countries themselves.

In regard to post-colonial political arrangements, decolonization has not enhanced Travel and Settlement Freedoms for either India or China, and political events such as wars or the disintegration of empires have not set in motion processes that enhance the values of their nationalities. In relation to the arrangements among countries themselves, unlike the availability of travel and settlement between Taiwan and China, for example, or their facilitation by other regional blocs such as the EU or the CIS, there are no such arrangements between India and China. The groups that India and China belong to — such as BRICS[1] and the G20 — do not contribute to their Travel and Settlement Freedoms. India is a member of the South Asian Association for Regional Cooperation,[2] but membership in this association does not affect either the Travel or Settlement Freedom of its members' respective nationalities. This explains why the countries discussed here that have relatively high Travel Freedom rankings — namely Hong Kong and Taiwan — have sought out bilateral arrangements.

56 Myanmar: The Unflinching Law of the Ethnic Citizen and the 'Mixed Blood' Other

By José-María Arraiza

There are many countries in our blood, aren't there, but only one person. Would the world be in the mess it is if we were loyal to love and not to countries?

Graham Greene, *Our Man in Havana*

Introduction: Burmese Identity and Nation-Building through Citizenship Laws

Myanmar's nationality is far from ideal, standing towards the bottom of *Kälin and Kochenov's Quality of Nationality Index*'s (QNI's) Low Quality tier. It ranked 139th with 23.1% in 2018, decreasing only slightly in value compared to the previous year (23.2%). The Myanmar citizenship framework, with its vintage color-coded ID cards, its long and exotic lists of ethnic groups, and its eyebrow-raising ancestry-analysis schemes, is perplexing for the outsider. Understanding it requires reflecting on its recent history and its particular politics of identity and nation-building in a post-colonial, multi-nation state suffering from the world's longest civil war.

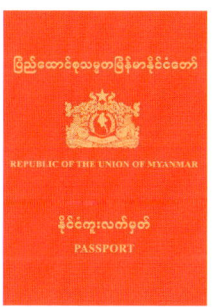

From a broader perspective, the utopian nationalist idea of constructing a state that corresponds in its geographic and human boundaries to a well-defined nation has resonated globally and given rise to all sorts of historical adventures and misadventures (Gellner 2016). Despite a violent track record, making a nation's political and ethno-national boundaries coincide and rejecting or expelling alien influences are still much-followed ideals (such as lately seen in the form of "taking back our country"). In such

a context, the search for ethnic purity in citizenship implies the rejection of anything considered impure, inauthentic, or foreign.

The present dystopia in the civil-war-torn areas of Myanmar such as the Kachin, Rakhine, and Shan states, with mass forced displacement within and across international borders — including more than a hundred thousand internally displaced in Kachin and North Shan, another hundred thousand Karen refugees in Thailand, and close to a million refugees in Bangladesh — is partly the result of just such a boundary-making enterprise (The Border Consortium 2018).[1] An ongoing peace process led by the country's de facto president, 1991 Nobel Peace Prize winner Aung San Suu Kyi, is aiming to put an end to such conflicts. However, progress has been disappointing so far due to the army's tight control. Some of the main actors, such as the Karen National Union, have temporarily withdrawn from the formal peace talks.

The making of modern Myanmar (which was known as Burma until 1989) and the foundations of its citizenship regime may be partly traced back to disgruntled Rangoon students, including soon-to-be General Aung San, weary of their British colonial masters, who followed with interest the campaigns of Sinn Féin in Ireland and used Sinn Féin as a model for the creation of the DoBamar Asiayone (in English, the 'We Burmans Association'). They stood the hierarchy upside down by calling themselves *Thakins* (which means 'masters', a word that had been used to refer to the English colonial rulers) (Khin 1998).

Along with the general opposition to alien rule by the British, there were also negative feelings toward the workers the British administration had brought along with it. Hence, grievances against the perceived or real privileges of Indian-origin workers in Yangon (which was named Rangoon at the time) led to intercommunal riots in 1930. These events were then used to stir up nationalist sentiments (Zaw Soe 2006).

Interestingly, since that time (and before) there had been an ambivalent attitude towards these recent or longstanding 'newcomers' on the part of the majority ethnic-Burmese Bamars. On the one hand, Bamar-centered nationalism sought Burma for the Bamar; on the other hand, it was necessary to integrate other ethnic groups in the border areas of Chin, Kachin, Rakhine, Shan, and the southeast, and persons of Indian and Chinese ancestries, into the new Burma.

Thus, the project of Burma (Myanmar) as a state could not be Bamar and Buddhist-only: the political boundaries of Myanmar included not only the Bamar and the Buddhist-dominated central plains but also the diverse peoples of the hills that surrounded it. These included what today constitute the states of Chin, Kachin, Karen, Kayah, Mon, Rakhine, and Shan. A broad range was to be found within these areas of ethnicities, languages, and religions, including where different strains of Christianity had been introduced by Baptist, Catholic, and Lutheran missionaries in the 19th and 20th centuries and had triumphed.

To successfully build a peaceful Myanmar (and Burmese citizenship) the inhabitants of these different ethnic areas had to be included as loyal nationals. Burma was therefore legally defined as including the "indigenous races of Burma". The initial citizenship framework provided for the naturalization of long-term residents and residents who came from other British colonial territories through double *jus soli*.[2] The 1947 Constitution included both this concept and provisions that conferred nationality on permanent residents, including those from other British-dominated territories. The Union Citizenship Act of 1948, art. 3.1, defined the indigenous races as "Burmese,

Chin, Kachin, Karen, Kayan, Mon, Shan, and any other group which may have settled in Burma before the first Anglo-Burmese war (1824–1826)". Such groups are considered to be *taingyintha*, that is, pure ethnic citizens who belong to the recognized national races.

In this sense, it is important to note that the demands for recognition of the non-Bamar ethnic groups are first and foremost demands for territorial self-government (such as in the form of a federal state). This territorial-claim linkage to group recognition explains, to a certain extent, the widespread and stubborn rejection of the recognition of the Rohingya in Northern Rakhine, as it includes a fear of secession of that border area.

Unfortunately, the first attempt at peacefully achieving a multi-national state failed, and the vision contained in the Panglong Agreement signed on 12 February 1947 by General Aung San (the father of Aung San Suu Kyi) and Chin, Kachin, and Shan representatives did not achieve the desired peace and stability. A series of civil wars between the Burmese Army (the *Tatmadaw*) and the Ethnic Armed Organizations that included the Karen National Union and others defined much of Burmese history in the following 70 years.

General Ne Win's Vision: The *Taingyintha* and the Others

In 1962, General Ne Win toppled the parliamentary democracy and established the military rule that would last, in one form or another, until the present day. His vision of Burma and Burmese citizenship meant another turn of the screw of the national vision towards isolation and ethnocentrism. He defined belonging to the union as being directly based on the purity of a person's 'blood', with the understanding that only the *taingyintha*, the national races, had the desired quality. In his vision, Burmese nationals were divided between 'pure blood' (the indigenous races and their descendants) and 'mixed blood', which meant anyone who did not belong to such races, including persons descended from Indian or Chinese ancestors or ancestors from other bordering countries. Such an approach, based on a nation-state scheme and its entrenchment through law, prevented the development of a more inclusive civic national identity that would incorporate the existing ethnic and religious diversity of Myanmar (Myint-U 2001).

Only by understanding Ne Win's point of departure is it possible to read the 1982 Burma Citizenship Law in context. Ne Win saw the country's complex social heterogeneity as a problem. As he stated during the presentation of the citizenship law, "the natives or Burmese nationals [were] unable to shape our own destiny. We were subjected to the manipulations of others from 1824 to 4 January 1948. … We then find that the people in our country comprised true nationals, guests, issues from unions between nationals and guests or 'mixed bloods', and issues from unions between guests and guests".

The problem faced by the legislator upon Myanmar's independence in 1948 was, as Ne Win asserted in the same speech, "how to clarify the position of guests and 'mixed bloods'". His solution was simple: "racially, only pure-blooded nationals will be called citizens", while others were to be classified as what has been translated into English as 'naturalized citizens' and 'associated citizens'. (Another plausible translation for the latter would be 'guest citizens').[3]

Integration of the Third 'Mixed' Generation as Citizens

Ne Win's regime did not trust people with 'mixed blood' (anyone of Indian or Chinese descent and Hindus and Muslims regardless of their descent). Having 'mixed blood' was perceived in this racial profiling narrative to include a tendency towards criminality. Ne Win asserted in 1982 that such persons, to whom he referred in his speech as "*kalas* [a derogatory term] to be frank", would engage in smuggling. "We have actually seen such smugglings", he continued. "We are aware of their penchant for making money by all means and, knowing this, how could we trust them in our organisations that decide the destiny of our country?"

In the same speech Ne Win went on to maintain, however, that the propensity of people not belonging to the eight recognized national races to smuggle would somehow become diluted by the third generation, when such 'mixed blood' persons would be more integrated into society. Hence, their grandparents' innate lack of trustworthiness would not be a problem for the grandchildren. In the general's words, "This blood relation will more or less cease to exist at the time of his or her grandchildren"; the descendants of people with 'mixed blood' would eventually become full citizens, after a third generation, when Ne Win assumed that the (real or perceived) 'newcomers' or 'guests' would be integrated into Burmese life. The ambivalence between exclusion and integration of the other was expressed by General Ne Win in his final advice: 'pure-blooded' Burmese should not mistreat these second-class citizens because "one day they will become one with us and all will be travelling in the same boat" (All quotes, Ne Win 1982). Not long after the enactment of the 1982 Citizenship Law, a list of 135 ethnic groups, developing the eight mentioned in the law's Article 3, was published and has since became a central piece in essentialist nation-building narratives. Posters that display the 135 groups are common in governmental offices and at ethnic festivals. Wooden figures representing each of the eight main groups are for sale in souvenir shops.

A Closed Regime: Criteria for Citizenship Acquisition and Loss

To prevent further external influences and 'mixing', the 1982 Citizenship Law therefore almost entirely removed existing *jus soli* and naturalization provisions (that is, citizenship by residence or birth in the territory) from the Burmese legal framework and created a closed system where naturalization of foreigners is not possible. The move towards closing naturalization avenues was clearly based on the rejection of potential alien rule and influence. This fear of the 'other' is best exemplified by the motto of the Ministry of Labour, Immigration and Population (MoLIP), which states that "an earthquake will not swallow a race to extinction but another race will" (Ministry of Labour, Immigration and Population 2002).

As an example, naturalization through marriage to a Burmese citizen is possible only if the date of marriage preceded the enactment of the 1982 Citizenship Law[4] and the non-citizen was issued with a Foreigner Registration Certificate.[5] It is no longer possible, therefore, for a foreign spouse to acquire Myanmar citizenship on the basis of his or her marriage to a Myanmar citizen after 1982.

Overall, eligibility for citizenship is based on the descent-based criteria of ethnicity and *jus sanguinis*. The ability to confirm or acquire citizenship depends on the individual providing sufficient evidence concerning the citizenship of his or her ancestors.

Myanmar recognizes three types of citizenship (Norwegian Refugee Council, United Nations Refugee Agency, United Nations Women, Institute on Statelessness and Inclusion, Statelessness Network Asia Pacific, The Seagull 2018, 5–10):

1. Full citizenship. Automatic acquisition is possible in four ways: First, the applicant was a citizen pursuant to the 1948 Union Citizenship Act and the 1948 Union Citizenship (Election) before the enactment of the 1982 Citizenship Law.[6] Second, the person is deemed to belong to the recognized national races, or *taingyintha* (Bamar, Chin, Kachin, Karen, Kayah, Mon, Rakhine, and Shan).[7] Third, children born to 'citizen' parents are automatically citizens irrespective of whether they are born in or outside the country.[8] Fourth, persons are full citizens whose parents are some combination of citizens, associate citizens, or naturalized citizens and who have at least one set of grandparents, both of whom are associate citizens, naturalized citizens, or a combination.[9]

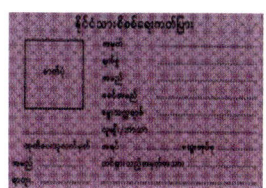

2. Associate citizenship. This 'second-class' citizenship may be acquired through application;[10] only persons whose application for nationality was pending at the time of the enactment of the 1982 Citizenship Law and who do not qualify for full citizenship (that is, who do not belong to the recognized national races) are eligible for associate citizenship.[11]

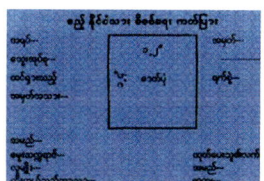

3. Naturalized citizenship. This form of citizenship may be acquired through application by three mechanisms. For the first, the person must have entered and resided in Myanmar prior to 4 January 1948;[12] for the second, a person born in or outside of Myanmar to parents who are a specific combination of citizen, associate citizen, naturalized citizen, or 'foreigner' may apply;[13] for the third, a child whose name is included in one of his or her parents' successful applications for naturalized citizenship is a naturalized citizen following a formal oath by the child upon reaching 18 years of age.[14]

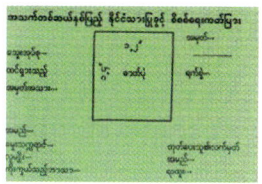

The law provides a safeguard against a citizen automatically losing citizenship merely by marriage to a foreigner.[15] However, such protection is applicable only to full citizens and not to associate citizens or naturalized citizens.[16]

Finally, an individual ceases to be a citizen, associate citizen, or naturalized citizen when he or she leaves Myanmar permanently, acquires citizenship or registers as a citizen of another country, or acquires a passport or "similar certificate of another country".[17]

Apart from its discriminatory aspects, the law has additional problems as it does not reflect the principles of separation of powers. Because the decisions of the Council of Ministers on matters concerning the 1982 Citizenship Law are final, its provisions prevent the judicial review of administrative decisions. In addition, Article 71 specifically states that "no reasons need to be given by organizations invested with authority under this law in matters carried under this law".[18] Thus no reasons are needed to justify the acts of the administration concerning citizenship.

Distance between Law and Practice

Unsurprisingly, the implementation of such a scheme did not lead to the perfect Burmese society envisioned by the military leader. The efforts of MoLIP to implement a highly impractical law did not yield the expected results. The obsession of the administration to achieve a citizenry of documented *taingyintha* — pure ethnic citizens — and second-class naturalized and associated citizens brought unexpected outcomes.

The resulting myriad bureaucratic requirements placed on individuals to prove their ancestry (or 'blood purity') combined with informal fees and arbitrariness led to a significant portion of the population being undocumented. Many persons who lost their documents during civil wars and natural disasters cannot prove their ancestry to the paper-based, control-oriented bureaucracy. Hence, during a census in 2014, MoLIP identified up to 11,000,207 persons who did not have valid identification documents (27.3% of Myanmar inhabitants over the age of 10) (Myanmar Ministry of Labour, United Nations Population Fund 2014, 207) In practice, the Bamar have relatively easier access to the pink 'Citizenship Scrutiny Card' of the full citizen.[19] Other ethnic groups, even if recognized, have additional difficulties. Those understood by the government to be not belonging to the *taingyintha* face highly unpredictable bureaucratic obstacles, regardless of whether they meet criteria for full citizenship (such as being a citizen at the moment the 1982 law was enacted) (Norwegian Refugee Council et al. 2018).

Apart from millions of undocumented or poorly documented persons, the 1982 Citizenship Law isolated and created the largest group of stateless persons worldwide: the Rohingya. The theoretical goal of integrating the 'mixed bloods' foreseen by Ne Win was abandoned by the administration's implementation of the citizenship law. While the 1982 law sought to create a temporary class of less empowered citizens (not necessarily stateless persons) whose grandchildren would be full citizens, its application was much harsher than envisioned. The consequences of such a policy are that a large portion of Myanmar inhabitants have become stateless, and a considerable portion bear the burden of an insecure legal identity, with either no valid documentation or temporary documentation of unclear legal value (such as Identity Cards for National Verification).

The Application of the Law in Rakhine State

Arguably, if the 1982 Citizenship Law had been implemented properly in Rakhine State, a large portion of its Muslim inhabitants would probably have had access to one of the three types of citizenship (with naturalized citizenship arguably the most common) (Nyi Kyaw 2017, 269–86).[20] However, a policy of naming Muslims in Rakhine (who normally self-identify as Rohingya) as 'Bengali' in official documents (linked to the earlier-mentioned rigid rejection of recognition) led to such communities in Rakhine refusing to participate in the process (Nyi Kyaw 2017, 270).[21] Members of the Muslim community argued that they were already citizens before 1982 and refused to participate in the national verification process unless their self-identifier was included in their ID cards. However, the policy in Rakhine State and elsewhere has been to deny such an option while offering to provide temporary documentation with unclear legal status (first, white Temporary Registration Cards, and more recently, interim Identity Cards for National Verification) pending a final decision on the citizenship scrutiny. As mentioned earlier, a large portion of these communities has been forcibly displaced across the border with Bangladesh without such verification taking place. In 2017, an Advisory Commission on Rakhine State led by the late Kofi Annan recommended fairer procedures on citizenship; to date, no changes have taken place (Advisory Commission on Rakhine State 2017).

The recommendations were presented in August 2017, on the same day that an attack by the Arakan Rohingya Salvation Army ignited a spiral of violence that generated further animosity and fears (including of terrorist attacks). Later, in early 2019, an escalation of a different conflict, one between the *Tatmadaw* and the ethnic Rakhine Arakan National Army, further worsened the situation.

Travel Freedom and Settlement Freedom

Myanmar's nationality ranked 158th with 11.4% on the External Value Ranking scale. In terms of freedom to travel, Myanmar citizens could enjoy visa-free or visa-on-arrival access to 44 states in 2018, most of them in Asia. As one might expect, the nationality of Myanmar ranked low on the Travel Freedom Ranking, taking only the 146th position with 22.8%. Myanmar is a member of the Association of Southeast Asian Nations (ASEAN), an organization that aims to promote economic cooperation and rule of law in the region and that also includes Brunei, Cambodia, Indonesia, Laos, Philippines, Singapore, Thailand, and Vietnam. Thanks to the ASEAN Framework Agreement on Visa Exemptions of 25 July 2006, regular Burmese passport holders can travel to the other member countries and obtain free-entry tourist visas for up to 14 days. But citizens of Myanmar cannot freely settle in any other country. Therefore, Myanmar's nationality was at the very bottom of the Settlement Freedom Ranking, in the 52nd position with 0%.

There are currently large Burmese migrant and refugee populations. Indeed, Myanmar is the largest regional source of migrants within the Greater Mekong Subregion. An estimated 4.2 million Burmese are migrants abroad or refugees, most of them (70%) in Thailand, where there are over 3 million, according to the International Organization for Migration (IOM). Other Burmese migrants live in Malaysia (15%), China (4.6%), Singapore (3.9%), and the US (1.9%) (IOM, n.d.). Settlement restrictions and work-permit requirements considerably increase the hardship for these migrants.

Conclusion

It is difficult to ascertain whether Ne Win's comparatively milder vision of citizenship in Myanmar (including a long-term integration strategy) would have led to the current dire situation: millions of undocumented persons and a whole category of denizens holding Interim Cards for National Verification of unclear legal value and with unclear rights or future prospects. After considering the recent history of citizenship law-making in Myanmar, it is not strange to see it at the bottom end of the QNI General Ranking (139th in 2018). Indeed, the current framework and its implementation belongs with the darker history of citizenship regimes. Hopefully this will change in future and Myanmar citizens — regardless of ethnicity and religion — will live to see happier days, but such reforms are not in sight at present. For the time being, paradoxically, the law is seen by a large portion of the Myanmar society as dogma, a central component of national identity and a necessary protection against undesirable influences and unwanted migration from neighboring countries. Proposing a citizenship framework that addresses such fears and national sentiments in a more rational, humane, and practical manner is a challenge for future law- and policy-makers.

Part 6

End Matter

Endnotes

1–36

1. *Nottebohm (Liechtenstein v. Guatemala)*, Second Phase, Judgment, 1955 I.C.J. 4, (April 6).

2. Article 1, "Convention on Certain Questions Relating to the Conflict of Nationality Laws," April 13, 1930, *League of Nations, Treaty Series*, vol. 179, 89, No. 4137. See also Article 2 of the Convention: "Any question as to whether a person possesses the nationality of a particular State shall be determined in accordance with the law of that State."

3. See in this regard *Advisory Opinion on Proposed Amendments to the Naturalization Provision of the Constitution of Costa*, OC-4/84, IACrtHR, 19 January 1984. But already in 1923 the PCIJ vaguely said that, 'generally speaking', nationality regulation remains within the jurisdiction of states, but this principle is subject to future treaty obligations; *Acquisition of Polish Nationality*, Advisory Opinion, 1923 P.C.I.J. (ser. B) No. 7 (Sept. 15), 16.

4. *Nationality Decrees Issued in Tunis and Morocco on Nov. 8th, 1921*, Advisory Opinion, 1923 P.C.I.J. (ser. B) No. 4 (Feb. 7), 24; *Acquisition of Polish Nationality*, Advisory Opinion, 1923 P.C.I.J. (ser. B) No. 7 (Sept. 15), 16.

5. *Nottebohm (Liechtenstein v. Guatemala)*, Second Phase, Judgment, 1955 I.C.J. 4, (April 6). Cf. (Spiro 2019b).

6. See, for example, (Donner 1994, 62; van Panhuys 1959, 158). See also *Soufraki v. United Arab Emirates*, ICSID Case No. ARB/02/7.

7. Notable examples of recent jurisprudence in sharp contrast with the *Nottebohm* dicta include *Feldman v. United Mexican States*, ICSID Case No. ARB(AF)/99/1. Even in the context of diplomatic protection, the 'genuine link' theory has questionable validity nowadays; see International Law Commission, "Draft Articles on Diplomatic Protection and Commentaries," *UN General Assembly Official Records*, 61st session, Supp. No. 10, UN Doc. A/61/10, 2006, 32–33. http://legal.un.org/ilc/texts/instruments/english/commentaries/9_8_2006.pdf.

8. For an overview, see Peters (2010).

9. For example, the Convention on the Settlement of Investment Disputes between States and Nationals of Other States, opened for signature March 18, 1965, *United Nations, Treaty Series*, vol. 575, 159, No. 8359. For an overview of relevant case law, see Sironi (2013).

10. The absurdity of the *Nottebohm* logic has been explained with abundant clarity already in the dissenting opinions in the same case. See, especially, the opinion of Judge Klaestad.

11. *Micheletti*, Case C-369/90, [1992] ECR I-4239.

12. Opinion of AG Tesauro, *Micheletti*, Case C-369/90, [1992] ECR I-4253, para. 5.

13. The best resource on this issue in Europe is the EUDO Citizenship Database of the European University Institute in Florence.

14. Article 9 Act No. 91 of 5 February 1992, Citizenship 15 August 1992; Zincone and Basili 2009, 13.

15. Among the instruments addressing this issue, see Protocol Relating to a Certain Case of Statelessness, April 12, 1930, entered into force July 1, 1937, League of Nations, No. 4138, 179 LNTS 115; Special Protocol Concerning Statelessness, April 12, 1930, *League of Nations*, C. 227.M.114.1930.V; Convention on the Reduction of Statelessness, August 30, 1961, entered into force December 13, 1975, *United Nations Treaty Series*, vol. 989, 175. The document is ratified by only a handful of states. For analysis, see Chan (1991, 2 et seq.), who is critical of the international legal developments in this area.

16. Convention on the Reduction of Cases of Multiple Nationality and on Military Obligations in Cases of Multiple Nationality, opened for signature May 6, 1963, Council of Europe, ETS No. 043; Additional Protocol to the Convention on the Reduction of Cases of Multiple Nationality and on Military Obligations in Cases of Multiple Nationality, November 24, 1977, Council of Europe, ETS No. 096.

17. The legal attitudes towards dual nationality are becoming less hostile: see, for example, European Convention on Nationality, November 6, 1997, Council of Europe, ETS No.166. In Article 14 the Convention allows double nationality in some cases. In the US, dual nationality became possible de jure after the Supreme Court ruling in *Afroyim v. Rusk*, 387 U.S. 253, (1967). Cf. Weil (2012). Also, the majority of Member States in the EU do not prohibit double nationality (Kochenov 2011; de Groot 2018).

18. On the analysis of the pros and cons of dual nationality see Martin (1999) and Spiro (1997). Cf. Bosniak (2002). See also Spiro (2010).

19. For a story of citizenship rights that does not fetishize the political entitlements, see Kochenov (2019b).

20. World Bank definition. https://www.qlik.com/us/products/qlik-data-market?q=all+provider%3Aworld-bank+tag%3Agdp.

21. Solemn Declaration on European Union, European Council, Stuttgart June 19, 1983, *Bulletin of the European Communities*, 6/1983, 24–29, http://aei.pitt.edu/1788/.

37 North versus South or Integrated versus Isolated? Notes on the Global Grouping of Nationalities

1. The World Bank also includes some economies that are recognized as sovereign nations. Category ranges are for 2019 (World Bank, n.d.b.; World Bank, n.d.c.). This model is much more interested in specifying degrees of poverty than in describing wealth. This can be seen by the large size and heterogeneity of the high-income category, which includes gaps of 6.6 to 1.0. (Switzerland had a GNI per capita of USD 80,560 in 2017, compared to countries that barely made the cut such as Argentina and Croatia which each have a GNI per capita of USD 12,500 to USD 13,000).

2. Development: Human Development Index (HDI) (United Nations Development Programme, n.d.) Security: State Fragility Index, compiled by Monty G. Marshall and Benjamin R. Cole (Center for Systemic Peace, n.d.); Democracy: Democracy Index compiled by the *Economist* Intelligence Unit (n.d.); *Freedom in the World Index* (Freedom House, n.d.); Travel Freedom: Henley & Partners.

3. An additional model of citizenship inequality is presented in Castles (2005).

4. There are some differences: my model also takes into account a country's democracy score, whereas the QNI also has a measure for the total size of a country's economy.

5   In the QNI, each country is also weighted in terms of its Gross Domestic Product (GDP). My model does not include this weighting because the unweighted and weighted indices, correlated at 0.99, are practically identical.

6   Citizens of four island nations may also enter the US visa-free: Bermuda, FS Micronesia, Northern Mariana Islands, and Palau.

7   My model of citizenship value (Harpaz 2019a, 2019b) does not treat settlement freedom as part of a country's citizenship value because of its derivative and transient character. Within the QNI model, however, it is a highly important and justifiable component of citizenship value.

39 The Quality of Statelessness

1   The 1954 Convention Relating to the Status of Stateless Persons defines a stateless person as someone who "is not considered as a national by any State under the operation of its law," Art. 1.

2   The idea that not all nationalities are equal and that divergence in the content of different nationalities may render certain international norms on nationality and statelessness rather empty is not new. In 1989, de Groot referred to the international concept of nationality as a "surprise package".

3   Unless a state issues its stateless persons travel documents that give them visa-free entry and possibly settlement rights in other countries — see, for example, the case of Latvian 'non-citizens' discussed below.

4   Examples of pre-UN international law on statelessness are the Hague Convention on Certain Questions Relating to the Conflict of Nationality Laws of 12 April 1930 and the Treaty between the Principal Allied and Associated Powers and Romania (Romanian Minorities Treaty) of 9 December 1919, Art. 7.

5   See, for example, *A Study of Statelessness*, UN Doc E/1112; E/1112/Add.1, (August 1949), and resolutions adopted by the UN Economic and Social Council during its sixth session (2 February to 11 March 1948), 18.

6   See more in *A Study of Statelessness*, UN Doc E/1112; E/1112/Add.1 (August 1949).

7   As of 1 March 2019.

8   See 1961 UN Convention on the Reduction of Statelessness, Art. 7(1).

9   As of 1 March 2019.

10 1954 Convention Relating to the Status of Stateless Persons, Art. 1(1).

11 Integration Act of Germany (*Integrationsgesetz*) of 31 July 2016.

40 Citizenship-by-Investment (*Ius Doni*)

1   The US nationality scored weaker than all EU nationalities but better than most other nationalities around the world, being ranked 25th in the 2018 QNI General Ranking, with a value of 70.0%.

2   The Mexican nationality was ranked 52nd in the 2018 QNI General Ranking, with a value of 45.7%.

3   The term *ius doni*, coined by the author, derives from the Latin expression used for a gift or a contribution (dōnum/gen. dōnī) and signifies the right to citizenship granted by making a contribution or by investing in the host state.

4   Other important aspects influencing decisions of potential investors, such as favorable taxation, residence requirements, weather conditions, or environmental cleanliness to mention only a few, must not be underestimated either. These aspects, however, go beyond the scope of this work.

5   These requirements are currently under review and are expected to change. It is expected that the overall cost will increase slightly.

6   C-300/04, *M. G. Eman and O. B. Sevinger v. College van burgemeester en wethouders van Den Haag*, [2006] ECLI:EU:C:2006:545 (*Eman and Sevinger*).

7   C-369/90, *Mario Vicente Micheletti and others v. Delegación del Gobierno en Cantabria*, [1992] ECLI:EU:C:1992:295 (*Micheletti*), para. 10.

8   The percentage is based on the total number of new EU citizenships granted each year provided by Eurostat (Eurostat, n.d.).

41 Twenty-Four Shades of Sovereignty and Nationalities in the Pacific Region

1   US Court of Appeals. 2015. *Leneuoti Tuaua v. USA*. No. 1:12-cv-01143. Washington DC: District of Columbia Circuit.

2   Government of the Cook Islands. 2014. Definitions of the Constitution. Constitution Amendment (no. 9) Act 1980-81.

3   Parliament of the Cook Islands. 2008. Laws of Cook Islands. Entry, Residence and Departure (Amendment) Act 2008. No. 3.

4   Government of the United States of America, and Government of the Republic of the Marshall Islands. 2003. Compact of Free Association, as Amended (Implementation) Act, 2004.

5   Art. 403 Sec. 402 (e)(f)(i), Republic of the Marshall Islands. 2010. Citizenship (Amendment) Act 2010. P.L.2010-40.

6   Art. 403 Sec. 402 (b), Republic of the Marshall Islands. 2010. Citizenship (Amendment) Act 2010. P.L.2010-40.

42 Passports, Free Movement, and the State in South America

1   Acuerdo sobre Documentos de Viaje y de Retorno de los Estados Partes del MERCOSUR y Estados Asociados, MERCOSUR/CMC/DEC. N° 46/15, Asunción, 20 December 2015. It was not ratified by all states.

2   Uruguay, Ley 19, 254, Publicada D.O. 4 September 2014.

3   Brazil, Resolução normativa no. 126, 2 March 2017, Dispõe sobre a concessão de residencia temporária a nacional de país fronteiriço.

4   *Portaria interministerial no 9*, 14 March 2018.

5   Colombia, Ministry of Foreign Affairs, Resolution 10677, 21 December 2018.

6   Ley 12/2015, de 24 de junio, en materia de concesión de la nacionalidad española a los sefardíes originarios de España. The original law set a deadline to apply in October 2018, which was later extended by another year. See Acuerdo por el que se prorroga el plazo de presentación de solicitudes de concesión de la nacionalidad española, en virtud de la Ley 12/2015, de 24 de junio, en materia de concesión de la nacionalidad española a los sefardíes originarios de España, Council of Ministers, 9 March 2018. See also Real Decreto 893/2015, de 2 de octubre, por el que se concede la nacionalidad española por carta de naturaleza a determinados sefardíes originarios de España, through which Spanish nationality was granted to 4,302 applicants who had initiated their procedure before the entry into force of the 2015 law.

7   Argentina, Disposición DI-2019-520-APN-DNM#MI, Buenos Aires, 29 January 2019.

8   Ecuador, Art. 1, Acuerdo Interministerial 000001, Quito, 21 January 2019.

43 The Quality of African Nationalities

1   Agenda 2063, the UN's Office of the Special Adviser on Africa. https://www.un.org/en/africa/osaa/peace/agenda2063.shtml.

2   See https://au.int/sites/default/files/treaties/36403-treaty-protocol_on_free_movement_of_persons_in_africa_e.pdf.

3   See http://www.dha.gov.za/WhitePaperonInternationalMigration-20170602.pdf.

44 Two Sticks, Half a Carrot: External and Domestic Divisions in the Post-Soviet Space

1   The CIS includes Armenia, Azerbaijan, Belarus, Kazakhstan, Kyrgyzstan, Moldova, the Russian Federation, Tajikistan, Ukraine, and Uzbekistan. In 2005 Turkmenistan withdrew from the CIS and is now classified as an associate member. Georgia has not been a formal CIS member since 2009, having left the organization after the Russo-Georgian War in 2008, but it is considered to be a part of the CIS region. In April 2018, Ukrainian president Petro Poroshenko announced plans to quit the CIS.

45 Post-Yugoslav Nationalities

1   The history of Yugoslavia started with the redrawing of the borders of Europe in 1918 as the Kingdom of Serbs, Croats, and Slovenes, renamed as the Kingdom of Yugoslavia in 1923. In 1941 the Kingdom was invaded by the Axis powers; in 1943 the Partisan resistance proclaimed Democratic Federal Yugoslavia, which was recognized by the King in 1944 only to see the monarchy itself abolished in 1945. In 1946 Yugoslavia became the FPRY (which included Istria, Rijeka, and Zadar, newly acquired from Italy). In 1963 the state was renamed again, to become SFRY. The last form of Yugoslavia was the Federal Republic of Yugoslavia (FRY), comprising a post-SFRY federation between Serbia and Montenegro. It existed under that name until 2003 when it was renamed State Union of Serbia and Montenegro, which ceased to exist in 2006 after Montenegro's referendum and formal declaration of independence.

2   See *Kurić and others v. Slovenia*, 2012-IV Eur. Ct. H.R. 1–92 (2012).

3   The Republic of North Macedonia is the new official name of the (now former) Republic of Macedonia. The name was changed in February 2019 to end the long-lasting dispute over the former name between that country and Greece. The name was changed after both parties signed and ratified the 'Prespa Agreement' despite high levels of dissatisfaction in both countries and an unsuccessful referendum in the (then) Republic of Macedonia.

4   A basis for acquisition of another citizenship may exist, for instance, where the other parent is a foreign citizen.

5   Article 10(1)(1.2) of the Citizenship Act of Kosovo stipulates the residence requirement that candidates for citizenship through naturalization need to fulfill. Namely, they should have resided for five years without interruption in Kosovo after obtaining permanent residence permits. The acquisition of permanent residence permits is regulated in Article 51 of the Law on Foreigners: Permanent stay shall be permitted to the foreigner who until the day of submission of application for permanent stay has either five years of uninterrupted temporary stay or has been married for three years to a citizen of Kosovo or to a foreigner with a permanent stay permit. In other words, naturalization through residence takes ten years, while facilitated naturalization through marriage takes eight years.

6   Article 8(3) Montenegrin Citizenship Act of 14 February 2008.

7   Article 10(3) Act on Citizenship of the Republic of Slovenia (as amended by Amending Act, Official Gazette No. 127/2006 of 7 December 2006).

8   Article 9(2) Law of 27 July 1999 on Citizenship of Bosnia and Herzegovina (consolidated version 2003).

9   Article 8(3) Law on Croatian Citizenship (as amended by law of 28 October 2011).

10   Article 7(2) Law on Citizenship of the Republic of Macedonia 67/92.

11   Article 14(3) Law on Citizenship of the Republic of Serbia (2004).

12   Article 8(2) Law on Croatian Citizenship (as amended by law of 28 October 2011).

13   Article 7(10) Law on Citizenship of the Republic of Macedonia 67/92.

14   Article 14(2) Law on Citizenship of the Republic of Serbia (2004).

15   Article 4 Law of 27 July 1999 on Citizenship of Bosnia and Herzegovina (consolidated version 2003).

16   Article 18 Montenegrin Citizenship Act of 14 February 2008.

17   Article 10(1)(2) Act on Citizenship of the Republic of Slovenia (as amended by Amending Act, Official Gazette No. 127/2006 of 7 December 2006).

18   Article 10(2) ibid.

19   By decision of the Swiss Federal Council the transitional period will be maintained until the end of December 2021.

20   Austria must remove its restrictions for Croatian nationals by the end of the third stage of the seven-year transitional period on 1 July 2020.

46 Citizenship of the European Union and Brexit

1   The score of the citizenship of the EU has been updated significantly in this edition to ensure that its intra-EU travel and settlement rights have not been counted as benefits of its nationality in the ranking, thus putting it on a par with any other federation in the world (as explained in more detail on pp. 42–43).

47 Canadian Nationality: The Value of Belonging

1   Canada has one of the most complicated and non-transparent sets of visa rules in the world (*World Economic Forum* 2017, 121).

2   The designation 'Indian' is now considered derogatory in Canada. The law has not been amended to reflect this (*Indian Act* RSC 1985, c I-5).

3   It would be misleading to overemphasize the rights granted by the *Indian Act*, as it "was premised on the paternalistic notion that, although Indian people were 'wards of the state' requiring 'protection', they would eventually become 'civilized' and assimilate into broader society" (Fiske 1995, 4–5).

4   'Landing' and acquiring 'Canadian domicile' have historically been used to mean 'permanent residence'.

5   S. 91 *Constitution Act* 1867; s. 3 *Act Respecting Aliens and Naturalization* SC 1868, c 66.

6   It prohibited the entry of foreigners who had not come by 'continuous journey' from their countries of citizenship (Kelley and Trebilcock 2010, 150–53).

7   For example, Japanese nationals hoping to migrate were impeded from entering (Ferguson 1975, 3).

8   S. 31(d) Order-in-Council PC 1962-86.

9   See, for example, s. 11(2), 12 and 16 of the 1869 *Immigration Act*; s. 3(c) of the 1910 *Immigration Act*; and s. (3)(1)(m) 1919 *Immigration Act*.

10 S. 34–39 IRPA SC 2001 c 27.

11 See, for example, s. 72(e)(i) *Immigration and Refugee Protection Regulations* (IRPR) (SOR/2002-227).

12 Immigration Regulations, Order-in-Council PC 1967-1616.

13 There are 11 economic sub-categories: six federal, one provincial, and four for Quebec: s 70(2)(b) IRPR (n 28).

14 Caregiver roles are considered unskilled and are low-paid and often riddled with abuse (Langevin and Belleau 2000).

15 S. 95 of the *Constitution Act* SC 30-31, c 3.

16 In issuing its own temporary visas, Canada is not as welcoming as many other high-scoring destinations: from 2012 to 2017, temporary visa refusals doubled to 22.6%; African and Middle Eastern nationals bore the brunt of this, with 75% refusal rates for some nationalities from these regions (York and Zilio 2018). In 2017, by contrast, Europe's Schengen Area visa refusal rate was 8.2% (European Commission, 2018b).

49 French Nationality

1   French Civil Code, Art. 18.

2   Fr. Civ. Code, Art. 19(3).

3   Fr. Civ. Code, Arts. 19, 19(1).

4   Fr. Civ. Code, Art. 21(11).

5   Fr. Civ. Code, Art. 22(1).

6   Fr. Civ. Code, Art. 21(12).

7   Fr. Civ. Code, Art. 21(13).

8   Fr. Civ. Code, Art. 21(13-1).

9   Fr. Civ. Code, Art. 21(2).

10 Fr. Civ. Code, Art. 21(22).

11 Fr. Civ. Code, Art. 21(16).

12 Fr. Civ. Code, Art. 21(24).

13 Fr. Civ. Code, Art. 21(23).

14 Fr. Civ. Code, Art. 23(4).

15 *Afroyim v. Rusk*, 387 U.S. 253 (1967).

16 French Civil Code, Art. 25.

17 Fr. Civ. Code, Art. 25(1).

18 CC 96-377 DC, 16 July 1996, *Loi tendant à renforcer la répression du terrorisme et des atteintes aux personnes dépositaires de l'autorité publique ou chargées d'une mission de service public et comportant des dispositions relatives à la police judiciaire*.

19 CC 2014-439 QPC, 23 January 2015, *Ahmed S.*

20 Fewer than 20 persons were deprived of their nationality between 1995 and 2015 (Geisser 2015, 3, 10).

21 Rodica Négroiu, a Romanian caregiver who had acquired French nationality by marriage, lost her French nationality in 2002 after being convicted for having slowly poisoned her husband since the beginning of their marriage, the French court inferring from this conviction that Négroiu never intended to stay married and could not therefore enjoy the benefits of the marriage in terms of nationality; Ilyes Hacène, an Algerian imam, lost his nationality in 2006 for preaching sermons considered dangerous to national security; Frédéric Minvielle lost his French nationality in 2007 after he applied for Dutch nationality. Since Minvielle had married

his same-sex partner in the Netherlands at a time when French law neither authorized nor recognized this form of marriage, the French government considered that the 1963 Convention between France and the Netherlands on conditions for dual nationality for married couples did not apply. The government gave back his French nationality in 2008 (Le Parisien 2016). It is to be noted that all these cases occurred in 2009, before French law was changed to make it possible for an individual to ask a court to refer a question of constitutionality concerning an act of Parliament already in force to the Constitutional Council (Constitutional bylaw no. 2009-1523 of 10 December 2009).

22 Law No. 96-647 of 22 July 1996.

23 Constitutional Bill No. 3381 of 23 December 2015, Art. 2.

24 French Civil Code, Art. 23(6).

25 Fr. Civ. Code, Art. 23(7).

26 Fr. Civ. Code, Art. 23(8).

27 Alexis Spire mentions the case of French-Polish citizens who went East after the Second World War to help build communism and who were stripped of their French nationality (Spire 2005).

28 Art. 349 of the TFEU. Saint-Barthélemy, also referred in this provision, has become an overseas country or territory by a decision of the European Council, in accordance with the Consolidated Version of the Treaty on the Functioning of the European Union [2008] OJ C115/47, Art. 355(6) (see endnote 30).

29 European Council Decision 2012/419/EU amending the status of Mayotte with regard to the European Union OJ [2012] L204/131.

30 Consolidated Version of the Treaty on the Functioning of the European Union [2008] OJ C115/47, art. 355(2); Consolidated Version of the Treaty on European Union [2008] OJ C115/13, Annex II; Consolidated Version of the Treaty on the Functioning of the European Union [2008] OJ C115/47, Annex II. Mayotte, also referred to in Annex II, has become an outermost region by a decision of the European Council, in accordance with the Consolidated Version of the Treaty on the Functioning of the European Union [2008] OJ C115/47, Art. 355(6) (see endnote 28).

31 European Council Decision 2010/718/EU amending the status with regard to the European Union of the island of Saint-Barthélemy OJ [2010] L325/4.

32 Consolidated Version of the Treaty on the Functioning of the European Union [2008] OJ C115/47, Art. 349.

33 Ibid., Art. 198.

34 Case C-260/90 *Bernard Leplat v. Territory of French Polynesia* [1992] ECLI:EU:C:1992:66.

35 Consolidated Version of the Treaty on the Functioning of the European Union [2008] OJ C115/47, Art. 198, 2nd sub-paragraph.

36 Ibid., Art. 202.

37 Case C-300/04 *M. G. Eman and O. B. Sevinger v. College van burgemeester en wethouders van Den Haag* [2006] ECLI:EU:C:2006:54, para. 29.

38 The customary civil status in New Caledonia is a personal civil status different from the ordinary French civil status. Persons holding this status are subject not to French Civil law but to New Caledonian customary Civil Law.

39 Art. 22 of Constitutional bylaw no. 99-209 of 19 March 1999 concerning New Caledonia.

40 Art. 62 of Constitutional bylaw no. 99-209, *cit*.

41 "Lois du pays" Art. 99 et seq. of Constitutional bylaw no. 99-209, *cit*.

42 Art. 104 of the Constitutional bylaw no. 99-209, *cit*.

43 The French Constitution, art. 61.

44 Art. 108 et seq. of Constitutional bylaw no. 99-209, *cit*.

45 Ibid., Art. 4.

46 C. 8 of the *British Overseas Territories Act* of 2002.

47 Art. 4 of Constitutional bylaw no. 99-209, *cit*.

48 Ibid., Art. 24.

49 Art. 217, 2nd sub-paragraph of Constitutional bylaw no. 99-209, *cit*.

50 Nationality of the Kingdom of the Netherlands

1 It has been noted that the granting of full Netherlands nationality to the population of Suriname and the Netherlands Antilles might have been an unintended consequence of the way the 1949 statute recognizing the independence of Indonesia was formulated (Hondius 2014).

2 Joined Cases C-35/82 and C-36/82 *Morson and Jhanjan* [1982] ECLI:EU:C:1982:368. For a discussion of this case, see Bierbach 2017, 277–78.

3 Case C-300/04 *Eman and Sevinger* [2006] ECLI:EU:C:2006:545. For commentary, see also Shaw 2008.

4 In Aruba, the *Landsverordening toelating en uitzetting*, which regulates the admission and expulsion of aliens, implicitly qualifies the right of settlement of bearers of Netherlands nationality without a qualifying connection to Aruba as subject to regulation (Art. 1(1)). The policy handbook implementing this law (*Toelatingshandboek 2018*, http://www.gobierno.aw/document.php?m=55&file-id=53209&f=71e120bba0731fafae8aef5917381903&attachment=0&c=40999)), provides that these persons can get a residence permit if they have sufficient means, housing, and no criminal record, and either have a job as a qualifying professional (para. 1.3.4) or have a job for which no Aruba-connected applicants could be found (para. 1.3.5). The other two Caribbean countries and the special municipal entities all have laws substantially continuing the former Antillean *Landsverordening toelating en uitzetting* (LTU), which declares bearers of Netherlands nationality without a qualifying connection to the former Antilles to have an automatic right of residence, and to be entitled to a declaratory residence document, provided only that they can demonstrate that they have sufficient financial means and housing and no criminal record (Art. 3(1)(f) of the LTU in Curaçao and Sint Maarten; Art. 3(5) *Wet toelating en uitzetting BES* in the special municipal entities).

5   Case *Gemeenschappelijk Hof van Justitie van Aruba, Curaçao, Sint Maarten en van Bonaire, Sint Eustatius en Saba* [2014] ECLI:NL:OGHACMB:2014:92.

6   In fact, it seems that in the 1950s, when freedom of movement of workers was being instituted in the EEC, the governments of Suriname and the then Netherlands Antilles specifically declined the option of introducing freedom of movement on their territories, fearing an influx of poor French citizens from the Caribbean and South American *départements d'outre-mer* (Goedings 2005, 285).

7   For a good summary of immigration law in Sint Maarten and Curaçao, see also Deelstra, Matroos-Piar, and van Houwelingen 2016, 43–52.

8   Letter from the Minister of Alien Affairs and Integration to the House of Representatives, 2005, *Tweede Kamerstukken 2004-2005*, 26283, 20. For a critical examination of her proposal, see van der Wal and Heringa, 2005.

9   See the answers of the Minister of Immigration and Asylum Gerd Leers to the parliamentary questions from the MPs Van Nieuwenhuizen and Bosman ("Kamervragen (Aanhangsel) 2010-2011, nr. 2435," *Tweede Kamer der Staten-Generaal 2011*, https://zoek.officielebekendmakingen.nl/ah-tk-20102011-2435.html).

10 *Tweede Kamerstukken* 20, 4, author's translation.

11 *Volkspartij voor Vrijheid en Democratie* (The People's Party for Freedom and Democracy).

12 *Tweede Kamer der Staten-Generaal 2013*, "Handeling 2012-2013, 33325 nr. 6: Voorstel van wet van het lid Bosman houdende regulering van de vestiging van Nederlanders van Aruba, Curaçao en Sint Maarten in Nederland (Wet regulering vestiging van Nederlanders van Aruba, Curaçao en Sint Maarten in Nederland)," https://zoek.officielebekendmakingen.nl/kst-33325-6.html.

13 Restrictions on the settlement of Netherlands nationals from the Caribbean special municipal entities of the Netherlands, on the other hand — that is, within the same country — would be nearly impossible politically.

14 Bosman, in the debate on his bill: "Dat is namelijk waar dit wetsvoorstel om draait: gelijk oversteken" (*Tweede Kamer der Staten-Generaal 2016*, "Handeling 2016–2017, nr. 5 item 4: Vestiging Nederlanders uit Aruba, Curaçao en Sint-Maarten in Nederland," https://zoek.officielebekendmakingen.nl/h-tk-20162017-5-4.html).

15 Case *Matos et al.* [2000] ECLI:NL:HR:2000:AA8448, in which the legality of the Antillean LTU was largely upheld. The Supreme Court noted that for purposes of application of Art. 12(4) of the International Covenant on Civil and Political Rights, providing for a right of unrestricted movement within one's 'own country', the Kingdom of the Netherlands had already clarified that the Antilles was a 'separate country'.

16 *Tweede Kamer der Staten-Generaal 2015*, "Kamerstuk 33325, nr. 11: Advice of the advisory division of the Council of State," https://zoek.officielebekendmakingen.nl/kst-33325-11.html.

17 All the special delegates actively participated in the debate during a recent legislative session and proposed amendments. One prominent source of irritation in Netherlands nationality law for the Caribbean countries is the requirement that aliens applying for naturalization in those countries have to pass an exam testing their knowledge of Dutch, a language that is little used in those countries compared to the local languages of Papiamento (in Aruba and Curaçao) and English (in Sint Maarten), on which applicants are also tested. During a recent legislative session, all of the special delegates sent by the Caribbean countries once more questioned the necessity of this double language requirement, and indeed (in the case of the special delegate from Aruba), the fact that the languages of the Kingdom do not have co-equal status. (For a critique of the double language requirement, see also de Groot and Mijts 2009, 366–71.) The questions of the special delegates are summarized and dismissed in a 2016 letter from the state secretary of security and justice to the chair of the house of representatives. *Tweede Kamerstukken* 33852 (R2023), no. 29.

18 *Tweede Kamer der Staten-Generaal 2014*, "Handeling 2013-2014, 33852-(R2023) nr. 2: Wijziging van de Rijkswet op het Nederlanderschap ter verlenging van de termijnen voor verlenging van het Nederlanderschap en enige andere wijzigingen," https://zoek.officielebekendmakingen.nl/kst-33852-2-n1.html.

19 Transcript of the plenary assembly of the Senate, second assembly, 2017.

20 *Tweede Kamer der Staten-Generaal 2015*, "Kamerstuk 34356, nr. 2: Wijziging van de Rijkswet op het Nederlanderschap in verband met het intrekken van het Nederlanderschap in het belang van de nationale veiligheid," https://zoek.officielebekendmakingen.nl/kst-34356-2.html.

21 "Deprivation of Nationality as an Anti-Terror Measure May Be 'At Odds with Human Rights'," Parliamentary Assembly of the Council of Europe, 2018, accessed 14 December 2018, http://assembly.coe.int/nw/xml/News/News-View-EN.asp?newsid=7310&lang=2&cat=5.

22 See, for the history of this debate from 1980 to 2004 and the general trend of antipathy in that period toward dual nationality in the politics of the Netherlands: de Hart 2007, 77–102.

23 Or in a civil union (*geregistreerd partnerschap*) with.

24 Idem.

25 Case C-135/08 *Janko Rottmann* [2010] ECLI:EU:C:2010:104. See for an analysis of this case: Bierbach 2017, 393–9.

26 Case C-221/17 *M.G. Tjebbes and Others v. Minister van Buitenlandse Zaken* [2019] ECLI:EU:C:2019:189.

27 On 12 March 2019, however, the Court handed down its decision.

28 Case C-221/17 *M.G. Tjebbes and Others v. Minister van Buitenlandse Zaken* [2019] ECLI:EU:C:2018:572 Opinion of AG Mengozzi.

29 Case C-133/15 *H.C. Chavez-Vilchez and Others v. Raad van bestuur van de Sociale verzekeringsbank and Others* [2017] ECLI:EU:C:2017:354.

30 See, for a discussion of the Case C-34/09 *Ruiz Zambrano* [2011] ECLI:EU:C:2011:124 that laid the groundwork for *Chavez-Vilchez*: Bierbach 2017, 399–403, 443–4.

31 Any increase in support for dual nationality, it seems, correlates to an increased perception of it as a benefit for emigrants from the Netherlands more than for immigrants to the Netherlands (Vink, Schmeets, and Mennes 2019).

32 "Governing Accord 'Vertrouwen in de Toekomst', VVD, CDA, D66, ChristenUnie," Kabinetsformatie (n.d.), accessed 14 December 2018, https://www.kabinetsformatie2017.nl/.

33 Letter from the State Secretary of Justice and Security to the Chair of the House of Representatives, 2018, *Aanhangsel van de Handelingen Tweede Kamer 2017–2018* no. 3105.

51 Bulgarian Nationality: Dire Straits?

1. Rick: "You want my advice?" Annina: "Oh yes, please." Rick: "Go back to Bulgaria." *Casablanca*, Michael Curtiz, dir. (Burbank, CA: Warner Bros. Pictures, 1942). http://www.moviequotedb.com/movies/casablanca/quote_28366.html.

2. Юридически речник, Авт.: Г. Хр.Георгиев, Л. Ст. Велинов С.: Отечество и Отворено общество, 1994 1во изд. 255. [Legal Dictionary, G. Georgiev, L. Sc. Velinov S., Fatherland and Open Society, 1st ed. 255.]

52 'Non-Citizens' of Latvia

1. Supreme Council of the Republic of Latvia, *Par Latvijas Republikas pilsoņu tiesību atjaunošanu un naturalizācijas pamatnoteikumiem* [On the Renewal of the Rights of the Citizens of the Republic of Latvia and on the Fundamental Principles of Naturalization] 1991, Latvijas Republikas Augstākās Padomes un Valdības Ziņotājs, 43.nr. (1991).

2. Constitutional Court of Latvia, Case No. 2004-15-0106, (2005), para 13. http://www.satv.tiesa.gov.lv/wp-content/uploads/2004/07/2004-15-0106_Spriedums_ENG.pdf.

3. Supreme Council of the Republic of Latvia, *Par Latvijas Republikas neatkarības atjaunošanu* [On the Restoration of Independence of the Republic of Latvia]. Latvijas Republikas Augstākās Padomes un Valdības Ziņotājs, 20.nr. (1990).

4. Constitutional Court of Latvia, Case No. 2007-10-0102, para.32.2 (2007), http://www.satv.tiesa.gov.lv/wp-content/uploads/2007/04/2007-10-0102_Spriedums_ENG.pdf (citations omitted). See also Krystyna Marek, *Identity and Continuity of States in Public International Law* 412 (1954) stating that "it may safely be concluded that the greater part of the international community has so far refused to recognize the Soviet annexation of [the Baltic States] and has, expressly or impliedly, upheld their continued legal existence"; Ineta Ziemele, *State Continuity and Nationality: The Baltic States and Russia – Past, Present and Future as Defined by International Law* 34 (2005), "*The Constitutional Law* thus confirmed the constitutional continuity and identity of the Latvian State of 18 November 1918."; James Crawford, *The Creation of States in International Law* 689–90 (2nd ed. 2006), discussing the proposition that annexation of the territory of a State as a result of the illegal use of force does not bring about the extinction of the State; Aleksejs Dimitrovs and Vadim Poleshchuk, *Kontinuitet kak osnova gosudarstvennosti i ètnopolitiki v Latvii i Èstonii*, in *Ètnopolitika Stran Baltii* (Vadim Poleshchuk & Valery Stepanov, eds., 2013) (Rus.).

5. Ibid., para. 2.

6. *Pilsonības likums* [Citizenship Law], Latvijas Vēstnesis, 93.(224.) nr. (1994).

7. *Par to bijušās PSRS pilsoņu statusu, kuriem nav Latvijas vai citas valsts pilsonības* [Law on the Status of Former USSR Citizens Who Do Not Have the Citizenship of Latvia or of Any Other State] 1995, Latvijas Vēstnesis, 63.(346.) nr. (1995).

8. Ibid., s. 1(1).

9. Ibid., s. 1(3).

10. In Latvian: "Latvijas nepilsoņi nav uzskatāmi ne par pilsoņiem, ne ārvalstniekiem, ne arī bezvalstniekiem." See Constitutional Court of Latvia, Case No. 2004-15-0106, para.15 (2005), http://www.satv.tiesa.gov.lv/wp-content/uploads/2004/07/2004-15-0106_Spriedums_ENG.pdf.

11. Ibid., para. 17. See also *Andrejeva v. Latvia*, App. No. 55707/00, Eur. Ct. H.R. para. 88 (2009).

12. Data by the Office for Citizenship and Migration Affairs as of 1 January 2019, https://www.pmlp.gov.lv/lv/assets/backup/ISVP_Latvija_pec_VPD.pdf.

13. In accordance with Section 8(2) of the *Law on the Status of Former USSR Citizens Who Do Not Have the Citizenship of Latvia or of Any Other State*, a child also becomes a 'non-citizen' if both of his/her parents are 'non-citizens', or one is a 'non-citizen' and the other one is stateless. This situation has been criticized by the UN Committee on the Rights of the Child and the CoE Commissioner for Human Rights. See *Concluding Observations of the Committee on the Rights of the Child: Latvia*, UN Doc. CRC/C/LVA/CO/3-5 (2016) and *Report following visit to Latvia from 5 to 9 September 2016*, CommDH(2016)41. In accordance with Section 3.1 of the Latvia *Citizenship Law*, however, either parent may register such a child as a citizen, but only if some administrative formalities are fulfilled. This is problematic from the point of view of the Convention on the Rights of the Child and the Convention on the Reduction of Statelessness, as the safeguard against statelessness is limited to children of whom both parents are 'non-citizens'/stateless and the parent registering the child is legally resident in the country. See Gérard-René de Groot, *Strengthening the Position of the Children: Council of Europe's Recommendation 2009/13*, in *Concepts of Nationality in a Globalised World* (Council of Europe 2011); Gérard-René de Groot, Katja Swider, Olivier Wonk, *Practices and Approaches in EU Member States to Prevent and End Statelessness* (European Parliament, 2015).

14. See *Concluding Observations of the Committee on the Elimination of Racial Discrimination: Latvia*, UN Doc. CERD/C/LVA/CO/6-12 (2018); nevertheless, in 2019 the Parliament adopted the President's bill, which will allow children born after 1 January 2020 to be automatically registered as citizens, if these children would otherwise qualify as 'non-citizens'.

15. If one of the parents is a 'non-citizen' and the other is a foreign national, the parents are entitled to choose 'non-citizen' status for the child instead of foreign nationality. (An administrative practice which imposed only foreign nationality for such cases was recognized as illegal by the Senate of the Supreme Court on 13 April 2005 in Case No. SKA-136.) See also Kristine Krūma, "Country Report: Latvia – Revised and updated January 2015," in *Eudo Citizenship Observatory* 21–23 (Eur. Univ. Inst. 2015), for a compelling overview of curious case law.

16. *Imigrācijas likums* [Immigration Law], section 1(1)1, Latvijas Vēstnesis, 169.(2744.) nr. (2002).

17. Ibid.

18. *Constitution of the Republic of Latvia*, Articles 8 and 101.

19. *Politisko partiju likums* [Law on Political Parties], section 12(1), Latvijas Vēstnesis, 107.(3475.) nr. (2006).

20. See, for example, *Likums par zemes privatizāciju lauku apvidos* [Law on Land Privatization in Rural Areas], section 29(2), Ziņotājs, 32. nr. (2000).

21. See, for example, *Valsts civildienesta likums* [State Civil Service Law], s. 7(1)1, Latvijas Vēstnesis, 331/333.(2242/2244.) nr. (2000).

22. *Likums par valsts pensijām, pārejas noteikumi* [Transitional Provisions of the Law on State Pensions], para. 1, Latvijas Vēstnesis, 182.(465.) nr. (2002).

23. *Buzajevs v. Masveida Bezpilsonība* [Mass Statelessness], Rīga, Latvijas Cilvēktiesību komiteja, 2016, 10–17.

24. *Atzinums Pārbaudes Lietā* (2008), http://www.tiesibsargs.lv/uploads/content/atzinumi/2008_10_08_atzinums_par_pilsonu_un_nepilsonu_tiesibam_2008_09_1507031817.pdf.

25 *Latvijas Republikas Advokatūras likums* [Advocacy Law], s. 14(1), Ziņotājs, 28. nr. (1993). *Patentu likums* [Patents Law], s. 26(4)1, Latvijas Vēstnesis, 34. (3610.) nr. (2007) — replaced by *Rūpnieciskā īpašuma institūciju un procedūru likums* [Law on Industrial Property Institutions and Procedures], s. 121(2)1, Latvijas Vēstnesis, 157.(5445.) nr. (2015).

26 *Apsardzes darbības likums* [Security Guard Activities Law], s. 6(1), Latvijas Vēstnesis, 83. (3451.), nr. (2006) — replaced by *Apsardzes darbības likums* [Security Guard Activities Law], s. 7(1), Latvijas Vēstnesis, 47, (5107.) nr. (2014).

27 *Detektīvdarbības likums* [Law of Detective Activity], s. 4(1), Latvijas Vēstnesis, 110 (2497) nr. (2001). Difference abolished since 1 October 2012.

28 *Likums par zemes reformas pabeigšanu pilsētās* [Law on Completion of Land Reform in the Cities], s. 3(1), Latvijas Vēstnesis, 333. (1394.) nr. (1998).

29 Atzinums Pārbaudes Lietā 5 (2008).

30 Par Nepilsoņu Tiesisko Statusu (2011), http://www.tiesibsargs.lv/uploads/content/atzinumi/tiesibsarga_viedoklis_par_nepilsonu_tiesisko_statusu_1507138132.pdf.

53 Georgian Nationality

1 Abkhazia and South Ossetia both prohibited Georgian passports in the 1990s yet failed to provide their citizens with internationally acceptable documents (Mühlfried 2010, 9).

2 The protection of Russian citizens was officially invoked by the then president Medvedev as the major reason behind Russia's intervention in Georgia in August 2008 (Artman 2013).

3 Article 6, *Draft Agreement between the Russian Federation and South Ossetia* (November 2014). http://osinform.org/48181-proekt-dogovor-mezhdu-rossiyskoy-federaciey-i-respublikoy-yuzhnaya-osetiya-o-soyuznichestve-i-integracii.html.

4 An amendment passed in 2013 precludes dual citizenship in Abkhazia, except in the case of Abkhaz-Russian citizenship (Kvarchelia 2014). The residence permits that were subsequently issued for Georgian citizens residing in the Gali district were suspended (allegedly temporarily) in November 2018.

5 Regulation (EU) 2017/372 of the European Parliament and of the Council Amending Regulation (EC) No. 539/2001, listing the third countries whose nationals must be in possession of visas when crossing the external borders and those whose nationals are exempt from that requirement (Georgia) [2017] OJ L61/7.

6 That is, the launch of a visa dialogue with a view to determining the conditions to be fulfilled to have the Schengen visa requirement lifted and the VLAP listing measures adopted and implemented.

7 The visa center processes visa applications and submits them to the Russian Federation Interests Section at the Embassy of Switzerland in Tbilisi.

54 Israel: Citizenship, Residence, Taxation: A View from Practice

1 Law No. 5712-1952, Citizenship Law, 5 September 1952. Most non-Jewish foreign spouses of Israeli citizens must undergo the naturalization process.

2 *Ius soli* is not applicable in today's Israel. That is to say, the very fact of being born within the territory of Israel gives no rights to an individual. If a child's mother or father was enjoying Israeli citizenship at the moment the child was born, however, Israeli citizenship is granted automatically, with a few minor exceptions.

3 Law No. 5710-1950, The Law of Return, 5 July 1950.

4 See HCJ 265/87, *Beresford v. Minister of Interior*, 43 PD (4) 793 (1989).

5 Ibid.

6 Ibid.

7 Law on Passports (Amendment No. 9) 2646-2017.

8 The mixture of conceptions of nationality and religion leads to a certain confusion in understanding the difference between the notions of 'Jewishness' and 'Judaism'.

9 Section 4B Law of Return (Amendment No. 2) 5730-1970. A person who has completed the procedure of religious conversion to Judaism (*giyur*) is also considered a Jew.

10 Or documents issued in other post-Soviet countries of the former Soviet Union.

11 Section 1 Law No. 5710-1950, The Law of Return, 5 July 1950.

12 Section 4A Law of Return (Amendment No. 2) 5730-1970.

13 Section 316(a) Immigration and Nationality Act of 1952. See also Kandel 2014, 5.

14 The principle of tax residence adopted by Israel is of European origin and is important for the taxation of global extraterritorial incomes. Whereas the US regards any US citizen as a tax resident and the Russian Federation's only criterion is staying in the country for at least 183 days in any consecutive 12-month period, the principle of 'center-of-vital interests' is applied in Israel, where individuals who stay in the country for 183 days per calendar year or more are seen to have their centers of life in Israel and are thus presumed to be tax residents in that year.

15 Section 14(a) Income Tax Ordinance 5721-1961.

16 Or to pay the tax difference, in cases where there is an agreement on avoidance of double taxation and if local income taxes have been paid out.

17 This area is regulated in Israel by a relatively advanced law on controlled foreign companies according to which avoiding taxation in Israel through veiling a separate legal entity in an offshore jurisdiction will not work out.

18 Section 14(a) Income Tax Ordinance 5721-1961.

19 Ibid., s. 1(a)(2)(a).

20. We do not mean the receiving of Israeli citizenship, but rather the moment of obtaining tax resident status. A standing joke told to HNWIs who ask when they will start paying taxes in Israel: "Never. Plus another 10 years."
21. Excluding, above all, direct incomes for consulting and hired labor.
22. Provided that the legislation on transfer pricing and payment of taxes in the country of deriving income is properly respected.

55 China and India

1. BRICS is an acronym for Brazil, Russia, India, China, and South Africa, five major emerging national economies known for their significant influence on regional affairs; all are members of the G20.
2. The member states of the South Asian Association for Regional Cooperation (SAARC) include Afghanistan, Bangladesh, Bhutan, India, the Maldives, Nepal, Pakistan, and Sri Lanka. Its secretariat is based in Kathmandu, Nepal.

56 Myanmar: The Unflinching Law of the Ethnic Citizen and the 'Mixed Blood' Other

1. According to UNHCR, as of February 2019 there were 909,235 Myanmar (Rohingya) refugees in Bangladesh, 740,476 of them arriving after the August 2017 crisis. According to the UN Office for the Coordination of Humanitarian Affairs, about 241,000 displaced people — of which 77% are women and children — remain in camps or camp-like situations in Kachin, Kayin, Rakhine, and Shan states.
2. Article 11 of the Constitution of the Union of Burma of 1947 allowed persons from other British colonial territories to acquire Burmese nationality if they resided eight years in Burma during the ten years prior to independence. In 1959, the Supreme Court of the Union confirmed in *Hasan Ali v. Union of Burma* that, under The Union of Burma Citizenship Act of 1948, no. LXVI, amended 1 December 1960, "[a] person descended from ancestors who for two generations have made Burma their permanent home, and whose parents and himself were born in Burma, is a statutory citizen."
3. The Burmese terms are *eh-naing-ngan-tha* (associate citizens) and *naingngan-tha-pyu-khwint-ya-thu* (naturalized citizens).
4. Burma Citizenship Law of 1982, art. 45.
5. Burma Registration of Foreigners Rules of 1948, art. 6(2).
6. Burma Citizenship Law of 1982, art. 6; Procedures relating to Myanmar Citizenship Law of 1983 No. 13/83, art. 7.
7. Burma Citizenship Law of 1982, art. 3; Procedures relating to Myanmar Citizenship Law of 1983, art. 5.
8. Burma Citizenship Law of 1982, art. 5.
9. Citizenship Law, art. 7.
10. Citizenship Law, art. 23.
11. Citizenship Law.
12. Citizenship Law, art. 42.
13. Citizenship Law, art. 43.
14. Citizenship Law, art. 47.
15. Citizenship Law, art.15.
16. Citizenship Law, art. 15(a). This is contained within Chapter II, applying *only* to type 1 'citizenship'.
17. Citizenship Law, arts. 16, 34, 57.
18. Citizenship Law, art. 71.
19. Citizenship Scrutiny Cards are color-coded pink for full citizens, green for naturalized citizens, and blue for associated citizens. These ID cards include information about a person's ethnicity and religion.
20. According to the Burma Citizenship Law of 1982, art. 6, persons who were citizens at the time of the entry into force of the law continue to be citizens.
21. The idea was also reflected in a Draft Rakhine State Action Plan of 2014.

Glossary

1. World Bank national accounts data and OECD National Accounts data files. License CC BY-4.0.

Bibliography

I. Treaties

Consolidated version of the Treaty on European Union [2016] OJ C202/1.

Consolidated version of the Treaty on the Functioning of the European Union [2016] OJ C202/1.

"European Convention on Nationality." Opened for signature November 6, 1997, entered into force March 1, 2000. Council of Europe, ETS No. 166.

"Additional Protocol to the Convention on the Reduction of Cases of Multiple Nationality and on Military Obligations in Cases of Multiple Nationality." November 24, 1977, entered into force October 17, 1983. Council of Europe, ETS No. 096.

"International Covenant on Civil and Political Rights." December 16, 1966, entered into force March 23, 1976. *United Nations, Treaty Series*, vol. 999, 171.

"Convention on the Settlement of Investment Disputes between States and Nationals of Other States." Opened for signature March 18, 1965, entered into force October 14, 1966. *United Nations, Treaty Series*, vol. 575, 159, No. 8359.

"Convention on the Reduction of Cases of Multiple Nationality and on Military Obligations in Cases of Multiple Nationality." Opened for signature May 6, 1963, entered into force March 28, 1968. Council of Europe, ETS No. 043.

"Convention on the Reduction of Statelessness." August 30, 1961, entered into force December 13, 1975. *United Nations, Treaty Series*, vol. 989, 175.

"The Dutch-American Friendship Treaty." March 27, 1956.

"Convention Relating to the Status of Stateless Persons." September 28, 1954, entered into force June 6, 1960. *United Nations, Treaty Series*, vol. 360, 117.

"Convention on Certain Questions Relating to the Conflict of Nationality Laws." April 12, 1930, entered into force July 1, 1937. *League of Nations, Treaty Series*, vol. 179, 89, No. 4137.

"Protocol Relating to a Certain Case of Statelessness." April 12, 1930, entered into force July 1, 1937. *League of Nations*, No. 4138. 179 LNTS 115.

"Special Protocol Concerning Statelessness." April 12, 1930, not yet entered into force. *League of Nations*, C. 227.M.114.1930.V.

"Treaty between the Principal Allied and Associated Powers and Romania." December 9, 1919. (Romanian Minorities Treaty).

II. Literature

Abu-Laban, Yasmeen. 1999. "Keeping 'em Out." In *Painting the Maple*, edited by Veronica Strong-Boag and Sherrill Grace, 69–84. Vancouver: UBC Press.

Acosta Arcarazo, Diego. 2018. *The National Versus the Foreigner in South America. 200 Years of Migration and Citizenship Law*. Cambridge: CUP.

Acosta Arcarazo, Diego, and Andrew Geddes. 2014. "Transnational Diffusion or Different Models? Regional Approaches to Migration Governance in the European Union and MERCOSUR." *European Journal of Migration and Law* 16 (1): 19–44.

Acosta Arcarazo, Diego, and Luisa F. Freier. 2015. "Turning the Immigration Policy Paradox Upside Down? Populist Liberalism and Discursive Gaps in South America." *International Migration Review* 49 (3): 659–96.

Ademmer, Esther. 2017. *Russia's Impact on EU Policy Transfer to the Post-Soviet Space – The Contested Neighbourhood*. Abingdon-on-Thames: Routledge.

Ademmer, Esther, and Laure Delcour. 2016. "With a Little Help from Russia? The European Union and Visa Liberalization with Post-Soviet States." *Eurasian Geography and Economics* (57) 1: 89–112.

Ademmer, Esther, and Tanja Börzel. 2013. "Migration, Energy and Good Governance in the EU's Eastern Neighbourhood." *Europe-Asia Studies* 65 (4): 591–608.

Adepoju, Aderanti. 2002. "Fostering Free Movement of Persons in West Africa: Achievements, Constraints, and Prospects for Intraregional Migration." *International Migration* 40 (2): 3–28.

Adepoju, Aderanti. 2009. "Migration Management in West Africa within the Context of ECOWAS Protocol on Free Movement of Persons and the Common Approach on Migration." In *Regional Challenges of West African Migration: African and European Perspectives*, edited by Marie Trémolières, OECD, and Sahel and West Africa Club, 17–47. Paris: OECD Publishing.

Advisory Commission on Rakhine State. 2017. "Final Report of the Advisory Commission on Rakhine State: Towards a Peaceful, Fair and Prosperous Future for the People of Rakhine." http://www.rakhinecommission.org/app/uploads/2017/08/FinalReport_Eng.pdf.

Agca, Fatma, and Ahmet Kaya. 2015. "*The Out-group Who Are No Longer the Out-group.*" In *Religion, Migration and Conflict*, edited by Carl Sterkens and Paul Vermeer, 73–87. Münster: Lit Verlag.

Aleinikoff, Alexander T., and Douglas B. Klusmeyer. 2002. *Citizenship Policies for an Age of Migration*. Washington D.C.: Carnegie Endowment for International Peace.

Alfonso, Adriana. 2012. *Integración y Migraciones: El Tratamiento de la Variable Migratoria en el MERCOSUR y su Incidencia en la Política Argentina*. Buenos Aires: IOM.

Apsītis, Romāns. 2008. "Atzinums Pārbaudes Lietā." Latvijas Republikas Tiesībsargs. http://www.tiesibsargs.lv/uploads/content/atzinumi/2008_10_08_atzinums_par_pilsonu_un_nepilsonu_tiesibam_2008_09_1507031817.pdf.

Arraiza, José-María. 2015. "Good Neighbourliness as a Limit to Extraterritorial Citizenship: The Case of Hungary and Slovakia." In *Good Neighbourliness in the European Legal Context*, edited by Dimitry Kochenov and Elena Basheska, 114–135. Leiden: Martinus Nijhoff.

Arrighi, Giovanni. 1994. *The Long Twentieth Century: Money, Power, and the Origins of Our Times*. London/New York: Verso.

Artman, Vincent. 2013. "Documenting Territory: Passportisation, Territory, and Exception in Abkhazia and South Ossetia." *Geopolitics* 18 (3): 682–704.

Babar, Zahra. 2011. "Free Mobility within the Gulf Cooperation Council." *Center for International and Regional Studies Occasional Papers* 8: 1–40.

Bagley, Chris. 2016. "Innovating Across Borders." *North Carolina Journal of International Law* 41 (4): 919–47.

Baker, Donnave. 1928. "'The Development of Citizenship." *Social Science* 3 (2): 122–25.

Baldacchino, Godfrey, and David Milne. 2009. *The Case for Non-Sovereignty. Lessons from Sub-National Island Jurisdictions*. Abingdon: Routledge.

Baldacchino, Godfrey. 2010. *Island Enclaves: Offshoring Strategies, Creative Governance, and Subnational Island Jurisdictions*. Montreal QC: McGill-Queen's University Press.

Baldacchino, Godfrey. 2018. "Autonomy Plus: The Policy Challenges and Opportunities Faced by Subnational (Mainly Island) Jurisdictions." In *The 21st Century Maritime Silk Road. Islands Economic Cooperation Forum. Annual Report on Global Islands 2017*, edited by James Randall, 99–118. Charlottetown, Canada: Island Studies Press at the University of Prince Edward Island.

Balibar, Étienne. 2001. *Nous, citoyens d'Europe? Les frontières, l'État, le peuple*. Paris: La Découverte.

Ballas, Dimitris, Danny Dorling, and Benjamin Hennig. 2017. *The Human Atlas of Europe: A Continent United in Diversity*. Bristol: Policy Press.

Bartlett, Richard. 1979. "Citizens Minus: Indians and the Right to Vote." *Saskatchewan Law Review* 44: 163–94.

Basheska, Elena. 2015. "(Mis)application of the Good Neighbourliness Principle in International and EU Law: The Case of the Republic of Macedonia." In *The Principle of Good Neighbourliness in the European Legal Context: Interpretation and Application*, edited by Elena Basheska and Dimitry Kochenov, 235–67. Leiden: Brill-Nijhoff.

Batchelor, Carol A. 1995. "Stateless Persons: Some Gaps in International Protection." *International Journal of Refugee Law* 7 (2): 232–59.

Bauböck, Rainer, and Sara Wallace Goodman. 2011. "Naturalisation." EUDO Citizenship Policy Brief No. 2.

Bauman, Zygmunt. 1998. *Globalization: The Human Consequences*. New York: Columbia University Press.

Beck, Ulrich. 2008. "Mobility and the Cosmopolitan Perspective." In *Tracing Mobilities: Towards a Cosmopolitan Perspective*, edited by Weert Canzler, Vincent Kaufmann and Sven Kesselring, 25–35. Aldershot/Burlington, VT: Ashgate Publishing.

Benhabib, Seyla. 2002. *The Claims of Culture: Equality and Diversity in the Global Era*. Princeton/Oxford, NJ: Princeton University Press.

Bennich Bjorkman, Li. 2017. "Post-Soviet Developments: Reflections on Complexity and Patterns of Political Orders." *Journal of Contemporary Central and Eastern Europe* 26 (1): 51–68.

Bianchini, Katia. 2018. *Protecting Stateless Persons. The Implementation of the Convention Relating to the Status of Stateless Persons across EU States*. Leiden/Boston: Brill-Nijhoff.

Bierbach, Jeremy. 2017a. *Frontiers of Equality in the Development of EU and US Citizenship*. The Hague: T.M.C. Asser Press.

Bierbach, Jeremy. 2017b. "Family Life as a Civil Right for Some EU Citizens, but Not All." *EUSA Conference Paper*. https://www.eustudies.org/conference/papers/download/335.8.

Blackstone, William. 1884. *Commentaries on the Laws of England: In Four Books*. Chicago: Callaghan and Co. Cited in Rubinstein, Kim, and Daniel Adler. 2000. "International Citizenship: The Future of Nationality in a Globalized World," 530. *Indiana Journal of Global Legal Studies* 7 (2): 519–48.

Bloom, Tendayi. 2017. "Members of Colonised Groups, Statelessness and the Right to Have Rights." In *Understanding Statelessness*, edited by Tendayi Bloom, Katherine Tonkiss and Phillip Cole. London: Routledge.

Blévis, Laure. 2001. "Les avatars de la citoyenneté en Algérie coloniale ou les paradoxes d'une catégorisation." *Droit et société 2* (48): 557–81.

Bonilla, Yarimar. 2015. *Non-Sovereign Futures: French Caribbean Politics in the Wake of Disenchantment*. London: University of Chicago Press.

Bonnet, Jean-Charles. "Les pouvoirs publics français et l'immigration dans l'entre-deux-guerres." Doc. thes., Lyon-II University, 1974.

Bosniak, Linda. 2000. "Citizenship Denationalized (The State of Citizenship Symposium)." *Indiana Journal of Global Legal Studies* 7 (2): 447–509.

Bosniak, Linda. 2002. "Multiple Nationality and the Postnational Transformation of Citizenship." *Virginia Journal of International Law* 42: 979–1004.

Bredbenner, Candice L. 1998. *A Nationality of Her Own: Women, Marriage, and the Law of Citizenship*. Berkeley: University of California Press.

van den Brink, Martijn, and Dimitry Kochenov. 2019. "Against Associate Citizenship of the European Union." *Journal of Common Market Studies* 54.

Broadberry, Stephen, and Alexander Klein. 2012. "Aggregate and per capita GDP in Europe, 1870–2000: Continental, Regional and National Data with Changing Boundaries." *Scandinavian Economic History Review* 60 (1): 79–107.

Brouillette, Martine. "Les Partenariats pour la mobilité: regards croisés sur un outil européen de gestion des migrations." PhD diss., Université de Poitiers, 2018.

Browne Gibson Harvey Lawyers. n.d. "Purchasing Land in the Cook Islands." http://www.cookislandslaw.com/faq.html.

Brubaker, Rogers. 1998. *Citizenship and Nationhood in France and Germany*, 2nd ed. Cambridge, MA: HUP.

Buzajevs, Vladimirs. 2016. *Masveida bezpilsonība* [Mass Statelessness]. Latvijas Cilvēktiesību komiteja. Rīga.

Cairns, Alan. 2011. *Citizens Plus: Aboriginal Peoples and the Canadian State*. Vancouver: University of British Columbia Press.

Cannon, Martin J. 2006. "First Nations Citizenship." *Canadian Review of Social Policy* 56: 40–71.

Capurri, Valentina. 2018. "The Montoya Case." *Disability Studies Quarterly* 38 (1).

Carens, Joseph H. 2000. *Culture, Citizenship, and Community: A Contextual Exploration of Justice as Evenhandedness*. Oxford: OUP.

Carens, Joseph H. 2013. *The Ethics of Immigration*. Oxford: OUP.

Castles, Stephen. 2005. "Nation and Empire: Hierarchies of Citizenship in the New Global Order." *International Politics* 42 (2): 203–24.

Castro, Maolis. 2018. El negocio del éxodo venezolano: miles de dólares por un pasaporte. *El País*, August 25, 2018. https://elpais.com/internacional/2018/08/24/america/1535121140_527084.html.

Centeno, Miguel, Nina Bandelj, and Frederick Wherry. 2011. "The Political Economy of Cultural Wealth." In *The Cultural Wealth of Nations*, edited by Nina Bandelj and Frederick F. Wherry, 23–46. Stanford, CA: Stanford University Press.

Center for Systemic Peace. n.d. "Center for Systemic Peace." Accessed February 22, 2019. http://www.systemicpeace.org.

Chamberlain, Lesley. 2006. *The Philosophy Steamer: Lenin and the Exile of the Intelligentsia*. London: Atlantic Books.

Chan, Johannes M.M. 1991. "The Right to a Nationality as a Human Right: The Current Trend Towards Recognition." *Human Rights Law Journal* 12: 1–14.

Chase-Dunn, Christopher, and Peter Grimes. 1995. "World-systems analysis." *Annual Review of Sociology* 21 (1): 387–417.

Chenery, Susan. 2016. "New Zealanders in Australia are Still Treated Like Second-Class Citizens." *Stuff*, April 16, 2016. https://www.stuff.co.nz/world/australia/78998518/New-Zealanders-in-Australia-are-still-treated-like-second-class-citizens.

Clarke Ey Lawyers, and Jones Lang LaSalle Real Estate. 2014. "Samoa Property Investment Guide." *Hospitality Edition*. http://www.joneslanglasallesites.com/investmentguide/uploads/attachments/2014AP_PropertyInvestmentGuide-Samoa_5kkzddtk.pdf.

Cohen, Miriam. 2017. "The Re-invention of Investment Immigration in Canada and Constructions of Canadian Citizenship." IMC WP 2017/2.

Cook-Martin, David. 2013. *The Scramble for Citizens: Dual Nationality and State Competition for Immigrants*. Stanford: Stanford University Press.

Corntassel, Jeff. 2012. "Re-envisioning Resurgence: Indigenous Pathways to Decolonization and Sustainable Self-determination." *Decolonization* 1 (1): 86–101.

Council of Europe. 2016. *Report by Nils Muižnieks, Commissioner for Human Rights of the Council of Europe, following visit to Latvia from 5 to 9 September 2016*. CommDH(2016)41.

Crawford, James R. 2006. *The Creation of States in International Law*. 2nd ed. Oxford: OUP.

Dados, Nour, and Raewyn Connell. 2012. "The Global South." *Contexts* 11 (1): 12–3.

Dang, T. Lam. 2011. "Relation associative, Les États fédérés de Micronésie: les spécificités de l'association." In *Destins des collectivités politiques d'Océanie – Volume 1: Théories et pratiques*, edited by Jean-Yves Faberon, Jean-Marc Regnault, and Viviane Fayaud, 373–6. Aix-en-Provence: Presses Universitaires d'Aix-Marseille.

Deelstra, Jojanneke, Darlene Matroos-Piar, and Thomas van Houwelingen. 2016. "Toelating in Koninkrijksperspectief: Één Koninkrijk, vier Landen, vijf Vreemdelingenwetten en Één Nationaliteit Deel I: Het Vreemdelingenrecht op Sint-Maarten en Curaçao." *Journaal Vreemdelingenrecht* 3 (20): 43–52.

Delcour, Laure. 2013. "Meandering Europeanisation – EU Policy Instruments and Patterns of Convergence in Georgia." *East European Politics* 29 (3): 344–57.

Delcour, Laure. 2017. *The EU and Russia in their Contested Neighbourhood: Multiple Influences, Policy Transfer and Domestic Change*. London: Routledge.

Delcour, Laure. 2018. "The EU's Visa Liberalisation Policy: What Kind of Transformative Power in Neighbouring Regions?" In *The Routledge Handbook of the Politics of Migration in Europe*, edited by Agnieszka Weinar, Saskia Bonjour, and Lyubov Zhyznomirska, 410–19. London: Routledge.

DeRosa, James. 1995. "The Immigrant Investor Program." *Case Western Reserve Journal of International Law* 27 (2): 359–405.

van Dijk, Ruud, William G. Gray, Svetlana Savranskaya, Jeremi Suri, and Qiang Zhai, eds. 2008. *Encyclopedia of the Cold War*. London/New York: Routledge.

Dimitrovs, Aleksejs, and Vadim Poleshchuk. 2013. "Kontinuitet kak osnova gosudarstvennosti i ètnopolitiki v Latvii i Èstonii." In *Ètnopolitika stran Baltii*, edited by Vadim Poleshchuk and Valery Stepanov. Moscow: Nauka.

Djackova, Svetlana. 2015. "Ending Childhood Statelessness: A Study on Latvia." European Network on Statelessness Working Paper No. 07/15.

Dobrowolsky, Alexandra. 2017. "Bad versus Big Canada." *Studies in Political Economy* 98 (2): 197–222.

Donner, Ruth. 1994. *The Regulation of Nationality in International Law*, 2nd ed. Leiden: Brill-Nijhoff.

Drumbl, Mark Anthony. 1994. "Canada's New Immigration Act." *Revue de droit de l'Université de Sherbrooke* 24 (2): 385–432.

Dugard, John. 1980. "South Africa's Independent Homelands: An Exercise in Denationalization." *Denver Journal of International Law & Policy* 10: 11–36.

Dumbrava, Costica. 2018. "The Ethno-demographic Impact of Co-ethnic Citizenship in Central and Eastern Europe." *Journal of Ethnic and Migration Studies* 45 (6): 958–74.

Dunn, Leslie. 2011. "The Impact of Political Dependence on Small Island Jurisdictions." *World Development* 39 (12): 2132–46.

Durand, Jorge. 2014. "Un 'Coyote' japonés en Ciudad Juárez (1905–1911)." *Desacatos* 46: 192–207. http://www.scielo.org.mx/scielo.php?script=sci_arttext&pid=S1607-050X2014000300015.

Dyer, L. 1897. "Anglo-Saxon Citizenship: A Proposition by Professor Dicey Looking to This End." *The Barrister* 3: 107.

Džankić, Jelena. 2012. "Country Report: Montenegro." *EUDO Citizenship Observatory* 2012/05.

Džankić, Jelena. 2017. "Dimensions of Citizenship Policy in the Post-Yugoslav Space: Divergent Paths." *Central and Eastern European Migration Review* 6 (1): 31–48.

Elwell, Frank W. 2013. "Wallerstein's World-Systems Theory." http://www.faculty.rsu.edu/users/f/felwell/www/Theorists/Essays/Wallerstein1.htm.

Espeland, Wendy N., and Michael Sauder. 2007. "Rankings and Reactivity: How Public Measures Recreate Social Worlds." *American Journal of Sociology* 113 (1): 1–40.

Espeland, Wendy N., and Mitchell L. Stevens. 1998. "Commensuration as a Social Process." *Annual Review of Sociology* 24 (1): 313–43.

European Bank for Reconstruction and Development. 2006. "Life in Transition Survey I: A Survey of People's Experiences and Attitudes." https://www.ebrd.com/news/publications/special-reports/life-in-transition-survey-i.html.

European Bank for Reconstruction and Development. 2010. "Life in Transition Survey II: After the Crisis." https://www.ebrd.com/cs/Satellite?c=Content&cid=1395237690999&d=&pagename=EBRD%2FContent%2FDownloadDocument.

European Bank for Reconstruction and Development. 2016. "Life in Transition Survey III: A Decade of Measuring Transition." http://www.ebrd.com/documents/oce/pdf-life-in-transition-iii.pdf.

European Commission. 2008. "Eastern Partnership" COM (2008) 823 final.

European Commission. 2017. "Visa Liberalisation with Moldova, Ukraine and Georgia." https://ec.europa.eu/home-affairs/what-we-do/policies/international-affairs/eastern-partnership/visa-liberalisation-moldova-ukraine-and-georgia_en.

European Commission. 2018a "Commission Staff Working Document Accompanying the Document Report from the Commission to the European Parliament and the Council Second Report Under the Visa Suspension Mechanism" COM (2018) 496 final.

European Commission. 2018b. "Visa Statistics." Last modified April 10, 2018. https://bit.ly/2vceW6Y.

European Commission. 2019. "Investor Citizenship and Residence Schemes in the European Union." COM (2019)12 final.

European Migration Network. 2016. "Statelessness in the EU." Version 4. Last modified November 11, 2016. https://ec.europa.eu/home-affairs/sites/homeaffairs/files/what-we-do/networks/european_migration_network/reports/docs/emn-informs/emn-informs-00_inform_statelessness_final.pdf.

European Network on Statelessness. 2013. "Good Practice Guide on Statelessness Determination and the Protection Status of Stateless Persons." Last modified December 2013. https://www.statelessness.eu/resources/ens-good-practice-guide-statelessness-determination-and-protection-status-stateless.

European Parliament. 2014. "European Parliament Resolution of 16 January 2014 on EU Citizenship for Sale (2013/2995(RSP))." P7_TA(2014)0038, OJ C 482/117.

Eurostat. 2018. "Asylum Quarterly Report." https://ec.europa.eu/eurostat/statistics-explained/pdfscache/13562.pdf.

Eurostat. n.d. "Eurostat – Your key to European Statistics." Accessed March 13, 2019. http://ec.europa.eu/eurostat/web/main/home.

Fabbrini, Federico. 2017. "The Political Side of EU Citizenship in the Context of EU Federalism." In *EU Citizenship and Federalism: The Role of Rights*, edited by Dimitry Kochenov, 271–93. Cambridge: CUP.

Fahrmeir, Andreas K. 1997. "Nineteenth-Century German Citizenships: A Reconsideration." *The Historical Journal* 40 (3): 721–52.

Faist, Thomas. 2013. "The Mobility Turn: A New Paradigm for the Social Sciences?" *Ethnic and Racial Studies* 36 (11): 1637–46.

Farran, Sue, and Donald Paterson. 2013. *South Pacific Property Law*. London: Routledge-Cavendish.

Ferguson, Ted. 1975. *A White Man's Country*. Toronto: Doubleday.

Firebaugh, Glenn. 2015. "Global Income Inequality." In *Emerging Trends in the Social and Behavioral Sciences: An Interdisciplinary, Searchable, and Linkable Resource*, edited by Robert A. Scott, Marlis C. Buchmann, and Stephen M. Kosslyn, 1–14. New York: John Wiley & Sons, Inc.

Firth, Stewart. 2018. *Instability in The Pacific Islands: A Status Report*. Lowy Institute. https://www.think-asia.org/bitstream/handle/11540/8550/Firth_Instability%20in%20the%20Pacific%20Islands_A%20status%20report_WEB.pdf.

Fiske, Jo-Anne. 1995. "Political Status of Native Indian Women." *American Indian Culture and Research Journal* 19 (2): 1–30.

Fix, Liana, Andrea Gawrich, Kornely Kakachia, and Alla Leukavets. 2019. "Out of the Shadow? Georgia's Emerging Strategies of Engagement in the Eastern Partnership: Between External Governance and Partnership Cooperation." *Caucasus Survey* 7 (1): 1–24.

Fourcade, Marion, and Kieran Healy. 2017. "Categories All the Way Down." *Historical Social Research* 42 (1): 286–96.

Fukuyama, Francis. 1992. *The End of History and the Last Man*. New York: Free Press.

Gastner, Michael T., and Mark E. J. Newman. 2004. "Diffusion-based Method for Producing Density Equalizing Maps." *Proceedings of the National Academy of Science USA* 101 (20): 7499-504.

Gauci, Gotthard Mark, and Kevin Aquilina. 2017. "The Legal Fiction of a Genuine Link as a Requirement for the Grant of Nationality to Ships and Humans – The Triumph of Formality over Substance?" *International and Comparative Law Review* 17 (1): 167–91.

Geisser, Vincent. 2015. "Déchoir de la nationalité des djihadistes '100 % made in France': qui cherche-t-on à punir?" *Migrations Société* 6 (162): 3–14.

Gellner, Ernest. 2008. *Nations and Nationalism*. New York: Cornell University Press.

Gel'man, Vladimir. 2015. *Authoritarian Russia. Analyzing Post-Soviet Regime Changes*. Pittsburg PA: University of Pittsburgh Press.

German, Tracey. 2016. "Russia and South Ossetia: Conferring Statehood or Creeping Annexation?" *Southeast European and Black Sea Studies* 16 (1): 155–67.

Gibney, Matthew. 2014. "Statelessness and Citizenship in Ethical and Political Perspective." In *Nationality and Statelessness under International Law*, edited by Alice Edwards and Laura van Waas, 44–63. Cambridge: CUP.

Gillis, Shelley, John Polesel, and Margaret Wu. 2016. "PISA Data: Raising Concerns with Its Use in Policy Settings." *The Australian Educational Researcher* 43 (1): 131–46.

Goedings, Simone A.W. 2005. *Labor Migration in an Integrating Europe: National Migration Policies and the Free Movement of Workers, 1950–1968*. Den Haag: Sdu.

Goesel-Le Bihan, Valérie. 1998. "La Nouvelle-Calédonie et l'accord de Nouméa, un processus inédit de décolonisation." *Annuaire français de droit international* 44, 24–75.

Government of Canada. 2015. "Reopening the Immigrant Investor Venture Capital Pilot Program." Last modified May 23, 2015. https://bit.ly/2rqgvcX.

Gramlich, John. 2017. "How Countries Around the World View Democracy, Military Rule and Other Political Systems." Pew Research Center, October 30, 2017. http://www.pewresearch.org/fact-tank/2017/10/30/global-views-political-systems/.

Griffith, Andrew. 2018. "What the Census Tells Us about Citizenship." *Policy Options*. https://bit.ly/2EQi7Vj.

de Groot, David A.J.G. 2018. "Free Movement of Dual EU Citizens." *European Papers* 3 (3): 1075–113.

de Groot, Gerard-René. 1989. *Staatsangehörigkeitsrecht im Wandel: Eine Rechtsvergleichende Studie über Erwerbs- und Verlustgründe der Staatsangehörigkeit*. The Hague: Asser Institute.

de Groot, Gerard-René. 2011. "Strengthening the Position of the Children: Council of Europe's Recommendation 2009/13." In *Concepts of Nationality in a Globalised World*, Council of Europe.

de Groot, Gerard-René. 2016. "Towards a Toolbox for Nationality Legislation." Valedictory Lecture at the Maastricht University. https://cris.maastrichtuniversity.nl/portal/files/5717469/Oratie_Groot.pdf.

de Groot, Gerard-René, and Eric Mijts. 2009. "De Onwenselijkheid van een Dubbele Taaltoets voor Naturalisandi in Aruba en de Nederlandse Antillen." *Migrantenrecht* 8: 366–71.

de Groot, Gerard-René, and Matjaz Tratnik. 2010. *Nederlands Nationaliteitsrecht*. Alphen aan den Rijn: Kluwer.

de Groot, Gerard-René, Katja Świder, and Olivier Wonk. 2015. "Practices and Approaches in EU Member States to Prevent and End Statelessness." Policy Department C: Citizens' Rights and Constitutional Affairs. European Parliament.

Gvalia, Giorgi, Bidzina Lebanidze, and Zurab Iashvili. 2011. *Political Elites, Ideas and Foreign Policy: Explaining and Understanding the International Behavior of Small States in the Former Soviet Union*. Tbilisi: Ilia State University.

Hale, Henry. 2015. *Patronal Politics: Eurasian Regime Dynamics in Comparative Perspective*. Cambridge: CUP.

Hanjian, Clark. 2003. *Sovereign: An Exploration of the Right to Be Stateless*. Vineyard Haven, Massachusetts: Polyspire.

Harpaz, Yossi. 2013. "Rooted Cosmopolitans: Israelis with a European Passport – History, Property, Identity." *International Migration Review* 47 (1) (Spring): 166–206.

Harpaz, Yossi. 2015. "Ancestry into Opportunity: How Global Inequality Drives Demand for Long-Distance European Union Citizenship." *Journal of Ethnic and Migration Studies* 31 (13): 2081–104.

Harpaz, Yossi. 2019a. *Citizenship 2.0: Dual Nationality as a Global Asset*. Princeton, NJ: Princeton University Press.

Harpaz, Yossi. 2019b. "Compensatory Citizenship: Dual Nationality as a Strategy of Global Upward Mobility." *Journal of Ethnic and Migration Studies* 45 (6): 897–916.

Harpaz, Yossi, and Pablo Mateos. 2019. "Strategic Citizenship: Negotiating Membership in the Age of Dual Nationality." *Journal of Ethnic and Migration Studies* 45 (6): 843–57.

de Hart, Betty. 2007. "The End of Multiculturalism: The End of Dual Citizenship? Political and Public Debates on Dual Citizenship in The Netherlands (1980–2004)." In *Dual Citizenship in Europe: From Nationhood to Societal Integration*, edited by Thomas Faist, 77–102. Farnham: Ashgate.

Hau'ofa, Epeli (1993). "Our Sea of Islands." In *Rediscovering our Sea of Islands*, edited by Eric Waddell, Vijay Naidu, and Epeli Hau'ofa, 2–17. Suva: University of the South Pacific (USP).

Hawkins, Freda. 1988. *Canada and Immigration*. Kingston & Montreal: McGill-Queen's University Press.

Heather, Ben. 2015. "Kiwis Sold 'Worthless' Insurance in Australia." *Stuff*, October 13, 2015. https://www.stuff.co.nz/business/money/72929434/Kiwis-sold-worthless-insurance-in-Australia.

Henley & Partners. 2017. *Global Residence and Citizenship Programs 2017–2018: The Definitive Comparison of the Leading Investment Migration Programs*. New York/London/Zurich/Hong Kong: Ideos.

Hennig, Benjamin. 2013. *Rediscovering the World: Map Transformations of Human and Physical Space*. Heidelberg/New York/Dordrecht/London: Springer.

Hennig, Benjamin, and Dimitris Ballas. 2018. "A Human Cartographic Approach to Mapping the Quality of Nationality Index." In *Quality of Nationality Index: Nationalities of the World in 2017*, 3rd ed., edited by Dimitry Kochenov and Justin Lindenboom, 37–39. New York/London/Zurich/Hong Kong: Ideos.

Hernández i Sagrera, Raül, and Oleg Korneev. 2012. "Bringing EU Migration Cooperation to the Eastern Neighbourhood: Convergence beyond the Acquis Communautaire?" European University Institute RSCAS Working Paper No 12/22.

Hobolth, Mogens. 2014. "Researching Mobility Barriers: The European Visa Database." *Journal of Ethnic and Migration Studies* 40 (3): 424–35.

Hondius, Dienke. 2014. *Blackness in Western Europe: Racial Patterns of Paternalism and Exclusion*. New Jersey: Transaction Publishers.

House of Commons of Canada. 2013. "Standing Committee on Official Languages: Evidence." No. 85 41st Parliament Session 1. Last modified June 13, 2013. http://www.ourcommons.ca/DocumentViewer/en/41-1/LANG/meeting-85/evidence.

Hudson, Manley O. 1952. "Nationality, Including Statelessness." *Yearbook of the International Law Commission* Volume II: 8–24. Doc. No. A/CN.4/50.

Huntington, Samuel P. 1996. *The Clash of Civilizations and the Remaking of World Order*. New York, NY: Simon and Schuster.

Hussen, Ahmed. 2018. "2018 Annual Report to Parliament on Immigration." Immigration, Refugees and Citizenship Canada. https://bit.ly/2AYdu86.

Institute on Statelessness and Inclusion. 2014. *The World's Stateless*. Oosterwijk: Wolf Legal Publishers.

Institute on Statelessness and Inclusion and European Network on Statelessness. 2017. "Joint Submission to the Human Rights Council at the 30th Session of the Universal Periodic Review (Third Cycle, May 2018), Federal Republic of Germany." Last modified October 5, 2017. http://www.institutesi.org/UPR30_Germany.pdf.

Instituto Nacional de Estadística. 2018. "Estadística del Padrón de españoles residentes en el extranjero (PERE)." Madrid. https://www.ine.es/dyngs/INEbase/es/operacion.htm?c=Estadistica_C&cid=1254736177014&menu=ultiDatos&idp=1254734710990.

International Law Commission. 2006. "Draft Articles on Diplomatic Protection and Commentaries." UN General Assembly Official Records, 61s session, Supp. No. 10, UN Doc. A/61/10, 2006. http://legal.un.org/ilc/texts/instruments/english/commentaries/9_8_2006.pdf.

International Monetary Fund. 2016. "St. Kitts and Nevis: 2016 Article IV Consultation – Press Release; and Staff Report." *IMF Country Report* No. 16/250.

IOM. 2018a. *Evaluación del Acuerdo de Residencia del MERCOSUR y su incidencia en el acceso a derechos de los migrantes.* Buenos Aires: IOM.

IOM. 2018b. "El número de refugiados y migrantes de Venezuela alcanza los 3 millones." Press Release. http://www.oim.org.co/news/el-n%C3%BAmero-de-refugiados-y-migrantes-de-venezuela-alcanza-los-3-millones.

IOM. n.d. "Myanmar." https://www.iom.int/countries/myanmar.

Ivanov, Martin, and Adam Tooze. 2007. "Convergence or Decline on Europe's Southeastern Periphery? Agriculture, Population, and GNP in Bulgaria, 1892–1945." *The Journal of Economic History* 67 (3): 672–703.

Ivković, Aleksandar. 2018. "What is Holding Kosovo's Visa Liberalisation Back?" *European Western Balkans*, December 26, 2018. https://europeanwesternbalkans.com/2018/12/26/holding-kosovos-visa-liberalisation-back/.

Izquierdo Escribano, Antonio, and Luca Chao. 2015. "Ciudadanos Españoles Producto de la Ley de Memoria Histórica: Motivos y Movilidades." In *Ciudadanía múltiple y migración: Perspectivas latinoamericanas*, edited by Pablo Mateos, 141–78. Mexico City: CIDE/CIESAS.

Jansons, Juris. 2011. "Par nepilsoņu tiesisko statusu." Latvijas Republikas Tiesībsargs. http://www.tiesibsargs.lv/uploads/content/atzinumi/tiesibsarga_viedoklis_par_nepilsonu_tiesisko_statusu_1507138132.pdf.

Joppke, Christian. 2010. *Citizenship and Immigration*. Cambridge: Polity Press.

Joppke, Christian. 2018. "The Instrumental Turn of Citizenship." *Journal of Ethnic and Migration Studies* 45 (6): 858–78.

Julien-Laferrière, François, and Catherine Teitgen-Colly. 1997. "Actes de terrorisme et droit des étrangers." *Actualité juridique – Droit administratif* 1: 86.

Kakachia, Kornely, and Salome Minesashvili. 2015. "Identity Politics: Exploring Georgian Foreign Policy Behaviour." *Journal of Eurasian Studies* 6: 1–10.

Kalinichenko, Paul. 2015. "Some Legal Issues of the EU-Russia Relations in the Post-Crimea Era: From Good Neighbourliness to Crisis and Back?" In *Good Neighbourliness in the European Legal Context*, edited by Dimitry Kochenov and Elena Basheska, 334–53. Leiden: Brill.

Kälin, Christian H. 2019a. *Ius Doni in International Law and EU Law*. The Hague: Brill-Nijhoff.

Kälin, Christian H. 2019b. "'Sovereign Equity' Launched as a Solution to Sovereign Debt and Financial Inequality in Davos Debate." *Global Citizenship Review* 59 (2).

Kamen, Deborah. 2013. *Status in Classical Athens*. Princeton, NJ: Princeton University Press.

Kandel, William A. 2014. "U.S. Naturalization Policy." Congressional Research Service Report 7-5700.

Keitner, Chimène I., and W. Michael Reisman. 2003. "Free Association: The United States Experience." *Texas International Law Journal* 39 (1): 1–63.

Kelley, Ninette, and Michael J. Trebilcock. 2010. *The Making of the Mosaic*. Toronto: University of Toronto Press.

Keppel, Gunnar, Clare Morrison, Dick Watling, Marika V. Tuiwawa, and Isaac A. Rounds. 2012. "Conservation in Tropical Pacific Island Countries: Why Most Current Approaches are Failing." *Conservation Letters* 5 (4): 256–65.

Khin, Yi. 1998. *The Dobama Movement in Burma (1930–1938)*. New York: South East Asia Program Publications.

Kim, Jaeeun. 2018. "Migration-Facilitating Capital: A Bourdieusian Theory of International Migration." *Sociological Theory* 36 (3): 262–88.

Kingsbury, Benedict. 1998. "Sovereignty and Inequality." *European Journal of International Law* 9 (4): 599–625.

Klein, Ruth. 2012. *Nazi Germany, Canadian Responses*. Montreal & Kingston: McGill-Queen's University Press.

Knowles, Valerie. 2007. *Strangers at Our Gates*. Toronto: Dundurn.

Kochenov, Dimitry. 2009. "*Ius Tractum* of Many Faces: European Citizenship and a Difficult Relationship between Status and Rights." *Columbia Journal of European Law* 15 (2): 169–238.

Kochenov, Dimitry. 2010a. "Rounding Up the Circle: The Mutation of Member States' Nationalities under Pressure from EU Citizenship." *EUI EUDO Citizenship Observatory RSCAS Paper* no. 2010/23: 1–34.

Kochenov, Dimitry. 2010b. "Regional Citizenships and EU Law: The Case of the Åland Islands and New Caledonia." *European Law Review* 35 (August): 307–24.

Kochenov, Dimitry. 2010c. "The Puzzle of Citizenship and Territory in the EU: On European Rights Overseas." *Maastricht Journal of European and Comparative Law* 17 (3): 230–51.

Kochenov, Dimitry. 2011. "Double Nationality in the EU: An Argument for Tolerance." *European Law Journal* 17 (3): 323–43.

Kochenov, Dimitry. 2017a. "EU Citizenship and Withdrawals from the Union: How Inevitable Is the Radical Downgrading of Rights?" In *Secessions from a Member State and Withdrawals from the European Union: Troubled Membership*, edited by Carlos Closa, 257–86. Cambridge: CUP.

Kochenov, Dimitry. 2017b. "On Tiles and Pillars: EU Citizenship as a Federal Denominator." In *EU Citizenship and Federalism: The Role of Rights*, edited by Dimitry Kochenov, 1–66. Cambridge: CUP.

Kochenov, Dimitry. 2017c. "The Citizenship of Personal Circumstances in Europe." In *Questioning EU Citizenship: Judges and the Limits of Free Movement and Solidarity in the EU*, edited by Daniel Thym, 37–56. Oxford/Portland, OR: Hart Publishing.

Kochenov, Dimitry. 2019a. "Interlegality – Citizenship – Intercitizenship." In *The Challenge of Interlegality*, edited by Gianluigi Palombella and Jan Klabbers, Cambridge: CUP.

Kochenov, Dimitry. 2019b. *Citizenship*. Cambridge MA: MIT Press.

Kochenov, Dimitry. 2019c. "Investor Citizenship and Residence: The EU Commission's Incompetent Case for Blood and Soil." *Verfassungsblog*, January 23, 2019. https://verfassungsblog.de/investor-citizenship-and-residence-the-eu-commissions-incompetent-case-for-blood-and-soil/.

Kochenov, Dimitry, and Martijn van den Brink. 2015. "Pretending There is No Union: Non-Derivative *Quasi*-Citizenship Rights of Third-Country Nationals in the EU." In *Rights of Third-Country Nationals under EU Association Agreements: Degrees of Free Movement and Citizenship*, edited by Daniel Thym and Margarite Zoetewij-Turhan, 65–100. The Hague: Brill-Nijhoff.

Kochenov, Dimitry, and Aleksejs Dimitrovs. 2016. "EU Citizenship for Latvian 'Non-Citizens': A Concrete Proposal." *Houston Journal of International Law* 38 (1): 55–97.

Kochenov, Dimitry, and Justin Lindeboom. 2017. "Empirical Assessment of the Quality of Nationalities." *European Journal of Comparative Law and Governance* 4 (4): 314–36.

Kochenov, Dimitry, and Justin Lindeboom. 2018. "Pluralism through Its Denial: The Success of EU Citizenship." In *Research Handbook on Legal Pluralism and EU Law*, edited by Gareth Davies and Matej Avbelj, 179–98. Cheltenham/Northampton, MA: Edward Elgar.

Korzeniewicz, Roberto P., and Timothy P. Moran. 2009. *Unveiling Inequality: A World-Historical Perspective*. New York: Russell Sage Foundation.

Kostakopoulou, Dora. 2018. "*Scala Civium*: Citizenship Templates Post-Brexit and the European Union's Duty to Protect EU Citizens." *Journal of Common Market Studies* 56 (4): 854–69.

Krasniqi, Gëzim. 2013. "Overlapping Jurisdictions, Disputed Territory, Unsettled State: The Perplexing Case of Citizenship in Kosovo." In *Citizenship after Yugoslavia*, edited by Jo Shaw and Igor Štiks, 353–66. London/New York: Routledge.

Krasniqi, Gëzim. 2015. "Country Report on Citizenship Law: Kosovo." *EUDO Citizenship Observatory* 2015/3.

Krensel, Andreas. 2017. *The Corporate Immigration Guide to Africa*. 2nd ed. Cape Town: IBN Business and Immigration Solutions.

Kroft, Steve. 2017. "Passports for Sale." *CBS News*, January 1, 2017. https://www.cbsnews.com/news/60-minutes-citizenship-passport-international-industry.

Krūma, Kristīne. 2013. *EU Citizenship, Nationality and Migrant Status: An Ongoing Challenge*. Leiden/Boston: Brill-Nijhoff.

Krūma, Kristīne. 2015. "Country Report: Latvia – Revised and Updated January 2015." *EUDO Citizenship Observatory* RSCAS 2015/6.

Kuisma, Mikko. 2007. "Nordic Models of Citizenship: Lessons from Social History for Theorising Policy Change in the 'Age of Globalisation'." *New Political Economy* 12 (1): 87–95.

Kvarchelia, Liana. 2014. *Abkhazia: Issues of Citizenship and Security*. Sukhum: Centre for Humanitarian Programmes.

Kymlicka, Will. 1995. *Multicultural Citizenship: A Liberal Theory of Minority Rights*. Oxford: Clarendon Press.

Lagarde, Paul. 2004. "Note sur les modifications du droit de la nationalité contenues dans la loi du 26 novembre 2003." *Revue critique de droit international privé* 2.

Lakner, Christoph, and Branko Milanovic. 2013. "Global Income Distribution: From the Fall of the Berlin Wall to the Great Recession." *Policy Research Working Paper* No. 6719, World Bank.

Lancaster, Alana, and Jill St. George. 2015. "The Organisation of Eastern Caribbean States." In *Latin American and Caribbean International Institutional Law*, edited by Marco Odello and Francesco Seatzu, 231–50.

Langbein, Julia. 2016. "(Dis-)integrating Ukraine? Domestic oligarchs, Russia, the EU, and the politics of economic integration." *Eurasian Geography and Economics* 57 (1): 19–42.

Langevin, Louise, and Marie-Claire Belleau. 2000. *Trafficking in Women in Canada*. Government of Canada.

Lataste, René. 2015. "Wallis et Futuna: le royaume de Sigave menace de demander son indépendance." *Franceinfo 1*, September 30, 2015. https://la1ere.francetvinfo.fr/wallisfutuna/2015/09/30/wallis-et-futuna-le-royaume-de-sigave-menace-de-demander-son-independance-291325.html.

Leblic, Isabelle. 2003. "Présentation: Nouvelle-Calédonie, 150 ans après la prise de possession." *Journal de la Société des Océanistes* (117): 135–45.

Le Parisien. 2016."Qui sont les derniers déchus de la nationalité française?" http://www.leparisien.fr/espace-premium/actu/qui-sont-les-derniers-dechus-de-la-nationalite-francaise-06-01-2016-5426243.php.

Lepoutre, Jules. 2015. "La déchéance de la nationalité, un outil pertinent?" *Esprit* 5 (May): 118–20.

Lepoutre, Jules. 2016. "L'article 23-7 du code civil: un dispositif de sanction de l'indignité ou de la déloyauté. Notes de recherche." *Le Blog de Patrick Weil*, February 22, 2016. http://weil.blog.lemonde.fr/2016/02/22/larticle-23-7-du-code-civil-un-dispositif-de-sanction-de-lindignite-ou-de-la-deloyaute/.

Leslie, Helen, and Gerard Prinsen. 2018. "French territories in the Forum: Trojan horses or paddles for the Pacific canoe?" *Asia Pacific Viewpoint* 59 (3): 384–90.

Levada. 2018a. "Gorizont planirovaniya budushhego." https://www.levada.ru/2018/11/08/gorizont-planirovaniya-budushhego/.

Levada. 2018b. "Pol'zovanie internetom." https://www.levada.ru/2018/11/13/polzovanie-internetom-2/.

Ley, David. 2003. "Seeking *Homo Economicus*." *Annals of the Association of American Geographers* 93 (2): 426–41.

Loda, Chiara. 2019. "Georgia, the European Union, and the Visa-Free Travel Regime: Between European Identity and Strategic Pragmatism." *Nationalities Papers* 47 (1): 72–86.

Makaryan, Shushanik, and Haykanush Chobanyan. 2014. "Institutionalization of Migration Policy Frameworks in Armenia, Azerbaijan and Georgia." *International Migration* 52 (5): 52–67.

Manby, Bronwen. 2016. *Citizenship Law in Africa. A Comparative Study*. 3rd ed. Open Society Foundation.

Mantu, Sandra. 2015. *Contingent Citizenship: The Law and Practice of Citizenship Deprivation in International, European and National Perspectives*. Leiden/Boston: Brill-Nijhoff.

Manyin, Mark E., Stephen Daggett, Ben Dolven, Susan V. Lawrence, Michael F. Martin, Ronald O'Rourke, and Bruce Vaughn. 2012. *Pivot to the Pacific? The Obama administration's rebalancing toward Asia*. Washington D.C.: Library of Congress Congressional Research Service. http://www.dtic.mil/get-tr-doc/pdf?AD=ADA584466.

Marambio, Helena-Ulrike. 2016. "Lack of data as an obstacle to addressing statelessness in the context of the refugee crisis in Germany." *ENS Blog*, October 19, 2016. https://www.statelessness.eu/blog/lack-data-obstacle-addressing-statelessness-context-refugee-crisis-germany.

Marek, Krystyna. 1954. *Identity and Continuity of States in Public International Law*. Geneva: Librairie Droz.

Maresceau, Marc. 2011a. "EU–Switzerland: *Quo Vadis*?" *Georgia Journal of International and Comparative Law* 39 (3): 727–55.

Maresceau, Marc. 2011b. "Very Small States and the European Union: The Case of Liechtenstein." In *A Constitutional Order of States? Essays in EU Law in Honour of Alan Dashwood*, edited by Anthony Arnull, Catherine Barnard, Michael Dougan, and Eleanor Spaventa, 500–27. Oxford: Hart.

Marques, Nicole Terese Capton. 2011. "Divided We Stand: The Haudenosaunee, Their Passport and Legal Implications of Their Recognition in Canada and the United States." *San Diego International Law Journal* 13 (1): 383–425.

Marshall, T.H. 1977. (1950). *lass, Citizenship, and Social Development: Essays*. Chicago: University of Chicago Press.

Martin, David A. 1999. "New Rules on Dual Nationality for a Democratizing Globe: Between Rejection and Embrace." *Georgetown Immigration Law Journal* 14 (1): 1–34.

Mateo, Juan José. 2018. "El Gobierno amplía hasta 2019 el plazo para que los sefardíes obtengan la nacionalidad." *El País*, March 5, 2018. https://elpais.com/politica/2018/03/05/actualidad/1520265130_351979.html.

Mateos, Pablo. 2017. "Aquí empieza la patria? Pliegues de la nación y doble nacionalidad en la frontera México–Estados Unidos." In *Migración internacional, interna y en tránsito: Actores y procesos: Nuevos procesos en la migración internacional y mercados de trabajo*, edited by Magdalena Barros and Agustín Escobar Latapí, 50–78. Mexico City: CIESAS.

Mateos, Pablo. 2018. "The Mestizo Nation Unbound: Dual Citizenship of Euro-Mexicans and U.S.-Mexicans." *Journal of Ethnic and Migration Studies*: 1–22.

Mau, Steffen, Fabian Gulzau, Lene Laube, and Natascha Zaun. 2015. "The Global Mobility Divide: How Visa Policies Have Evolved over Time." *Journal of Ethnic and Migration Studies* 41 (8): 1192–213.

McDonald, Caroline. "Decolonisation and Free Association: The Relationships of the Cook Islands and Niue with New Zealand." PhD diss., Victoria University of Wellington, 2018.

McElroy, Jerome L., and Courtney E. Parry. 2012. "The Long-Term Propensity for Political Affiliation in Island Microstates." *Commonwealth & Comparative Politics* 50 (4): 403–21.

McLean, Lorna. 2004. "To Become Part of Us": Ethnicity, 'race,' literacy and the Canadian Immigration Act of 1919." *Canadian Ethnic Studies/Études ethniques au Canada* XXXVI(1), 1-28.

Medved, Felicita. 2012. "Country Report: Slovenia." *EUDO Citizenship Observatory* 2012/24.

Melnykovska, Inna, Rainer Schweickert, and Tetiana Kostiuchenko. 2011. "Balancing National Uncertainty and Foreign Orientation: Identity Building and the Role of Political Parties in Post-Orange Ukraine." *Europe-Asia Studies* 63 (6): 1055–72.

Meyer, John W., John Boli, George Thomas, and Francisco O. Ramirez. 1997. "World Society and the Nation-State." *American Journal of Sociology* 103 (1): 144–81.

Milanovic, Branko. 2016. *Global Inequality: A New Approach for the Age of Globalization*. Cambridge, MA: Belknap Press of Harvard University.

Milloy, John S. 1999. *A National Crime*. Winnipeg: University of Manitoba Press.

Ministry of Immigration and Population (Myanmar). 2002. "Government & Policy." http://www.modins.net/myanmarinfo/ministry/population.htm.

Morrison, Sean. 2013. "Foreign in a Domestic Sense: American Samoa and the Last US Nationals." *Hastings Constitutional Law Quarterly* 41 (1): 1–150.

Moshes, Arkady, and Andras Racz. 2019. *What Has Remained of the USSR: Exploring the Erosion of the Post-Soviet Space*. FIIA Report 58.

Moya, Jose. 1998. *Cousins and Strangers. Spanish Immigrants in Buenos Aires 1850–1930*. Berkeley and Los Angeles: University of California Press.

Mulalap, Clement. 2016. "Federated States of Micronesia." *The Contemporary Pacific* 28 (1): 172–84.

Munshi, Sherally. 2017. "Immigration, Imperialism, and the Legacies of Indian Exclusion." *Yale Journal of Law & the Humanities* 28 (1): 51–104.

Myanmar Ministry of Labour, United Nations Population Fund. 2014. "Myanmar Housing and Population Census." http://themimu.info/sites/themimu.info/files/documents/Census_Atlas_Myanmar_the_2014_Myanmar_Population_and_Housing_Census.pdf.

Myint-U, Thant. 2001. *The Making of Modern Burma*. Cambridge: CUP.

National Ombudsman of the Netherlands. 2016. *Rapport verlies Nederlanderschap: "En Toen was ik Mijn Nederlanderschap kwijt..."* Report No. 2016/446. https://www.nationaleombudsman.nl/system/files/onderzoek/Rapport%20Verlies%20Nederlanderschap_0.pdf.

New Zealand Parliament Foreign Affairs Defence and Trade Committee. 2010. *Inquiry into New Zealand's Relationships with South Pacific Countries*. https://www.parliament.nz/resource/0000140225.

Niboyet, Jean-Paulin. 1938. *Traité de droit international privé français*. Paris: Recueil Sirey.

Niles, Chavon. 2018. "Who Gets In? The Price of Acceptance in Canada." *Journal of Critical Thought and Praxis* 7 (1): 148–62.

Nizhnikaŭ, Ryhor. 2018. *EU Induced Institutional Change in Post-Soviet Space: Promoting Reforms in Moldova and Ukraine*. Abingdon-on-Thames: Routledge.

Norwegian Refugee Council, United Nations Refugee Agency, United Nations Women, Institute on Statelessness and Inclusion, Statelessness Network Asia Pacific, The Seagull. 2018. "A Gender Analysis of the Right to a Nationality in Myanmar." https://www.nrc.no/globalassets/pdf/reports/myanmar/cedaw-report-web-7-march-2018.pdf.

Novoe Vremya. 2018. "V Polshe rabotaet bolee 2 millionov ukraincev." https://nv.ua/ukraine/events/v-polshe-rabotajut-bolee-2-mln-ukraintsev-kak-etot-potok-mihrantov-povlijal-na-obe-strany-2511040.html.

Nyi Kyaw, Nyi. 2017. "Unpacking the Presumed Statelessness of Rohingyas." *Journal of Immigrant & Refugee Studies* 15 (3): 269–86.

O'Brien, Charlotte. 2017. "Union Citizenship and Disability: Restricted Access to Equality Rights and the Attitudinal Model of Disability." In *EU Citizenship and Federalism: The Role of Rights*, edited by Dimitry Kochenov, 509–39. Cambridge: CUP.

Office for Citizenship and Migration Affairs (Latvia). 2019. "Latvija siedzīvotāju sadalījums pēc valstiskās piederības." https://www.pmlp.gov.lv/lv/assets/backup/ISVP_Latvija_pec_VPD.pdf.

O'Leary, Síofra. 1996. *The Evolving Concept of Community Citizenship: From the Free Movement of Persons to Union Citizenship*. The Hague: Kluwer Law International.

Osborne, Michael J. 1983. *Naturalization in Athens: The Testimonia for Grants of Citizenship*. Brussels: AWLSK.

Oskanian, Kevork. 2016. "The Balance Strikes Back: Power, Perceptions, and Ideology in Georgian Foreign Policy, 1992–2014." *Foreign Policy Analysis* 12 (4): 628–52.

Overton, John, Warwick E. Murray, Gerard Prinsen, Tagaloa Avataeao Junior Ulu, and Nicola Wrighton. 2018. *Aid, Ownership and Development. The Inverse Sovereignty Effect in the Pacific Islands*. Abingdon: Routledge.

Palandt, Otto. 2012. *Bürgerliches Gesetzbuch*, 71st ed. Munich: Beck.

van Panhuys. H. F. 1959. *The Role of Nationality in International Law: An Outline*. Leiden: A.W. Sijthoff.

Paskalev, Vesco. 2018. "Free Movement Emancipates, but What Freedom Is This?" In *Debating European Citizenship*, edited by Rainer Bauböck, 117–120. Cham: Springer.

Perham, Elisabeth. 2011. "Citizenship Laws in the Realm of New Zealand." *New Zealand Yearbook of International Law* 9: 219–40.

Peters, Anne. 2010. "Extraterritorial Naturalizations: Between the Human Right to Nationality, State Sovereignty, and Fair Principles of Jurisdiction." *German Yearbook of International Law* 53: 623–725.

Pew Research Center. 2011. "The American–Western European Values Gap: Survey Report." Pew Research Center. Last modified February 29, 2012. http://www.pewglobal.org/2011/11/17/the-american-western-european-values-gap/.

Pew Research Center. 2012. "Most Muslims Want Democracy, Personal Freedoms, and Islam in Political Life." Pew Research Center, July 10, 2012. http://www.pewglobal.org/2012/07/10/most-muslims-want-democracy-personal-freedoms-and-islam-in-political-life/.

Prinsen, Gerard, and Séverine Blaise. 2017. "An Emerging 'Islandian' Sovereignty of Non-Self-Governing Islands." *International Journal* 72 (1): 56–78.

Radio New Zealand. 2015. "French Polynesia gets land court." *RNZ Pacific*, January 14, 2015. https://www.radionz.co.nz/international/pacific-news/263668/french-polynesia-gets-land-court.

Ragazzi, Francesco, Igor Štiks, and Viktor Koska. 2013. "Country Report: Croatia." *EUDO Citizenship Observatory* 2013/12.

Rakotoarison, Sylvain. 2010. "L'intégralité du discours de Nicolas Sarkozy le 30 juillet 2010 à Grenoble." http://rakotoarison.over-blog.com/article-doc-54866609.html.

Rava, Nenad. 2013. "Country Report: Serbia." *EUDO Citizenship Observatory* 2013/9.

Reding, Viviane. 2014. "Citizenship must not be up for sale." Speech by Viviane Reding. *European Commission, Plenary Session Debate of the European Parliament on 'EU Citizenship for Sale'*, Strasbourg, January 15, 2014.

Reicher, Stephen, Clare Cassidy, Ingrid Wolpert, Nick Hopkins, and Mark Levine. 2006. "Saving Bulgaria's Jews: An Analysis of Social Identity and the Mobilisation of Social Solidarity." *European Journal of Social Psychology* 36 (1): 49–72.

RIA Novosti. 2018. "Lukashenko poruchil uregulirovat' protivorechiia s Rossiey." https://ria.ru/world/20180111/1512418739.html.

Risse, Thomas. 2010. *A Community of Europeans? Transnational Identities and Public Spheres*. Ithaca: Cornell University Press.

Rodrik, Dani. 2014. "The Past, Present, and Future of Economic Growth." *Challenge* 57 (3): 5–39.

Ruiz Parra, Catalina. 2018. "Chile modifica requisitos para la visa de residencia temporal a los venezolanos." *El Nuevo Herald*, June 9, 2018. https://www.elnuevoherald.com/noticias/mundo/america-latina/venezuela-es/article212877824.html.

Rundle, Kristen. 2009. "The Impossibility of an Exterminatory Legality." *University of Toronto Law Journal* 59 (1): 65–125.

Sahgal, Neha. 2018. "Religion in Western Europe: 10 Key Insights." World Economic Forum, May 31, 2018. https://www.weforum.org/agenda/2018/05/10-key-findings-about-religion-in-western-europe.

Sahia Cherchari, Mohamed. 2004. "Indigènes et citoyens ou l'impossible universalisation du suffrage." *Revue française de droit constitutionnel* 4. (60): 741–70.

Sandel, Michael J. 2010. *Justice: What's the Right Thing to Do?* London: Penguin Books.

Sarajlić, Eldar. 2013. "Country Report: Bosnia and Herzegovina." *EUDO Citizenship Observatory* 2013/7.

Schengenvisainfo.com. 2018. "Georgia's Visa Liberalization with European Union Comes Under Threat." https://www.schengenvisainfo.com/news/georgias-visa-liberalization-with-european-union-comes-under-threat/.

Schiek, Dagmar. 2017. "Perspectives on Social Citizenship in the EU: From *Status Positivus* to *Status Socialis Activus* via Two Forms of Transnational Solidarity." In *EU Citizenship and Federalism: The Role of Rights*, edited by Dimitry Kochenov, 341–70. Cambridge: CUP.

Schneider, Dorothee. 2000. "Symbolic Citizenship, Nationalism and the Distant State: The United States Congress in the 1996 Debate on Immigration Reform." *Citizenship Studies* 4 (3): 255–73.

Secretaría de Relaciones Exteriores (Mexico). 2009. *Reforma constitucional sobre la no pérdida de la nacionalidad mexicana*. Mexico DF. Secretaría de Relaciones Exteriores, SRE.

Secretary-General of the Pacific Islands Forum. 2018. "Statement by Pacific Islands Forum to the APEC Ministers Responsible for Trade Meeting." Delivered May 26, 2018. Suva, Fiji. https://www.forumsec.org/statement-by-pacific-islands-forum-to-the-apec-ministers-responsible-for-trade-meeting/.

Selee, Andrew. 2018. "How Guadalajara Reinvented Itself as a Technology Hub." *Smithsonian.com*, June 12, 2018. https://www.smithsonianmag.com/innovation/how-guadalajara-reinvented-itself-technology-hub-180969314/.

Selee, Andrew, Jessica Bolter, Betilde Muñoz-Pogossian, and Miryam Hazán. 2019. *Creativity amidst Crisis. Legal Pathways for Venezuelan Migrants in Latin America*. Washington: Migration Policy Institute.

Serrano, Silvia. 2007. *Géorgie: Sortie d'Empire*. Paris: CNRS Éditions.

Shachar, Ayelet. 2009. *The Birthright Lottery: Citizenship and Global Inequality*. Cambridge, MA: HUP.

Shachar, Ayelet. 2013. "Citizenship and Global Distribution of Opportunity." In *Citizenship Between Past and Future*, edited by Engin F. Isin, Peter Nyers, and Bryan S. Turner, 139–49. Abingdon: Routledge.

Shachar, Ayelet. 2018. "The Marketization of Citizenship in an Age of Restrictionism." *Ethics & International Affairs* 32 (1): 3–13.

Shamir, Ronen. 2005. "Without Borders? Notes on Globalization as a Mobility Regime." *Sociological Theory* 23 (2): 197–217.

Shaw, Jo. 2007. *The Transformation of Citizenship in the European Union: Electoral Rights and the Restructuring of Political Space.* Cambridge: CUP.

Shaw, Jo. 2008. "The Political Representation of Europe's Citizens: Developments." *European Constitutional Law Review* 4, no. 1: 162–86.

Sironi, Alice. 2014. "Nationality of Individuals in Public International Law: A Functional Approach." In *The Changing Role of Nationality in International Law*, edited by Alessandra Annoni and Serena Forlati, 54–75. London: Routledge.

Skwiriwski, Piotr. 2018. "Zły sen polskich pracodawców. Widmo odpływu Ukraińców." *Rzeczpospolita*. https://www.rp.pl/Biznes/310289935-Zly-sen-polskich-pracodawcow-Widmo-odplywu-Ukraincow.html.

Sloane, Robert D. 2009. "Breaking the Genuine Link: The Contemporary International Legal Regulation of Nationality." *Harvard International Law Journal* 50 (1): 1–60.

Smith-Spark, Laura. 2018. "EU Parliament Urges Visas for US Citizens Visiting Europe." *CNN*, June 20, 2018. https://edition.cnn.com/2017/03/03/europe/eu-america-visa-trnd/index.html.

Snyder, David, and Edward L. Kick. 1979. "Structural Position in the World System and Economic Growth, 1955–1970: A Multiple-Network Analysis of Transnational Interactions." *American Journal of Sociology* 84 (5): 1096–126.

Spaskovska, Ljubica. 2012. "Country Report: Macedonia." *EUDO Citizenship Observatory* 2012/06.

Spinks, Harriet, and Michael Klapdor. 2016. "New Zealanders in Australia: A Quick Guide." *Research Papers Series 2016–17*. Canberra: Parliamentary Library.

Spire, Alexis. 2005. *Étrangers à la carte: l'administration de l'immigration en France (1945–1975)*. Paris: Grasset.

Spiro, Peter J. 1997. "Dual Nationality and the Meaning of Citizenship." *Emory Law Journal* 46 (4): 1411–86.

Spiro, Peter J. 2010. "Dual Citizenship as Human Right." *International Journal of Constitutional Law* 8 (1): 111–30.

Spiro, Peter J. 2011. "A New International Law of Citizenship." *American Journal of International Law* 105 (4): 694–746.

Spiro, Peter J. 2016. *At Home in Two Countries: The Past and Future of Dual Citizenship*. New York: New York University Press.

Spiro, Peter J. 2019a. *Citizenship: All You Need to Know*. Oxford: OUP.

Spiro, Peter J. 2019b. "*Nottebohm* and 'Genuine Link': Anatomy of a Jurisprudential Illusion." *IMC Research Paper* 2019/1: 1–23. www.investmentmigration.org/academic.

Štiks, Igor. 2010. "A Laboratory of Citizenship: Shifting Conceptions of Citizenship in Yugoslavia and its Successor States." *CITSEE Working Paper Series* 2010/02.

Štiks, Igor. 2015. *Nations and Citizens in Yugoslavia and the Post-Yugoslav States: One Hundred Years of Citizenship*. London/New York: Bloomsbury.

Stora, Benjamin. 1992. *Ils venaient d'Algérie. L'immigration algérienne en France 1912–1992*. Paris: Fayard.

Sumption, Madeleine, and Kate Hooper. 2014. *Selling Visas and Citizenship: Policy Questions from the Global Boom in Investor Immigration*. Washington, D.C.: Migration Policy Institute.

Surak, Kristin. 2016. "Global Citizenship 2.0 – The Growth of Citizenship by Investment Programs." *IMC Research Paper* No. 2016/03: 1–44. www.investmentmigration.org/academic.

Swider, Katja. 2017. "Why End Statelessness?" In *Understanding Statelessness*, edited by Tendayi Bloom, Katherine Tonkiss, and Phillip Cole, London: Routledge.

Swider, Katja. "A Rights-Based Approach to Statelessness." PhD diss., University of Amsterdam, 2018.

Tintori, Guido. 2012. "More Than One Million Individuals Got Italian Citizenship Abroad in Twelve Years (1998–2010)". *EUDO Citizenship Observatory*, November 21, 2012. https://www.academia.edu/2517536/More_than_one_million_individuals_got_Italian_citizenship_abroad_in_twelve_years_1998-2010_.

Tomlinson, B.R. 2003. "What Was the Third World?" *Journal of Contemporary History* 38 (2): 307–21.

Torbakov, Igor. 2013. "The European Union, Russia and the "In-between' Europe: Managing Interdependence." In *The European Union Neighbourhood*, edited by Teresa Cierco, 173–91. Farnham: Ashgate.

Torpey, John. 2010. *The Invention of the Passport. Surveillance, Citizenship and the State*. Cambridge: CUP.

Trauner, Florian, and Imke Kruse. 2008. "EC Visa Facilitation and Readmission Agreements: Implementing a New EU Security Approach in the Neighbourhood." CEPS Working Document No. 290.

Triadafilopoulos, Triadafilos. 2013. "Dismantling White Canada." In *Wanted and Welcome?*, edited by Triadafilos Triadafilopoulos, 15–37. New York: Springer.

Troper, Harold. 1993. "Canada's Immigration Policy Since 1945." *International Journal* 48 (2): 255–81.

Türk, Volker. 2014. "Foreword." In *Handbook on the Protection of Stateless Persons*, 1–3. UNHCR: Geneva.

UN Ad Hoc Committee on Refugees and Stateless Persons, A Study of Statelessness (August 1949) UN Doc E/1112; E/1112/Add.1.

UN Commissioner for Refugees (UNHCR). n.d. "Population Statistics. Persons of Concern." Accessed March 1, 2019. http://popstats.unhcr.org./en/persons_of_concern.

UN Committee on the Elimination of Racial Discrimination. 2018. *Concluding Observations on the Combined Sixth to Twelfth Periodic Reports of Latvia*. UN Doc. CERD/C/LVA/CO/6-12.

UN Committee on the Rights of the Child. 2016. *Concluding Observations on the Third to Fifth Periodic Reports of Latvia*. UN Doc. CRC/C/LVA/CO/3-5.

UN Development Programme: Human Development Reports. n.d. "Human Development Reports." Accessed February 22, 2019. http://hdr.undp.org.

UN High Commissioner for Refugees (UNHCR). 1948. Report of the Second Session of the Commission on Human Rights. UN Doc. E/RES/116(VI).

UN High Commissioner for Refugees (UNHCR). 2010. "Compilation Report – Universal Periodic Review: Latvia, Submission for the Office of the High Commissioner for Human Rights." Last modified November 2010. https://lib.ohchr.org/HRBodies/UPR/Documents/session11/LV/UNHCR_UNHighCommissionerforRefugees-eng.pdf.

UN High Commissioner for Refugees (UNHCR). 2014a. *Handbook on the Protection of Stateless Persons*. UNHCR: Geneva.

UN High Commissioner for Refugees (UNHCR). 2014b. *Global Action Plan to End Statelessness 2014–2024*. UNHCR: Geneva.

US Census Bureau. 2015. "Current Population Survey (CPS)." http://www.census.gov/programs-surveys/cps.html.

US Department of State. 2012. "The Continued Free Association with the Republic of Palau Act of 2012. Testimony Before the House Committee on Natural Resources Subcommittee on Fisheries, Wildlife, Oceans, and Insular Affairs." https://2009-2017.state.gov/p/eap/rls/rm/2012/09/197539.htm.

Utkin, Sergey. 2017. "The Russian-Georgian Visa Paradox: A Long Path to Normal." In *Georgia and Russia: In Search of Ways for Normalisation*, Project Director Kakha Gogolashvili, 12–16. Tbilisi: GFSIS.

Vink, Maarten, Hans Schmeets, and Hester Mennes. 2019. "Double Standards: Attitudes Towards Immigrant and Emigrant Dual Citizenship in the Netherlands." *Ethnic and Racial Studies* 42 (16): 83–101.

Visek, Richard C. 1997. "Creating the Ethnic Electorate Through Legal Restorationism: Citizenship Rights in Estonia." *Harvard International Law Journal* 38 (2): 315–373.

Vonk, Olivier. 2014. *Nationality Law in the Western Hemisphere. A Study on Grounds for Acquisition and Loss of Citizenship in the Americas and the Caribbean*. Leiden/Boston: Brill-Nijhoff.

Vonk, Olivier, Maarten Vink, and Gerard-René de Groot. 2013. "Protection against Statelessness: Trends and Regulations in Europe." EUDO-Citizenship Comparative Report 2013/01. Badia Fiesolana: European University Institute.

Voronia, N.A. 2013. "Sojuznoje gosudarstvo Rossija – Belarus': opyt pravovogo regulirovanija." *NB: Mezhdunarodnoje parvo* 3: 52.

van Waas, Laura. 2008. *Nationality Matters. Statelessness under International Law*. Antwerp: Intersentia. Vigni, Patrizia. 2017. "The Right of EU Citizens to Diplomatic and Consular Protection: A Step Towards Recognition of EU Citizenship in Third Countries?" In *EU Citizenship and Federalism: The Role of Rights*, edited by Dimitry Kochenov, 584–612. Cambridge: CUP.

van der Wal, Gerald, and Jilles Heringa. 2005. "Excellentie, er zijn geen Antillianen." *Migrantenrecht* 19 (7): 216–25.

Wallerstein, Immanuel. 1974. *The Modern World-System: Capitalist Agriculture and the Origins of the European World-Economy in the Sixteenth Century*. New York: Academic Press, Inc.

Ward, Peter. 2002. *White Canada Forever*. Montreal & Kingston: McGill-Queen's University Press.

Weil, Patrick. 2012. *The Sovereign Citizen: Denaturalization and the Origins of the American Republic*. Philadelphia PA: University of Pennsylvania Press.

Willsher, Kim. 2016. "Hollande Drops Plan to Revoke Citizenship of Dual-National terrorists." *The Guardian*, March 30, 2016. https://www.theguardian.com/world/2016/mar/30/francois-hollande-drops-plan-to-revoke-citizenship-of-dual-national-terrorists.

Win, Ne. 1982. "Presentation of the Citizenship Law." Speech of October 8, 1982, Myanmar. https://www.scribd.com/document/162589794/Ne-Win-s-Speech-1982-Citizenship-Law.

Wolf-Phillips, Leslie. 1987. "Why 'Third World'?: Origin, Definition and Usage." *Third World Quarterly* 9 (4): 1311–27.

Wood, John R. 1978. "East Indians and Canada's New Immigration Policy." *Canadian Public Policy* 4 (4): 547–67.

Woodcock, George. 1989. *A Social History of Canada*. Markham: Viking.

World Bank. n.d.a. "GINI Index." Accessed March 5, 2019. https://data.worldbank.org/indicator/SI.POV.GINI?end=2017&start=1979.

World Bank. n.d.b. "World Bank Country and Lending Groups." Accessed February 22, 2019. https://datahelpdesk.worldbank.org/knowledgebase/articles/906519.

World Bank. n.d.c. "How Does the World Bank Classify Countries?" Accessed February 22, 2019. https://datahelpdesk.worldbank.org/knowledgebase/articles/378834-how-does-the-world-bank-classify-countries.

World Economic Forum. 2017. "The Travel & Tourism Competitiveness Report 2017." https://bit.ly/2oEuKeL.

Worldmapper. n.d. Accessed April 3, 2019. https://worldmapper.org.

Worster, William T. 2018. "Brexit and the International Law Prohibitions on the Loss of EU Citizenship." *International Organizations Law Review* 15 (2): 341–63.

York, Geoffrey, and Michelle Zilio. 2018. "Access Denied: Canada's Refusal Rate for Visitor Visas Soars." *Globe & Mail*, July 8, 2018. https://www.theglobeandmail.com/world/article-access-denied-canadas-refusal-rate-for-visitor-visas-soars/.

Zaw Soe, Min. 2006. "Emergence of the DoBamar Asiayone and the Thakins in the Myanmar Nationalist Movement." *Journal of Humanities and Social Sciences* 27 (3): 103–21.

Ziemele, Ineta. 2005. *State Continuity and Nationality: The Baltic States and Russia – Past, Present and Future as Defined by International Law*. Leiden: Martinus Nijhoff Publishers.

Zincone, Giovanna and Marzia Basili. 2009. "Country Report: Italy." *EUI EUDO Citizenship Observatory RSCAS Paper*.

Methodological Annex

Human Development

Standard Formula

$$\text{Normalized Human Development} = \frac{\text{(HDI score of country granting nationality [X])}}{\text{(HDI score of highest scoring country, the nationality of which is also included in the QNI)}} \times 15$$

Primary Source

- United Nations Human Development Index http://hdr.undp.org/en/data

Deviations

Destination	HDI Last Available Data	Source (Countries Not Calculated by UN)
Chinese Taipei (Taiwan)	2015	Taiwan government database calculated according to same method as UNDP
Korea (DPRK)	2008	David A. Hastings, "Filling Gaps in the Human Development Index: Findings for Asia and the Pacific" (UNESCAP Working Paper, 2009) https://web.archive.org/web/20111005100501/http://www.unescap.org/pdd/publications/workingpaper/wp_09_02.pdf
Isle of Man	2008	Hastings, "Filling Gaps in the HDI"
Kosovo	2016	Kosovo Human Development Report 2016 http://www.ks.undp.org/content/kosovo/en/home/library/poverty/kosovo-human-development-report-2016.html
Macao	2015	Government of Macao (published 2017) http://www.dsec.gov.mo/Statistic.aspx?lang=en-US&NodeGuid=ba1a4eab-213a-48a3-8fbb-962d15dc6f87
Monaco	2017	Given score of Norway
San Marino	2017	Given score of Italy
Nauru	2008	Hastings, "Filling Gaps in the HDI"
Palau	2015	UNDP HDI 2015
Somalia	2012, 2008	0.285: UNDP, Somalia Human Development Report 2012
Tuvalu	2008	Hastings, "Filling Gaps in the HDI"
Jersey	2008	Hastings, "Filling Gaps in the HDI"
Guernsey	2008	Hastings, "Filling Gaps in the HDI"
Aruba, Curaçao, Sint Maarten, Dutch municipalities overseas (Bonaire, Saba, Sint Eustatius)	2008	Hastings, "Filling Gaps in the HDI"

Economic Strength

Standard Formula

$$\text{Normalized Economic Strength value of nationality [X]} = \frac{\text{(GDP(PPP) – NRR of nationality [X])}}{\text{(GDP(PPP) – NRR of nationality of the country with highest (GDP(PPP) – NRR))}} \times 15$$

With

$$\text{GDP(PPP) – NRR of nationality [X]} = \frac{\text{GDP(PPP) of country granting nationality [X] – ((NRR of country granting nationality [X] × GDP(PPP) of country granting nationality [X])}}{100}$$

Primary Source
World Bank data for 2017 GDP figures, updated 28 June 2018.

Supplementary Sources
IMF estimates, *CIA World Factbook* estimates, UN Data, previous year's WB GDP PPP value.

Deviations from Main Source

Country	Last Available Data	Source	GDP PPP/Non-PPP Data
Andorra	2015	CIA World Factbook estimate*	2012 USD
Chinese Taipei (Taiwan)	2017	IMF estimate	PPP
Cuba	2016	CIA World Factbook estimate*	2016 USD
Djibouti	2017	IMF estimate	PPP
Eritrea	2017	IMF estimate	PPP
Korea (DPRK)	2008	CIA World Factbook estimate*	2015 USD
Isle of Man	2015	World Bank	Non-PPP in USD
Liechtenstein	2014	CIA World Factbook estimate*	PPP
Monaco	2015	CIA World Factbook estimate*	2015 USD
Somalia	2017	IMF estimate	PPP
South Sudan	2016	World Bank	PPP
Syrian Arab Republic	2014	CIA World Factbook estimate*	2015 USD
Venezuela	2017	IMF estimate	PPP
Yemen	2016	World Bank	PPP
Jersey	2015	CIA World Factbook estimate*	2015 USD
Guernsey	2015	CIA World Factbook estimate*	2015 USD

* Same as QNI 2018

Peace and Stability

Standard Formula

$$\text{Normalized Peace and Stability value of nationality [X]} = \frac{\text{(GPI score of highest scoring country on GPI, the nationality of which is also included in the QNI} - \text{Minimum GPI value)}}{\text{(GPI score of country granting nationality [X]} - \text{Minimum GPI value)}} \times 10$$

With Minimum GPI value = 5.000

Source

Institute for Economics and Peace's Global Peace Index

Deviations from Main Methodology

Andorra: Average of France and Spain
Antigua and Barbuda: Average for the region: Cuba, Dominican Republic, Haiti, Jamaica, and Trinidad and Tobago
Bahamas: Average for the region: Cuba, Dominican Republic, Haiti, Jamaica, and Trinidad and Tobago
Barbados: Average for the region: Cuba, Dominican Republic, Haiti, Jamaica, and Trinidad and Tobago
Belize: Average of Guatemala, Honduras, and Mexico (changed in 2017)
Brunei Darussalam: Average of Indonesia and Malaysia (changed in 2017)
Cape Verde: Average of Gambia, Guinea-Bissau, Mauritania, and Senegal (changed in 2017)
Commonwealth of Dominica: Average for the region: Cuba, Dominican Republic, Haiti, Jamaica, and Trinidad and Tobago
Comoros: Average of Madagascar, Mozambique, and Tanzania
Grenada: Average for the region: Cuba, Dominican Republic, Haiti, Jamaica, and Trinidad and Tobago
Guernsey: Given UK GPI
Isle of Man: Given UK GPI
Hong Kong, China (SAR): Value for China
Jersey: Given UK GPI
Liechtenstein: Average of Austria and Switzerland
Luxembourg: Average of Belgium, France, and Germany
Macao: Value for China
Maldives: Average of Mauritius and Sri Lanka (changed in 2017)
Malta: Value for Italy
Monaco: Value for France
Pacific Islands: Fiji, Kiribati, Marshall Islands, Micronesia, Nauru, Palau, Samoa, Solomon Islands, Tonga, Tuvalu, and Vanuatu: All given world average score of 2.103
Saint Kitts and Nevis: Average for the region: Cuba, Dominican Republic, Haiti, Jamaica, and Trinidad and Tobago
Saint Lucia: Average for the region: Cuba, Dominican Republic, Haiti, Jamaica, and Trinidad and Tobago
Saint Vincent and the Grenadines: Average for the region: Cuba, Dominican Republic, Haiti, Jamaica, and Trinidad and Tobago
San Marino: Value for Italy
São Tomé and Príncipe: Average of Equatorial Guinea and Gabon
Seychelles: Value for Mauritius (changed in 2017)
Suriname: Average of Brazil and Guyana (changed in 2017)

Diversity of Travel Freedom

Standard Formula

Normalized Diversity of Travel Freedom of nationality [X] = $\dfrac{\text{Diversity of Travel Freedom of nationality [X]}}{\text{Diversity of Travel Freedom of highest scoring nationality}}$ × 15

With

Diversity of Travel Freedom of nationality [X] = Number of countries that holders of nationality [X] can visit visa-free or by visa-on-arrival for tourist or business purposes

Weight of Travel Freedom

Standard Formula

Normalized Weight of Travel Freedom of nationality [X] = $\dfrac{\text{(Weight of Travel Freedom of nationality [X])}}{\text{(Weight of Travel Freedom of highest scoring nationality)}}$ × 15

With

Weight of Travel Freedom of nationality [X] = Sum of the destination values of the destinations that holders of nationality [X] can visit visa-free or by visa-on-arrival for tourist or business purposes

Destination Value for Weight of Travel Freedom

The weighed destination value of a travel destination is normalized on a 0–30 scale, comprising the normalized Human Development value (0.0–15.0) and the normalized Economic Strength value (0.0–15.0) of the respective territory. It is given by the following formula:

Weighted score of country [X] = Normalized (GDP(PPP) of country [X] − NRR of country [X]) + Normalized (HDI of country [X])

Diversity of Settlement Freedom

Standard Formula

Normalized Diversity of Settlement Freedom of nationality [X] = $\dfrac{\text{(Weight of Settlement Freedom of nationality [X])}}{\text{(Weight of Settlement Freedom of highest scoring nationality)}}$ × 15

With

Diversity of Settlement Freedom of nationality [X] = Number of countries to which holders of nationality [X] have full access

Weight of Settlement Freedom

Standard Formula

Normalized Weight of Settlement Freedom of nationality [X] = $\dfrac{\text{(Weight of Settlement Freedom of nationality [X])}}{\text{(Weight of Settlement Freedom of highest scoring nationality)}}$ × 15

With

With Weight of Settlement Freedom of nationality [X] = Sum of the destination values of all destinations to which holders of nationality [X] have full access

Destination Value for Weight of Settlement Freedom

The weighed destination value of a settlement destination is normalized on a 0–30 scale, comprising the normalized Human Development value (0.0–15.0) and the normalized Economic Strength value (0.0–15.0) of the respective territory. It is given by the following formula:

Weighted score of country [X] = Normalized (GDP(PPP) of country [X] − NRR of country [X]) + Normalized (HDI of country [X])

Minimum Destination Values for Travel Freedom and Settlement Freedom

The minimum weighed destination value for territories having independent immigration controls but not being included in the QNI is 10.99 on a 0–30 scale. It is calculated by taking the normalized value of the HDI world mean (0.0–15.0) and an infinitesimal economic Strength value (0.001):

$$\left(\dfrac{\text{Latest world mean HDI}}{\text{HDI of highest scoring country}} \times 15 \right) + 0.001$$

World mean HDI = 0.696 (excluding EU score)
Highest HDI value: 0.95 (Norway)

$$\left(\dfrac{0.696}{0.950} \times 15 \right) + 0.001 = 10.9904737$$

Glossary of Terms

Business Access
See Tourist and Business Access.

Camouflage Passport
A passport issued in the name of a non-existent country, which cannot therefore attest to the possession of any existing nationality. Camouflage passports are mostly used for false identification and/or criminal activities and are generally issued under the name of a country no longer in existence.

See also Fantasy Passport.

Cut-Off Date
The measurement time for the elements of the QNI of a particular year. This edition represents the status quo on 1 July 2018. Where up-to-date data as of 1 July is not available, the most recently available data is used.

Diversity of Settlement Freedom
The number of countries to which a nationality grants its adult holders full access. This means that the adult holder of a nationality is allowed to work without permission or by permission obtained virtually automatically.

The following aspects are not considered in determining whether someone has full access to another country:

- Entitlement to public pension systems
- Entitlement to healthcare
- Entitlement to social security benefits
- Specific skill qualifications required to perform certain professions, particularly of a qualitative nature, for example bar qualifications to practice as a lawyer, medical qualifications to practice as a doctor, or construction-worker qualifications.

Diversity of Travel Freedom
The number of countries to which a nationality gives its holders visa-free or visa-on-arrival tourist and business access. Tourist and business access to a country is limited to a short period, usually between one and three months. Almost all countries now require visas from certain non-nationals who wish to have tourist and business access to their territory.

See also Tourist and Business Access, Visa, Visa-Free Tourist and Business Access, and Visa-on-Arrival Tourist and Business Access.

Economic Strength
The Economic Strength of a nationality represents the scale of the economy to which the nationality is attached. This is measured by the country's share of world Gross Domestic Product (GDP) at Purchasing Power Parity (PPP), excluding rents from the exploitation of natural resources — known as Natural Resources Rents (NRR).

See also Gross Domestic Product (GDP), Natural Resources Rents (NRR), and Purchasing Power Parity (PPP).

External Value
The value of a nationality in terms of the diversity and quality of opportunities that it allows us to pursue outside our countries of origin. External Value is composed of Diversity of Settlement Freedom, Weight of Settlement Freedom, Diversity of Travel Freedom, and Weight of Travel Freedom.

See also Diversity of Settlement Freedom, Weight of Settlement Freedom, Diversity of Travel Freedom, and Weight of Travel Freedom.

External Value Ranking
The External Value Ranking of the QNI ranks nationalities on the basis of four parameters which measure External Value on a 0%–100% scale. Each parameter accounts for 25%.

See also Diversity of Settlement Freedom, Weight of Settlement Freedom, Diversity of Travel Freedom, and Weight of Travel Freedom.

Fantasy Passport
A passport issued in the name of a non-existent country, which therefore cannot attest to the possession of any existing nationality. Fantasy passports are used mostly to make political statements.

See also Camouflage Passport.

Full Access
An adult holder of a nationality is allowed to work without permission or by virtually automatic permission. The following aspects are not considered in determining whether a person has full access to another country:

- Entitlement to public pension systems
- Entitlement to healthcare
- Entitlement to social security benefits
- Specific skill qualifications required to perform certain professions, particularly of a qualitative nature, for example, bar qualifications to practice as a lawyer, medical qualifications to practice as a doctor, or construction-worker qualifications.

See also Diversity of Settlement Freedom and Weight of Settlement Freedom.

General Ranking
The General Ranking of the QNI ranks nationalities on the basis of seven parameters, which gauge both Internal Value (40%) and External Value (60%). The three parameters for Internal Value are Human Development (15%), Economic Strength (15%), and Peace and Stability (10%), and the four parameters for External Value are Diversity of Settlement Freedom (15%), Weight of Settlement Freedom (15%), Diversity of Travel Freedom (15%), and Weight of Travel Freedom (15%).

See also Internal Value, External Value, Human Development, Economic Strength, Peace and Stability, Diversity of Settlement Freedom, Weight of Settlement Freedom, Diversity of Travel Freedom, and Weight of Travel Freedom.

Global Peace Index
The Global Peace Index published by the Institute for Economics and Peace is an annual ranking that measures the peacefulness, stability, and harmony of countries by looking at 23 indicators of peace divided into three domains: ongoing domestic and international conflict, the level of harmony within a nation, and the degree of militarization.

Gross Domestic Product (GDP)
The 'sum of gross value added by all resident producers in an economy plus any product taxes and minus any subsidies not included in the value of the products'.[1]

Human Development
One of the three elements of the Internal Value of a nationality. The level of Human Development of a nationality is derived from the country of origin's score in the United Nations Development Programme's Human Development Index, which is today's most authoritative ranking of basic Human Development.

See also Human Development Index.

Human Development Index
The United Nations Development Programme's Human Development Index is an annual ranking measuring the degree of basic Human Development of countries by looking at health (life expectancy at birth), education (number of years of schooling), and standard of living (gross national income per capita).

IATA Timatic

The largest and most reliable database of travel information in the world. IATA Timatic is administered by the International Air Transport Association. It contains a comprehensive overview of visa regimes that is not publicly available.

See also International Air Transport Association (IATA).

Internal Value

The value of a nationality in terms of the quality of life within the nationality's country of origin. Internal Value comprises three parameters: Human Development, Economic Strength, and Peace and Stability.

See also Human Development, Economic Strength, and Peace and Stability.

International Air Transport Association (IATA)

The International Air Transport Association (IATA) is the trade association of the overwhelming majority of airlines. IATA maintains IATA Timatic, the world's largest and most reliable database of travel information, including a comprehensive overview of visa regimes that is not available publicly.

See also IATA Timatic.

Mean

An average of a set of numbers calculated as the sum of the set divided by the number of numbers in the set. In the QNI, the mean of a set of nationalities is the sum of the values of those nationalities divided by the number of nationalities in the set.

Median

The midpoint in a set of numbers ordered by value, in which half the numbers are above the median and half below. In the QNI, the median of a set of nationalities is the value for which half of the nationalities in the collection have a higher value and half of the nationalities have a lower value.

Nationality

An inheritable legal status of attachment to a public authority — usually a state — that entitles the holder to a passport or a passport-like travel document.

Natural Resources Rents (NRR)

The sum of oil rents, natural gas rents, hard and soft coal rents, mineral rents, and forestry rents. Natural Resources Rents are part of GDP but are excluded in measuring the Economic Strength of a nationality.

See also Economic Strength.

Passport

A travel document issued by a public authority — usually a state — that certifies the identity and nationality of its holder.

See also Camouflage Passport and Fantasy Passport.

Peace and Stability

One of the three elements of the Internal Value of a nationality. The level of Peace and Stability of a nationality is derived from the country of origin's score in the Global Peace Index published by the Institute for Economics and Peace.

Purchasing Power Parity (PPP)

The rates of currency conversion that equalize the purchasing power of different currencies by eliminating the differences in price levels between countries. In measuring the Economic Strength of a nationality, Purchasing Power Parity is applied to convert the country of origin's GDP into international dollars. An international dollar possesses the same purchasing power that a US dollar has in the US.

See also Economic Strength and Gross Domestic Product (GDP).

Settlement Access

See Full Access.

Settlement Freedom Ranking

The Settlement Freedom Ranking of the QNI ranks nationalities on the basis of Diversity of Settlement Freedom (50%) and Weight of Settlement Freedom (50%) on a 0%–100% scale.

See also Diversity of Settlement Freedom and Weight of Settlement Freedom.

Timatic

See IATA Timatic.

Tourist and Business Access

A holder of a nationality is allowed to visit another country for a short period, usually between one and three months. Almost all countries now require visas for certain non-nationals who wish to have tourist and business access to their territory.

See also Visa, Visa-Free Tourist and Business Access, and Visa-on-Arrival Tourist and Business Access.

Travel Freedom Ranking

The Travel Freedom Ranking of the QNI ranks nationalities on the basis of Diversity of Travel Freedom (50%) and Weight of Travel Freedom (50%) on a 0%–100% scale.

See also Diversity of Travel Freedom and Weight of Travel Freedom.

Visa

A document allowing a person to travel to a destination country as far as its port of entry (airport, seaport, or land border crossing) and to ask an immigration official to permit entry to the country. In most countries the immigration official has the final authority to permit entry. He or she usually also decides how long the person may stay for any particular visit.

See also Visa-Free Tourist and Business Access and Visa-on-Arrival Tourist and Business Access.

Visa-Free Tourist and Business Access

No visa is required to enter the country for tourist or business purposes.

Visa-on-Arrival Tourist and Business Access

A visa granting tourist and business access to a country is required, but it can be acquired at the port of entry of the country itself.

Weight of Settlement Freedom

The combined value of all countries to which a nationality grants its adult holders full access. This is calculated by the sum of these countries' weighted scores on Human Development and Economic Strength, which are each given 50% weight. Full access to a country means that an adult holder of the relevant nationality is allowed to work without permission or by permission obtained virtually automatically. In determining whether a person has full access to another country, entitlement to public pension systems, healthcare, social security benefits, and specific skill qualifications required to perform certain professions are not considered.

Weight of Travel Freedom

The combined value of all the countries to which a nationality gives its holders visa-free or visa-on-arrival tourist and business access. This is calculated by the sum of these countries' weighted scores on Human Development and Economic Strength, which are each given 50% weight. Tourist and business access to a country is limited to a short period, usually between one and three months. Almost all countries now require visas from certain non-nationals wishing to have tourist and business access to their territories.

See also Visa-Free Tourist and Business Access and Visa-on-Arrival Tourist and Business Access.

Alphabetical Index of Nationality Quality Charts Included in the Text

Afghanistan 103
Albania 94, 115, 249
Algeria 123
Andorra 22, 78
Angola 24
Antigua and Barbuda 110, 165
Argentina 17, 96, 108, 184
Armenia 117, 205
Australia 2, 103, 121, 123, 128, 176
Austria 12
Azerbaijan 202
Bahrain 112
Bangladesh 103
Belarus 117, 202
Belgium 4, 144
Benin 193
Bolivia (Plurinational State of) 96, 186
Bosnia and Herzegovina 214
Brazil 108, 184
British overseas territories 32
Brunei Darussalam 119
Bulgaria 18, 82, 169, 248, 249
Cameroon 122, 196
Canada 11, 27, 78, 115, 144, 222
Cape Verde 60, 197
Central African Republic 11, 196
Chad 80, 144, 196
Chile 186
China (People's Republic of) 5, 12, 22, 27, 55, 130, 143, 265
Chinese Taipei (Taiwan) 265
Columbia 83, 183
Comoros 23, 101
Côte d'Ivoire 14
Croatia 81, 94, 106, 213
Cuba 110
Cyprus 78, 107, 121, 164
Czech Republic 107
Denmark 3, 11
Ecuador 185
Egypt 195
Equatorial Guinea 194
Eritrea 14
Estonia 59
European Union 217
Eswatini (formerly Swaziland) 198
Ethiopia 192
Fiji 121, 181
France 14, 23, 59, 60, 129, 144, 175, 176, 234
Gabon 196
Gambia 197
Georgia 79, 85, 202, 256, 258
Germany 14, 55, 106, 130
Ghana 100
Grenada 84, 111, 165
Guatemala 13
Guyana 184
Haiti 139
Hong Kong, China (SAR) 104, 265
Hungary 19, 59
Iceland 5, 27, 56
India 57, 266
Iraq 28
Ireland 107
Israel 98, 263
Israeli Laissez-passer 263
Italy 17, 107
Japan 62, 128

Jersey 107
Jordan 167
Kazakhstan 117, 123, 140, 159
Kenya 198
Kiribati 181
Korea (Republic of) 62, 103
Kosovo 210, 215
Kuwait 112
Kyrgyzstan 11, 117, 205
Lao People's Democratic Republic 104
Latvia 106, 254
Latvia ('Non-Citizen') 106, 159, 254
Lesotho 12, 122
Liberia 144
Libya 87
Liechtenstein 4, 12, 13, 125
Lithuania 206
Luxembourg 115
Macao 265
Madagascar 4, 33
Malawi 122
Malaysia 104
Malta 12, 107, 164
Marshall Islands 126, 176
Mauritius 101, 192
Mexico 18, 55, 139, 162, 228, 230
Micronesia (Federated States of) 176
Moldova (Republic of) 19, 85, 167, 202, 206, 249
Mongolia 22
Montenegro 167, 213
Morocco 195
Myanmar 269
Namibia 193
Nauru 122
Netherlands 24, 59, 128, 239
New Zealand 11, 174, 176
Nicaragua 11
Nigeria 191
North Macedonia 18, 213, 249
Norway 22, 52
Oman 112
Pakistan 23, 121
Palau 63, 176
Papua New Guinea 179
Paraguay 109
Peru 84, 185
Philippines 24
Poland 59, 107
Portugal 24
Qatar 88, 98
Romania 19, 52, 59, 82
Russian Federation 11, 12, 63, 117, 130, 144, 201, 258
Rwanda 101, 193
Saint Kitts and Nevis 62, 111, 125, 165
Saint Lucia 111, 165
Samoa 122, 179
San Marino 3, 125
São Tomé and Principe 126, 194
Saudi Arabia 98, 130
Serbia 210
Seychelles 101, 191
Singapore 53, 119, 122
Slovakia 19
Slovenia 27, 94, 169, 213, 215
Solomon Islands 181
South Africa 100, 193
South Sudan 195

Sudan (Republic of the) 195
Suriname 24, 184
Sweden 28, 128
Switzerland 23, 127
Syrian Arab Republic 56, 87
Tajikistan 104
Thailand 119
Timor-Leste 85, 181
Trinidad and Tobago 111
Turkey 94, 115, 167
Turkmenistan 4, 201
Uganda 122, 140

Ukraine 2, 79, 201
United Arab Emirates 83, 98, 112
United Kingdom 43, 107, 127, 221
United Kingdom 'Hard Brexit' 43, 221
United States 3, 18, 24, 53, 123, 129, 143, 162, 217, 230
Uruguay 109
Uzbekistan 201
Vanuatu 167
Venezuela (Bolivarian Republic of) 3, 109, 187
Viet Nam 119
Yemen 52, 86
Zambia 62, 215

Acknowledgments

Every reasonable effort has been taken to contact the appropriate copyright holders.

All passport cover vectors were drawn by Michelle van den Berg. The cover of a German Third Reich passport stamped with the letter "J" (Jude) identifying its holder as a Jew (p.15): United States Holocaust Memorial Museum, courtesy of Walter Jacobsberg. IATA logo (p.61): https://www.iata.org. Unless otherwise indicated, all photographs in Part 5 Expert Commentary (pp.136–275): Gallo/Getty Images; Figure 1. The Three Worlds of the Cold War Period (p.137): from *The Clash of Civilizations and the Remaking of World Order* by Samuel P. Huntington. Copyright © 1996 by Samuel P. Huntington pp.24–25. For publication and distribution of the Work in the English language in the US, its territories and dependencies, Canada, and the Open Market: reprinted with the permission of Simon & Schuster, Inc. All rights reserved. For publication in the UK/British Commonwealth in print format: reprinted with the permission of Simon & Schuster UK. All rights reserved. For World Digital rights: reproduced by permission of GEORGES BORCHARDT INC. Redrawn by Liezel Bohdanowicz; Figure 2. Samuel Huntington's World of Clashing Civilizations (p.138): From *The Clash of Civilizations and the Remaking of World Order* by Samuel P. Huntington. Copyright © 1996 by Samuel P. Huntington.pp.26–27. For publication and distribution of the Work in the English language in the US, its territories and dependencies, Canada, and the Open Market in print format: reprinted with the permission of Simon & Schuster, Inc. All rights reserved. For publication in the UK/British Commonwealth in print format: reprinted with the permission of Simon & Schuster UK. All rights reserved. For World Digital rights: reproduced by permission of GEORGES BORCHARDT INC. Redrawn by Liezel Bohdanowicz; Figure 3. World's Countries by Visa-free Access to the US and the EU (p.142): Author's calculation based on data from the EU (https://ec.europa.eu) and the U.S. Department of State (https://travel.state.gov); Figure 4. World Map with Citizenship Tiers (p.143): Harpaz, Yossi. 2019. Citizenship 2.0: Dual Nationality as a Global Asset. Princeton University Press. p.24. Reprinted by permission of Princeton University Press through Copyright Clearance Center; MERCOSUR emblem (p.186): https://www.mercosur.int/en/ Reprinted by permission of MERCOSUR; ECOWAS emblem (p.196): https://www.ecowas.int/; EAC emblem (p.197): https://www.eac.int/; SADC emblem (p.197): https://www.sadc.int/; Figure 1. Birthplace of Spanish Citizens living in Mexico (2009–2019) (p.229): Produced with figures from Spanish Register of Citizens Living Abroad (PERE), National Institute for Statistics, Madrid 2019, https://www.ine.es/; Three photographs of Myanmar identification documents (p.273): Supplied by the author.